INTERNATIONAL
PROPAGANDA
AND
COMMUNICATIONS

INTERNATIONAL
PROPAGANDA
AND
COMMUNICATIONS

THE PRESS
AND WORLD AFFAIRS

By

ROBERT W. DESMOND

ARNO PRESS
A New York Times Company
New York • 1972

LIBRARY
University of Texas
At San Antonio

Reprint Edition 1972 by Arno Press Inc.

Reprinted from a copy in The Newark Public Library

International Propaganda and Communications
ISBN for complete set: 0-405-04740-1
See last pages of this volume for titles.

Manufactured in the United States of America

Library of Congress Cataloging in Publication Data

Desmond, Robert William, 1900–
   The press and world affairs.

   (International propaganda and communications)
   Reprint of the 1937 ed.
   Bibliography: p.
   1. Press. 2. Foreign news. I. Title.
II. Series.
PN4731.D45 1972   070   72-4665
ISBN 0-405-04746-0

THE PRESS
AND WORLD AFFAIRS

FOUR NEWSPAPERS WHICH MIRROR THE WORLD

For description see List of Illustrations

THE PRESS
AND WORLD AFFAIRS

By

ROBERT W. DESMOND

With an Introduction by

HAROLD J. LASKI

Professor of Political Science
in the University of London

ILLUSTRATED

D. APPLETON - CENTURY COMPANY

INCORPORATED

NEW YORK   LONDON

1937

TO

DOROTHY

WITH APPRECIATION

PREFACE

THE WORLD has become so close-knit that it is difficult for a nation to find isolation or to solve its problems independently. Affairs that affect one people seem eventually to affect others. On such matters the alert citizen or student keeps himself well informed. In practice he does so by reading the newspapers. But few persons know how the reports upon which they depend reach the pages of the newspapers, especially the reports of world affairs as distinct from local affairs. Concerning that there is limited and confused understanding.

This volume strives to clear up that confusion by describing the processes and influences involved in reporting the news of the world. It is a book intended to help the average person to read his newspaper with more comprehension.

The histories of some national presses have been written. The technical processes of gathering and writing and editing the news, locally and domestically, have been described. There have been numerous critical studies of the practices and ethics of the press. Biographies and autobiographies of journalists and publishers are many. This volume, however, is the first detached study of the contemporary press as it operates on the broad stage of international affairs.

Into the preparation of the book have gone considerable personal experience in gathering, writing, and editing news, numerous conversations with journalists and students of public affairs, and extensive reading in libraries and private collections. In pursuit of relevant facts the writer has visited and at times worked professionally in such news centers as London, Paris, Geneva, Rome, Berlin, Washington, New York, and other cities. The material first was organized as a doctoral dissertation for the University of London (School of Economics and Political Science) but has been edited to bring it into a somewhat more compact form.

Acknowledgments are due to so many friends and acquaintances for their patience in answering questions and providing material that it would be quite hopeless to try to list them all individually, but I do express to them my sincere thanks.

R. W. D.

CONTENTS

ix

LIST OF ILLUSTRATIONS

With Explanatory Notes

FOUR NEWSPAPERS WHICH MIRROR THE WORLD   *Frontispiece*

In the pages of these papers public affairs receive balanced presentation. All have excellent news services, attain a high degree of impartiality, are free of any improper control, publish a large volume of authoritative material, and encourage their readers to take a broad and intelligent interest in matters of significance, wherever they may occur. There are other fine newspapers, but none better than these four. Published in London, Buenos Aires, Boston, and New York, they are known, read, and respected throughout the world.

Several styles of type are used to convey information to the diverse peoples of the globe. German script is one. It is used in the *General Anzeiger* of Berlin (at the top) and by many other German-language newspapers throughout the world. Some of them prefer the Roman alphabet, accepted by most newspapers of Europe, including the *Aftenposten* of Oslo (second from the bottom), and papers of the western hemisphere and all English-speaking parts of the world.

The Cyrillic alphabet, derived from the Greek, is used by papers in Russia, Bulgaria, parts of Yugoslavia, and other Slavic regions. The *Vechernaya Moskva* ("Evening Moscow") (second from the top) illustrates the type. Chinese and Japanese newspapers use characters such as appear in the popular literary paper of Tokyo, *Yomiuri Shimbun* (center). Arabic is used by many papers in the Near East and Middle East, including the Cairo paper *Al Balagh* (at the bottom). Both the Arabic and the Chinese-Japanese papers must be read from right to left and from back to front. There are other alphabets, but these five are the most widely used.

This is a carbon of the first page of a long cable reporting a day's developments at the Reparations Conference in Paris on May 11, 1929. It was written by Leland Stowe, then Paris correspondent for the New York *Herald Tribune*. Mr. Stowe was awarded the Pulitzer Prize a year later for "the best foreign correspondence" of 1929. The basis for the award was his work in reporting these Paris meetings, and this dispatch was one of those instrumental in earning him the distinction. As he says in his prefatory note to Mr. Holcombe, then

At the top left appears the first page of a dispatch describing a storm in London. Below is an "insert," cabled later, for inclusion in the report as used.

The right-hand page shows part of the rewritten version of the original dispatch, with its translation from cablese. That version was handled by the copy desk and appeared on page one of the New York *Herald Tribune*.

The clipping shows that the "insert" was added after the original rewrite job was completed. The last two lines of the clipping are the beginning of the insert, as it appears on the left-hand page.

At the right are the first two pages of a story cabled from Paris to the New York *Times* and mimeographed in the New York office for distribution to the correspondents there who file telegrams for newspapers subscribing to the *Times'* syndicate service. That portion of the published story appearing in the pages shown is at the left. The full story ran on for several pages of copy and nearly a column of type.

The *Times'* foreign correspondents file dispatches which are not much condensed, and the clipped story shows expansion in the ratio of only about two words for one in the cable.

At a control bureau messages are received from native correspondents, sometimes in the language of the country or perhaps in another language. Before such a message can be relayed or used, it must be translated. One such telegram received at the New York *Herald Tribune* bureau in Paris, from a correspondent in Nice, was translated, used in the Paris edition, and a carbon copy of the rewritten Paris-edition story made available for transmission to New York. The original telegram and the printed Paris version appear above.

A staff correspondent has been sent from the Paris bureau to Brussels to report a royal wedding. Part of his telegram as received in the Paris bureau is shown below, while a clipping of the story as it appeared in type is above. The portion represented by the sheet of the telegram shown begins just under the divisional "Chimes Ring Out."

This map shows how the news centers of the world are linked by the service of a large press association. Correspondents are stationed in permanent bureaus in the key places, native correspondents are on call in the less important places, and the entire structure is united by

culations. They are "journals of information," rather than "journals of opinion."

The six shown at the top are more or less strongly political and may be described as "journals of opinion," as distinct from the type of "journals of information" shown in Figure 22. The four at the bottom are the most widely read of the afternoon newspapers, with *Paris Soir* and *L'Intransigeant* leading.

A conservative and important Paris evening newspaper. Although large in size and rather dull, it is read with care particularly because of its "Bulletin du Jour," or leading editorial, in column one. This often is taken as representing the views of the government, especially on matters of foreign affairs.

Any of these papers might be useful to a correspondent at one time or another in providing him with information or tips. They represent special political groups, sports, literary and artistic interests.

L'Action Française represents the Royalist group in France. *Le Populaire* is the Socialist party organ, and is directed by M. Léon Blum. *Le Petit Journal* is one of the Patenotre papers. *L'Auto* is concerned with sports. *Gringoire* is a weekly, largely devoted to political and literary subjects.

Probably more papers are published in Paris than in any other city in the world. Most of them are quite small, and usually have some special interest or bias, yet any one may contain some nugget for a correspondent, and obscure papers sometimes blossom into prominence.

Political matters provide the *raison d'être* for most of these papers. *La Journée Industrielle* is a business and industrial daily, however; *Comœdia* is a weekly paper concerned with the theater, art, and literature; and *Excelsior,* a daily owned by Mme. Paul Dupuy, is much concerned with social affairs and local Parisian topics. The others in this group express shades of political opinion.

Whether in Geneva or elsewhere, any meeting summoned by the League of Nations finds the Information Section of the League Secretariat ready to help the press. The agenda for the meeting is distributed in mimeographed form (top of left-hand page) in advance of the meeting itself. A mimeographed account of what happened is ready a few moments after adjournment (left center), and duplicate releases of everything are always available in French, the second official language of the League, for the benefit of those who do not understand English.

paper offices in Rome, or to the offices maintained there by correspondents for provincial newspapers, who telephone the dispatches
to their offices.

The Agenzia di Roma, a semi-official agency which is concerned
with financial and political news and interpretation, distributes its
reports in the mimeographed form shown at the bottom of the right-
hand page.

News of the Vatican, which is important to correspondents in
Rome, is available through a privately syndicated service. A carbon
copy of one release from that service appears at the top of the right-
hand page.

The Ministry of Foreign Affairs issues a yellow-covered pamphlet
containing reprints of reports, editorials, and articles culled from
the press of the world which refer in favorable terms to what the
Fascist government is doing in Italy. This pamphlet, a copy of which
appears at the top of the left-hand page, is distributed every week
to Italian newspapers in order that the items may be reprinted
therein, so indicating to the people how favorably their government
is regarded in other countries.

The topmost paper is published in Vatican City. The next three
below are published in Rome. The two below that group are published in Turin, and the two at the bottom are published in Milan.

The *Corriere della Sera* long has been regarded as Italy's finest
newspaper, and is one of the best known outside the country. *Il
Popolo d'Italia* was founded by Benito Mussolini, and is regarded
as expressing his views with especial authority. It is edited by his
nephew, Vito Mussolini. *Il Giornale d'Italia* of Rome, edited by Dr.
Virginio Gayda, also is considered to reflect the government's views
with accuracy.

All of these papers circulate throughout Italy, and some of them
beyond.

These papers, although somewhat circumscribed in their circulations, reflect the views of leading men or of sections of the country,
and hence are important to correspondents. They are published, as
shown from top to bottom, in Naples, Genoa, Cremona, Rome, Rome
again, Ferrara, and Bologna.

Roberto Farinacci, former secretary of the Fascist party and a life
member of the Grand Council, is proprietor and editor of *Il Regime
Fascista* of Cremona. *Il Piccolo* is a noon edition of *Il Giornale
d'Italia* (see Figure 32). The *Corriere Padano* of Ferrara is owned
by Italo Balbo, and is presumed to express some of his ideas.

All these papers are published in Moscow. The *Moscow Daily
News,* English-language paper, appears at the bottom. The others,
printed in the Cyrillic alphabet (see Figure 1) are, reading up,
Izvestia (meaning "News"), *Pravda* ("Truth"), *Za Industrialaziu*

INTRODUCTION

THE SCIENTIFIC STUDY of public opinion is still in its infancy. To the development of that study I believe that Dr. Desmond has made a contribution of signal interest and illumination. He has the advantage of a practical newspaperman's first-hand experience of how news is gathered and presented, as well as the academic training necessary to assess the meaning of that experience. His book brings a wealth of material for the student of affairs, here, as I believe, gathered together in reasonable compass for the first time. To have organized into a coherent and orderly whole this massive body of facts will, I think, be everywhere recognized to be a service of outstanding importance.

The reader will not go far in Dr. Desmond's pages before he sees that getting the truth in foreign news is a matter of intricate complexity. There is unconscious deception in reporting, as well as conscious deception; which of the two is responsible for the greater amount of false judgments it would be difficult to say. It is clear enough that the simple hopes of a "free" press as a source of right opinions, hopes with which Jeremy Bentham and his disciples started, are unlikely to be fulfilled in any period of time we can foresee.

There are four things which need to be understood by the average reader of the newspapers: (1) that there is no government in the world not engaged in "weighting" the news in its own interest; (2) that there are many news-gathering organizations, some of which add their own bias to what they report; (3) that correspondents have what Mr. Justice Holmes called their "inarticulate major premisses" which necessarily color the reports they send; and (4) that the editorial offices have also their own special values to contribute to the work of selection and presentation of news. Once these points are generally appreciated, perhaps a more critical audience will demand greater respect for objective truth than now obtains in the press. But that day is far ahead.

The essential result that emerges from Dr. Desmond's study is, I suggest, that so long as there is an unequal interest in the result of what impact the news may make, just so long will it pay the purveyors of news to report events with an emphasis deliberately calculated to serve those interests in a position to influence its supply. Our news system, in a word, is a reflection of our social system; there will be no vital change in the one unless there is also a vital change in the other.

That is a hard conclusion. But I think any reader who reflects upon the facts Dr. Desmond has collected will find it difficult to evade. It is a grim conclusion if only because it becomes daily more obvious that public liberty is a direct function of an honest supply of news. We cannot really think correctly on national or international affairs unless the facts reported to us correspond to the reality that they are supposed to depict. The volume of correspondence is too often pitifully small, too often, also, deliberately so. And our power to transcend the influence of what we read is also alarmingly small. Once interest is engaged in coloring the facts, the chance of unprejudiced judgment on the reader's part is, with rare exceptions, dangerously small also. It may be true that, in the end, truth will prevail; but before it wins its victory, incalculable damage may be, indeed has been, done to human relationships.

Nothing is gained by attacking the journalists. Indeed, I think it would be true to say that one of the most heartening things in the post-war world is the number of foreign correspondents who have genuinely tried to keep the public honestly informed. Certain of the better correspondents give one a sense of the potential dignity of the journalist's profession. But behind them, and perhaps even controlling them, is an immense machinery whose definite purpose is deliberate distortion in the service of sinister interest. Dr. Desmond shows how powerful that machinery is. Can we defeat its influence?

The temptation is to say that education will achieve this result.

I have no such confidence for two reasons. In the first place, the results of educational progress are too slowly gathered to make in any brief period a serious impact on the proportions of the problem. To take a simple instance: the methods of Mr. W. R. Hearst have been publicly exposed a hundred times, but the public still continues to buy, and to be influenced by, his papers. And, in the second place, any rapid development of the kind of education we need is conditioned by the necessity of other changes in our social system. The press, in a sentence, is a fundamental weapon in the social conflict, national and international, in which we are all, despite ourselves, combatants. We shall have truthful news when untruthful news does not pay, but it will not pay only when the major causes of social conflict, national and international, have been removed.

That, for me at least, is the essential lesson of Dr. Desmond's able analysis. It is not a lesson which tends to optimism. But here, as elsewhere, if we can get from books of this quality the vital sense of how intricate our problems are, how useless is the search for simple remedies, we shall at least have set our foot on the right road. The supreme value of Dr. Desmond's book is the degree to which it makes it irresistibly evident that the problem of the foreign news service lies at the heart of the major problems of the modern state. If that is grasped by those who translate its implications to the student of affairs, it is bound to help in a real degree to the urgent clarification of these grave issues.

HAROLD J. LASKI

The London School of Economics
and Political Science

THE PRESS
AND WORLD AFFAIRS

They were passing through the Strand as they talked, and by a newspaper office, which was all lighted up and bright. Reporters were coming out of the place, or rushing up to it in cabs; there were lamps burning in the editor's rooms, and above, where the compositors were at work, the windows of the building were in a blaze of gas.

"Look at that, Pen," Warrington said. "There she is—the great engine—she never sleeps. She has her ambassadors in every quarter of the world—her couriers upon every road. Her officers march along with armies, and her envoys walk into statesmen's cabinets. They are ubiquitous. Yonder journal has an agent, at this minute, giving bribes in Madrid; and another inspecting the price of potatoes at Covent Garden. Look, here comes the foreign express galloping in. They will be able to give news to Downing Street tomorrow; Funds will rise or fall, fortunes be made or lost; Lord B. will get up, and holding the paper in his hand and seeing the noble Marquis in his place, will make a great speech; and —and Mr. Doolan will be called away from his supper at the back kitchen; for he is foreign sub-editor, and sees the mail on the newspaper sheet before he goes to his own."

W. M. THACKERAY, *Pendennis*

THE PRESS
AND WORLD AFFAIRS

CHAPTER I

THE PRESS COMES OF AGE

THE PRESS not only reports the history of the world, day by day, but helps to make it. Almost all that any person knows about public affairs is gleaned from newspapers. As it is not possible for him to have personal knowledge of activities outside a limited circle, he is obliged to depend upon others to keep him informed. In practice, it is the press which does this. It is equally certain that what any person knows, or thinks he knows, determines how he behaves. His opinion and his behavior, multiplied by the opinions and behavior of all those of his fellow-men, who are similarly influenced, determines the history of the world.

Local affairs or the policy of a nation, economic practices or social justice, the issues of war or peace, may be governed, in the final analysis, by the character of the information habitually provided by the press. The happiness of millions of persons, including those yet unborn, rests in the balance. It is this circumstance which gives importance to the news, as provided by the press. The news is the stuff of civilization, the substance of to-day, the echo of yesterday, the shadow of to-morrow.

Intelligent journalists cannot fail to be aware of the general responsibility of the press in the matter of relationships between peoples. Diplomats likewise know that news can be dynamite. Nor can thoughtful citizens ignore the press as a force in society, or remain indifferent to its influence and to the factors which shape that influence. Oddly enough, truth is unpalatable to many persons. This circumstance puts both journalists and their employers in a delicate position, since a penalty may be attached to telling the truth; yet if they play carelessly with such explosive material, and make truth secondary to popular prejudices, or deliberately create items which tend to provoke bad feelings or mislead readers, then they are betraying humanity.

The world to-day is acting on the basis of information more plentiful than ever before, but still much distorted by prejudice, censorship and propaganda. Few countries have newspapers that are free of government control. There is a certain amount of poison in the news stream, and sometimes a sleeping potion is added. It behooves every individual who considers himself intelligent to keep awake to the persuasions of the press, as exercised through its news columns even more than through its editorials, or leaders. He must learn to make discounts in reading the news, estimating its sources and the influences that have touched it. He must demand more and better information-services, and cast his own weight on the side of good journalism, as a measure of self-protection, if for no more altruistic reason.

* * *

This book is an examination of the press as an existing world force. It examines its growth in enterprise and technical competence in pursuit of the news. It examines the organization for gathering and distributing the news of the present-day world. It examines two obstacles to the free flow of the news, that is, censorship and propaganda. And, finally, it considers obstacles existing in the minds of journalists, publisher-owners, and readers, with implications as to how all may contribute toward safeguarding human rights, where they yet survive.

§ 1. NEWS FUNDAMENTALS

EVENTS are news; so are trends and tendencies, forecasts and reviews, summaries and interpretations. The journalist makes it possible for persons in all parts of the world to know about and understand what occurs at home and abroad. He is trained to know "news values," is experienced in the means of gathering the news-facts and in writing them concisely and interestingly.

He is one of the more essential, although least appreciated, cogs in the modern world machine.

It is the reporter-journalist who comes into contact with the men and women who *make* the news by their thoughts, words and deeds. Upon him, for the most part, the editors in the office must depend. It is the editor-journalist at home, however, who prepares the written matter for actual publication, selects and rejects, and comments on it editorially. From his desk it goes to the mechanical department, which translates it into metal and sends it whirling from the presses as a part of the finished newspapers.

News falls into certain general categories: Personalities, politics, government administration, including news of crime and the courts; economic, commercial, or financial; sports, Labor-class news, social problems, the arts. Whether at home or abroad, most of this news flows in certain channels, which the journalist knows and has charted. Looking to the channels simplifies news gathering and, although it tends to standardize the newspapers somewhat, it has proved a generally.satisfactory method. It is elastic enough so that any fresh type of news may promptly be included in the system. The result is that most news is anticipated and journalists are ready to "cover" a "story" when it "breaks," to use the technical jargon.

*   *   *

Once having obtained any desired information, the journalist writes it into a report and then gets the report to the home office for publication. Good present-day news writing, in the American press at least, usually results in the presentation of a story in some one of perhaps five fairly distinct ways:

(*a*) A "straight" account of the news. This means that the first paragraph or so, called the "lead" of the story, gives a summary of the essential points involved; the who, what, when, where, why and how of it, and the details follow, usually in the order of diminishing importance or of interest. The writing is kept as simple, factual, and yet as effective as possible. This is journalism of information, primarily.

(*b*) An "interpretative" account of the news. This is much like the first in structure, but with the addition to plain facts of impartial explanations of the event or trend under consideration, in its present, future, and possibly in its historical significance. This may be called a "situation" story, or "think stuff." It may be journalism of ideas, to a greater or less extent.

(*c*) A "feature" story. This is a short or moderate length account intended primarily to entertain, and usually dealing with a matter of no great intrinsic importance. It is likely to be a "sidelight" on a news event, to be about persons or places of news interest, or merely intended to arouse a smile or a tear.

(*d*) A "news feature" story. This is a fairly long account of a matter of some importance, but written with the intent to entertain and at the same time to inform, with the emphasis on the entertainment side.

(*e*) A "special article." This is a relatively long consideration, analysis, or review of an important trend, tendency, or situation, rather than of an isolated event. Usually serious and partaking of the nature of an article in a magazine, it is not commonly so dependent for its reader-appeal upon trigger-like timeliness, although it probably is topical, at least.

*   *   *

News writing fashions have changed during the four centuries since the central European banking-houses began to receive letters of information from correspondents in other places. Doubtless they will change again.

The earliest printed sheets retained many of the characteristics of those first news-letters, offering a collection of paragraphs, usually brief, grouped according to the sources of the information. It was not until early in the eighteenth century that Addison and Steele, in England, introduced something new in their "essay papers," which were word-sketches of contemporary events, persons, and places. This style won the tribute of imitation in England and in the American colonies.[1]

[1] Benjamin Franklin was one of those influenced by the *Spectator,* in which the Addison-Steele papers appeared. He tells in his *Autobiography* of

The so-called "human interest" formula brought a more important change. It consisted in selecting the news or aspects of the news that could be so written as to move the reader to feel some emotion—amusement, excitement, sorrow, even grief. The method seems to have been originated by John Wight in his "Mornings at Bow Street," a series of brief little word-pictures, dramatized and fiction-like versions of cases in London's Bow Street police court. They appeared in the *Morning Herald* of London, beginning about 1820, and sent its circulation climbing.[2]

It was a method to be widely used and extended, with application to the reports of many aspects of life in addition to police-court incidents. It was given a constant new zest by the use of larger type, colored paper, colored inks, and pictures. It proved so appealing that papers which were clever in the use of the human interest formula attained great circulations and great wealth. It explains the material success of all the mass-circulation papers of England and America. It is the key to the power exercised by the James Gordon Bennetts, Joseph Pulitzer, E. W. Scripps, William Randolph Hearst, Lord Northcliffe, Lord Beaverbrook, Lord Rothermere, Colonel Robert McCormick, Joseph Patterson and others.[3]

how he had read and admired the *Spectator* from the time he was 12 years old, and patterned his own writing upon it. His brother, James Franklin, as editor of the *New England Courant* in Boston, reprinted essays from the *Spectator* and printed original articles written in the same general style.

[2] A compilation is in print under the title of *Mornings at Bow Street*, by J. Wight. See also: James Grant, *The Newspaper Press*, V. 1, pp. 318-320; H. R. Fox Bourne, *English Newspapers*, V. 2, pp. 17-19 (somewhat inaccurate); W. G. Bleyer, *Main Currents in the History of American Journalism*, pp. 156-158.

[3] F. M. O'Brien, *The Story of the Sun* (rev. ed.) Chs. 15, 16; Don Seitz, *The James Gordon Bennetts;* Frederic Hudson, *Journalism in the United States.* A compilation of successful human interest stories published in the New York *Tribune* are issued under the title, *Hot Corn: Life Scenes in New York, Illustrated*, by Solon Robinson. These little stories by Mr. Robinson began to appear in the *Tribune* in 1853; N. D. Cochrane, *E. W. Scripps;* Gilson Gardner, *Lusty Scripps;* Don Seitz, *Joseph Pulitzer: His Life and Letters;* W. E. Carson, *Northcliffe, Britain's Man of Power;* Max Pemberton, *Lord Northcliffe: A Memoir;* R. M. Wilson, *Lord Northcliffe: A Study;* Hamilton Fyfe, *Northcliffe, an Intimate Biography;* Tom Clarke, *My Northcliffe Diary;* J. K. Winkler, *W. R. Hearst, an American Phenomenon;* Ferdi-

Despite the frequent misapplication of the human interest formula, it remains innocent and even praiseworthy in itself. Correctly used, it provides a means for giving wider interest to what might otherwise be dull matters by portraying them in their warm, personalized aspects, both from the standpoint of those involved and of those reading about them.[4] It reclaims many a story from stodginess and wins for it an attention that it perhaps deserves. A combination of human interest journalism and the more serious style has resulted in some of the "best" newspapers.

A variant of the human interest story is the "interview," first used, so some reports say, by the New York *Herald* in 1859 at the time of the John Brown Raid at Harper's Ferry. Others credit its invention to J. B. McCullagh of the St. Louis *Globe-Democrat*.[5] In any event, it was in wide use soon after the Civil War. Its adoption in other countries followed slowly; it was approximately 1890 before it was used in Great Britain, and then especially by W. T. Stead. It had been held in derision for many years as lacking in dignity. The style has always given great latitude in subject matter and in writing, and it does not necessarily depend for its effectiveness upon a "news peg," that is, upon the excuse of a conspicuous current incident or trend.[6]

Fashions in news writing have been shaped, to some extent, by

nand Lundberg, *Imperial Hearst, A Social Biography;* Oliver Carlson and E. S. Bates, *Hearst, Lord of San Simeon;* Emile Gauvreau, *Hot News;* Silas Bent, *Ballyhoo: The Voice of the Press*, Ch. 7.

[4] An interesting criticism of news writing "fashions" appears in Silas Bent's *Ballyhoo: The Voice of the Press*, Ch. 1.

[5] E. P. Bell, "The Interview is a Mirror Held Up to a Remarkable Personality," *Editor and Publisher* (Jan. 22, 1927), p. 42. Also appears in E. P. Bell, "Interviewing—Its Principles and Functions," *An Introduction to Journalism*, pp. 133-139.

[6] For British references to the American "novelty," as the interview was considered then, see: James Grant, *The Newspaper Press*, V. 2, pp. 427-428. For reference to the origin of the interview style, see: Frederic Hudson, *Journalism in the United States*, pp. 567-584. For more on the history and technique of the interview, see: L. M. Salmon, *The Newspaper and the Historian*, Ch. 10. There is a considerable literature on the "art" of the interview, but most of it seems to have been said first, in one way or another, by Henri de Blowitz in his *Memoirs*. See also: I. F. Marcosson, *Adventures in Interviewing;* Emil Ludwig, "Emil Ludwig, Famed for His Reporting, Tells the Art of the Interview," *Editor and Publisher* (July 18, 1936), pp. 3-4, 44.

economic necessity. During the Civil War the electric telegraph came into general use as a means to speed the news to an eager public. But the telegraph was expensive to use. News writing prior to that date had tended to be somewhat florid and wordy. But it cost too much to be florid and wordy by telegraph. Correspondents were induced, therefore, to confine their dispatches to unadorned facts. These facts were necessarily the answers to the questions, What has happened? When? Where? Who was involved? How did it come to happen just so? Why did it happen so? In other words, the summary lead was born, due to a need for economy.

Much the same thing happened during the Great War. Cable costs were high, there was more factual material to be sent, and correspondents were permitted to sacrifice some details. So the what-when-where-why-how convention was further trimmed. Instead, correspondents would present in the leading paragraph only the absolute double-distilled essence of the story. In one brief sentence they told what had happened; that sentence was packed with as much drama, suspense, color and significance as it would hold in a line or two. It assumed that the reader was somewhat acquainted in advance with what was going on, and omitted what might have been unnecessary points from the lead, although they may have been included in the "body" of the story. While this new form of "lead" has not supplanted the summary lead in American journalistic practice, it has taken its place in accounts of some "big" events.[7]

In the British press, unlike the American, it is common to find stories written to present the facts of the news in chronological order, without any attempt to startle readers in the first sentence, but rather to interest them and then to build up to a climax, in-

---

[7] As a further refinement in news writing, there has developed the so-called "sweep line," in which an entire situation is strikingly characterized and summarized in a single typewritten line, so that the reader may presumably grasp the full significance at a glance. This style is not so much used in newspapers, but is a device used by writers of the modern style "news-letter," as prepared in Washington and perhaps in other places, purporting to give subscribers a real comprehension of public affairs as they are known to those privy to the secrets of state. See: W. M. Kiplinger, "Interpret the News," *Journalism Quarterly* (Sept. 1936), pp. 289-94.

stead of beginning with one. These two opposing schools of news writing have their proponents in both countries, and either method might be used in writing individual stories in either country, but, generally speaking, the one is more common in Great Britain and the other in the United States. Newspapers in most other countries accept one or the other of these patterns for their own use.

*   *   *

What the future may bring in the way of changed methods of news writing can be mere speculation. It is reasonable to suppose, however, that these will continue to change, as they have in the past, always striving toward a more effective means of portraying the world for the benefit of the reading public. The trend toward an interpretative style of writing seems likely to wax stronger, and brevity may be more sought after.

Interpretation in news writing may, and does, take two forms.

In one form it is an *editorial interpretation*. Some newspaper editors object to so-called "interpretative" news writing because they believe it must be this type, involving editorializing. Readers and editors alike are quite right in objecting to any critical appraisal by the reporter of the original facts. It would mean having the opinion of some individual foisted upon one instead of receiving facts, as accurate, impartial, and clearly defined as it is possible to make them. The good reporter wants facts, facts, and more facts, and then seeks to make those facts utterly clear. Readers then may have them as a basis for forming proper judgments and opinions.

The other form is *factual interpretation*. This is not merely legitimate, but useful. No opinions are expressed by the writer, directly or indirectly, but the event is put in its proper perspective, historically and otherwise, and the background, together with its possible meaning, is sketched in with clinical objectivity. There is no serving the reader with a ready-made opinion, but only an attempt to help him "place" and evaluate the news, relating it to what has gone before and linking it with its essential phases of human affairs.

In American newspaper offices there was for some years an almost fanatical insistence upon facts served so entirely without background as to be practically unintelligible to any save experts. This method of writing discouraged most readers from taking an interest in events occurring very far beyond their own personal ken. Almost nobody read foreign news, even national affairs left most persons apathetic, while economics and science were too difficult for consideration. In Great Britain the cult of pure factualism never was so widespread, and a certain amount of the second type of interpretation has characterized writing in the best papers for many years.

Perhaps it was the increasing complexity of all public affairs following the Great War that demanded a change of policy even in the United States. Efforts began to be made to explain the developments of science, then the workings of economics, later the operations of both national and foreign affairs so that more persons could understand them. At first the trend was confined to a few newspapers, directed by enlightened editors and publishers, and to a few feature syndicates. Its more general acceptance may be ascribed to efforts by the United Press and the Associated Press to "humanize" the news, that is, to give it increased interest and meaning, without distortion. The result was publication of far more news of a sort that might be described as "significant" rather than merely "interesting." Although some critics spoke of over-simplification, readers began to be much better informed through the press.

Editors took notice of the generally favorable public response to this new policy, so that factual interpretation of the news has, in theory at least, been generally accepted as desirable.

§ 2. IN PURSUIT OF THE NEWS

EXPANSION of trade and political affairs bred an early demand for information. Proprietors of coffee houses, such as Lloyds in London and less prominent ones not only in London, but in Paris, Amsterdam, and other great cities, found correspondents who would provide them with budgets of news. The printers of the corantos and news-books made similar arrangements on a limited scale.

The young newspapers in England and in the United States depended for non-local news almost entirely upon items reprinted from other newspapers published abroad or at home. This always meant a delay in news presentation, sometimes as much as several months, but the readers, unaccustomed to anything better, seemed not to mind. Only a very few of the richer newspapers had their own letters from correspondents, but even they were definitely not "staff" or "special" men sent by the newspapers in question to the cities from which they wrote. Rather, they were regularly employed at some task in that community, journalistic or otherwise, and their correspondence with the newspaper was more or less incidental.

The change that has occurred since then has been gradual and is to be attributed to a combination of circumstances. Before 1800, as well as since, mere curiosity supported much of an individual's interest, if any, in events removed from his own immediate orbit. Only a few persons had any special interest in far events, and they usually were business men, traders, some scholars, and especially money-lenders and speculators.

But better communications, better transportation, more general education, and the improved service of news established by the world press, especially by the Anglo-Saxon press, made information and ideas available to all, and this helped to create a further appetite for more and more information—News.

The history of the hunt for news is as exciting as the history of the world itself, and entirely inextricable from that history. It was about 1800 when the press began to develop enough independence of government restraint, economic strength, tradition and leadership to pursue the ends it considered right and desirable. This new freedom, it must be made clear, was almost exclusive to the press of Great Britain and the press of the United States, for in other countries the newspapers were held under so sharp a government supervision, or were so economically restricted, as to prevent any important display of enterprise. It is for this reason that the more dramatic portion of the history of

FIG. 1. SOME ALPHABETS OF THE WORLD

For description see List of Illustrations

press development during the nineteenth century and the first part of the twentieth century is concerned almost entirely with Anglo-American journalistic ventures.

Early in the nineteenth century, and even before, enterprising newspapers were laying the groundwork for the present-day system of news gathering. It was relatively simple to arrange to have letters of news written for publication and sent from Vienna, Paris, and other important capitals. It was far less simple and much more costly to send special correspondents to report specific events or to gather news in given places, or to make special arrangements for spreading the news, once obtained. It never had been done; there was no precedent.

When newspapers depended for their reports of foreign affairs upon other newspapers, published in foreign cities, rewriting or summarizing the reports given therein, translation of the news items often was necessary. An ability to translate such items brought some important figures into journalism. M. Charles Havas was one of them.[8]

Early examples of journalistic enterprise concerned means by which certain newspapers were able to obtain copies of foreign newspapers more quickly than their competitors. This continued to be a factor of importance in newspaper publishing, particularly in the New World, up to the successful operation of the Atlantic cable in 1866.[9]

[8] A Monsieur Tansky, early in the nineteenth century, prepared a letter known as *Le Petit Papier*, copies of which were circulated in London. It presented a summary of foreign news and was the basis for all or most of the foreign accounts at that time elaborated and published by leading newspapers, including *The Times*. J. Hall Richardson, *From the City to Fleet Street*, pp. 169-71.

[9] A classic story of how important the prompt receipt of information can be is that of Nathan Rothschild, of the famed banking house of that name. He has been reported to have made a fortune on the London Stock Exchange in 1815, a time when the service of news from the Continent was none too rapid, because he had the news of Napoleon's defeat at the Battle of Waterloo some twenty-four hours before the Government itself received the news.

One account of this incident is that a Rothschild courier, by rushing to the coast and taking a fast sailing boat across the Channel to Dover, was able to get the information to the London banking house most quickly. See H. M. Collins, *From Pigeon Post to Wireless*, pp. 25-26.

When events were moving rapidly in Europe at the end of the eighteenth century, British readers were especially anxious for news. Hence, after England declared war on France in 1793, and the importation of French newspapers was halted as contraband of war, the British newspapers and readers were left without a good supply of news from the Continent. John Walter, of *The Times,* which had been established in 1785, had a light cruiser crossing the Channel almost constantly. It would bring communications from *Times* correspondents, who had been engaged in Brussels and Paris in 1792,[10] and all the French and Belgian papers that could be obtained. These would be sent to the office of *The Times* by special messenger. Although the government sometimes interfered with the delivery of the foreign mail, this system enabled *The Times* to publish some most important news, including an eye-witness account of the execution of King Louis XVI, the surrender of Flushing in 1809, and the reports of Napoleon's rise and fall in the years up to 1815.[11]

*   *   *

Another version has it that Nathan Rothschild himself was present at the battle and when he was sure of the outcome he returned to England in an open boat on a stormy Channel. See Com. Frank Worsley and Capt. Glyn Griffith, *The Romance of Lloyds: From Coffee House to Palace,* pp. 211-12.

The authentic story, on the authority of Nathan Rothschild's grandson, Leopold, was that the news came to Nathan Rothschild in a small Dutch newspaper published at Amsterdam and brought to him promptly by the captain of one of the ships he owned. He is said to have passed on the information to Lord Liverpool of the British Treasury, without saying how he got it, but the news was not believed at the Treasury. See J. Hall Richardson, *From the City to Fleet Street,* pp. 169-71.

Nevertheless, it was upon this information that Nathan Rothschild is said by his grandson to have acted in the Stock Exchange. The Rothschilds did, in 1870, get news from besieged Paris by carrier pigeon, and knew two weeks in advance that the city was fated to surrender to the Prussians.

[10] Anon., *The History of The Times: "The Thunderer" in the Making. 1785-1841,* pp. 42-43.

[11] *Ibid.,* Ch. 7. Describes difficulties with Government over getting mail and newspapers, which often were addressed to merchants and firms in the City to avoid interference; W. D. Bowman, *The Story of "The Times,"* pp. 72-79, 82-86; J. W. Croker, *The Croker Papers,* V. 1, pp. 36-38. Mr. Croker was Secretary of the Admiralty in 1809 and received Mr. Walter's complaints.

The first war correspondent actually to be sent out by a newspaper appears to have been an unidentified representative of the *Swedish Intelligencer,* among the earliest European newspapers. He went into the field in 1807 with the forces of King Gustavus Adolphus.[12]

The Times, continuing in its enterprising way, would seem to have been the first British newspaper, not merely to engage resident correspondents in European cities, as it had done in 1792 and 1794, but also to send out its own special correspondent to represent it specifically in a foreign place.

It was partly as a means to overcome interference with its news service by the Government, which resented the paper's political independence, that *The Times* sent Henry Crabb Robinson to Altona, Germany, in 1807. Altona and Hamburg were at that time important clearing centers for news of Northern and Central Europe, although they were not news sources in themselves. From Altona, Robinson went to Sweden. Then he returned to London, but in 1808 and 1809 he was in Spain for six months and observed matters leading up to and including the Battle of Corunna.

Both in Germany and in Spain Robinson was reporting wars, and his assignment seems to represent both the first major special correspondence and the first war correspondence.[13] On the first assignment he devoted himself chiefly to preparing a summary of news from the newspapers published in the country of his residence, be it Germany or Sweden. In the later period he was somewhat more active in the pursuit of news facts.[14]

Actually, Crabb Robinson, as he is generally known, took a most important part in improving foreign news service. While at

[12] S. T. Sheppard, "In Memoriam: William Howard Russell. The Genesis of a Profession," *The United Service Magazine* (March 1907), V. 155, pp. 569-75, especially p. 570.

[13] W. D. Bowman, *The Story of "The Times,"* pp. 98-108.

[14] In addition to mention of Robinson in all standard histories of *The Times* and of British journalism, see: *Diary, Reminiscences, and Correspondence of Henry Crabb Robinson, F.S.A.* Barrister-at-law. Selected and edited by Thomas Sadler, 3 vols. 3rd ed. As this indicates, Mr. Robinson left journalism for the law.

Altona he urged upon John Walter an organization to gather news from abroad in time of peace as well as of war. He outlined his ideas of how such an organization should be formed and how the foreign news should be written. Mr. Walter appears to have liked the idea and to have liked Robinson, for he recalled him to London and made him the first Foreign Editor, and for a brief time virtual editor-in-chief of *The Times*. Under Robinson's direction and supervision, a system for obtaining foreign news was developed between 1807 and 1809, during part of which time he was at Corunna, Spain, for the campaign there.[15]

Charles Lewis Gruneisen, representing the *Morning Post* of London, went to cover the Carlist wars in Spain in 1837.[16] It was his work there, as much as anything, that soured the Duke of Wellington on war correspondents, and made difficulties for William Howard Russell some years later in the Crimean War, in which the British Army was directed by officers who had served with Wellington in Spain and had been taught to share his views, at least on this subject.[17]

Despite the precedents set by Robinson and Gruneisen, no English papers covered the Afghan campaigns of 1838-1842, or the first and second Punjab wars, and it was not until the Crimean War of 1854 that the practice was resumed.

By about 1840 the cost of obtaining foreign news had increased

[15] Anon., *The History of The Times: "The Thunderer" in the Making, 1785-1841*, pp. 137-146.

[16] The *Morning Post* of April 24, 1905, calls Mr. Gruneisen "the first regular war correspondent for a daily paper in the sense in which the duties have been discharged by such men as Sir W. H. Russell, the late Archibald Forbes, and Mr. E. F. Knight." Mr. Robinson's prior claim is discounted because "he never considered that his duty required his presence on the field of battle, and he never saw a shot fired unless it were at a very great distance." Mr. Gruneisen went to Spain along with the so-called Spanish Legion, made up of 10,000 men recruited in Great Britain to fight for Spain and which did so from 1835 to 1837.

[17] For the part that the Press played in the Peninsular campaign, and the attitude of the Duke of Wellington, see: W. F. P. Napier, *History of the War in the Peninsula and in the South of France from 1807 to 1814* (new rev. ed.), 6 vols.; J. H. Stocquelar, *The Life of Field Marshal the Duke of Wellington*, V. 2, pp. 151-52. The Press had conveyed to the enemy damaging information about the operations and disposition of the English troops, and it had undoubtedly lied about Wellington and libeled him.

so much that Mr. Walter permitted the *Morning Chronicle* and the *Morning Post* to share *The Times'* news—and the expenses involved in getting it.[18] The *Morning Herald,* which was excluded from this arrangement, set about building its own foreign service and succeeded so well that it won a wide reputation in Europe for quick and accurate accounts of foreign affairs.

Governments continued to interfere with the news dispatches, however. Guizot, in France, detained *The Times* courier in Paris in 1845 to delay delivery to the paper of messages from the Far East. This was to repay *The Times* for its unfavorable remarks about the government of Louis Philippe. *The Times,* however, re-routed its dispatches on an alternative course through Germany and so not only found itself able to avoid further French interference, but also to outstrip rival newspapers, notably the *Morning Herald.* This incident may be said to have *marked the beginning of competition* in rapid news delivery.[19]

About 1850 the *Morning Post* was represented in Paris by Mr. Algernon Borthwick, son of the owner. He was one of the first special correspondents and eventually became editor of the paper, subsequently assuming the title of Lord Glenesk. In later years, under his direction, the paper developed a rather good foreign service.

The Times also had Henry Reeve as Paris correspondent in 1848. When suffering from gout, and unable to be about, he engaged John Palgrave Simpson to substitute for him. The letters that Simpson wrote to *The Times* concerning the revolutionary outbreaks in Europe, especially as they were reflected in Paris, now form a standard historical work on the events of that stormy period.[20]

* * *

Although it is common to say that there was no extensive newspaper correspondence of importance, and, above all, no war correspondence, until William Howard Russell went to the

[18] T. H. S. Escott, *Masters of English Journalism,* p. 192.
[19] S. V. Makower, *Notes Upon the History of "The Times,"* *1785-1904,* pp. 19-21.
[20] J. P. Simpson, *Pictures from Revolutionary Paris.*

Crimean War for *The Times* in 1854, this is not accurate. Quite apart from the expeditions of Robinson and Gruneisen, which are perhaps more important than usually is implied, marked honors must go to the press of the United States for progress between 1808 and 1854.

James Gordon Bennett, who started the New York *Herald* in 1835, was responsible for the chief developments in American news enterprise during these years. At that time, when most foreign news was reprinted from London papers, American newspapers sent representatives in fast boats to board incoming ships and get the papers. Bennett's impatience with existing means of meeting incoming ships to obtain news led him to set the pace with faster news boats. He organized the first American system, and the first extensive world system, of foreign correspondence, so setting a standard for other newspapers to follow for many years to come.[21]

Mr. Bennett went to London to witness the coronation of Queen Victoria, which event he reported for the *Herald*. He organized in Europe, during 1838, a service of foreign news for the paper. Six regular correspondents were engaged, including Mr. Dionysius Lardner, who achieved a certain fame as head of the Paris office.[22] Later he augmented this service with correspondents in Texas,

[21] Mr. Bennett "obtained by wire from Washington the first speech ever thus reported in full, that of John C. Calhoun on the Mexican War. During the Civil War he brought the modern war correspondent into prolific existence by employing a staff of sixty-three persons to write dispatches about the battles, and otherwise to attend in newspaper fashion to the business of the conflict." See: A. S. Crockett, *When James Gordon Bennett Was Caliph of Bagdad*, p. 2.

It was in 1848 that the *Herald* "scooped" all other papers by printing the treaty of peace with Mexico, and also by reporting that Louis Philippe was certain to be ousted as France's ruler nearly a week before that event occurred. See: D. C. Seitz, *The James Gordon Bennetts, Father and Son*, p. 126. See also: Frederic Hudson, *Journalism in the United States*, Chs. 27, 28. Intimate contemporary picture of the *Herald*. L. M. Salmon, *The Newspaper and the Historian*, Chs. 8, 9. References to the special correspondent and the war correspondent, his evolution, and the part of the *Herald* in that evolution. Albert E. Coleman, "New and Authentic History of the *Herald* of the Bennetts," *Editor and Publisher*, V. 56 to V. 58. (Serialized from March 29, 1924, to June 13, 1925.)

[22] Frederic Hudson, *Journalism in the United States*, pp. 450-51.

then a foreign state; Mexico, Canada, and the larger cities of the United States.

In 1845 regular transatlantic passenger ship service began and ships called first at Halifax, N. S. Here some of the newspapers attempted to get the dispatches and foreign periodicals and rush them to New York ahead of the ship, but the *Herald* usually won the race, although not without competition, and finally was driven, partly as a measure of economy, perhaps, to subscribe to the service that Daniel H. Craig had arranged.[23]

The New York *Sun* was the particular rival of the *Herald* in news enterprise at that time, and in 1843 it established a correspondent in London. He ran a special horse express to carry his dispatches from London to Bristol to get the very latest foreign news on to ships there just before departure for New York. Other American newspapers did not enjoy being "beaten" by the *Herald* any more than did the *Sun,* and in 1846 sixteen papers in several cities conspired to get in the fastest possible time the first news of the arbitration decision in the Oregon boundary dispute with England, which had given rise in America to the slogan, "54-40 or Fight!" These newspapers combined to charter a swift pilot boat, which was dispatched with the greatest secrecy across the Atlantic to get the news and speed it back to American shores. The cost of this enterprise to the group, which the *Herald* ironically called "The Holy Alliance," was about $10,000, and all to no purpose, for the *Herald* had the news first despite the opposing plans.[24]

In England also the more enterprising newspapers went out to meet incoming ships. The ships from America were commonly met off Plymouth. Cape mail steamers also were watched for and boarded off that port.[25]

During the Mexican War of 1846 to 1848 Mr. Bennett's correspondence system functioned very well, especially with the telegraph, which had become practicable only in 1844, speeding

[23] Anon., *Life and Writings of James Gordon Bennett.*

[24] Frederic Hudson, *Journalism in the United States,* pp. 529-35.

[25] William Hunt, *Then and Now: Fifty Years of Newspaper Work,* pp. 46-47. Mr. Hunt began his career on the Plymouth *Western Courier* staff in 1846, and was Plymouth correspondent for the London *Daily News.*

news from Washington to New York. But A. S. Abell of the Baltimore *Sun* established his own overland express between New Orleans and Baltimore, with sixty blooded horses housed at relay stations along the way. During the War dispatches received by water at New Orleans were carried by this pony express to Baltimore. All other transport was far outdistanced, and even the Government dispatches sometimes arrived more than thirty hours later.[26]

From 1840 to 1850, a decade during which steam railroads and telegraph wires were being extended, the newspapers used both of them increasingly.[27] As the transition was being made the old and the new methods were combined. The news boats meeting incoming ships off Sandy Hook would carry their messages to a nearby telegraph station and from there the messages would be wired the rest of the way into New York City, so saving considerable time. Similarly Daniel H. Craig, with a news service built upon speedy delivery of news from Halifax or from ships between Boston and Halifax, was able to hasten the news to New York by wire from Boston, where the telegraph line then reached.

Despite all of these methods, however, the normal time required for European news to see print in New York was from ten days to two weeks, until 1866, when the Atlantic cable went into successful operation. The first cable, laid in 1858, had broken almost at once, and the coming of the Civil War in America prevented the completion of another or the mending of the first until after the termination of hostilities.

* * *

After the Mexican War the New York *Tribune*, which had been established by Horace Greeley in 1841, joined the *Herald* and the *Sun* in the maintenance of several foreign correspondents. By 1850 it had four permanent European correspondents, two

[26] F. L. Bullard, *Famous War Correspondents*, Ch. 13.
[27] D. C. Seitz, *The James Gordon Bennetts, Father and Son*, pp. 120-21, descriptive of the development of the telegraph in the United States, and the use of news boats. Frederic Hudson, *Journalism in the United States*, Ch. 37, "The Telegraphic Era," presenting an excellent description of the extension of the telegraph.

correspondents in Canada, and one each in Mexico, Cuba, and Central America.[28]

Few foreign correspondents, however, whether for American or British newspapers, were natives of the country for whose newspapers they wrote, nor did they view impartially the events of which they wrote. It was considered preferable at that time, however, to engage as a correspondent some person long a resident and acquainted not only with the language, but with the intimate details of political and other affairs in the country in question. This usually resulted in the appointment of a native, preferably one able to write and speak English. Usually it was only at times of crisis, such as during wars, that staff members were sent from the home office to report events from a definitely national viewpoint.

Under such circumstances, therefore, occurred the next great stride in the history of bold news reporting. That came in 1854, when William Howard Russell, long a staff member of *The Times* of London, and previously its correspondent in Ireland, was sent to the Crimea to cover the war in which British and French forces met Russian forces.

Although he was coldly received and shunned by British staff officers, trained under Wellington in the Peninsular Campaign to regard war correspondents in the field as a distinct liability, he wrote a series of letters so vivid, so outspoken, and so powerful that they had far-reaching results. They won him fame, if no popularity, among military men at the time, but they also resulted in a much-needed reorganization of the British Army and its administration.

[28] F. L. Bullard, *Famous War Correspondents*, Ch. 13; W. G. Bleyer, *Main Currents in the History of American Journalism;* Victor Rosewater, *History of Coöperative News Gathering in the United States;* L. M. Salmon, *The Newspaper and the Historian*, Ch. 9. The *Morning Chronicle* of London is shown by its accounts to have maintained a staff correspondent in Paris as early as 1850, and to have paid varying sums to correspondents or agents in ten other European cities, in New York, and Montreal; to agents in Boston and Halifax, and to correspondents in Bombay, Singapore, in China, Jamaica, Malta, and Alexandria. Agents at ports also were paid to gather news and facilitate its transmission to London. F. K. Hunt, *The Fourth Estate*, V. 2, pp. 197-98.

As another result, Miss Florence Nightingale went to the Crimea and laid the foundation for the great Red Cross organization and for numerous important advances in public sanitation.[29]

Mr. Russell's experiences in the Crimea are said to have started war correspondence. Mr. Atkins's biography describes him on the fly-leaf as "The First Special Correspondent," and a memorial bust to Russell in the crypt of St. Paul's Cathedral, London, calls him "The first and greatest of war correspondents." Without wishing to detract in any way from Russell's accomplishments, which won him his knighthood, neither of these descriptions is accurate. Henry Crabb Robinson and Charles Lewis Gruneisen

[29] J. B. Atkins, *The Life of Sir William Howard Russell*, V. 1, Chs. 12-21. Relates to the Crimea and aftermath; A. W. Kinglake, *Invasion of Crimea* (6th ed.), V. 4, p. 169, V. 7, pp. 204-54. Contains references to the part of the press in reporting the Crimean War and the effects of the reports, with special attention to *The Times*, for which this historian of the war has praise. At that time the telegraph reached only as far as Vienna, so the correspondents had to depend on other means to get their dispatches to London and elsewhere.

I. B. O'Malley, *Florence Nightingale, 1820-1856*. A study of her life down to the end of the Crimean War. Miss Nightingale, then Lady Superintendent of the Establishment for the Care of Gentlewomen in Sickness, in upper Harley Street, read Russell's dispatches in *The Times* in the summer and autumn of 1854. It was his account of the inadequate treatment of those British soldiers wounded at the Battle of the River Alma, of the hardships of the army on the march to Sebastopol, and of the poor British hospital facilities at Scutari, across the Bosphorus from Constantinople, that roused her professional interest. An article on October 12, 1854, and another on October 14, asking why the British had no Sisters of Charity like the French, at last decided Miss Nightingale to go to the Crimea. With great energy she acted to obtain money, nurses, and official authority; left London on October 21st, landed at Constantinople November 4th, and so started the Red Cross.

See also: W. H. Russell, *The War*. A volume containing Mr. Russell's dispatches to *The Times*, printed practically without alteration; W. H. Russell, *The British Expedition to the Crimea* (rev. ed.). This is Mr. Russell's postwar résumé of the war, and is not his correspondence; Rollo Ogden, *Life and Letters of Edwin Lawrence Godkin*, 2 vols. Godkin, as a man of 22 years, was sent late in 1853 to cover the Crimean War for the *Daily News* of London. He remained in the field for two years, returning to London in 1855. In 1856 he went to the United States, where his greater journalistic career opened up. He and a representative of the *Morning Chronicle* arrived in the Crimea before Russell, but their dispatches apparently did not equal Russell's, for whom Godkin had great admiration.

were war correspondents before him by many years, and Gruneisen, at least, had seen some real fighting. So had George Wilkins Kendall of the New Orleans *Picayune,* who reported the Mexican War in 1846 to 1848, along with other American correspondents.[30]

The distinction has been made between Gruneisen as the first definitely "commissioned" war correspondent, and Russell as the first "professional" war correspondent, but Kendall and some of his colleagues deserve recognition as setting the pace for the so-called "modern" war correspondence. Russell, however, was the first "professional" correspondent in that he was to continue as a journalist specializing on wars, and he was one of the first actually to go into the field, instead of writing from somewhere well behind the lines. Russell subsequently reported the British campaigns in India in 1857, the American Civil War during 1861, the Franco-Prussian War of 1870, and other engagements.

The *Daily News* of London had Jesse White Mario in Italy from 1857 to 1860, or thereabouts, reporting the liberation of Italy. The *Daily News* continued to be prominent during the 'sixties and 'seventies for its excellent coverage of news, both relating to war activities and peace activities.[31]

Henry J. Raymond, first editor of the New York *Times,* and one of its founders, was himself a witness of the battle of Solferino in 1859, with his Paris correspondent, Dr. W. E. Johnston, and contrived to get a good account of it to New York for publication in the *Times* ten days before any other paper had any news of it whatever.[32] William Howard Russell also was a witness of this battle.[33]

[30] J. B. Atkins, *The Life of Sir William Howard Russell,* 2 vols.; F. L. Bullard, *Famous War Correspondents,* Chs. 1, 2, 13, 14. The experiences of Mr. Kendall are described in Ch. 13; W. D. Bowman, *The Story of "The Times,"* Ch. 9; Sir Edward Cook, *Delane of The Times,* V. 1, Ch. 6. The last two references deal with the part Delane took during the Crimean War in supporting Russell in his fearless journalism, despite pressure from high places to halt the criticism of the army administration.

[31] Justin McCarthy and Sir John R. Robinson, *The "Daily News" Jubilee,* Chs. 5-9.

[32] Elmer Davis, *History of the New York Times, 1851-1921,* pp. 40-44.

[33] J. B. Atkins, *The Life of Sir William Howard Russell,* V. 2, Ch. 5.

The American Civil War brought the war correspondent into active service. George W. Smalley, representing the New York *Tribune,* was one of the more famous. That war called Russell to the United States for a short and not especially happy time. Reuters, then a youthful British news agency, scored some of its most striking journalistic triumphs during the period and so helped to establish itself firmly. But Reuters' dispatches were interpreted in the North of the United States as biased in favor of the Southern cause, which was sympathetically viewed in England until the last year of the war. In fact, the only London newspaper that was favorable to the North in its dispatches was the *Daily News,* for which Edwin L. Godkin was correspondent in America.

Naturally, American newspapers covered the war in detail. The increasing use of the electric telegraph, as it was called, helped speed dispatches and fed the fires of public interest in the struggle, and sent American newspaper circulations mounting rapidly. This introduced a period of new prosperity and development for the American press.[34] The New York *Herald,* always enterprising, had a particularly fine service, spending $500,000 on coverage during the period of the war, a tremendous sum in those times.

* * *

[34] Allan Nevins, *The Evening Post: A Century of Journalism,* pp. 315-25. Presents details about Civil War correspondence for New York papers; F. M. O'Brien, *The Story of the Sun,* Ch. 8; Elmer Davis, *History of the New York Times, 1851-1921,* Pt. I, Ch. 2; D. C. Seitz, *The James Gordon Bennetts, Father and Son,* Chs. 8, 9; G. W. Smalley, *Anglo-American Memories,* Ch. 14, also some references in Chs. 15, 16, 17; J. B. Atkins, *The Life of Sir William Howard Russell,* V. 2, Chs. 1-8; Royal Cortissoz, *The New York Tribune: Incidents and Personalities in Its History,* pp. 22-25; Frederic Hudson, *Journalism in the United States,* Ch. 48. Discusses war correspondence in general, and the Civil War coverage in particular, with some attention to the fate of correspondents, some of whom were killed, wounded, or captured; L. M. Salmon, *The Newspaper and the Historian,* Ch. 9; Henry Villard, *Memoirs of Henry Villard,* 2 vols. (He was a Civil War correspondent.) F. L. Bullard, *Famous War Correspondents,* Chs. 1, 14; G. H. Payne, *History of Journalism in the United States,* Chs. 23, 24; Ida M. Tarbell, *A Reporter for Lincoln;* Havilah Babcock, "The Press and the Civil War," *Journalism Quarterly* (March, 1929), pp. 1-5.

After the Civil War, Mr. Smalley was sent to Europe to head a
newly established London bureau to serve the New York *Tribune*
and to apply to the coverage of European news some of the
American practices of news gathering.[35] He arrived in 1866 at the
beginning of the brief war between Prussia and Austria, and he
sent to the *Tribune* one of the first news cable dispatches, reporting a break in peace negotiations and the threat of renewed
hostilities. His hundred-word dispatch cost $500. Altogether, the
paper spent $125,506.97 on cable tolls during the short conflict,
which was more than it had spent on telegraph tolls during the
entire Civil War.[36]

Mr. Smalley brought about a change in the technique of covering foreign news for American newspapers, and played an important part in the coverage of the War of 1870 between France
and Prussia. Although he remained in his London office, it was his
enterprise that brought some of the greatest news coverage of the
war and revitalized British news practices into the bargain.

[35] The New York *Tribune* balance-sheet reveals that it spent for news
gathering the following sums in 1865 and 1866, the last year of the Civil
War and the year following:

Purpose	1865	1866
Editorial expense	$ 51,844.05	$ 81,775.40
Correspondence	41,073.76	49,300.57
News by telegraph	22,044.76	58,776.04
Harbor news	1,875.20	2,112.34
	$116,837.77	$191,964.35

From D. C. Seitz, *Horace Greeley: Founder of the New York Tribune*, pp.
111-12: "Not only was the *Tribune* foremost in its reports of the Franco-
Prussian War, with Mr. Smalley directing the service in London, but it had
been almost as enterprising as the *Herald* in seeking foreign news reports.
So in 1848 it had sent Charles A. Dana to France to report the Revolution
that drove Louis Philippe from his throne and brought in the Second Republic, with Napoleon III as President." *Ibid.*, pp. 112-13.

[36] G. W. Smalley, *Anglo-American Memories*, pp. 144-49; James Grant,
The Newspaper Press, V. 2, pp. 341-49. Refers to the early use of the Atlantic cable by American newspapers. The *Pall Mall Gazette* of London caused
something of a sensation in 1870 by having cabled from New York, at
great expense, a column-long story of Mrs. Harriet Beecher Stowe's defense
of a statement she had previously made about Lord Byron. See: Frederic
Hudson, *Journalism in the United States*, p. 606; Harry Baehr, Jr., *The New
York Tribune Since the Civil War*.

Late in 1866, after his first arrival in Europe, Mr. Smalley returned to New York. But in 1867 he was sent to London again by the *Tribune* under an agreement to remain until 1870. His previous experience had convinced him that the introduction of the cable into the news equation called for a revision of the system for covering international affairs. Just as Crabb Robinson in 1807 had suggested fundamental changes in news-gathering methods and so paved the way for the extension of *The Times* service, which set standards for other papers to follow, so Smalley just sixty years later brought about another change in foreign news-handling methods.

Mr. Smalley believed London should be the distributing center of European news destined for publication in the United States. He maintained that the London correspondent, as the responsible agent in charge, ought to have increased authority, permitting him to organize the news service, appoint and dismiss correspondents, and exercise complete supervision over the European staff and the gathering of European news. Previously all direction had centered in the New York office but Mr. Smalley felt that the London correspondent was in a more advantageous position to sense a situation and to act quickly and wisely. When he returned to England, he was empowered to act on this theory. Other New York newspapers looked upon such an arrangement as tantamount to setting up a rival office, and considered it a mistaken policy. James Gordon Bennett was one who ridiculed the plan, but he was to adopt it later for the *Herald*.

The emergencies arising in connection with the coverage of the Franco-Prussian War in 1870 brought a test of the plan's value. In that year Mr. Smalley formed the first international alliance of newspapers when he arranged with the *Daily News* of London to exchange with the *Tribune* the news of the war. Both papers had men in the field. Mr. Smalley also found it advantageous to know what Reuters was distributing and what the Associated Press was sending to New York, so that unwarranted duplication would not occur in his own dispatches, involving waste of money on cable tolls.

The alliance turned out to be fortunate for both papers. Remarkable news dispatches by Holt White, Gustave Muller, M. Mejanel, a Mr. Hands, and Moncure D. Conway, a Unitarian pastor of Washington, D. C., who witnessed the Battle of Gravelotte, all *Tribune* representatives, when published by the *Daily News*, through its exchange arrangement with the *Tribune*, gave the *Daily News* a favorable reputation throughout Europe.[37] The *Tribune* later benefited similarly by its right to the dispatches of Mr. Archibald Forbes, sent into the field for the *Daily News*, and by the communications of Mr. Henry Labouchere, trapped in Paris when the French capital was surrounded by the Prussians, but whose dispatches were smuggled out by balloon post.[38] These dispatches remain as remarkable historical documents.

The *Tribune* spent a great deal of money on its service, and the expenditure of the *Daily News* for war telegrams, exclusive of the salaries and expenses of correspondents, amounted to £1,200 a month. The entire tempo of the war correspondence was greatly speeded up, due to the general use of the telegraph, and the risk to the individual correspondent in the field was far greater than

[37] Fulsome praise is given the New York *Tribune* and Mr. Smalley, although he is not named, by A. W. Kinglake, the historian, in *The Invasion of the Crimea*, 6th ed. In V. 7, p. 204, note No. 4 refers to p. 449 of the Appendix, where appear these sentences: "In justice toward the great nation which I like to call 'English,' and sometimes refuse to call 'foreign' I ought perhaps to acknowledge that the extraordinary triumphs of European journalism at the time of the Franco-Prussian War of 1870-71 were due, in no slight degree, to the vigor, the sagacity, and the enterprise that were brought to bear on the objects from the other side of the Atlantic. The success of the 'partnership for the purpose of war news' which had been formed between one of our London newspapers and the New York *Tribune* was an era in the journalism of Europe, though not in that of the United States, where the advance had an earlier date, deriving from their great Civil War. I cannot speak of the New York *Tribune* without thinking of one of its conquests achieved in another direction ... years ago, it established in London a kindly, highly-gifted correspondent, whose charming house has done more than the stateliest embassies could well have achieved towards dispersing old, narrow prejudices, and creating and maintaining good-will, affection, and friendship between the two great English nations."

[38] These dispatches later were collected in book form, with several new letters, all very lively and interesting, covering the period from Sept. 18, 1870, to Feb. 10, 1871. See: Henry Labouchere, *Diary of a Besieged Resident in Paris*. (*By H. L.*), 3rd ed. See also: Algar Labouchere Thorold, *The Life of Henry Labouchere*. A biography, by his grandson.

ever before because of the long-range rifles that had come into use.[39]

William Howard Russell again went into the field for *The Times* during that conflict. As the "dean" of the correspondents, he took a prominent position and was made much of, so much, in fact, that he drew the fire of Matthew Arnold, in a satirical essay that lampooned the entire British press.[40]

[39] Reference to the coverage of the Franco-Prussian War: F. L. Bullard, *Famous War Correspondents*, Chs. 2, 3; Sir John Robinson, *Fifty Years of Fleet Street*. Robinson, editor of the *Daily News*, sent Archibald Forbes to the war; G. W. Smalley, *Anglo-American Memories*, Chs. 23, 24, 25. Accounts of his new theory of foreign news handling, and of the great dispatches of the War of 1870; Royal Cortissoz, *The Life of Whitelaw Reid*, V. 1, Ch. 12. How the New York *Tribune* covered the War, and built up its foreign service, from the New York end; Justin McCarthy and Sir John R. Robinson, *The "Daily News" Jubilee*, Chs. 5-9; A. I. Dasent, *John Thaddeus Delane: Editor of The Times*, V. 2, Ch. 14; G. M. Fenn, *George Alfred Henty*, Chs. 21-25; T. H. S. Escott, *Masters of English Journalism*, pp. 249-51. Mr. Escott implies that Mr. White was selected by Frederick Greenwood of the *Pall Mall Gazette* to cover the War, and credits Mr. Greenwood with a shrewd choice; Royal Cortissoz, *The New York Tribune: Incidents and Personalities in Its History*, pp. 26-34. Asserts that Smalley was second only to Henri de Blowitz in European fame; James Grant, *The Newspaper Press*, V. 2, Ch. 10. Describes history of war correspondence up to the time of the Franco-Prussian War; Archibald Forbes, *Memories and Studies of War and Peace*, Chs. 1, 10. He says that Hands's telegraphed half column about the Battle of Gravelotte "has the right to stand monumentally as the first successful attempt in the old world to describe a battle over the telegraph wires" (p. 220). He gives great praise to the New York *Tribune* and its correspondents for enterprise; Archibald Forbes, *My Experiences of the War Between France and Germany*, 2 vols.; Archibald Forbes, *The War Correspondnce of the Daily News, 1870;* J. B. Atkins, *The Life of Sir William Howard Russell*, V. 2, Chs. 13-18; Harry Baehr, Jr., *The New York Tribune Since the Civil War.*

[40] Matthew Arnold, *Friendship's Garland*, pp. 111-12. A fanciful scene in Versailles, described in part as follows: "...Dr. Russell of *The Times* was preparing to mount his war-horse. You know the sort of thing—he has described it himself over and over again. Bismarck at the horse's head, the Crown Prince holding his stirrup, and the old King of Prussia hoisting Russell into the saddle. When he was there, the distinguished public servant waved his hand in acknowledgment, and rode slowly down the street, accompanied by the *gamins* of Versailles, who even in their present dejection could not forbear a few involuntary cries of '*Quel homme!*' Always unassuming, he alighted at the lodgings of the Grand Duke of Oldenburg, a potentate of the second or even the third order, who had beckoned to him from the

The excellent handling of the news of the Franco-Prussian War marked the beginning of a lavish policy of sending almost all news by the fastest means, regardless of expense, and reduced the dependence upon the mails.

*   *   *

Although not a war exploit, the accomplishment of Henry Morton Stanley, who, on a commission for James Gordon Bennett, Jr., of the New York *Herald,* went into the heart of Africa in 1869 seeking some trace of Dr. David Livingstone, stirred wide interest. Dr. Livingstone, a missionary and an explorer, had gone into the Equatorial regions of what was then a "Dark Continent" in March, 1868, and had not been heard of since. The *Daily Telegraph* of London shared with the New York *Herald* both the expense and the glory of the expedition. Stanley was gone from 1869 to 1872 on what has been called by some the greatest assignment in journalistic history, but which at first was considered a joke, if not a hoax, by certain London and New York papers. In November, 1871, he found Dr. Livingstone, but it was 1872 before he himself returned to civilization. When he did so his reports occasioned a new sensation.[41]

Previous to this African adventure, Stanley had taken part as a correspondent in General Hancock's expedition against the Indians in the great American plains. As a correspondent for the New York *Herald,* he also had gone to Abyssinia in 1868 with an Anglo-Abyssinian expedition sent to subdue King Theodore and to obtain the release of Consul Cameron and other officers and missionaries. The expedition was a success and Stanley managed to get his account to the New York *Herald* weeks be-

---

window...." In reference to this satirical "dig," see: J. B. Atkins, *The Life of Sir William Howard Russell,* V. 2, p. 202. Although the picture as painted by Arnold was exaggerated, Atkins says that Russell was indeed "treated with great consideration and friendliness" by the "powerful personages" who had come to Versailles, including the King of Prussia, Bismarck, and Moltke.

[41] D. C. Seitz, *The James Gordon Bennetts, Father and Son,* Ch. 12; Dorothy Stanley, ed., *The Autobiography of Sir Henry Morton Stanley, G.C.B.,* edited by his wife; Anon., *Life and Finding of Dr. Livingstone;* Priscilla Price, *The Life of Sir Henry Morton Stanley.*

fore any other report appeared, and so he took rank with the best war correspondents. In 1869 he roved about the Mediterranean countries, doing special articles, before he returned to Paris to receive the Livingstone assignment.

After that great adventure he accompanied the British campaign against the Ashantees, in 1873-1874, again for the New York *Herald;* and in 1875 the *Daily Telegraph* once more joined with the *Herald* to send Stanley to Africa on a new expedition, this time of discovery. The journey and the well-publicized reports that followed, were important in opening up Africa.[42]

The *Daily Telegraph,* in fact, was partial to expeditions of discovery. Acting independently, it had sent Mr. George Smith to Nineveh in June, 1873, and there he discovered missing fragments of the cuneiform account of the Deluge as recorded in the Bible. It likewise supported Sir Harry Johnston's exploration of Kilimanjaro in 1884-1885, and Lionel Decla's march from the Cape of Good Hope north to Cairo in 1899-1900.[43]

Following Stanley's two sensational journeys, which occupied the journalistic spotlight, there were a number of wars of limited extent which attracted some attention. First was the Serbian campaign of 1876, followed by the Russo-Turkish conflict of 1877-1878, and other campaigns in the Balkans and the Near East, in which participated such famed war correspondents as Archibald Forbes, Januarius Aloysius MacGahan, and Frederic Villiers. The first two represented the *Daily News* of London, Villiers was a war artist for the London *Graphic.*

Some of the revelations by MacGahan of Turkish atrocities in Bulgaria in 1876 aroused vast indignation in Great Britain and elsewhere, and were almost as far-reaching in effect as William Howard Russell's Crimean dispatches had been twenty years earlier. MacGahan was an American and originally correspondent for an American newspaper, but most of his important work was done for the *Daily News* of London. Gladstone was greatly

[42] H. M. Stanley, *Through the Dark Continent,* new ed., 2 vols. In this work is presented Stanley's own version of the journey.

[43] J. C. Francis, *Notes by the Way,* with memoirs of Joseph Knight, F.S.A., p. 198.

aroused by MacGahan's letters and, although Lord Beaconsfield tried to dismiss them as mere "coffee house babble," they were verified, and Turkish rule in Europe was circumscribed in 1878 by the Treaty of Berlin.[44]

William Howard Russell, who left *The Times* several years earlier to edit the *Army and Navy Journal,* in 1879 was sent out to cover the Zulu War for the *Daily Telegraph,* an assignment notable because it is said to have marked the departure from a rule of anonymity for correspondents. Russell was given a "by-line," that is, a signature with his reports.

It was at about this time, too, that Henri de Blowitz was making a reputation for himself and for *The Times* by his correspondence from Paris. He joined *The Times* in Paris in 1871 and continued there for many years. In addition to forestalling what was at least a possible war between France and Germany in about 1875, he attended the Congress of Berlin in 1878 and managed to obtain the Treaty ending the Russo-Turkish War and to have it published in *The Times* even before it was signed in Berlin.[45]

There were Near-Eastern and Balkan adventures during the late years of the nineteenth century, in which Edmond O'Donovan, for one, took an active part.[46] There were the Egyptian campaigns of 1883, in which some of the correspondents already mentioned again were active, and in which Bennet Burleigh of

[44] Archibald Forbes, *The War Correspondence of the Daily News, 1877-1878;* Archibald Forbes, *Souvenirs of Some Continents.* A series of papers based upon his experiences and acquaintances; J. A. MacGahan, *The War Correspondence of the "Daily News," 1877-1878* (see above); J. A. MacGahan, *Campaigning on the Oxus, and the Fall of Khiva,* 4th ed.; J. A. MacGahan, *The Turkish Atrocities in Bulgaria;* J. A. MacGahan, *Under the Northern Lights;* Frederic Villiers, *Villiers: His Five Decades of Adventure,* 2 vols.; Frank Scudmore, *A Sheaf of Memories.* He was a correspondent for *The Times* and the *Daily News* in the Greco-Turkish War, the Sudan campaign, etc.

[45] These and many other amazing exploits he recounts in his *Memoirs* with such a singular lack of reserve that the irreverent have been known to make a pun on his name in the phrase, "Blowitz own horn." Henri de Blowitz, *Memoirs of M. de Blowitz.*

[46] Edmond O'Donovan, *The Merv Oasis. Travels and Adventures East of the Caspian During the Years 1879-80-81.* 2 vols.

the *Daily Telegraph* [47] and Moberly Bell, Egyptian correspondent for *The Times*, gained fame, among others. And there were more peaceful, but no less important exploits of other correspondents in the political realm.[48]

The Boer War, or South African War, of 1899 to 1901, brought further reputation to Burleigh, and also to George Warrington Steevens, of the *Daily Mail;* Winston Churchill, then representing the *Morning Post;* and to one or two American correspondents, such as Julian Ralph and Richard Harding Davis.[49] *The Times* of London gave very fine coverage to that war, including an excellent series of letters from the besieged Ladysmith, an exclusive account of the signature of peace at Pretoria on June 1, 1902, and some special and excellent accounts of important battles. Earlier, the *Daily Mail*, through its representative, Edgar Wallace—later to become widely known as a writer of mystery tales—and thanks to an ingenious system of signals and cable codes, was able to announce that satisfactory peace terms

[47] Bennet Burleigh is supposed to be the correspondent described in Rudyard Kipling's *The Light that Failed*. See also: Bennet Burleigh, *The Natal Campaign;* Bennet Burleigh, *Empire of the East; or Japan and Russia at war, 1904-5.* This covers his later experiences in the Russo-Japanese War.

[48] Julius Chambers, *News Hunting on Three Continents.* Recounts experiences serving the New York *World* and the New York *Herald* in the United States and in Europe, and in starting the Paris edition of the New York *Herald;* A. S. Crockett, *When James Gordon Bennett Was Caliph of Bagdad.* References to the New York *Herald* and the Paris edition of the *Herald;* Frank Dilnot, *The Adventures of a Newspaper Man.* Service for a London newspaper, especially in Russia; W. J. Stillman, *The Autobiography of a Journalist,* 2 vols. *The Times* correspondent in Rome and the Balkans, also served the New York *Tribune;* Charles Lowe, *The Tale of a "Times" Correspondent.* Correspondent in Berlin for *The Times* from 1878 to 1891. L. M. Salmon, *The Newspaper and the Historian,* Ch. 8; Joseph Hatton, *Journalistic London;* W. D. Bowman, *The Story of The Times;* Henri de Blowitz, *Memoirs of M. de Blowitz;* Lady Grogan, *The Life of J. D. Bourchier;* Wickham Steed, *Through Thirty Years, 1892-1922,* 2 vols.

[49] Winston Churchill, *My Early Life: A Roving Commission;* Ernest Smith, *Journalism: By Some Masters of the Craft* (see Anon.). A lecture, "Reminiscences of a War Correspondent," covering the period from the Boer War to the World War; C. B. Davis, *Adventures and Letters of Richard Harding Davis;* Julian Ralph, *The Making of a Journalist;* F. A. MacKenzie, *The Mystery of the Daily Mail, 1896-1921,* Ch. 2; see H. W. Nevinson, under n. 53.

had been concluded. This paper was two days ahead of all other news reports.[50] Reuters' report of the relief of Mafeking, coming well in advance of any official announcement, was one of the great journalistic triumphs of the War and a great credit to the organization, although the name of the correspondent responsible is not known.

The Spanish-American War of 1898 had brought fame, among others, to Richard Harding Davis, James Creelman, Ralph Paine and Stephen Crane.

The Russo-Japanese War of 1904 brought together again many of the correspondents who had covered the Spanish-American and the Boer wars. It was during the Russo-Japanese War, too, that Lionel James of *The Times* put wireless to one of its first important tests in news gathering.[51]

The Balkan Wars were reasonably well covered,[52] but it was

[50] Anon., *Modern Journalism. A Guide for Beginners.* By a London Editor, pp. 61-64.

[51] Lionel James, *High Pressure*, Chs. 17-21; C. B. Davis, *Adventures and Letters of Richard Harding Davis;* R. D. Paine, *Roads of Adventure;* O. K. Davis, *Released for Publication;* D. C. Seitz, *The James Gordon Bennetts, Father and Son*, p. 371; M. E. Stone, *Fifty Years a Journalist*, pp. 228-30, in reference to the Spanish-American War, and pp. 278-84 in reference to the Russo-Japanese War. Mr. Stone says the Associated Press cable tolls for reporting the encounter between the American Navy and Cervera's fleet were $8,000, while the costs for reporting the entire war exceeded $300,000; J. K. Winkler, *W. R. Hearst: An American Phenomenon*, pp. 133, 143-45, and Ch. 7. James Creelman, *On the Great Highway;* R. H. Davis, *The Cuban-Porto Rican Campaign;* Fairfax Downey, *Richard Harding Davis: His Day;* R. H. Davis, *A Year from a Correspondent's Note-Book;* F. M. O'Brien, *The Story of the Sun*, pp. 353-56, in reference to Spanish-American War, and pp. 376-77 in reference to the Russo-Japanese War; Elmer Davis, *History of the New York Times, 1851-1921*. The *Times* took no part in special coverage of the Spanish-American War because it was not, at the time, financially able. For its part in the Russo-Japanese War, see pp. 228-31, 283-84. Edgar Mels, "War News. Its Collection and Cost," *Sat. Eve. Post* (July 2, 1904), pp. 16-17. Stanley Washburn, *The Cable Game.* Experiences of a Chicago *Daily News* correspondent covering the Russo-Japanese War and other stories of the period.

[52] Lady Grogan, *The Life of J. D. Bourchier*, Chs. 2-4. See also: Sir Philip Gibbs, H. W. Nevinson, and others in n. 53, below, as some of the same correspondents covered both the Balkan Wars and the Great War. Percival Phillips, "Out in the Cold: The Tragedy of the War Correspondent," *Sat. Eve. Post* (Feb. 1, 1913), pp. 14-15; (Feb. 15), pp. 26-28. G. Marvin,

the Great War that brought one of the greatest tests of the war correspondence system, and gave added luster to the names of Frederick Palmer and H. W. Nevinson, and world-wide reputations to such men as Sir Philip Gibbs, Sir Percival Phillips, and Edwin L. James.[53]

Those wars which have occurred since the War of 1914-1918 have received uneven coverage. During the Manchurian campaign of the Japanese Army, and Japan's temporary occupation of Shanghai, the Anglo-American press, particularly, went to great lengths to cover it. On the other hand the Chaco War between Bolivia and Paraguay received relatively little attention from the press. Revolutions in South American countries were sketchily covered, except as they became manifest in Buenos Aires and Rio de Janeiro, where there was some measure of press organization. Italy's campaign in Ethiopia in 1935-1936, however, received a great deal of press attention, and correspondents went

"Chroniclers of the Balkan War: How the Modern War Correspondent Gets His News—or Fails To," *Independent* (June 19, 1913), V. 74, pp. 1390-96.

[53] F. A. MacKenzie, *The Mystery of the Daily Mail, 1896-1921,* Ch. 10; Philip Gibbs, *Adventures in Journalism,* Chs. 15-21; I. F. Marcosson, *Adventures in Interviewing.* He interviewed many of the important wartime figures, chiefly for the *Saturday Evening Post;* J. W. Barrett, *The World, the Flesh, and Messrs. Pulitzer,* pp. 70-73. Refers to Herbert Bayard Swope's wartime feats of news gathering; T. M. Johnson, *Without Censor;* Frederick Palmer, *My Year of the War;* Frederick Palmer, *Our Greatest Battle—the Meuse-Argonne;* Frederick Palmer, *With the New Army on the Somme: My Second Year of the War;* Frederick Palmer, *With My Own Eyes;* Frederick Palmer, *America in France: The Story of the Making of an Army.* Also: Frederick Palmer, *Going to War in Greece,* and Frederick Palmer, *With Kuroki in Manchuria;* H. W. Nevinson, *Last Changes, Last Chances;* also H. W. Nevinson, *Changes and Chances,* and H. W. Nevinson, *More Changes, More Chances;* Elmer Davis, *History of the New York Times, 1851-1921,* Chs. 5, 6, and pp. 187-88; M. E. Stone, *Fifty Years a Journalist,* pp. 299-330; Royal Cortissoz, *The New York Tribune: Incidents and Personalities in Its History,* pp. 31, 67-68; Sir Edward Cook, *The Press in War Time;* J. M. de Beaufort, *Behind the German Veil;* Arno Dosch-Fleurot, *Through War to Revolution;* George Seldes, *You Can't Print That!* George Seldes, *Can These Things Be!* Wilbur Forrest, *Behind the Front Page;* C. S. Lord, *The Young Man and Journalism,* Ch. 13; Webb Miller, *I Found No Peace;* Harry Baehr, Jr., *The New York Tribune Since the Civil War;* H. W. Nevinson, *Fire of Life;* Granville Fortescue, *Front Line and Deadline;* Wythe Williams, *Dusk of Empire.*

there in considerable numbers, but found the news so meager and so difficult to obtain that most of them left early in 1936.[54]

The Spanish Civil War, again, presented unique problems for the press, beginning in the summer of 1936. It involved hazards for correspondents, censorship obstacles, a scattered news field, and it required mobilization of all facilities to give it coverage.[55]

* * *

What the wars from 1850 to 1870 did to stir newspaper enterprise was continued from 1870 to 1890 by the Stanley journeys into Africa, wars in the south of Europe, and by interests built upon expanding world trade and travel.

During the following twenty years, from 1890 to 1910, new wars were important in stimulating correspondence, but hardly more so than was the further extension of commercial enterprise and the fact that the development of a complete world system of telegraph and cable lines made communication easy and comparatively cheap. It was in these two decades, under Mr. Moberly Bell, that *The Times'* system of foreign correspondence was built to such notable heights.[56]

[54] Anon., "War in Ethiopia Will Test Reporters," *Editor and Publisher* (July 27, 1935), p. 26; J. W. Perry, "Writers Mobilize for War Coverage," *Editor and Publisher* (Aug. 31, 1935), pp. 9, 12; Webb Miller, "Webb Miller Tells of Hardships of News Men in Ethiopia," *Editor and Publisher* (Nov. 9, 1935), p. 11; Anon., "Newshawks, Seals," *Time* (Oct. 14, 1935), pp. 40-42; R. H. Markham, "News Hunting Poor Sport in Ethiopia," *Christian Science Monitor* (Jan. 31, 1936), pp. 1, 3; Wynant Davis Hubbard, *Fiasco in Ethiopia;* W. W. Chaplin, *Blood and Ink;* Webb Miller, *I Found No Peace;* John T. Whitaker, *And Fear Came;* George Steer, *Cæsar in Abyssinia.*

[55] Robert U. Brown, "Smuggling Undoes Spain's Censors," *Editor and Publisher* (Aug. 29, 1936), p. 11. An early appraisal of the situation confronting American correspondents; Anon., "Official Falsehood and Censorship Prevent Clear Picture From Spain," *Editor and Publisher* (Aug. 29, 1936), pp. 11, 42; Oestreicher, J. C., "Getting the News Out of Spain," *The Quill* (Aug., 1936), p. 10; Anon., "Carney's Uncensored Times' Dispatch Reveals Dangers of Madrid Coverage," *Editor and Publisher* (Dec. 12, 1936), p. 11.

[56] W. D. Bowman, *The Story of "The Times,"* Ch. 13; E. H. C. Moberly Bell, *Life and Letters of C. F. Moberly Bell;* F. H. Kitchin, *Moberly Bell and His Times.*

Then came the busy years from 1910 to 1930, and since, with wars of previously unrivaled action on the broadest possible scale, with a succession of major and minor crises following. Beginning with the Balkan Wars and the Great War, the period was marked by a quick growth in all facilities and organizations for gathering news.[57]

Post-war developments in the realm of news included aviation exploits, exploration stories, and crime stories. Transocean flights, beginning with Charles A. Lindbergh's New York-Paris flight in 1927, resulted in the expenditure of vast sums of money and energy by the press.[58]

When Byrd, Wilkinson, Ellsworth and other explorers, went to the North and South Poles, press coverage followed them. The short wave radio began to play a part, particularly when Admiral Byrd went to the South Pole in 1929-1930. On that expedition he was accompanied by Russell Owen, reporter for the New York

[57] It had cost the New York *Herald,* then in the forefront of newspaper enterprise, $3.25 gold, per word, to cable 2,000 words from Jamaica to New York, rushed at double the commercial rate, to gain precedence over other press messages giving details of the destruction of Cervera's fleet in 1898. This, in addition to the cost of the dispatch boats and ordinary cables, made war coverage very expensive. See: Elmer Davis, *History of the New York Times, 1851-1921,* p. 230.

The Times of London spent £50,000 during 1898 to obtain a satisfactory supply of foreign news, and a single telegram concerning a revolution in Argentina had cost £1,200. Although *The Times* is reticent as to its expenses, these figures were revealed in evidence given before the Select Committee in the Copyright Bill of 1898. See: S. V. Makower, *Notes upon the History of "The Times," 1785-1904,* p. 34.

The Chicago *Daily News* won wide fame for its reports of the World War. How that service was organized, as described by Mr. Victor Lawson, the publisher, was printed in *Editor and Publisher,* and reprinted in *Newspaper Building,* by Jason Rogers, pp. 145-52. It describes the development of the Chicago *Daily News* foreign service from the time it was established in 1899 until 1918. During the first years of the Great War the service cost from $148,000 to $170,000 a year, and the dispatches were widely syndicated.

[58] John F. Roche, "Von Wiegand Tells Graf Flight Plans," *Editor and Publisher* (Aug. 10, 1929), pp. 7, 36; Vernon McKenzie, ed., *Behind the Headlines,* pp. 251-63; E. L. James, "When Lindbergh Reached Paris: a Tale of Newspaper Hardships," *Ibid.,* pp. 27-51; Frederick Griffin, "Everything Goes—When You Cover a Story Like the *Bremen* Flight," *Ibid.*

Times, a two years' assignment called the longest in the annals
of journalism, and an assignment that Owen covered so ably as to
win the Pulitzer Prize for 1930.[59]

*   *   *

In the century since 1838, when Mr. Bennett set up his skeleton
foreign staff in Europe, it may be said that there has been a
constant growth in the service of information provided for the
public, especially by certain newspapers and press associations in
Anglo-Saxon countries.

The imperial interests of Great Britain, rapidly expanding,
brought demands in that country for news on a world scale, and
this was made possible by the advance in communication methods
and the development of press associations such as Reuters, the
Associated Press, Havas, and others of somewhat less importance,
all coöperating in the exchange of information.

Scandinavian and Dutch newspapers never have been far behind
in any forward journalistic steps, but either the available histories
have been unfair to them, or they did not choose to attempt the
more striking kind of enterprise, such as brought fame to English
and American newspapers and journalists. In any event, details
of their exploits are difficult to obtain. Nor were French, German
and Italian journalists unheard of in the race for better news
service, but the fact remains that the history of such progress
appears to be almost entirely a history of the British and American presses.

By the time of the Boer War, the Spanish-American War, and
the Russo-Japanese War more newspapers, and more press associations, were sending special correspondents afield. But it remained for the Great War and its aftermath to provide the more
decided impulsion which virtually forced agencies and papers to
establish permanent systems of correspondence covering the
world. Able correspondents, especially trained, so far as possible,
were sent to key positions in all important countries, and permitted to remain there. Much patience was devoted to organizing
an almost faultless communications system, at the mercy only of

[59] Russell Owen, *South of the Sun.* His own account of the adventure.

cataclysms of nature or of censorship. It is such a system, somewhat humbled by years of economic dislocation and an increasing
severity of censorship, that exists in these times.[60]

[60] Correspondents have moved rapidly with the course of events. Men
such as the late Frank Simonds, Sir Philip Gibbs, William Henry Chamberlin, Walter Duranty, Sir Willmott Lewis, Leland Stowe, H. R. Knickerbocker, Paul Scott Mowrer, Edgar Ansel Mowrer, Webb Miller, and others,
both British and American, have won attention not merely as good reporters,
but as keen interpreters of public affairs. Some of them have become known
through their books, some appear only in the columns of their newspapers,
and some hide their lights under the cloak of anonymity.
    Among the personal experience books that some of the post-war journalists
have produced, bearing on their work, are the following: Anon., *Washington Merry-Go-Round*, Ch. 15; Anon., *Not to Be Repeated: Merry-Go-
Round of Europe;* George Seldes, *You Can't Print That!*; George Seldes,
Can These Things Be!; Larry Rue, *I Fly for News;* Vincent Sheean, *Personal History;* Wilbur Forrest, *Behind the Front Page;* Anon., *Journalism:
By Some Masters of the Craft.* Lectures, including "The Lobby Corre-
spondent," by Alan Pitt Robbins, pp. 73-84; and "The Special Correspond-
ent," by Edgar Wallace, pp. 103-109; Ralph D. Blumenfeld, *R.D.B.'s Pro-
cession;* H. J. Greenwall, *Scoops: Being Leaves from the Diary of a Special
Correspondent;* Walter Duranty, *I Write as I Please;* Philip Gibbs, *More
That Can Be Told;* Negley Farson, *The Way of a Transgressor;* George
Slocombe, *The Tumult and the Shouting;* Webb Miller, *I Found No Peace!*;
H. J. Greenwall, *Round the World for News;* R. D. Blumenfeld, *The Press
in My Time;* John T. Whitaker, *And Fear Came;* David Darrah, *Hail
Cæsar;* Miles Vaughn, *Covering the Far East;* George Steer, *Cæsar in
Abyssinia;* Robert Bernays, *Special Correspondent;* Wythe Williams, *Dusk
of Empire;* Eugene Lyons, ed., *We Cover the World,* by Fifteen Foreign
Correspondents.

CHAPTER II

GATHERING THE WORLD'S NEWS

PEOPLE make news. Where people go, there news develops. From north of Spitzbergen to south of Little America, from Irving, Kansas, to Irkutsk, Siberia, and back again, news is predictable in some of its movements, unreliable as quicksilver in others.

But whether it is news long foreseen and prepared for, or news that breaks unexpectedly, the world seldom needs to wait very long for full details. A widespread organization of correspondents, plus almost instantaneous communication, and very rapid transportation, bring the facts to all larger cities and most of the smaller ones within a few moments, and usually within a few hours even from the more remote places. Newspapers and press associations have charted the news areas of the world and have spread a net to ensnare virtually anything that may be classified as news.

This network is comprised of telephone and telegraph lines, railroads, radio channels and ship lanes. Where these converge most thickly it is safe to assume that social, artistic, commercial, financial and governmental activities are greatest. And in those very places in which populations center, news is certain to grow luxuriantly. There journalists foregather.

The leading news centers of the world are London, Washington, New York, Paris, Berlin, Geneva, Rome, Madrid, Vienna, Moscow, Shanghai, Tokyo and Buenos Aires. In these thirteen cities press associations and newspapers concentrate their efforts.

Other important centers are Brussels, Lisbon, Copenhagen, Amsterdam, Stockholm, Oslo, Riga, Sofia, Budapest, Athens, Belgrade, Milan, Prague, Warsaw, Bucharest, Istanbul, Ankara, Jerusalem, Cairo, Cape Town, Bombay, Calcutta, Delhi, Bangkok,

Singapore, Manila, Nanking, Peiping, Hong Kong, Hsingking, Canton, Melbourne, Wellington, Honolulu, Montreal, Ottawa, Havana, Mexico City, Rio de Janeiro, Lima, Santiago. Still others become important from time to time.

Staff correspondents are stationed in some of these secondary cities, particularly in such as Warsaw, Cairo, Bombay, Peiping, Mexico City and Rio de Janeiro, but it is far commoner to depend upon native correspondents, often regularly employed by some local paper, or upon aliens resident there for business or personal reasons. They send to the nearest "control bureau" of the foreign newspaper or press association served, a report of any matter which their experience tells them may be desired by that paper or agency. Every such "part time" correspondent is instructed as to what constitutes news in the view of the foreign paper, and he even receives instructions as to how to cover that type of news, how to write it, and how to transmit it.

The basis for world news collection is the press association. There is one association, and often more than one, in almost every country. About thirty of these national associations maintain an exchange arrangement by which each has its own correspondents covering the news of a certain area. The news gathered more or less independently is made available to all of the other associations. A representative of each may select, from this mass of information, such matter as he believes will be of interest to his own people. He verifies it if necessary, edits it, and possibly rewrites it before sending it for use at home. Or he may merely use it as a springboard for an entirely new story which he himself writes on the basis of information obtained from primary sources.

If a report comes to a control point bureau from some locality within the sphere of its interest, and circumstances seem to warrant, a special correspondent for the foreign newspaper may leave his bureau and journey to the place where the event has occurred to report upon it at first hand. This was particularly common, as a method, in the nineteen-twenties, when some correspondents were so constantly on the move about the continent of Europe that they sometimes were referred to as "swing men." International conferences in the capitals and watering places of Europe

since 1920 have sent small armies of correspondents stampeding
back and forth across the map.

§ 1. THE CORRESPONDENT AND HIS WORK

THERE must be efficient men in all strategic news centers. This
is axiomatic and expensive, but it is the only way in which prompt
and intelligent news coverage is possible. Accordingly, correspondents are at work twenty-four hours a day, around the world,
in order that the newspaper reader may be well informed.

Just as no man ignorant of football could understand the game
or write about it intelligently, so no man ignorant of public affairs
could understand them, write about them, or edit reports about
them without making mistakes in facts or perspective that would
mislead and confuse readers, while injuring the reputation of the
newspaper itself with persons who recognize its shortcomings.[1]

Facts are what the good correspondent wants, and facts make
news, although what looks like news when published is not always
fact, unhappily for the reader.[2] Much depends upon the discern-
ment of the correspondent, who needs to understand the country
in which he is living; and fully as much depends upon the common
sense and social responsibility of the employing newspaper.

How to keep the home office happy is one problem of the correspondent, for that office occasionally seems to ask the impossible! Correspondents have been ordered by their offices to
interview Kings, Emperors, Premiers, Generals, Chief Justices

[1] Karl H. von Wiegand, "In Europe: Reporter vs. Correspondent," *Cir-
culation* (Aug., 1925), pp. 12-13, 37; Sisley Huddleston, "Correspondent in
Paris," *Blackwood's Magazine* (Sept., 1924), V. 216, pp. 321-31; Anon.,
"Your Mirrors of Europe" (by a Foreign Correspondent), *Sat. Eve. Post*
(Dec. 9, 1922), pp. 5, 145-50.

[2] There also is the type of correspondent who says, "I don't want facts;
I want news." His editor wants from him, and he provides, stories which
are less often comprised of authenticated facts than of rumors, suggestions
of intrigue, perversions of the truth, reflections of prejudices, sensational
statements and implications—in short, reports that make spicy reading,
regardless of the harm they may do through poisoning the public mind.
Such reports may be written without the slightest investigation, entirely
from imagination, and they sometimes are so written, but reputable papers
shun them.

and all manner of high officials. Such exalted personages hold no awe for the far-off newspaper editor, secure in his own little half-acre, but rarely are they themselves free to grant press interviews, even if willing to do so.[3]

Up to about 1895 a correspondent in London or Paris for an American newspaper often sent his own opinion, his own editorial interpretation of events, rather than the bare facts. But in writing to-day, bowing to a demand for objectivity, the correspondent either presents the facts as unadorned as possible, as for a press association, or he confines himself to factual interpretation, as distinguished from editorial interpretation, for a newspaper or syndicate.[4]

To report the news without bias, intentional or otherwise, requires that the correspondent retain enough detachment so that he may see things not only objectively, but in the light of his own national interests. That is assuming him to be a native and a citizen of the country to which his dispatches go. This is not always the case, but there is a tendency to make it so, increasingly, on the supposition that only under such circumstances can readers feel the greatest confidence in the impartiality of the facts they are receiving, and only thus can the correspondent himself make clear to his readers—his countrymen—the reasons and the meanings underlying the news as it appears on the surface. To do this successfully he needs, actually, to keep free of personal or national prejudices, pro or con, and of influences that might corrupt impartiality.[5]

* * *

[3] E. S. Dithmar, "European Correspondent," *Bookman* (N. Y., May, 1904), V, 19, pp. 244-57. Washington correspondents have received grotesque orders from their editors, such as "We have information that there is something in the air. Get it and send us 1,000 words." "Get interview with President on local political situation. Tell him to make it short." "Please rush immediately names of all unknown dead soldiers from this state." J. Fred Essary, *Covering Washington*, pp. 56-57.

[4] See Ch. I, pp. 8-9, for explanation of these terms.

[5] Some Paris correspondents for newspapers in the United States have felt that their best efforts to present a fair view of France and French affairs have been nullified, on occasions, by an attitude held to be common in American newspaper offices. There, proprietors and editors, for some reason,

Well-recognized sources to which correspondents turn for news at any post include the newspaper and periodical press of the city or country itself, representing various shades of opinion, where variety is politically possible; the service of a local press association; the government offices, especially the ministry of foreign affairs; parliament and its members, foreign embassies, legations, and consulates; commercial attachés, banks and business houses, hotels, clubs, bars, educational institutions, the offices and homes of persons active in the affairs of the country or acquainted with the local situation in its various aspects, and willing to talk about it.

The foreign correspondent must, to an extent, make his own assignments; he must make his own decisions. His output of copy may not be great and sometimes his merit is in knowing when *not* to send a story. Quality is more important than quantity in his product. He may produce much in the way of private reports to editorial writers and other editors, reports which do not appear in print, but which guide the editors in what they themselves write. This system helps to explain the exceedingly well-informed editorials, or leaders, which appear, for example, in *The Times* of London.

Because of the important position that a correspondent occupies in interpreting one country to another, he has been correctly referred to as an "unofficial ambassador." As such, his position can be as powerful as his sense of responsibility, his ability, and the reputation of his paper. Sir Willmott Lewis, as Washington correspondent for *The Times* of London, offered ten suggestions to correspondents: [6]

consider the Paris correspondents to be pro-French, and so discount what they send. They sometimes neutralize accurate and good articles by the editing, the display, the editorials, and by reports from Washington.

Washington correspondents have been sardonically termed "oracles of journalism" in the United States, and often they have been said to hold slightly anti-French prejudices. This is attributed to (a) lack of knowledge of Europe and the world from any sufficient first-hand experience, (b) traditionally uncordial press relations with the French embassy in Washington, and (c) absence of bureau heads with European experience.

[6] In Block Foundation lecture at Yale University, New Haven, Dec. 8, 1931. Reported in *Editor and Publisher* (Dec. 12, 1931), p. 12.

1. Take your work, but never yourself, seriously.
2. Know that there is no simple or immediate solution for any national or international problem.
3. Never forget that 99 times out of 100 the issue is not between right and wrong, but between right and right; but also that those who explain too much prepare the way for those who excuse too much.
4. Remember always that prejudice is dishonesty—patriotic prejudice as much as any other kind.
5. Be chary of moral exaltation, and of moral indignation no less, for good and evil mingle in the best and worst of causes.
6. Remember that if you do not like a country, there are a thousand chances that the fault is not in the country, but in you.
7. Be prepared to find that the best and the worst give way under closer scrutiny.
9. Pray nightly that the generalizing and abstracting habit of mind may not prevail over the practical.
9. Be very sure that of all the influences which seek to destroy your independence of mind, the most respectable will be the most dangerous.
10. Know that the sort of patriot who maintains that the women of his country are more chaste and the statesmen of his country more stupid than those of any other country, is wrong on both these counts and may be wrong on every count.

The correspondent must be *persona grata* in the country to which he is assigned. If he is not well liked, he cannot hope for success. He needs to be a gentleman, in every sense of the word, and he needs to be well educated, whether through formal university instruction or otherwise. Modern languages are indispensable, although correspondents often learn a tongue only after having been assigned to a post requiring it. Some even have maintained that it is possible for a correspondent to act without a speaking and reading knowledge of the language of the country in which he is working. While correspondents may have succeeded thus handicapped, there can be no argument about the desirability of knowing languages. History, economics, logic, philosophy and finance are other subjects considered of the greatest value. In most instances, newspapers and press associations prefer to have the correspondent serve an apprenticeship in the home office because it teaches him home office needs, conditions and attitudes.[7]

One notably successful correspondent and bureau chief has advocated this preparation as ideal for foreign work: A good liberal arts training, with history, economics and modern languages prominent in the curriculum. After leaving college, join a paper in as big a city as possible. Get on the city hall run, covering municipal affairs and politics, learning all about methods and operations. Then get to the state capital and ultimately to Washington as a correspondent. Then go abroad with any press association or newspaper bureau, and work up to the directorship of the bureau.

This correspondent believes that there will be increased opportunities for journalists with an interest in foreign work.

In general, a foreign correspondent is paid at a somewhat better rate than the reporter at home. That is necessary because living costs are, greater, if requirements of comfort and convenience are equal, and it often is necessary to do considerable entertaining and to maintain a standard sufficiently high to command the respect of those persons with whom he must deal. It is almost essential for a foreign correspondent to follow such a policy because the name of his paper probably means nothing in the foreign land, and his prestige and reception will depend upon his own manner, personality, acquaintanceships, and style of living.[8]

[7] Lord Northcliffe is credited with having said that a journalist should know how to ride a horse and wear a monocle. James Gordon Bennett said a special correspondent of the right kind should be "half diplomat, half detective."

[8] In Europe any person of the slightest standing in the newspaper world is a "journalist." A "reporter," as American journalists of prominence often delight to call themselves, in self-conscious modesty, frequently is regarded in Europe and most other parts of the world as a mere keyhole-peeper, free-lance tipster, gossip-monger and blackmailer. If a European journalist has a title, military, academic, or otherwise, he uses it, and, if he can claim to be a special editor of any sort, that is on his formal card. All the prestige that he can muster is scarcely enough to overcome an inherent distrust, dislike and, in some cases, contempt, for the press. Only a few exceptions are made.

The correspondent needs to be level-headed, not only to avoid being deceived by propagandists and by those trying to escape unwelcome publicity, but to avoid yielding to personal temptations and to keep from seeing stories where none exist and so becoming an unwitting sensationalist. If he knows the local situation thoroughly he is less likely to fall victim to rumors and statements deliberately intended to mislead him. This attitude of independent judgment is stressed by many good correspondents. It means independence of all groups and individuals interested in shaping his opinions and so influencing his writing. Sir Willmott Lewis has expressed it by saying that a correspondent must protect his "intellectual virginity" at any cost, adding that, in forming judgments, he must keep trying to discern the great tidal movements underlying the froth on the sea of public affairs. The ability of the correspondent to recognize the tidal movements and to differentiate those movements from the waves and the spray on the surface is the measure of his success. Also, he must report both the people and the government; almost any people is likable; but governments seldom are.

So far as concerns the Anglo-Saxon press, Sir Willmott notes a tendency to sentimentalize the news reports. This he considers objectionable because it represents a love of emotion for its own sake, manifested in a growing drift to "features," and feature treatment of the news. He does not object to proper *sentiment*, but finds that *sentimentality*, as distinct from the other, is not merely contaminating the domestic news reports, but also the foreign correspondence, which is a more serious matter because the spark of emotion is thus introduced into the tinder box of international relations and increases the possibility and danger of an explosion.

Much the same view as to the need for utter independence of thought on the part of the foreign correspondent was held by the late William Bolitho (Ryall), correspondent for the Manchester *Guardian* and the New York *World*. He contended that the correspondent should put aside all prejudice, stop all wishful-thinking, and, instead of letting his emotions dictate his judgments and his reports, that he should analyze his own prejudices, ruthlessly, so that he could discount them and thus come nearer impartiality. The next step was to learn to judge how others would act in the light of the prejudices and habits of thought that he was able to discern *in them.* This attitude Mr. Bolitho passed on to Walter Duranty, who attained fame as correspondent in Russia for the New York *Times,* and Mr. Duranty put it to use and acknowledged his debt to Bolitho.[9]

Even though the modern correspondent is writing much of the time about events and trends that are technical, he cannot ignore the human element involved in the news and encountered in getting the news. So he must be a diplomat, he must be tactful, he must learn how to persuade people to do things and tell him things, chiefly because he has won their trust, made them like him personally. He forms sincere friendships, but he must know how to play off one individual against another, or one group against another.

The best and most successful correspondents often win that reputation because they know how to deal with people. In contacts with officials the correspondent should, as one of the number has said, be sufficiently well informed himself so that he can *give* information as well as *ask* it. If he can do that regularly, he is sure of a welcome whenever he calls. Otherwise, he becomes a nuisance to be tolerated or to be "used." In fact, officials sometimes call, themselves, upon the correspondent who has something to give and who does not limit his interest in their affairs to mere receiving.

Yet, when persons, and especially persons in official positions, are more than naturally communicative, correspondents have learned that it is wise to verify all statements with extra care, lest they be made avenues for propaganda, or be used simply to help launch a "trial balloon." [10]

[9] Walter Duranty, *I Write as I Please,* pp. 93-106, 303-304.

[10] Great Britain, for example, was anxious that the United States should view Gandhi and his actions in a light more sympathetic to the British policy. Knowing that the American people, like the British people, are prone to judge news on a sentimental basis, great care was taken that American correspondents in London should be "properly" informed on the Indian situation in which Gandhi was the central figure.

Similarly, correspondents find that they must exercise the greatest patience, and frequently ingenuity as well, on some stories which require long periods of waiting and physical inactivity. This is true, for example, of so-called "death-watches" set up when prominent persons are very ill, and it is true, also, of many conferences and meetings at Geneva or elsewhere.

* * *

The new correspondent at a post is instructed carefully in his work, if time and circumstances permit. He is given a few days to go about and become familiar in a general way with the city and its people, if his introduction happens to be under ideal conditions. Perhaps he may accompany an experienced correspondent, observe his methods, and meet officials of news importance. Then, the older correspondent permits the new man to act independently, but corrects his mistakes and makes suggestions when they are in order. Or the new man spends a sufficient time in the office, first handling copy, writing and rewriting dispatches, and otherwise familiarizing himself with the work and conditions. It requires more time to become accustomed to some countries than to others, certain situations are far more complex, languages more difficult, customs more involved, and general living conditions either more or less agreeable.

Political and economic circumstances in the country must be mastered by the correspondent, and any change from one country to another requires a new study. China and Japan, Russia and Italy probably are the most difficult countries for an American or British correspondent to understand. Two years is none too much to devote to learning what it is necessary to know to deal intelligently with the news in any one of them, whereas six months to a year may suffice in London or New York, although no thorough knowledge would be possible even there in so brief a time.

It is the need for this long training which makes it desirable that correspondents be left at posts for considerable periods— three to ten years, or longer. Some have remained twenty-five years and more. If a correspondent does not enjoy living in a country, he should not stay there, but if he *does* enjoy it, his value is likely to increase with time, especially if he keeps his own national perspective. Under such circumstances, however, employers at home occasionally come to believe that the correspondent is so sympathetic to the point of view of the country in which he lives that he no longer sees affairs there with the perspective they want him to maintain. Sometimes there is a basis for the belief, but other times the attitude is unfair and dictated by local prejudices instead. It is true, however, that a correspondent needs to leave a country from time to time to refresh his viewpoint, and to keep his impartial outlook. This may mean a national change of scene as frequently as once in six weeks in some stormy countries, but certainly the intervals should be no greater than three years in any case.

There are times, of course, when a correspondent does not have the leisure to study a country or a situation. A crisis arises in some city or country remote from his usual base, and he must hasten to the new scene, round up the story as quickly as possible, and get it off. Then he will need to use his ingenuity and intelligence to the fullest extent.

Under such conditions, as a general thing, he spends time on the way to the scene of activity reading what he can about the situation he is to report. He tries to gain an understanding of both sides, if it is a controversy. This may mean reading books, reports, periodicals, newspapers. On arriving, he visits such persons and offices as he believes may be able to give him useful information. That probably means certain government offices, it means interviews with officials, with spokesmen for the opposition views, with local editors and journalists representing various groups, with some foreign diplomats and business men, or other resident foreigners who may be presumed to be neutral and yet to have some familiarity with local conditions. Thus he gathers his threads, and presently he is able to weave them together to form a tapestry picturing the situation. The clarity of the picture, and its accuracy, will depend largely upon his ability.

The foreign correspondent for the newspaper with a serious view of the news is constantly on the watch for several types of stories. A classification prepared, by way of suggestion, for representatives abroad for the Chicago *Daily News,* especially the non-American correspondent, indicates in general the kind of thing that concerns all correspondents of the better newspapers.[11]

(*a*)   News events of truly international significance. . . . Be careful to avoid stories of merely local interest, especially local political stories, which seem big on the spot, but are of little consequence to our readers. In treating international news events, we should dwell particularly on their international significance, especially as affecting the United States. [Or, in other cases, the people of the country where the report is to be published.]

(*b*)   There is no part of the world in which the United States has not, at present, important interests—economic, moral, cultural, diplomatic, social, political. We should discover and analyze out these interests, whether actual or potential—and write about them.

(*c*)   A story is frequently welcome explaining the national viewpoint of the country in which one is stationed—the national viewpoint, that is, regarding some truly international problem of great general interest, but especially when this national viewpoint is interesting or significant in itself.

(*d*)   Original interviews with well-known political, scientific, financial, industrial, artistic or literary personalities. It has, however, never been our policy to pay for interviews.[12]

(*e*)   Scientific inventions, discoveries or movements, when they are of really international significance.

(*f*)   Social problems and experiments, especially when analogous to our own social problems in America [or other countries where reports are to be published], and therefore apt to contain a lesson for us.

[11] Derived from *Principles and Instructions of the Foreign Service of the Chicago Daily News* (see Anon.).

[12] This suggests another problem of the foreign correspondent. In some countries, especially in Europe, public figures sometimes demand that they be paid if they grant an interview. By this requirement they save themselves from having to endure numberless interviews. As some of them are themselves writers, too, they consider that they are entitled to a return if they reveal their ideas instead of writing them and selling them as articles for their own profit.

(g)   Stories of the activities and the unusual experiences of Americans, especially of Chicagoans, living or travelling in Europe. [Again to be considered with appropriate changes for newspapers serving other communities.]

The easier it is to obtain and verify facts, the more accurately the press can report events. Journalists, particularly, have demanded freer access to information. One result has been the establishment by most governments of "press bureaus," "news departments" or "information sections," under the direction of "press officers" or "intelligence officers," to answer questions about the affairs of government, sometimes to arrange interviews, and to aid the press in general. Most of these bureaus have been organized since the Great War, during which period the need for information sources became especially obvious, not only as a service to journalists, but so that governments might be represented favorably and accurately in the press at home and abroad.

Helpful as these offices frequently are, each naturally is working primarily in the interests of its government. This is admitted and tacitly understood by all parties concerned. No such office will give out information unfavorable to the purposes or reputation of the government. The correspondent is obliged to find another, more impartial source for such data. This may be in a liberal or opposition press, at a foreign embassy, or it may come from an intelligent and communicative person of whatever connection.

Nowadays, at international conferences, for example, a correspondent usually is able to discover what happens even though a meeting is secret. Usually some one who has attended the secret session will talk, possibly because he is dissatisfied with the course of the negotiations, or more likely, because he is indifferent to the subject under consideration, or, again, because he is seeking to satisfy his own diplomatic purposes and reveals what has occurred on the understanding that his own anonymity is to be protected.

So it is that vague phrases, such as "it is learned on high authority," need not necessarily be regarded as evidence that the news report is of doubtful authenticity. Nor, on the other side, are official government denials of reports, or refutations by officials of statements or views attributed to them, necessarily to be accepted unquestioned. The public often is ready to doubt or discredit even the reputable press on such denials. But as between a responsible correspondent, interested primarily in presenting the facts, and a government bureau or official aware that a certain action or remark was inexpedient, or its announcement premature, which is the more likely to be dependable? [13]

The correspondent is an exile from his own people. Whatever the cynical may think, usually he is sincere in trying to give an honest picture of events or trends to stay-at-home persons. Thoughtful correspondents understand the responsibility they bear, and they accept it conscientiously.

Journalists, in organizing to advance their own interests and work, have thereby aided the entire press. Such organizations include particularly the Association of Correspondents Accredited to the League of Nations, the Anglo-American Press Association in Paris, the Anglo-American Press Association in Vienna, the Anglo-American Press Association in Geneva, the Institute of Journalists and the National Union of Journalists in Great Britain, the Foreign Press Association in London, the Association of Foreign Correspondents in the United States, the National Press Club in Washington, the American Newspaper Guild, and the American Society of Newspaper Editors. Some of these groups have worked to raise journalistic standards, have dealt with local government officials, and have won their coöperation in simplifying news-gathering problems or clearing the news channels.

§ 2. PRESS ASSOCIATIONS

THE PRESS ASSOCIATION of to-day had its origin in the handwritten news-letters provided in medieval times for individuals, for business firms, and for groups of nobles. Aside from governments, which needed information and which themselves distributed in-

---

[13] Some light on the relations of the press with diplomats appears in: Richard Washburn Child, "International Show Windows," *Sat. Eve. Post* (Dec. 20, 1924), pp. 21, 105-110.

formation in the routine of administration, bankers and traders found the greatest value in information services. In Europe and, later, in North America it was marine news and news of trade that brought the "reading room" into being as an essential part of coffee houses, and the more enterprising houses went to considerable trouble and expense to provide a good service of news.[14]

It was about 1725 that Edward Cave, inspector of the franks in London, and so able to use the mails freely, set up a system for the exchange of news between the London press and provincial newspapers. He sold the news service thus obtained for a guinea a week, and his news-collecting organization was fundamentally like that of a present-day press association. In the United States the earliest press associations were concerned more with obtaining foreign news and distributing it, than with domestic news, although they accomplished that exchange also. It was in 1827 that some New York newspapers formed a combination to defray the costs of meeting incoming ships to obtain European news.[15]

But the roots of the press associations go deeper in both England and America than these eighteenth and nineteenth century developments. Edward Lloyd had established a coffee house in Tower Street, London, in 1686 or 1687. He prospered, and the coffee house, situated in the center of the mercantile world of that time, became a center for business and social groups of a respectable and established character. It was a sort of club, and like some other early coffee houses, it also became a clearing-house for news and advertisements. The newspaper press was not highly developed at that time, but as the years went along it was the custom to have available in the coffee houses collections of newspapers, such as they were, not alone those published locally, but also newspapers brought from other countries.

This was particularly true at Lloyds, which was a center for seagoing men and for merchants and others with foreign trade

---

[14] A concise summary of the history of press associations appears in: L. M. Salmon, *The Newspaper and the Historian*, Ch. 5; M. A. Shaaber, *Some Forerunners of the Newspaper in England, 1476-1622;* Victor Rosewater, *History of Coöperative News-Gathering in the United States.*

[15] L. M. Salmon, *The Newspaper and the Historian*, Ch. 5.

interests, even as it became true somewhat later of coffee houses in New York and Boston. In 1696, partly to satisfy his customers, Edward Lloyd began the publication of a daily paper, *Lloyd's News,* which continued for seventy-six numbers, ceasing publication by government order on February 23, 1697. In 1713 Edward Lloyd died and in 1720 the business passed out of the control of his family, but continued under the same name, nevertheless. In 1734 the firm began the publication of *Lloyd's List,* which has continued ever since. It specialized in shipping news and built up a rather extensive foreign news service of its own, with thirty-two correspondents in twenty-eight ports sending both shipping news and general news. The service was in full working order by 1788, if not before, and later *Lloyd's List* achieved several journalistic "scoops." [16]

* * *

What Lloyd's meant to England, Samuel Topliff meant to the United States. As a young man he became proprietor of Gilbert's Coffee House and Marine Diary in Boston. The name later was changed to the Merchants' Reading Room, which was a sort of club where shipping news and general news was available to members through a file of domestic and foreign newspapers, and later through what was called Topliff's Private Marine Journal, consisting of seven large books in which were entered items of shipping information and of news brought in from foreign ports or from other ports in the United States. [17]

[16] Com. Frank Worsley and Capt. Glyn Griffith, *The Romance of Lloyd's: From Coffee-House to Palace,* Chs. 7, 12, 13.

[17] The seven books were as follows: 1. General record of news, in which is recorded daily all information of a general nature, and such as is particularly interesting to the merchants of the place, as may be received from correspondents by land and water, and by arrivals at the port. 2. Record of all arrivals from foreign ports or places, with cargoes particularly specified to each consignee. 3. Record of all arrivals from other ports in the United States similarly noted as the second. 4. Record of all vessels clearing for foreign ports, time of sailing, etc. 5. Record of all vessels cleared for other ports in the United States. 6. Record of all arrivals and clearances from or for foreign ports in all parts of the United States, except Boston. 7. Record of names of all gentlemen introduced by the subscribers, the places whence they came, and the name of the subscriber introducing them. The

The Topliff service was well established by 1811, but Mr. Topliff's desire to see his patrons more adequately provided with news led him to set up what was the first real system for gathering foreign news for American use, and his system continued from 1820 to 1850. Henry Ingraham Blake, who had for years been a ship news reporter for the Boston *Mercury-Palladium,* began also to serve the Topliff coffee house with news. He would row out to ships entering Boston harbor, get packets of newspapers, ask questions of the Captain and other officers, and perhaps interview one or two passengers. Then he would bring the news to the coffee house, where it would be posted, and whence it would be forwarded to New York by pony express. The European vessels put in at Boston first, so Boston heard the news before New York.

Some newspapers commonly credited "Mr. Topliff's correspondent" for much of their foreign news. He sent news to them, and they may be assumed to have been among his subscribers, which meant that he was running a sort of press association, and possibly it should be considered the first in the United States. As the years passed the system for getting news improved and the service was extended. Topliff himself went to Europe in 1828 and spent a year in travel. His letters were published in American newspapers so that, in a sense, he was the first special correspondent for American newspapers.[18]

A venture somewhat like Topliff's was tried at Charleston, South Carolina, by Aaron Smith Willington. Meeting one incoming ship, Willington received the positive news that the Treaty of Ghent had been signed, ending the War of 1812 between the United States and Great Britain. This he announced to his readers on February 14, 1815, the treaty having actually been signed at Ghent on December 28, 1814. In the meantime, General Andrew Jackson had defeated the British forces at New Orleans on Janu-

place also boasted several maps useful to shipowner or merchant, and a good clock, among other things.

Samuel Topliff, *Topliff's Travels.* Letters from abroad in the years 1828 and 1829. From the original manuscript. Edited with a memoir by Ethel Stanwood Bolton, pp. 67-68.

[18] Victor Rosewater, *History of Coöperative News-Gathering in the United States,* pp. 5-8, 10.

ary 8, 1815. Some years later James Gordon Bennett, a recent immigrant from Scotland, found employment with Willington, starting a career that was to lead him to establish the New York *Herald* and usher in a new era in journalistic enterprise, as already described.

It was common enough for merchants and newspapers in Atlantic port cities to share the expenses of having some qualified person row out to newly arrived ships to get newspapers and information and then deliver the same to mercantile and editorial offices. This method was well developed before 1820. In about 1830 warmer competition between certain New York newspapers led to the use of clipper ships and schooners to meet the incoming ships farther at sea. One newspaper tried to outdo another until the costs of ship news collection threatened to outstrip any possible advantage that early publication of that news might involve. This expensive rivalry continued, nevertheless, for some years, but the costs to individual newspapers were somewhat mitigated, especially after 1837, by the formation of several so-called coöperative "harbor associations" sharing the expenses of meeting the ships and rushing the news to shore. Even so, however, some newspapers chose to act independently and, as they often were the more successful papers, they also were able to equip ever-faster boats.

In some instances a signaling system of bells or semaphores displayed prominently on masts was arranged in port cities. Lighthouse-keepers or others on the eastern headlands, seeing incoming ships, might signal the news on the land-semaphores. Then those who were to meet the ships went out into the bay or beyond. The news thus obtained was published in the New York or the Boston newspapers, which in turn were sent to inland cities.

Pony express services expedited the news, even so early as 1781, and regularly before 1830. They ran between Boston and Salem, Boston and New York, New York and Philadelphia, Baltimore and Washington. Some New York newspapers, notably the *Sun* and the *Herald*, used not only pony expresses but carrier pigeons and such short stretches of railroad as then existed, to rush the news from Washington and from Boston to New York.

The rivalry in news collection was intense through the third decade of the nineteenth century in the United States. The advent of the telegraph brought a new phase of press rivalry in the following decade.[19]

*   *   *

In Europe the matter of news dissemination also was receiving attention. Individual newspapers had engaged correspondents on the Continent, or sent staff men there early in the nineteenth century. But the more systematic collection of news is associated with the names of Charles Havas and Julius Reuter.

Charles Havas established the Agence Havas, which has become both an important news agency and a successful advertising agency. Napoleon died at St. Helena on May 5, 1821; Paris heard about it on July 6th. Most persons did not mind the two months' delay, nor think much about it, being accustomed to such a time lag, but it suggested to M. Havas the need for improved news service. He was a native of Portugal, but had taken up residence in Paris. In 1825 he offered to supply certain Paris newspapers and government departments with extracts from newspapers published in England, Germany, Italy, Spain and Russia. While the news still would be late, the idea of such a daily service appealed to some nonetheless.

M. Havas ultimately found his sources of information insufficient for the needs of his clients, and he felt the need of assistance to keep up the service. So in about 1836 he engaged several translators, and used all the most advanced means to disseminate his news to government ministries, embassies, banks, and commercial houses. Newspapers, at that time, scarcely subscribed at all.

Although the Agence Havas generally is said to have been set up as a press agency in 1836, it was not until 1840 that it was firmly established, and only after 1845 did it prosper notably. In the latter year the agency opened a little office in the rue Jean Jacques Rousseau. To enrich his service of news after 1836, M.

[19] D. C. Seitz, *The James Gordon Bennetts, Father and Son*, pp. 61-65, 90-93; M. E. Stone, *Fifty Years a Journalist*, pp. 204-18.

Havas had arranged to contribute news of France gratuitously to foreign newspapers in exchange for the free use of news from their columns. In this way the exchange of news between France, Belgium and England was developed to quite an extent. Correspondents were engaged in England, Germany, Italy, Spain, Belgium and Holland, while every effort was made to speed the messages.

It was in 1840, when M. Havas was in some financial difficulties, that he began to use carrier pigeons to transmit the news between Brussels and Paris every day. This method had been adopted at about the same time by Julius Reuter, a young bank clerk in Aix-la-Chapelle. Reuter had observed the eagerness with which bankers, brokers and merchants awaited the arrival, by mail coach or mounted courier, of the stock market prices from Brussels. He instituted a carrier pigeon service between Aix-la-Chapelle, the starting point of the German communications system, and Brussels, which was in direct communication with Paris. So he was able to get the Paris Bourse prices over this gap in the communications system and into all the big German towns several hours before the regular mail service could bridge it. Reuter's enterprise was rewarded by generous patronage, enabling him to extend his service.

The carrier pigeon method enabled M. Havas to have the important news appearing in the London morning papers reach Paris in time for use in the evening papers there. The French press, and his other clients, were pleased, and his subscribers increased in number. After that the Havas agency grew rapidly. By 1845 it was necessary to establish sub-agencies in Brussels, Rome, Vienna, Madrid and even in the United States. After that date, also, the bureau began to develop quite rapidly as an advertising agency, differing in important respects, however, from the advertising agencies now known in Anglo-Saxon countries. The telegraph, cable and radio were adapted by the Havas agency as they became practicable and facilitated the handling of news.[20]

[20] M. Eugene Legigan, *L'Agence Havas*. Conference a l'école des Sciences morales et politiques; A. G. Laney, "Havas World Power in News and Advertising," *Editor and Publisher* (June 19, 1928), pp. F.8-F.10.

After M. Havas borrowed Reuter's carrier-pigeon idea for news transmission, the two men began to work together in providing a full exchange of news between Brussels and Paris, and in 1849 Reuter went to Paris to help Havas. In 1851 Reuter went on to London to establish his own agency there, but Reuters and Havas always have coöperated closely since that time.

* * *

The Agence Havas differs from the Reuters' agency in that it is an advertising agency, as well as a news agency.[21] After 1860 the Agence Havas offered to 200 French provincial newspapers, unable to afford a news service, a daily news review without cash payment, but it asked in exchange the exclusive right to a certain amount of advertising white space on the third and fourth pages, this space to be sold or disposed of by the Agence Havas as it saw fit. Havas then turned about and sold this space for its own advantage. Most of the papers accepted the plan, which since has been extended and altered so that some newspapers sell their advertising space to Havas for a flat sum. The agency, in addition to distributing the news, therefore controls about 80 per cent of the advertising space in French papers, both Paris and provincial, and acts as advertising representative, solicits advertisements and prepares advertising copy. This gives Havas a position of unique influence and importance in French journalism.[22]

After the coming of the telegraph, Havas obtained control from

[21] The fact that the Agence Havas is devoted largely to the advertising business, and did not develop its service to the general press until after 1860, is the basis for a claim by the Reuters' agency to the distinction of being the first modern *news* agency. It began its service to newspapers in London in 1858.

[22] "Most of the commercial advertising is handled by Havas. To alienate Havas may mean for a newspaper the loss of practically all its advertising revenue. This power of one advertising agency is of tremendous importance for the press and for the public, for it is known that in several cases advertising patrons have objected to editorial policies and interfered directly or indirectly with them, stopped campaigns and tabooed topics." Pierre Denoyer, New York correspondent for *Le Petit Parisien*, speaking at the Princeton Conference on the Press in 1931. Anon., *Conference on the Press*, p. 129.

the State of special telegraph wires connecting its Paris headquarters with the editorial departments of practically all important newspapers in France. Ticker news services later were
installed in some of these offices, as well as in some of the Paris
newspaper offices. To others the news was delivered by mail or
by messenger.

Charles Havas was succeeded by his son, Auguste, as head of
the Agence Havas in 1860. In 1897 M. Charles Lafitte succeeded
Auguste Havas and, in 1924, upon the death of M. Lafitte,
M. Leon Renier became head of the agency. In 1925 the Agence
Havas was capitalized at 50,000,000 francs (about $2,000,000).
Its special wires extend about 3,500 miles, altogether, and the
agency transmits approximately a million words a day. It deals
quite largely in texts and official communications.

*   *   *

Julius Reuter opened a small office in London in 1851, the
year in which the first cable across the Channel provided a wire
between Paris and London. He hired an office boy to help him.
At first he devoted his efforts to the transmission of Stock
Exchange information and to obtaining clients for that service,
but he was working on the idea of a daily news service to the
press of London and the provinces.

Up to 1858 the London newspapers were receiving no regular
service of news dispatches from the Continent. *The Times,* the
Morning Post, and one or two other morning papers, had correspondents in Paris, Berlin, Vienna, Constantinople and some other
capitals, but unless war was in progress or imminent, or unless
there were other very important events to report, even those
correspondents wrote very little or nothing. But Reuter had other
ideas about the reporting of foreign news.

In Paris Reuter's chief agent was on confidential terms with
the secretary of Napoleon III, another of his staff had entrée to
the French Government departments, a third handled assignments
requiring careful work of special kinds, a fourth sought news and
rumors appearing in newspapers published in all parts of the
continent, a fifth prepared all the news matter for transmission,

while a sixth actually sent it over the wire.[23] This staff provided Reuter with a schedule of interesting and often exclusive news, quickly available.

Ultimately, late in 1858, M. Reuter was ready with his plan, and he approached Mr. John Walter of *The Times* first, but without success. Next, he chose to call upon Mr. James Grant, editor of the *Morning Advertiser,* then an important London paper. Mr. Grant has written of how, as a result of that call, the *Morning Advertiser* and other London papers, except *The Times,* gave M. Reuter's service a two weeks' trial at no cost to them. They tested his claim that he could provide a better service of foreign news at a lower cost (£30. a week to the *Morning Advertiser* instead of £40. for its existing service of dispatches). The trial satisfied all of the papers, which thereafter accepted his proposals and subscribed to his service. *The Times* followed suit a little later. Subsequently, Reuter extended the service to embrace other parts of the world, charging proportionately more, quite soon reaching £1,000 a year for morning papers, and £250 a year for afternoon papers, and the newspapers were compelled by competition to buy his service, even though sometimes at a cost greater than they wished to pay.[24]

The reputation of the agency was enhanced by its reports of the American Civil War and of the campaign of Solferino, but long before that it may be said to have been well established. Reuter himself ultimately became a British citizen, and the agency grew constantly in the extent of its news coverage under the name of Reuter's Telegram Co. Ltd., although known colloquially as Reuters, Limited.

M. Havas may be called the "father" of the modern news agency, but the Reuter agency became the most extensive and most important in the world. Reuter, like Havas, was quick to make use of the newest and best means of communication, and, in fact, Reuter financed the first section of the first cable from England to India. The Reuter agency organized virtually the only

---

[23] H. A. B., *About Newspapers: Chiefly English and Scottish,* pp. 115-17, quoting *Hubbard's Newspaper Press Directory of the World* (see Hubbard).

[24] James Grant, *The Newspaper Press,* V. 2, Ch. 13.

service of news from Africa, the Near and Middle East, and the Far East.

The Havas agency covered France, Italy, Switzerland, Belgium, Spain, Portugal, parts of Northern Africa and South America. The Wolff bureau, later formed in Germany, reported the news of that country and of other Central European countries, including Austria, Poland, the Balkans, the Netherlands, and Scandinavian countries. In the years since 1914 North American agencies have extended their services to overlap those of the Agence Havas in France and Latin America, Reuter in the Eastern countries and of Wolff (now DNB) in Central Europe. These three European agencies and the Associated Press of the United States also formed an arrangement for the exchange of news, later joined by other associations.[25]

* * *

Just as Reuters later was to gain and retain great prestige by its one week's "beat" on the assassination of President Abraham Lincoln and by exclusive accounts of some of the engagements of the American Civil War, so, several decades earlier, American

[25] Data on the Reuter service also appears in: Andrew Wynter, *Our Social Bees*, pp. 297-303. One of the earliest printed references to the Reuter service; H. M. Collins, *From Pigeon Post to Wireless;* J. D. Symon, *The Press and Its Story*, pp. 87-97; H. E. Wildes, *Social Currents in Japan*, Ch. 7. Presents a partial history of the Reuter service in Japan; Anon., "The Romance of Reuters in the Making," *The Graphic* (May 26, 1923), pp. 754-55, 780; F. D. Bone, "Reuter's Are Always Right: The History and Organization of Great News Agency with World-Wide Ramifications," *World's Press News* (July 4, 1929); Philip Schuyler, "Reuters' Connection with Old Jewry: Incidents in the History of a Great Agency. Reuters' Deeds Seen as Romance by Sir Roderick Jones," *Editor and Publisher* (Oct. 13, 1923); V. Prodzky, "Live Wires of Reuters," *World's Press News* (Mar. 31, 1932), pp. 14-15; Sir Roderick Jones, "The Romance of Reuters," lecture by Sir Roderick Jones at Hall of Institute of Journalists, London, Oct. 21, 1930. *Journal of the Institute of Journalists* (Dec., 1930), V. 18, pp. 223-24.

Also the following four pamphlets published by the Reuter's Telegram Co. Ltd.: *A Note on Reuters.* (For private information only. Confidential); *International Conference on the Press.* "News Agencies and Their Work." Address by Sir Roderick Jones, K.B.E. (Chairman of Reuters), London, July 6, 1927; *Reuters.* Address by Sir Roderick Jones, K.B.E., before Cardiff Business Club, Cardiff, April, 1932; *Reuters,* Address by Sir Roderick Jones, at School of Military Engineering, Chatham, Oct. 25, 1928.

news agencies developed out of a rivalry to get and distribute European news first. The same competition actuated individual newspapers and, in some instances, they were so eager to offer their readers "exclusive" foreign news that they invented it themselves. This inventiveness gave rise to three notable "hoaxes" in the history of New York journalism alone.

The first was the so-called "moon hoax," perpetrated by Richard Adams Locke in the New York *Sun* in 1835. It was reported, in great detail and in the most plausible way, that a South African astronomer had discovered vegetable and animal life, buildings and winged people on the moon, all thanks to the marvelous capacity of a new telescope. To verify this report it was necessary to wait for slow ships in regular trade to go, not merely to Great Britain, where the accounts were said to have appeared in a scientific journal published in Edinburgh, but to South Africa, and return. During the long weeks intervening before the hoax was exposed, the subject was a matter of awe-stricken discussion in some quarters, although it was scoffed at in others, and Locke kept it going in several installments. So much interest attached to the articles that the *Sun* sold 19,380 copies on August 28, 1835, which was the largest circulation up to that time for any daily in the world. *The Times* of London then had 17,000 circulation.[26]

The second deception was Edgar Allan Poe's so-called "balloon hoax," in the New York *Sun* on April 13, 1844. It concerned a three-day trip across the Atlantic Ocean in a "steering balloon." [27] The third was the "wild animal hoax" printed by the New York *Herald* on Sunday, November 9, 1874. It told of events following an escape of the wild animals in the Central Park Zoo, New York.[28] No such escape had occurred.

[26] F. M. O'Brien, *The Story of the Sun,* Ch. 3.
[27] *Ibid.,* pp. 148-53.
[28] D. C. Seitz, *The James Gordon Bennetts, Father and Son,* Ch. 13.
A hoax that was inspired by mischief alone was that perpetrated upon the *Packet,* a weekly paper of Hull, England, in 1864. Through a devious arrangement, the *Packet* received what seemed a bona fide message from the telegraph office announcing under the heading, "The War in Denmark," that "the enemy had taken Umbrage," and giving the geographical position

The first stage in the development of press associations in the United States had been the formation of rather kaleidoscopic harbor news associations in New York. With the advent of the telegraph, the field of competition was extended somewhat, for ships were met at Halifax, rather than at Boston or New York, and from there the news was rushed to Boston and New York newspapers by carrier pigeons or by combinations of pony express and telegraph, where it existed. The Mexican War, from 1846 to 1848, resulted in similar efforts for speedy news delivery from those Southern battlefields, usually by ship to New Orleans and from there overland by pony express and telegraph, wherever lines were to be found in operation.[29]

Peace was reached in the New York harbor rivalry with the formation in 1849 of the Harbor News Association. Instrumental in bringing about this truce was the fact that Daniel H. Craig of Boston was forestalling even the fastest of the New York newspaper boats.[30] He had arranged with correspondents in European countries to send him the latest news aboard the passenger steamships which began to make regular scheduled Atlantic crossings in 1845. His agents met the ships at Halifax and had carrier pigeons taken aboard. As the ships neared Boston, they released the pigeons, which flew to Boston, where Craig's assistants sent the news on by other pigeons to New York, and papers there subscribing to the service had a "beat" on the European news.

The New York newspapers that were being "beaten" tried to prevent Craig getting the pigeons aboard incoming ships, but they never succeeded in breaking up the system, so that in the end the *Herald* and the *Courier and Enquirer,* unable to combat him successfully, commissioned Craig to act for them in obtaining

of "Umbrage" in such a way as to place it somewhere in the middle of the North Sea, and noting its population and other data. The paper accepted the report as true, and printed it. William Hunt, *Then and Now. Fifty Years of Newspaper Work,* pp. 85-87.

[29] F. M. O'Brien, *The Story of the Sun,* Chs. 6, 7. Illustrates rivalry for news among New York newspapers about the time of the Mexican War.

[30] For further reference to Craig's service see: Frederic Hudson, *Journalism in the United States,* pp. 612-14; Victor Rosewater, *History of Co-operative News-Gathering in the United States,* Ch. 11; A. F. Harlow, *Old Wires and New Waves.*

European news. Thus it may be said that Daniel H. Craig, who previously had been unsuccessful in starting a penny paper in Boston, was to sponsor the second news service in the United States, the first having been the Topliff service already mentioned.[31]

Most of the New York newspapers agreed to share the expenses of the Harbor News Association in 1849. Later, the Telegraphic and General News Association was formed on a similar basis to gather news from inland points. In 1856 these two Associations were merged to form the General News Association of New York. Out of this grew the New York Associated Press, a coöperative news-gathering organization of New York papers, something like the present City News Bureaus in Chicago and New York, except that it also sold to newspapers outside of New York the news collected by its member papers.

During the Civil War, particularly, other regional associations grew up, and after the War many of these continued the relationship already worked out. In 1872 the New York Associated Press was serving telegraphic news to more than 200 dailies in the United States, and it paid out more than $200,000 in the year for cable dispatches alone. By 1880 it served 30 per cent of all dailies in the country with both foreign and domestic news, at a cost of $500,000 a year.[32] This was the lineal ancestor of the present Associated Press, which is the oldest existing press association in the United States.[33]

Regional or sectional news agencies that grew up were based on a plan similar to that used by the New York association. There were the New England Associated Press, Southern Associated Press, and Western Associated Press. These came to coöperate so

---

[31] M. E. Stone, *Fifty Years a Journalist*, pp. 204-18.

[32] S. N. D. North, *History of the Periodical Press of the U. S. A.*, House of Representatives, 47th Congress, 2nd Session. Misc. Doc. Part 8, Dept. of Interior. Census Office. Census of 1880, p. 107. A full report of news transmission methods by the Associated Press and by newspapers appears on pp. 105-10.

[33] Frederic Hudson, *Journalism in the United States*, Ch. 38. A more or less contemporary account of the history of the Harbor News Association and the New York Associated Press and rivals.

closely in the exchange of news as to form what was in effect one association, until internal rivalries and politics caused the Western Associated Press to break away in 1893. It set up as the Associated Press of Illinois, which soon grew so strong and so efficient that it drove the Associated Press of New York out of business and began to serve newspapers in all parts of the United States.

In 1900 the success of the Associated Press of Illinois was seriously threatened by a decision of the Illinois Supreme Court. The agency dissolved voluntarily as an Illinois organization, but reorganized itself under the Membership Corporation Law of New York State, a law intended to apply to social clubs, by which the organization was permitted to limit its membership. The Illinois Court had ruled that it must sell its news to all comers, whereas the Associated Press of Illinois felt that its chief advantage lay in being able to promise an exclusive news service to a newspaper in a certain community. Under the New York law it could, and can, do that, and membership may be restricted, just as in a social club. That is the present situation in the Associated Press and, therefore, the existing organization, while tracing its ancestry back to 1849, really was born in May, 1900.[34]

The new Associated Press extended its service not only throughout the United States, but to all other parts of the world. It set up bureaus in the most important capitals, opened foreign countries to modern methods of news reporting, and engaged literally hundreds of correspondents to "protect" it on events in their communities.[35]

* * *

[34] Inter-Ocean Pub. Co. v. Associated Press, 184 Ill. 438, 56 N.E. 822, 46 L.R.A. 568, 75 Am.St.Rep. 184; Victor Rosewater, *History of Coöperative News-Gathering in the United States*, Chs. 21, 22.

[35] For data on the Associated Press see: Victor Rosewater, *History of Co-operative News-Gathering in the United States*. This book also traces the entire history of news gathering in the United States; M. E. Stone, *Fifty Years a Journalist;* M. E. Stone, *News Gathering,* a pamphlet published by the Associated Press; W. G. Bleyer, *Main Currents in the History of American Journalism,* pp. 402-404; Anon., "(AP)" (Associated Press), *Fortune* (Feb. 1937), pp. 88-93, 148-62.

It is not to be supposed that other press associations did not arise even in the nations served by Reuters, Havas, and the Associated Press. The histories of journalism reveal that some have been short-lived and others have merged with more vital organizations.[36] But some have survived and gained high respect.

So in the United States, there is the independent and strong United Press.[37] The Hearst-owned International News Service is enterprising, although more limited in its news coverage. In Great Britain the Press Association of the United Kingdom is a branch of Reuters devoted to covering news of Great Britain and Northern Ireland alone. The Central News and the Exchange Telegraph also are reputable agencies serving British newspapers.[38] In France there is the Agence Télégraphique Radio, which is allied to Havas, and some minor agencies.

In other countries press associations were developed, usually patterned after one of the first three—Havas, Reuters, or the Associated Press. Generally speaking, they make little effort to report the news outside their own countries but depend for such coverage upon affiliations with other agencies.[39]

Thirty principal news agencies, in as many countries, form an unofficial but effective World League of Press Associations for the exchange of news.[40] The original membership included Reuters (Great Britain), Havas (France), Associated Press

[36] The Laffan News Bureau, for example, was set up by the New York *Sun* in the late 'eighties, and continued as an independent bureau until 1916.

[37] M. A. McRae, *Forty Years of Newspaperdom*, Ch. 7. Stephen Vincent Benét, "The United Press," *Fortune* (May, 1933), V. 7, No. 5, pp. 67-72, 94-104. N. D. Cochrane, *E. W. Scripps.*

[38] H. Simonis, *The Street of Ink*, Ch. 15. Covers history and organization of Reuters, Central News, Exchange Telegraph Co., London News Agency; J. D. Symon, *The Press and Its Story*, pp. 87-97.

[39] Sir Roderick Jones, *International Conference on the Press*, "News Agencies and Their Work." Address by Sir Roderick Jones, K.B.E., Chairman of Reuters, London, July 6, 1927.

[40] The members of the World League are indicated in "The Press as a Factor in International Relations," by Paul F. Douglass and Karl Bömer. *Annals of the American Academy of Political and Social Science* (July, 1932), V. 162, pp. 265-68. Also in *Documents Relating to the Preparation of the Press Experts Committee* (Anon.). League of Nations Publication, C. 399, M. 140 (1928), pp. 12-13.

(United States), Wolff (Germany), Westnik (Russia), Kokusai (Japan), Stefani (Italy), Fabra (Spain), and others. Westnik or the Petrograd News Agency became known as Rosta and later as the Tass agency under the Soviets. Kokusai in 1926 was transformed into the Rengo agency and in 1936 it was known as the Domei agency. Wolff became known in 1933 as the Deutsches Nachrichten Büro.

Specifically, the thirty members of the world league, or alliance, of press associations, country by country, with status of the agencies and the cities in which they have their main offices, now are as follows: [41]

MEMBERS OF THE WORLD LEAGUE OF PRESS ASSOCIATIONS

AUSTRIA	Amtliche Nachrichtenstelle (Official)	Vienna
BELGIUM	Agence Télégraphique Belge (Belga) (Semi-official)	Brussels
BULGARIA	Agence Télégraphique Bulgare (Official)	Sofia
CANADA	Canadian Press, Ltd. (Coöperative, Independent)	Toronto, Ontario
CHINA	Reuters (Branch of British Agency)	Shanghai
CZECHOSLOVAKIA	Československa Tisková Kancelář (Czechoslovak Press Bureau)	Prague
DENMARK	Ritzaus Bureau (Ritzaus), (Dansk Telegrambureau) (Independent)	Copenhagen
ESTONIA	Eesti Telegraafi Agentuur A.S. (Eta) (Estonian Telegraph Agency Ltd.)	Tallinn
FINLAND	Finska Notisbyran	Helsingfors
FRANCE	Agence Havas (Semi-official)	Paris
GERMANY	Deutsches Nachrichten Büro G.m.b.h. (DNB), (Official)	Berlin
GREAT BRITAIN	Reuters, Ltd. (Independent)	London
GREECE	Agence d'Athènes (Semi-official)	Athens
HUNGARY	Magyar Távirati Iroda (Ungarisches Telegraphen-Korrespondenz Büro), (Hungarian Telegraphic Agency), (Semi-official)	Budapest
ITALY	Agenzia Stefani (Official)	Rome
JAPAN	Domei Tsushin Sha (Allied News Association), (Semi-official)	Tokyo
LATVIA	Latvijas Telegrafa Agentura (Leta), (Latvian Telegraph Agency)	Riga

[41] Compiled from *Associated Press Handbook, Political Handbook of the World, Europa* (see Anon.), and sources listed in n. 40, p. 65.

MEMBERS OF THE WORLD LEAGUE OF PRESS ASSOCIATIONS
(Continued)

LITHUANIA	Agence Télégraphique Lithuanienne (Lithuanian Telegraphic Agency)	Kovno
NETHERLANDS	Algemeen Nederlandsch Persbureau (ANP), (Official agency of Netherlands Daily Press Association)	Amsterdam
NORWAY	Norske Telegrambyrå (Norwegian News Agency), (Independent)	Oslo
POLAND	Polska Agencja Telegraficzna (PAT), (Polish Telegraph Agency) (Official)	Warsaw
PORTUGAL	Agence Havas (Branch of French Agency)	Lisbon
RUMANIA	Agence Orient Radio (Rador) (Official)	Bucharest
RUSSIA (U.S.S.R.)	Tass (Telegrafnoje Agentstwo Ssojusa), (Telegraphic Agency of the Soviet States), (Official)	Moscow
SPAIN	Agencia Telegrafica Fabra (Official—Controlled by Havas)	Madrid and Barcelona
SWEDEN	Tidningarnas Telegrambyrå (Telegram Agency of Newspapers) (Semi-official)	Stockholm
SWITZERLAND	Agence Télégraphique Suisse, S.A. (Schweizerische Depeschenagentur A.G.), (Swiss Telegraphic Agency)	Berne
TURKEY	Anodolu Ajansi (Agence d'Anatolie) (Anatolian News Agency), (Semi-official)	Ankara
UNITED STATES OF AMERICA	Associated Press (Coöperative, Independent)	New York
YUGOSLAVIA	Agence Avala (Semi-official)	Belgrade

Almost every country represented in the world alliance has one or more news agencies in addition. The exceptions are the smallest countries, or countries under dictatorships or other arrangements wherein the press associations have been consolidated and made official or semi-official, or countries where no association exists.[42] It will be observed that no South American press associations are members of the world alliance. This is because South American news is covered by the United Press, Associated Press, International News Service, and Agence Havas,

[42] A convenient source in which to find these and other press associations is the *Political Handbook of the World*. Published annually, it lists the most recent nomenclature and organization of the press of each country.

and finds its way into the news stream through these agencies. Domestic press associations are not developed in Latin America. The same is true of Australia, so far as concerns national associations, and of most other countries not represented. Although China has several press associations, a local branch of Reuters provides the news of that country to the rest of the world.

It may be said that there is a smaller, and quite new affiliation, including the United Press (United States), the British United Press (Great Britain and Canada), Agence Télégraphique Radio (France), and Tass (Russia). The French agency is allied to Havas, and Tass also is in the larger affiliation.

Although each of the agencies forming the "world league" originally was restricted, by mutual agreement, to the sale of news entirely in its own country or in well defined territories, that arrangement was "liberalized" at a London meeting in 1932, between the heads of Reuters, the Associated Press, Havas, and the Wolff agency. By this agreement any one of the agencies was permitted to sell its service independently to any newspaper or other clients wanting it in a country normally served by one of the other member agencies.

In practice, the four biggest agencies have arranged coverage of most of the world in the following way, with an exchange of news among them:

ASSOCIATED PRESS.—Covers the United States, Central America, and coöperates with Havas to cover South America.

HAVAS.—Covers France, the French Colonies, Romanic countries of Europe, and coöperates with the Associated Press to cover South America, and with Reuters to cover the Near East.

REUTERS.—Covers Great Britain and the British Empire, the Netherlands, the Far East, and coöperates with Havas to cover the Near East.

DNB.—Covers Germany and Austria.[43]

---

[43] Paul F. Douglass and Karl Börner, "The Press as a Factor in International Relations," *Annals of the American Academy of Political and Social Science* (July, 1932), Ch. 2. "The International Combination of News Agencies," pp. 265-68. This was before the Wolff agency had been reorganized as DNB.

Among the other press associations of the world, not members of the league of agencies, but some of them very important, are the following: [44]

OTHER LEADING PRESS ASSOCIATIONS

ALBANIA	Albanian Press Bureau and Telegraph Agency	Tirana
AUSTRALIA	Australian Associated Press, Proprietary, Ltd.	Melbourne
	Australian Newspapers Cable Service	Sydney
	Provincial Press Association of South Australia	Adelaide
	Queensland Country Press Association	Brisbane
	Tasmanian Provincial and Country Press Association	Launceston
	Country Press Coöperative Company, Ltd.	Melbourne
	Victorian Provincial Press Association	Melbourne
	West Australian Provincial Press Association	Perth
	Australian United Press Ltd.	Sydney
	Australian Provincial Press Association	Sydney
	Country Press, Ltd.	Sydney
	New South Wales Country Press Association	Sydney
AUSTRIA	Korrespondenz Wilhelm (Semi-official)	Vienna
BRAZIL	Agencia Brasiliera (Independent)	Rio de Janeiro
	União Telegrafica Brasileira (Independent)	Rio de Janeiro

[44] Adapted from *Political Handbook of the World* (1937 edition). Unless otherwise noted, an agency is to be regarded as independent, at least nominally. If a nation is unrepresented on this list or on the previous list of associations forming the world league of news agencies, it may be assumed that it has no press association of its own, but is dependent upon press associations of other countries for its news service. Also, while some of these associations are important and devoted to providing a general service of news, many of them are concerned only with the news of a certain section or province, or with special kinds of news, such as news and interpretation of political and diplomatic affairs, news of business, etc., and some of them are little more than propaganda agencies.

OTHER LEADING PRESS ASSOCIATIONS (*Continued*)

CHINA	Central News Agency (Kuomintang Official)	Nanking
	Kuo Min (Chinese Semi-official)	Shanghai
	Shun Shih (Chinese)	Shanghai
	Domei Tsushin Sha (Allied News Association),[45] (Japanese)	Shanghai
	Agence Havas (French) [45]	Shanghai
	Reuters (British) [45]	Shanghai
	Transozean-Nachrichten (German) [45]	Shanghai
	Tass (Russian) [45]	Shanghai
	Associated Press (American) [45]	Shanghai
	United Press (American) [45]	Shanghai
CZECHOSLOVAKIA	Central European Press	Prague
	Radio Central	Prague
FINLAND	Suomen Tietotoimisto (STT), (Semi-official)	Helsingfors
	Presscentralen	Helsingfors
	Työväen Sanomalehtien Tietotoimisto (TST), (Social-Democratic)	Helsingfors
FRANCE	Agence Économique et Financière (Economic and financial news)	Paris
	Agence Fournier (Financial and political news)	Paris
	Agence Télégraphique Radio (Controlled by Havas), (Political and financial news)	Paris
GERMANY	Deutsche Diplomatisch-Politische Korrespondenz (Semi-official— political news)	Berlin
	Transozean-Nachrichten (Semi-official. For radio and overseas service)	Berlin
GREAT BRITAIN	British United Press Ltd.	London
	Central News, Ltd.	London
	The Central Press Ltd. (Correspondence and features for provincial and overseas papers)	London
	Exchange Telegraph Co., Ltd.	London
	Press Association Ltd. (Affiliated with Reuters for domestic news)	London

[45] China represents rather a special case for there a number of foreign press associations maintain independent offices, as indicated, due to the fact that the Chinese press associations are not well organized, nor are they always reliable or impartial in their handling of the news. The situation is similar in Uruguay, although on a smaller scale.

OTHER LEADING PRESS ASSOCIATIONS (*Continued*)

GREAT BRITAIN	British Continental Press	London
(*cont.*)	London General Press (News of economics, finance, politics, science)	London
GREECE	Hellenic Press Association	Athens
HONDURAS	Asociación de la Prensa Hondureña	Tegucigalpa
INDIA	Associated Press of India (Independent)	Calcutta, Delhi, etc.
	United Press of India (Independent)	Calcutta, Delhi, etc.
ITALY	Agenzia di Roma (Semi-official—political news)	Rome
	Agenzia Volta (Economic news)	Rome
	Agenzia Telegrafica Orientale	Rome
	Radio Nazionale	Rome
JAPAN	Teikoku Tsushinsha (Imperial News Agency)	Tokyo
MEXICO	Agencia Noticiosa Telegrafica Americana (ANTA), (Semi-official, controlled by Havas)	Mexico City
MONACO	Agence Télégraphique	Monte Carlo
NETHERLANDS	Persbureau Vaz Diaz	Amsterdam
	Persbureau Aneta (Colonial news service)	Batavia
	Nederlandsch Correspondentie-bureau (Semi-official)	The Hague
	Persbureau Aneta-Holland (Colonial news)	The Hague
NEW ZEALAND	United Press Association of New Zealand	Wellington
NORWAY	Avisernes Oslokontor A/S	Oslo
	Myres Pressebyraa	Oslo
POLAND	Agencja Telegraficzna Express (ATE)	Warsaw
	Agencja Eschodnia (EST)	Warsaw
	Iskra (Semi-official)	Warsaw
RUMANIA	Interbalkan	Bucharest
SOUTH AFRICA (Union of)	Reuters Ltd. (Branch of British agency)	Pretoria & Cape Town
SWEDEN	Svensk-Amerikanska Nyhetsbyrån (Swedish-American News Agency)	Stockholm
	Svensk-Internationella Pressbyråm	Stockholm
TURKEY	Turkish Press Association (Independent, but recognized by the Government)	Ankara
UNITED STATES	United Press Associations (UP), (Independent)	New York

OTHER LEADING PRESS ASSOCIATIONS (*Continued*)

UNITED STATES (*cont.*)	International News Service (INS), (Hearst service)	New York
	Universal News Service (US), (Hearst service)	New York
	Federated Press (FP), (A labor service)	New York
	North American Newspaper Alliance (NANA)	New York
URUGUAY	Associated Press (Branch of American Agency)	Montevideo
	Circulo de la Prensa (Independent)	Montevideo
	United Press Associations (Branch of American Agency)	Montevideo

The larger press associations, especially in important centers such as London, Paris, and New York or Washington, maintain staffs organized as in a newspaper office, each with an executive equivalent to a city editor, or news editor, as he would be termed in Great Britain, assigning reporters to various events.

* * *

Apart from the feature services, which have arisen as adjuncts to the news reports, press associations are expected to deal primarily in pure facts.

The special correspondent, representing an individual newspaper or several newspapers, or a special syndicate, often writing under his own name, sometimes does much the same thing, but if he touches a story at all he frequently sends more detail and gives more emphasis to the interpretation.[46]

Certain press associations are not quite impartial, however. They serve governments or private interests. Some of them are subsidized by governments and are, in effect, agencies of those governments. This status sometimes is recognized, and the agency

[46] For example, the Associated Press sent 200 words from London about the Unemployment Commission report of Nov. 7, 1932. The New York *Times* wanted more, so Charles A. Selden, its correspondent, sent 1,000 words and made page one. Such papers as the New York *Times* and *La Prensa* of Buenos Aires are unique in the world of journalism because of their appetite for details, but this very complete handling of the news is what has given them their splendid reputations.

is frankly held to be "official" or "semi-official," but even some of those agencies which pretend to be "independent" are not beyond suspicion. They are, potentially at least, propaganda organizations. Some of these groups, as members of the world league, may feed into the news stream a certain amount of propaganda, despite the conscientious efforts of foreign agencies to keep it out.

It is not that governments necessarily pay money across the counter to persuade press associations to disseminate favoring news. But a properly disposed press association may enjoy favorable financial terms in its use of communication and transmission facilities. Or extremely generous payments may be made to the association for special service of news to out-of-the-way colonial-military, or governmental posts, or radio service to ships at sea and foreign countries. At the same time, payment for such services is not necessarily evidence that the association is "official," much less that it is engaged in distributing propaganda.[47]

It sometimes is assumed that because a government issues official statements and communiqués which are distributed verbatim, through a press association, that such an association is clearly government-owned or controlled. This is not necessarily so. Press associations sometimes coöperate with their governments out of national loyalty. Reuters, Havas, the former Wolff agency of Germany, Stefani of Italy, the former Rengo agency of Japan and others have received exclusive news releases from their governments and in return have provided the governments with advance copies of incoming foreign dispatches before distribution. This sometimes has given government departments opportunity to re-word or revise dispatches to accord with the official

[47] To avoid any such appearance of lending itself to propaganda purposes, the Canadian Press Association refused in May, 1920, to accept a joint British and Canadian Government subsidy increased to $50,000 or $60,000. The association, for about fifteen years prior to that date, had received a smaller subsidy, which was regarded as almost essential if it were to continue in business, but it had not "been very happy in the fact." John W. Dafoe of the Manitoba *Free Press,* so remarked at the Second Imperial Press Conference, Ottawa, 1920. Robert Donald, ed., *The Imperial Press Conference in Canada, 1920,* pp. 168-69.

viewpoint and, in some cases, to withhold the news completely until a time that seemed more suitable for its release.

There are occasions when this relationship of government and press is unfortunate. In France the Foreign Office prefers to have Havas communicate to the French press only those comments from foreign newspapers which are favorable to the actions or purposes of the French Government. Unless a French newspaper maintains its own foreign correspondents—and few do so—who can and will send other versions, readers may gain a totally incorrect view of foreign opinion on some subjects. Then, when events prove that they have been misled, instead of feeling annoyance with their government or the press, they vent their displeasure unjustly on the foreign peoples.

The same is true where a government maintains an absolute censorship over its press, as in Russia, Italy, and Germany. Opposition or unwelcome views never receive publicity in those countries unless with a propaganda purpose.

*   *   *

A phase of press association development has been the so-called "syndicates" dealing with long feature stories of the magazine variety, with fiction and short articles, puzzles, cartoons, et cetera, usually with emphasis on entertainment.

In the United States the syndicate idea seems to have begun with Henry Villard, who, as a reporter for the Associated Press in Springfield, Illinois, proposed a news-reporting system from Washington in 1881. He suggested a syndicate to gather and provide the same "political and other news by mail and telegraph to a number of papers in different parts of the country, geographically situated so that they would not interfere with each other by the simultaneous publication of the same matter. . . . My enterprise was to be a sort of supplement to the Associated Press. . . . It was indeed the beginning in this country of the news syndicates or agencies, of which scores now exist in Washington and New York. I think I am fairly entitled to be considered the pioneer in this business. . . ." [48] He went to Washington and

[48] Henry Villard, *Memoirs of Henry Villard*, V. 1, pp. 153-54.

formed such a syndicate, serving the Cincinnati *Commercial,* Chicago *Tribune* and New York *Herald.*

The syndicate idea began in England in about 1870, when Tillotson & Son, Bolton publishers, undertook to sell fiction serials to other British newspapers. This was a different type of material from that in which Villard was to deal, which was strictly news, and it suggested similar syndicates in other countries, including the United States.

In about 1884 Charles A. Dana syndicated some short stories by Bret Harte and Henry James, stories that he had purchased for the New York *Sun.* Samuel S. McClure, then of the *Century Magazine,* found in this his inspiration and in the autumn of 1884 he began a weekly syndication of 5000 words, consisting of short stories. His scope of material and his list of clients expanded phenomenally, and syndicates soon were well established in the United States. Edward W. Bok also established one of the early American syndicates and carried it on for a time.[49] Since then, numerous syndicates have been formed.

§ 3. WRITING THE NEWS FOR TRANSMISSION

ALL CORRESPONDENTS must consider the costs of news transmission. The increased use of the telephone has changed the aspect of this matter somewhat, but judicious economy governs that verbal style of transmission, too. Much that the correspondents write may go by mail, hence is almost without restriction as to volume, so far as that is related to expense. But telegraphic messages usually are written with some attention to brevity, while matter which must go at once by cable, usually spanning a greater

[49] S. S. McClure, *My Autobiography;* Edward W. Bok, *The Americanization of Edward Bok,* pp. 78-88; M. A. McRae, *Forty Years in Newspaperdom;* W. G. Bleyer, *Main Currents in the History of American Journalism,* pp. 399-402; Elmo Scott Watson, *A History of Newspaper Syndicates in the United States, 1865-1935;* Irving Bacheller, "The Rungs in My Literary Ladder," *American Magazine* (April, 1918), V. 85, p. 19; V. V. McNitt, "Sam McClure Started Something," *Editor and Publisher* (July 21, 1934), pp. 89-90; Richard H. Waldo, "The Genius of S. S. McClure," *Editor and Publisher* (July 21, 1934), pp. 80, 88; S. S. McClure, "And McClure Tells How He Did It," *Editor and Publisher* (July 21, 1934), pp. 82, 90.

distance, is prepared in a form known as "cablese," intended to save money by saving words.

This curious language has been much simplified in recent times due to somewhat reduced transmission rates and agreements accompanying the reductions, and due also to the need for more rapid handling of the news at the receiving end, where the extensive editing that "cablese" required slowed up the process. A few offices have ceased to use even a modified form of "cablese," permitting their correspondents to write, apparently, without much regard for expense. Such lavishness still is far from common, however.

In cablese, articles are omitted, identifications are omitted, and condensations or combinations are used to make one word do the work of two or more. For example, "this morning" becomes "smorning," "delivered an oration" becomes "orated," "all those present agreed," would become "omniagreed," and "The Prime Minister has gone to Paris" would become "Premier Parisward." If he "will not go," he will "ungo," and if France is "in favor of the treaty," it is "protreaty." [50]

Yet this is simple compared to the Phillips code, patented in 1879, which was used by telegraph operators as a sort of telegraphic shorthand wherein combinations of letters stood for groups of words. Thus, "SCOTUS" would mean "Supreme Court of the United States," "ICW" would mean "in connection with," "SOT" meant "Secretary of the Treasury," "POTUS" meant "President of the United States," "POW" meant "Prince of

[50] The Western Union Telegraph Co. sought to end this sort of cablese, beginning Jan. 1, 1928. Such word contractions were forbidden on the ground that the press services wanted clearer messages, and it was announced that cables violating the rule would be refused or reworded. An earlier revision downward of press rates, the Western Union maintained, was to have been accompanied by a practice of writing news messages in full, without contractions or evasions, but this change had not been made by correspondents, it was contended, which made it necessary for the Company to establish rules in the matter. It was true that some correspondents had started to write their dispatches more fully, and this tendency has continued, so that the cable companies have no cause to complain, although a certain amount of condensation, as apart from contraction, continues and is regarded as permissible.

Confirmation of Cable sent VIA COMMERCIAL.

5/11/29

Note holcombe following is exclusive absolutely authentic summary experts plan for bank international settlements xxxx stowe step For more than two months plans for establishment new powerful and unprecedented international banking institution to manage and dominate all germanys future reparations payments have been outstanding task of second reparations conference step this propos quote bank for international settlements unquote will inaugurated as entirely new xxxx financial experiment on widespread farreachin lines as never before attempted worlds history comma if experts succeed step twill stand out clearly as the heart and by all odds greatest achievement of what may one day known as quote young plan unquote but even if experts failx reach agreement on total amount and annuities germanys to pay this pioneering conception of an international bank will remain as core and substance and most significant contribution of young committees report step herald tribune today is able xxx publish for first time and exclusively the summary and outline of projected bank for intl settlements and xxxx details of many its most important functions which of primar interest to bankers world over step this summary constitutes firs authentic firsthand report of what experts have evolved in three months of unceasing labor step it amounts to advance presentation of quote kernel of the quote young plan unquote it should emphasized that plan for bank intl settlements in past weeks has drafted redrafted and revised with all painstaking care of worlds foremost banking

FIG. 2. THE CORRESPONDENT WRITES FOR THE CABLE

For description see List of Illustrations

Wales," "UNL" was "unconstitutional" and "SAK" was "shot and killed." [51]

In present-day cabling the first word or numeral, apart from the address, usually is a "time slug" or a figure indicating the time of filing, followed by the name of the correspondent, unless the name is at the end, and then the message follows. The exact sequence of figures differs between organizations, but the purpose is always the same.

For example, a cable from Leland Stowe, when Paris correspondent for the New York *Herald Tribune,* filed in Paris on the 17th day of the month, the 20th hour of the day (8 P.M.) and in the first ten-minute period after the hour, would reach the cable desk in New York, as follows:

PRESS VIA COMMERCIAL
TRIBUNE NEW YORK 17201 STOWE HERRIOT LEADER RADICAL PARTY AND ONETIME PREMIER FRANCE OUSTED FROM LYONS MAYORALTY YESTERDAY AS RESULT MUNICIPAL ELECTIONS STOP WHOLE RADICAL ADMINISTRATION CITY WILL BE REPLACED BY SOCIALISTS RESULT LATTERS SWEEPING VICTORY IN BALLOTING STOP HERRIOT BEEN MAYOR MANY YEARS STOP AS RESULT SIMILAR ELECTIONS ALSACE COMMA STRASBOURG AND OTHER IMPORTANT ALSATIAN MUNICIPALITIES TO BE COMPLETELY CONTROLLED BY COMMUNISTS IN COALITION WITH AUTONOMISTS STOP

Translated, this cable would appear in print somewhat as follows:

By LELAND STOWE
(*Special Cable to The New York Herald Tribune*)
PARIS, Oct. 17.—M. Edouard Herriot, leader of the Radical Party, and former Premier of France, was ousted as Mayor of the important industrial city of Lyons yester-

[51] Walter P. Phillips, who devised this code, was general manager of the old United Press.

Telbermefte:

Berzögerungsbermerkt:

Gebühren: ....RA........ Rpf | Telegramm and | **Deutſche Reichspoſt** | Tag | Beſtellt Zeit
Ungen........ | (Aufgabenſtell) | an | durch

Nr. .... mit .... W. 19 ...... den .... um .... Uhr | Weg-angabe | **VIA DAT**

Presse Chicagonews Newyork

american diplomatic circles raised *quizzical* eyebrows today
when learned one important function of new ministry for
propaganda and popular enlightenment which just been created and
placed hands of paul joseph goebbels will be broadcasting *special*
programs to american people *particularly those of* german origin stop
so fars can yet be learned these programs will given in
both english german thereby being aimed to catch unonly
german americans *but all who will* listen stop tis explained
subect matter largely of cultural type including music
but that occasionally quote objective news bulletins unquote
will be interpolated stop germans explain this practice
began two years ago in bruening days that recently *such*
programs been broadcasted three times weekly that will
made daily *beginning* april first stop programs are sent direct
on shortwave without cooperation of american senders dash or
so twas stated smorning stop germans cant quite understand
american *emotion nearly because* attempt should be made to
urge german americans to keep close touch with their former
country or to influence american public opinion directly
rathern through *turgid* channels of american
newspaper reports stop americans answer this practice
been outcarried by soviet russia and
poland and that germans been so *little* enthusiastic about receiving
profganda from abroad in german that they immediately
strengthened their own senders in hope shutting it out stop
poles say their own programs occasionally sent abroad in
english french german languages that they dont know whether
can be recéived in america or not stop last program was
about six weeks ago therefore *that* practice cant compared with
german plan of daily broadcast stop rumor dash now

Bu Fauben fur **Chicago Daily News**
Unſchlußamt: **A 1 Jäger 0130**

Wohnung: **Unter den Linden 25**

Ubſender (Name): **Chicago Daily News**

Zuſtell-Poſtanſtalt: **Berlin W 8**

Vom Abſender zu beachten:

Die von ſtarkpunktierten
Linien (♦♦♦♦♦♦) umgebenen
8 Teile hat der Abſender aus-
zufüllen.

*) Entſprechendes durchſtreichen.

Ubſender (Name): **Chicago Daily News**

Wohnung: **Unter den Linden 25**

Anſchlußamt: **A 1 Jäger 0130**

Zuſtell-Poſtanſtalt: **W 8**

Liefert am Schalter gegen Gebührenſtund.*) ein Telegramm auf

am .... an Chicagonews .... in New York

Nr. des Telegramms | Beſonderer Bermerk | Wortzahl | Name des Beamten | Gebühren:

Presse .... RA .... Rpf.

FIG. 3. THE CORRESPONDENT WRITES FOR THE TELEPHONE

For description see List of Illustrations

day as a result of the municipal elections. The entire Radical party administration of the city will be replaced by Socialists as a result of the Socialist party's sweeping victory in the balloting.

M. Herriot had been Mayor of Lyons for many years. Not only was he defeated, but similar elections in Alsace, Strasbourg, and other important Alsatian municipalities mean that those cities will be completely controlled by Communists in coalition with Autonomists.

Occasionally a message may be written in code to escape the vigilance of the censor or for some other reason. One such code resulted in a press association sending out a message disguised as a report of a sports event. An unusual use of code occurred in a message from Russell Owen, correspondent of the New York *Times* with the first Byrd South Pole expedition. Owen's messages were radioed direct from Little America to the New York *Times* and syndicated by that paper all over the world. Another newspaper, however, served notice that it would pick up the radio messages and use them. So it was that when Byrd and his associates actually flew over the South Pole on Nov. 28, 1929, the message was radioed from the plane in flight to Little America, and from Little America to the *Times* in New York. The message, as received in code, read:

213 WFA AIRPLANE FLOYD BENNETT IN FLIGHT 155 PMGMT NOV. 29 1929 NEW YORK TIMES NEW YORK CITY MY CALCULATIONS INDICATE WE HAVE REACHED VICINITY SUGAR FISHING HUMIDITY FOR SURVEY ATKINSON CRAMP WELL STOP WILL SOON TURN NOMINATE PINEY ONALASKA TRIGGER FLUNKEY DIAMOND SUGAR BILLETT 5:23 P.M.

This message, translated, appeared in the New York *Times* of Nov. 29, 1929, and was on the street in New York one-half hour after the message had been sent from the plane in flight over the South Pole. It read:

BERLIN   Thompson's   Vienna   32000

Via   Budapest.   Quote   Communications
strike   necess-ary   consequence   long
reconstruction   program   and   Austrian
governments   policy   said   foreign
Minister   Grunberger   Ledger   interview
Chancellor   Seipel   intends   keep   his
word   to   unadd   item   budget
Chancellor   definitely   rejected   socialists'
demand   bonuses   equally   divided
employes   regardless   length   service
age   or   position   Socialists   since
foundation   Republic   sought   establish
need   rathern   service   as   basis
pay   present   government   while
wishing   be   humane   and   recognizing
regretfully   condition   Austrian   finances
prevents   adequate   wages   public
servants   insists   service   rathern
personal   needs   reestablished   as
basis   fixing   wages   believing   any
other   system   uneconomic   Seipel   also
protecting   middle   classes   who   been
among   worst   sufferers   Austria   and
recognized   need   of   educated   man
for   something   moren   food   unquote
Asked   whether   any   prospect
socialists   entering   government   ending
continual   fight   wherefrom   whole
population   suffers   Grunberger   said
saw   unway   admitting   socialists
without   fundamental   changes   policy
whereto   Austria   pledged.   by
League   Protocols   unquote   Seipel
referred   whole   problem   to
Parliament   where   socialists   control
twofifths   votes   compromise   yet
unfound   estimated   sixmillion   letters
await   delivery   industrial   life
practically   standstill.

Conger.

8Pm.

FIG. 4. THE CORRESPONDENT WRITES FOR THE WIRELESS

For description see List of Illustrations

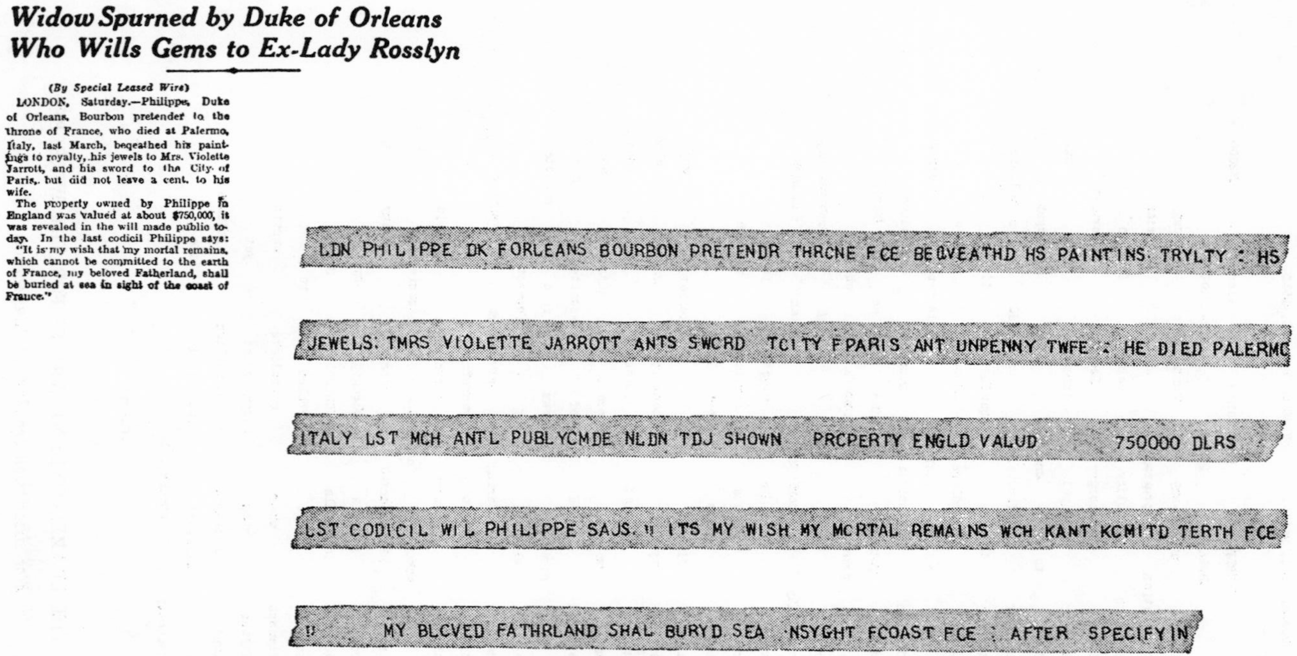

Widow Spurned by Duke of Orleans Who Wills Gems to Ex-Lady Rosslyn

(By Special Leased Wire)

LONDON, Saturday—Philippe, Duke of Orleans, Bourbon pretender to the throne of France, who died at Palermo, Italy, last March, bequeathed his paintings to royalty, his jewels to Mrs. Violette Jarrott, and his sword to the City of Paris, but did not leave a cent. to his wife.

The property owned by Philippe in England was valued at about $750,000, is was revealed in the will made public to-day. In the last codicil Philippe says:

"It is my wish that my mortal remains, which cannot be committed to the earth of France, my beloved Fatherland, shall be buried at sea in sight of the coast of France."

LDN PHILIPPE DK FORLEANS BOURBON PRETENDR THRONE FCE BEQVEATHD HS PAINTINS TRYLTY : HS

JEWELS: TMRS VIOLETTE JARROTT ANTS SWORD TCITY FPARIS ANT UNPENNY TWFE : HE DIED PALERMO

ITALY LST MCH ANT'L PUBLYCMDE NLDN TDJ SHOWN   PRCPERTY ENGLD VALUD   750000 DLRS

LST CODICIL WIL PHILIPPE SAJS. " ITS MY WISH MY MORTAL REMAINS WCH KANT KCMITD TERTH FCE

MY BLCVED FATHRLAND SHAL BURYD SEA NSYGHT FCOAST FCE : AFTER SPECIFY IN

!'

FIG. 5.   A MESSAGE FROM A PRESS ASSOCIATION

For description see List of Illustrations

ABOARD THE AIRPLANE FLOYD BENNETT, IN FLIGHT, 1.55
P.M. GREENWICH MEAN TIME, Friday, Nov. 29.—My
calculations indicate that we have reached the vicinity of
the South Pole flying high for a survey. The airplane is
in good shape, crew all well. Will soon turn north. We can
see almost limitless polar plateau. Our departure from
the Pole was at 5:23 P.M.

* * *

To "send" a message, a foreign correspondent decides whether
it is to go by telegraph, cable or radio. Or perhaps he telephones
it himself, either direct to his office or to some other point for
use or for relay. If not, however, a messenger takes the dispatch
to the proper office for transmission. The differences in time and
the probable interval required for delivery need to be considered
by the correspondent.

It is noon in London or Paris five hours before it is noon in
New York, six hours before it is noon in Chicago, seven hours
before it is noon in Denver, eight hours before it is noon in San
Francisco, and so on. This time difference permits the American
correspondent in Europe to work on a fairly leisurely schedule.
If, on the other hand, the message is going from New York or
Washington to London the correspondent is rather rushed to get
his copy into the London newspaper office in time for the morning
edition, because when it is 6 P.M. in Washington, for example, and
the day is over, it already is 11 P.M. in London.

Press associations, which have a deadline to make somewhere
at almost every hour of the day or night, cannot rest at all, however, and they do not always wait to construct well-rounded
stories. Instead, the big agencies serving North and South America, particularly, have transmission keys and automatic printer
keyboards in their main control bureaus, and keep a series of
bulletins, flashes, new leads, and adds flowing, especially between
Europe and New York, leaving it for the cable desk in New York
to convert the fragments into smooth-reading stories for distribution over the national wire circuits.

During a dock strike in London, for example, these two wire-

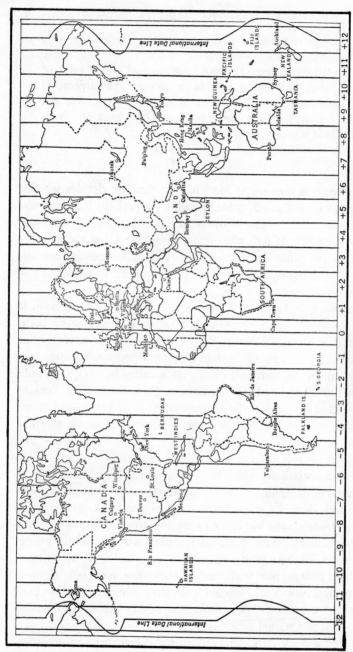

FIG. 6. HOW TIME AFFECTS THE WORK OF A CORRESPONDENT

For description see List of Illustrations

less dispatches were sent from London to New York by the International News Service: [52]

DOCKERS CONFERENCE ADJOURNED MONDAYWARD UNAGREEMENT DELEGATES RETURNING HOMEWARD CONSULT MEMBERS

BEVIN ANNOUNCES DELEGATES RECOMMENDING MEMBERS ACCEPT SETTLEMENT.

The story, as constructed by the cable desk in New York from these brief messages, combined with what was already known of the situation, read:

LONDON, Feb. 22.—Despite the agreement reached Wednesday, the British dock strike still dragged on to-day.

Representatives of the dock workers met again in an attempt to reach a settlement satisfactory to all factions.

London leaders favor acceptance of the terms agreed upon Wednesday, but the provincial strikers are opposed. They are demanding the full wage increase at once, instead of taking half now and the balance in three months.

Unless the strike is settled completely by to-morrow the week-end food shortage is going to prove acute.

Ernest Bevin, leader of the strikers, said that the delegates at to-day's conference are recommending to the rank and file of the dock workers' unions to accept the terms of Wednesday's agreement.

When a story is sent piecemeal, of course, special care must be taken to insure proper identification, so that the various parts may be brought together accurately at the control bureau, whether that be Berlin, London or New York. The key is in the "time slug." So a message sent to the London bureau of the Associated Press at five minutes after noon on the fourth day of the month, would bear the time slug "41205," the entire address being

PRESS ASSOCIATED LONDON 41205

[52] Charles W. Miller, "How the Cable Is Translated," *Circulation* (July, 1924), pp. 33, 48.

8 04 Ks

London 356/357   9/650pm.   Dec 9, 1929.

Press Tribune, NewYork.

Rapid rise Thames in upper reaches with menace to London of rise
equal great flood of last year today added peril to gales and rains
which for four days without cease have pounded England stop After
few hours comparative quiet gales during afternoon evening again
lashed coast and shipping paid toll stop Royal train bringing
King Queen from Sandringham London struck eightymile gale beyond
Cambridge stop Its progress effectively checked and for first time
memory royal train ran behind schedule stop Arrived eighteen
minutes late stop Additional King Queen aboard were King Queen
Denmark Duke Gloucester most royal entourage stop At heighth gale
afternoon BBC broadcast SOS from Spanish steamer Marojo drifting
rocks near Hastings stop Manchester regiment reported shed rescued
fortyfive from steamer believed Volumnia from Glasgow sinking
several hundred miles out Atlantic stop Channel steamer Alberta
arriving Guernsey after making usual eight hour trip in twentyhours
reported passing two thrilling rescues in Channel stop Lifeboats
Ramsgate braved gale search four men adrift open boat after
collision near Goodwin Sands stop Several Channel steamers
took advantage morning lull make first crossings since Saturday stop

WU TRIBUNE

160L M2258 LONDON 151   1117pm Dec 9

Insert Gale stop At request ministry fisheries BBC tonight
broadcast appeal all vessels north sea keep lookout for fleet
sailing trawlers belonging lowestoft stop Also ten herring drifters
unheard from since gale began stop They believed southern part
North Sea STOP Deal where proximity goodwin sand made sea disasters
almost part daily routines never witnessed more thrilling battle
elements than that which could seen pier today STOP Within easy
sight swedish steamer Frieda could seen drifting on sands after
collision stop Smallboat swung over side vessel with four aboard
instantly whisked away in cloud spray with deal ramsgate lifeboats
pursuit stop Nightfall those ashore wereat certain rescue affected
stop Unknown vessel which struck Frieda believed drifting stop
Channel steamers fought gale manfully and though all delayed they
managed relieved some congestion ports stop Nearly 900 passengers
crossed to Continent stop Hundred families homeless somerset
result floods 09225

SCARBOROUGH

720p

FIG. 7. THE STAFF CORRESPONDENT
For description see

London Faces Flood As Gale Toll Rises; 69 Ships Helpless

King's Train Delayed by 80-Mile Wind; 100 Are Homeless in Somerset; Dunkirk Under Water

Storm to Continue Throughout Today

34 Lost as Italian Ship Sinks; Volumnia Founders in Mid-Atlantic; 2 Go Down After Collision

From the Herald Tribune London Bureau
Copyright, 1936, New York Tribune Inc.

LONDON, Dec. 9.—The rapid rise of the River Thames in its upper reaches, with the menace to London of a rise equal to the great flood of last year, added new peril today to the gales and rains which for four days have pounded England and much of the European coastline, with a loss of lives believed tonight to have exceeded 100.

After a few hours' of comparative quiet, the gales during this afternoon and evening again lashed the coast, and shipping paid toll.

Gale Strikes King's Train

A royal train bearing King George and Queen Mary from Sandringham to London struck an eighty-mile gale beyond Cambridge. Its progress was effectively checked, and for the first time within memory a royal train ran behind schedule, arriving eighteen minutes late. In addition to the King and the Queen, there were aboard it the King and Queen of Denmark, the Duke of Gloucester, and most of the royal entourage.

Thirty members of the crew of the Italian freighter Chiari, which foundered early Sunday morning, have perished, according to a report by the trawler Gascogne, which arrived tonight at La Rochelle, France, with six of the Chiari's survivors, including her master. The Gascogne had stood by all day Sunday off Ushant Light, but saw no other survivors.

The steamship Manchester Regiment reported that she had rescued forty-five persons from a ship believed to be the Volumnia, from Glasgow for Boston and Philadelphia, sinking several hundred miles out in the Atlantic.

First Crossings Since Sunday

Perhaps the most remarkable feat of the gale was that of a little pilot boat, which has circled Dungeness without touching land since Friday, offering pilots or assistance to many ships in difficulties in those waters.

At the request of the Ministry of Fisheries the British Broadcasting
(Continued on page sixteen)

Scarborough - J.Price

From the Herald Tribune London Bureau
Copyright, etc.

LONDON, Dec. 9. — The rapid rise of the River Thames in its upper reaches, with the menace to London of a rise equal to the great flood of last year, added new peril today to the gales and rains which for four days without cease have pounded England.

After a few hours of comparative quiet, the gales during this afternoon and evening again lashed the coast, and shipping paid toll.

A royal train bringing King George and Queen Mary from Sandringham to London struck an eighty-mile gale beyond Cambridge. Its progress was effectively checked, and for the first time within memory a royal train ran behind schedule, arriving eighteen minutes late. In addition to the King and the Queen, there were aboard it the King and Queen of Denmark, the Duke of Gloucester, and most of the royal entourage.

At the height of the gale this afternoon the British Broadcasting Company broadcast an S.O.S. from the Spanish steamer Maroje, drifting on the rocks near Hastings. The Manchester Regiment reported that she had rescued 45 persons from a steamer believed to be the Volumnia, from Glasgow, sinking several hundreds miles out in the Atlantic.

The Channel steamer Alberta, arriving at Guernsey after making her usual eight-hour trip in twenty hours, reported passing two thrilling rescues in the Channel. Lifeboats at Ramsgate braved the gale to search for four men adrift in an open boat after a collision near Goodwin Sands Sands.

Several Channel steamers took advantage of this morning's lull to make their first crossings since Saturday. Some were caught in mid-Channel, and arrived badly battered. One Folkstone boat could not enter the harbor, and was forced to proceed to Dover.

Perhaps the most remarkable feat of the gale was that of a little pilot boat, which has circled Dungeness without touching land since Friday, offering pilots or assistance to numerous ships in difficulties in those waters.

Larger ships rescued the crews of two vessels sinking in the Channel during the afternoon. The Cunarder Alaunia, arriving from New York, lost nine hours in the Channel standing by the steamer Tyne Bridge.

AND THE WORK OF THE CABLE DESK

List of Illustrations

A running file of messages to New York from London, sent on the sixth of the month, beginning at 8:30 A.M. and, stripped of address, would read thus: [53] First message:

60830 BRITISH GOVERNMENT ISSUED INVITATIONS FRENCH ITALIAN GERMAN GOVERNMENTS FOR CONFERENCE LONDON 6/4 ON DANUBIAN PROBLEM

The second message would begin:

SECOND 60830 THE GOVERNMENTS etc.

The third message would begin:

THIRD 60830 etc.

The last one, assuming that there were only four, would read:

FOURTH LAST 60830 etc.

If later developments arose and made unexpected additions necessary, the message would be slugged:

FIRST ADD 60830
SECOND ADD 60830
THIRD LAST ADD 60830

No "take," or section of a story sent in fragments this way exceeds 200 words, under usual conditions. If a story is not so urgent as to require that sort of fragmentary handling, however, it will be written in full before being sent, and this is the general practice among correspondents for newspapers, rather than for press associations. However, now that many correspondents are using the telephone to reach their control or relay points, they will report as much information as they have been able to gather and leave it for the control point to send the message as given, or to break it up for transmission in shorter portions.

The use of the time slug also permits economies, for when an event is anticipated much of the detail and background material

---

[53] These examples from *A Guide for Foreign Correspondents: Practices and Principles in the Collection and Dissemination of AP News Dispatches.* (Published by the Associated Press to instruct correspondents.)

PARIS THROWS OFF CARE AT NEW YEAR

Old Spirit of "Who Cares?" Revived for First Time in Many Years.

By P. J. PHILIP.

Special Cable to THE NEW YORK TIMES.

PARIS, Jan. 2.—There was no trace of pessimism or business depression in the way Paris brought in the New Year. There was rather a real revival for the first time in many months, indeed years, of that old spirit of "who cares?" which used to be characteristic of Paris before it began taking life seriously. Somehow everybody suddenly seems to be convinced that it was utterly silly to pay any attention to whether there was any Bolshevik menace, whether Germany was really going to start a new war or whether Premier Mussolini was the only real pacifist in Europe.

Taking life so seriously, as has been done these past ten years, has not led anywhere anyhow, and for one night at least the whole capital seemed determined to be as gay as possible. It was far gayer than on Christmas night for Christmas has still here its sobering midnight mass. Burying 1930 in oblivion was an occasion for real rejoicing.

Wettest Year on Record.

It was the wettest year there ever had been in Paris, and that in itself was reason for dumping it joyfully on the scrap heap of time. It was a year when nobody ever seemed to get what he wanted, when the Bourse remained consistently depressed, when politics went all wrong, when while business was bad the cost of living kept on rising, when despite André Tardieu there was nothing joyous about it. It just had no character except of unrest and crossness. "So let's bury it gayly," everybody said, and went to it with zest.

POSTAL TIMES COPYRIGHT

7J3,0A,706 PRESS COLLECT

PARIS 820PM, JAN 1 31

PRESS TIMES NY

11931, PHILIP WEEKEND THERE WASNT ANY TRACE PESSIMISM OR BUSINESS DEPRESSION IN WAY PARIS BROUGHT IN NEW YEAR STOP THERE WAS RATHER REAL REVIVAL FOR FIRST TIME MANY MONTHS INDEED YEARS THAT OLD SPIRIT QUOTE WHO CARES UNQUOTE WHICH USED BE CHARACTERISTIC PARIS BEFORE IT BEGAN TAKING LIFE SERIOUSLY STOP SOMEHOW ALL SUDDEN EVERYBODY SEEMS CONVINCED THAT TWAS UTTERLY SILLY PAY ANY ATTENTION WHETHER OR NOT THERES ANY BOLSHEVIK MENACE WHETHER OR NOT GERMANY REALLY GOING START NEW WAR WHETHER OR NOT MUSSOLINI ONLY REAL PACIFIST EUROPE STOP TAKING LIFE SO SERIOUSLY AS BEEN DONE THESE PAST TEN YEARS HASNT LED ANYWHERE ANYHOW AND FOR ONE NIGHT AT LEAST WHOLE CAPITAL SEEMED DETERMINED BE GAY AS POSSIBLE STOP TA TWAS FARXH GAYER THAN ON XMAS NIGHT FOR XMAS HAS STILL HERE ITS SOBERING MIDNIGHT MASS STOP BURYING 1930 IN OBLIVION WAS OCCASION FOR REAL REJOICING STOP TWAS WETTEST YEAR THERE EVER BEEN IN PARIS AND THAT IN ITSELF WAS REASON FOR DUMPING IT JOYFULLY ON SCRAPHEAP SXSX TIME STOP TWAS YEAR WHEN NOBODY EVER SEEMED GET WHAT WANTED WHEN BOURSE REMAINED CONSISTENTLY DEPRESSED WHEN POLITICS WENT ALL WRONG WHEN WHILE BUSINESS WAS BAD COST LIVING KEPT ON RISING WHEN DESPITE ANDRE TARDIEU THERE WAS NOTHING JOYOUS ABOUT IT STOP IT JUST HADNT ANY CHARACTER EXCEPT OF UNREST AND CROSSNESS STOP SO LET'S BURY IT GAILY EVERY-

FIG. 8. A MESSAGE AS OFFERED FOR SYNDICATION

For description see List of Illustrations

Indications de service.

PC....	= Réponse payée.
RP....	
TC....	= Télégramme collationné.
MP....	= Remettre en mains propres.

JOUR... = Remettre seulement pendant le jour.
... = Remettre même pendant la nuit.
OUVERT = Remettre ouvert.

Dans les télégrammes imprimés en caractères romains par l'appareil télégraphique, le premier nombre qui figure après le nom du lieu d'origine est un numéro d'ordre, le second indique le nombre de mots dans le premier le mot imprimé. la date et l'heure de dépôt.
Dans le service intérieur et dans les relations avec certains pays étrangers, l'heure de dépôt est indiquée au moyen des chiffres de o à 24.

L'État n'est soumis à aucune responsabilité à raison du service de la correspondance privée par la voie télégraphique. (Loi du 29 novembre 1850, art. 6.)

ORIGINE.	NUMÉRO.	NOMBRE DE MOTS.	DATE.	HEURE DE DÉPÔT.	MENTIONS DE SERVICE.

PRESSE NICE 822 212 21 19H20

UN INGENIEUR DE CEBU L UNE DES ILES PHILIPPINES M AUGUSTIN GEREZA
QUI EFFECTUE UN VOYAGE EN EUROPE AVAIT FAIT LA CONNAISSANCE A
ROME D UN AUSTRALIEN DONT IL NE SE RAPPELLE MEME PAS LE NOM ET QU IL
RETROUVA ENSUITE A GENES A MONTECARLE ET ENFIN A NICE M GEREZA ETAIT
AVEC LUI LORSQU IL SE RENDIT HIER DANS UNE BANQUE POUR CHANGER
DEUX MILLE CINQ CENTS DOLLARS ON LUI REMIT QUATRE VINGT MILLE FR QU IL
PLACA DANS UNE ENVELOPPE AVEC DEUX CENTS AUTRES DOLLARS ET DEUX
BAGUES VALANT VINGT CINQ MILLE F EN SORTANT DE LA BANQUE L AUSTRALIEN
RENCONTRA UN AMI QU IL PRESENTA A M GEREZA TOUS TROIS ALLERENT DANS
UN CAFE BOIRE DES RAFRAICHISSEMENTS ET AU BOUT DE QUELQUES INSTANTS L AMI
DE L AUSTRALIEN PRETEXTA UNE COURSE A FAIRE IL DEMANDA A SON AMI DE
L ACCOMPAGNER TOUS DEUX PARTIRENT LAISSANT A M GEREZA UNE VALISE A
GARDER APRES UNE BONNE HEURE D ATTENTE L INGENIEUR EUT QUELQUES SOUP
-CONS IL PORTA LA MAIN A LA POCHE DE SON PANTALON OU IL AVAIT PLACE
L ENVELOPPE CONTENANT SON AVOIR ELLE AVAIT DISPARU IL COMPRIT ALORS
QU IL AVAIT EU AFFAIRE A DES ESCROCS ET IL S ADRESSA A LA POLICE MAIS
LES VOLEURS N ONT PU ETRE RETROUVES

FIG. 9. A MESSAGE REACHES A CONTROL POINT

For description see List of Illustrations

may be sent on ahead by mail. The order of march at a public ceremony would be an example. Then, in the cabled message on the day of the ceremony itself, this advance matter could be confirmed, or alterations noted, and the whole picked up in the publication office and added to the timely cabled news to make a complete story. Or, instead of writing at length that a noted person died at such-and-such a time on such-and-such a day, and the funeral will be held at such-and-such a time on such-and-such a day, the message may simply be sent:

60830 BRIAND DIED 52350 FUNERAL SET FOR 11430 etc.

All of this is part of the technical consideration for a foreign correspondent. Experience teaches him how to combine speed with economy in covering the news.

In years past, when rates were higher, cable dispatches were extremely brief and it was considered a virtue for an editor to be able to convert a few words into a fairly long story.[54] But this is no longer a favored practice. Articles, some conjunctions, prepositions, familiar given names and titles are omitted, but little more, whereas some punctuation marks are included if needed for clarity.[55]

*   *   *

[54] Dr. Fitzgerald of the New York *Herald,* it was said, could convert five words of cable into a hundred words of text, and a hundred words of cable would make a column of text. Joseph I. C. Clarke, *My Life and Memories,* pp. 125-26.

Such expansion, however, was greater than was considered wise, even then, when two words for each word in the cable was regarded as an average nearer correct. Dr. Fitzgerald's "crowning effort," as described by Mr. Clarke, was his rewrite in 1872 of a cable stating merely, "Alice's cold better." This referred to Queen Victoria's second daughter, and the London cable became: "The royal sore throat which the Court physicians diagnosed upon examining the laryngeal processes of Her Majesty Queen Victoria's second daughter, the Princess Alice, as of mild character, is rapidly improving." This is in the ratio of one-to-ten.

[55] The Associated Press received at New York on Feb. 1, 1923, in all, 10,119 words of cable matter, and that did not include cables received at San Francisco from the Far East. This means six or seven columns of news when rewritten and set in type. When explanatory matter, if not

One duty of an important control point, such as London or
Paris, is the handling of relay messages, which come in and must
be put through to New York or Buenos Aires, if the editor at the
control point believes they warrant it.

So an event that occurs in Southern Europe may be wired or
telephoned to London, and if it is cleared there even so late as
3 or 4 A.M. it still will be in time to make editions of New York
morning papers, because it is only 11 P.M. in New York when it
is 4 A.M. in London, and transmission is almost instantaneous.

An important story received in New York up to 2 A.M. may
still go into the late morning editions there. It is 7 A.M. in London at that time. An event in London at 11 A.M., if given instant
transmission, is known in New York at 5 A.M. and the late afternoon papers, appearing at about 4 P.M. in New York, can carry
reports of events occurring as late as 8 or 9 P.M. in London.

Papers published in Chicago or San Francisco have from one
to three hours more time than the New York papers. It is such
circumstances as these that keep the press associations, particu-

---

actually sent, is added, it commonly follows a break or a dash-line in the
type, sometimes giving it the name of "dash matter."

The New York *Times* received the following cable files for ten days in
1923:

Jan. 30	12,610 words	Feb. 4	8,751 words
Jan. 31	12,479	Feb. 5	7,505
Feb. 1	12,486	Feb. 6	8,419
Feb. 2	8,827	Feb. 7	9,509
Feb. 3	4,898	Feb. 8	6,890

This was a total of 92,274 words, and a daily average of 9,000 words, equal
to a full eight-column page of foreign news. See: Anon., "Cable News Is No
Longer Inflated from Skeleton Dispatches," *Editor and Publisher* (Feb. 17,
1923), p. 12.

These daily totals have been increased in the years since. By 1931, for
example, the Associated Press was receiving 1,800,000 words a year by
cable from Latin America alone, or about five newspaper columns a day,
and Europe always has yielded far more news than Latin America. In 1936
it spent about $315,000 for cables, and distributed about 25,000 words of
foreign news daily over its national wire circuits. See: Anon., "(AP)" (Associated Press), *Fortune* (Feb. 1937), pp. 88-93, 148-62.

While no newspaper prints all the foreign news provided daily by a press
association, the amount that is published has been increasing gradually in
volume as the importance of foreign affairs has become more apparent.

ASTRID AND LEOPOLD WED; 400,000 CHEER PROCESSION

Pomp and Splendor of Preceding Festivities Offset by Simple Religious Ceremony.

(Herald's Special Correspondence)

BRUSSELS, Wednesday.—Before the altar in the century-old church of Saints Michael and Gudule Princess Astrid of Sweden this morning became the wife of Crown Prince Leopold of Belgium and First Princess of Belgium.

Though the wedding was staged with Royal splendor and magnificent pomp only the simple marriage service of the Catholic Church was read by the Archbishop of Malines and Primate of Belgium, who officiated. Instead of High Mass, which is not permitted by Catholic rite as the Princess is a Protestant, the Archbishop addressed the young couple in a kindly tone and gave them his blessing before performing the ceremony.

To-night, the dark-haired Swedish Princess, although married a week ago by the civil ceremony in Stockholm, is the Duchess of Brabant and the future Queen of Belgium. She and Prince Leopold are established in their own house, which is in the west wing of the Royal Palace, overlooking the Place Royale and the gardens of the square.

There has been great rejoicing in Brussels to-day, and though the people were not enthusiastic over the coming of the Princess last week, since her triumphant entrance into the city on Monday the populace of the Belgian capital has gradually taken her to its heart. Her conquest to-day reached a climax when nearly 400,000 people lined the route from the palace to the church to cheer her and their Prince.

Chimes Ring Out.

From the spires the ancient chimes peel forth to Brussels the message of the wedding, while the notes of the hymn sung by a hundred voices float through the vaulted interior. Slowly the procession makes its way with solemn step to the altar, where Princess Astrid and Prince Leopold step out alone to stand before the Archbishop of Malines, while the Royal family groups around the bridal couple.

The organ dies and there is a hush. The Archbishop is speaking in low, soft tones—he gives blessings instead of a mass. He comes forward and Princess Astrid and Prince Leopold kneel as four pages, all counts, drape the bride's train on the steps of the altar. He reads the marriage ceremony and stoops to bless the wedding rings which the Prince and Princess exchange, as is the custom, and they rise man and wife.

Their appearance on the steps outside is greeted with a tumultuous roar and they paused for a brief moment while Princess Astrid replies to the roaring crowd with a wave, and the Duke of Brabant salutes.

ÉPUBLIQUE FRANÇAISE. **TÉLÉGRAMME** POSTES ET TÉLÉGRAPHES.

M: PRESSE = HERALD PARIS =

2 feuilles

LE PORT EST GRATUIT. Le facteur doit délivrer un récépissé à souche lorsqu'il est chargé de recouvrer une taxe.

À DÉCHIRER

Signification des principales indications éventuelles pouvant figurer en tête de l'adresse.

D...... = Urgent.
AR...... = Remettre contre reçu.
PC...... = Accusé de réception.
RP ...... = Réponse payée.
XPx.... = Exprès payé.
NUIT... = Remettre même pendant la nuit.
JOUR... = Remettre seulement pendant le jour.
OUVERT = Remettre ouvert.

N°.........

= BRUXELLES 1625 223 10º 22H39 =

FROM SPIRES ANCIENT CHIMES PEEL FORTH TO BRUSSELS MESSAGE WEDDING WHILE NOTES HYMN FROM HUNDRED VOICES FLOAT THROUGH VAULTED INTERIOR STOP SLOWLY PROCESSION MAKES ITS WAY WITH SOLEMN STEP TO ALTAR WHERE ASTRID LEOPOLD STEP OUT ALONE TO STAND BEFORE ARCHBISHOP MALINES WHILE ROYAL FAMILY GROUPS AROUND THEIR SON AND DAUGHTER PARAGRAPH BEHIND ARE SOVERIEGNS PRINCES PRINCESSES NOBILITY AND MINISTERS NEARLY EVERY LAND BRILLIANT IN UNIFORMS AND DECORATIONS AND JEWELS ON HANDS AND IN CROWNS OF WOMEN SPARKLE MAGNIFICENTLY AS SUNS RAYS PLAY UPON THEM PARAGRAPH ORGAN DIES AND THERS HUSH STOP ARCHBISHOP IS SPEAKING LOW SOFT = TONES DASH HE GIVES BLESSINGS INSTEAD MASS STOP HE COMES FORWARD AND ASTRID AND LEOPOLD KNEEL AS

FIG. 10. A MESSAGE FROM A SPECIAL CORRESPONDENT

For description see List of Illustrations

larly, on the watch at all hours. In practice, however, the news-paper bureaus in London or Paris send very little after midnight, which is 7 P.M. in New York; and the press associations, although operating on a 24-hour basis, transmit little between 4 and 8 A.M.

Upon reaching the newspaper or press association office, the message goes to the foreign editor or cable editor, who glances at it to estimate its importance, schedules it, and then passes it to a rewrite man or to the cable desk for building up. Either by rewriting or by careful editing, the missing words are inserted, full names and titles are worked in, mistakes are corrected, and the whole is made to read smoothly and to tell as much as pos-sible, accurately and vividly. To help him in his work, the rewrite man or editor will have at hand certain reference books, a card index and clippings. Ideally, he will possess a broad background of experience and reading, combined with a controlled imagina-tion, a love of accuracy, and a strong sense of objectivity.

When the rewriting or editing process is completed in a news-paper office the story is given a headline and subheads and is sent to the composing room, just like any other piece of copy. In a press association office, when the story is written from frag-mentary cables and edited, the copy is put on the wires to bureaus all over the country, from which it is distributed in turn to news-papers, and in each office is handled over the copy desk like a local story.

The press association may have wired an advance schedule, or forecast, of known stories to come, regardless of original source. Such a brief summary helps the news editor plan his paper for the day. Any story not scheduled in advance will be called to the special attention of editors, when it is sent out, by the prefixed word "Bulletin," or, if something particularly striking has hap-pened, by the word "Flash." Such messages are accompanied by the sounding of bells on the printer-telegraph machines. Some-thing so extremely important that all Associated Press papers are entitled to use it, whether their memberships cover morning service alone or evening service alone, is marked "EOS" meaning "extraordinary service."

A cable editor, whether for a newspaper or a press association, keeps a record of all stories on hand or expected. On his schedule, he may note the subject, source, and slug of each story, the writer's name, the time filed, the time received, the method of transmission (radio, cable, telegraph, mail), the number of words, the number of words actually used, and, in the case of a newspaper editor, where in the paper it appeared, under what size of headline. Not every editor keeps so complete a schedule, but all keep some record.

A correspondent, especially if he serves a newspaper, is informed by mail or by cable as to what has happened to his dispatches. He is told how many words have been printed out of the total sent, on what page of the paper, and sometimes the size of the headline as well. In addition, he receives by mail a complete file of his own and of opposition papers so that he can see exactly how his stories have been used, and how his work compares with that of other correspondents.

CHAPTER III

THE NEWS NETWORK

WHILE the *statistics* of news communication are rather forbidding, they carry implications that are great indeed. Who shall say whether some obscure incident in Europe or America or China may not hold the key to new possibilities for mankind, to changes perhaps no more remote than next year, or next week? Yet, if the cost of transmitting a dispatch between Europe and America is $25, and the cost for a message of the same length between China and Europe or America is more than $100, it is clear that the editor who has a budget to observe will give his readers rather less news about China. But history, in the making, recognizes no such budgetary limitations.

§ 1.   HOW THE WORLD GREW SMALLER

WHAT POWER over the thoughts of the peoples of the world are hidden in the ownership and control of transmission facilities! Does the land that owns the cables rule the world? Certainly the nation whose radio towers receive from and send to far-away parts of the earth never can be ignored in international relations! It is too well informed; its own voice informs too many others.

Only a century ago, the nations lived in comparative isolation. Mail alone carried intelligence between peoples, and between men at home. There was then no telegraph, no cable, no telephone, no wireless. There was no newspaper comparable to those of to-day, and most persons on the globe feared and were ignorant of what was beyond their physical or mental horizons. In the statistics of communication, therefore, concerned with miles of wire and costs per word, a great romance is hidden, and its conclusion no man knows even now.

The present-day communication, remarkable as it seems, has developed from the most primitive transmission methods, and its progress continues. Polynesian and African log-drumming, Indian smoke signals, the "runners" of ancient Greece, these and other means have revealed man's desire to know more about his neighbor, and his need to know. Some of the later methods, such as the heliograph, semaphore, and signal flags, are used even now on some occasions.

When the forerunners of the newspaper came into existence, a mail system already was operating in Europe. This was much used as a means to obtain newspapers from other places, with their reports of local affairs, and to convey letters from correspondents to their papers.

The growth of a large literate population, stirred by events and served by an alert press, caused newspaper circulations to mount ever higher. Journalists became ardent news gatherers, fired with the intent to get information first, to write it and present it with the greatest possible effect. Enterprise and progressive thought came to characterize the press. Individual journalists braved dangers and hardships to get the news quickly and to get it correctly.[1]

Each new means of communication was seized upon to speed dispatches—carrier pigeons, faster ships, cruisers owned by the papers themselves, horse-and-rider relays, trains, the telegraph, submarine cables, the telephone, the automobile, the wireless, the airplane, the printer-telegraph, the radio, the radio telephone, the teletype, the short-wave radio, the teletypesetter, picture transmitting devices, and all others.

For quick service the press owes most to the telegraph, which came into wide use after 1844; to the establishment of regular cable and telegraphic communication between London and parts of the European Continent after 1851, to the Atlantic ocean cable

[1] A good history of the development and present state of international communications appears in *The Background of International Relations*, by Charles Hodges, Ch. 22. Helpful bibliography and notes, pp. 720-21. See also: F. Knight Hunt, *The Fourth Estate*, V. 2, pp. 205-14, describing early handling of foreign mails in London. See also: James C. Herring and Gerald C. Gross, *Telecommunications: Economics and Regulation*.

after 1866, to the telephone after 1900, to the wireless after 1907, to the radio after 1920, to the beam system of radio transmission after 1924, to the radio telephone after 1930, to short-wave radio after 1931, and to the wire transmission of pictures after 1934.

Even for these methods, the great developments did not follow immediately upon their invention or discovery, but most often upon the crisis-born need for the speed they offered, at whatever cost. The press use of the telegraph in the United States grew with the public desire for news of the Mexican War, from 1846 to 1848; and of the Civil War, from 1860 to 1865. In England it was first used for the dispatch of news in May 1845, and was quickly extended so that by 1847 Queen Victoria's speech at the opening of Parliament in that year was telegraphed to the chief towns in the United Kingdom.[2]

On the continent of Europe the telegraph had linked London to Paris in 1851, by way of the first successful submarine cable, which was laid in that year from Dover, England, to Cap Gris Nez, France. This cable, some persons supposed to be operated like a bell-pull, by jerking at one end of it! The telegraph had been extended to Vienna by 1856, and before the Atlantic cable was completed in 1866 a land-and-water line between England and India was completed, while from 1866 to 1870 cables were laid plentifully, but without much publicity.

*   *   *

The telegraph, flashing news overland, had the added effect of permitting newspapers to be established to some purpose even though far from London or New York, which, as cities where news originated or centered, had previously enjoyed almost complete monopolies on newspaper publication in their respective countries. Creditable journals developed in various parts of Great

[2] William Hunt, *Then and Now: Fifty Years of Newspaper Work*, pp. 109ff. An interesting first-hand account of the growth of the telegraph and its use by the press of the United Kingdom; A. F. Harlow, *Old Wires and New Waves*. Describes development of the telegraph in the United States and elsewhere.

Britain and the United States, as well as in less central parts of France, Germany and Italy, while the number of informed persons multiplied everywhere. In this way, the telegraph has had an incalculable effect for good.[3]

Telegraph rates were high for some years, and transmission was slow and unsatisfactory, at least in England, until 1868, when the Press Association was formed to protect the press interests. It continued to do so, in addition to organizing a domestic news service, until 1870, when the government took over the telegraph and cables.

The high costs of transmission, and the element of time involved, resulted in the dispatch of summaries, to be expanded in the newspaper office, instead of full reports. Even so late as 1860, when Abraham Lincoln was nominated for President at the Republican national convention in Chicago, one lone telegraph operator was able to dispatch all of the press matter offered him. At present-day conventions a hundred or more operators are taxed to handle the news copy.

The rates are much lower now, of course. Yet even in 1870, more than twenty years after the telegraph was in considerable use, the cheapest night press rate was 10 cents a word from California to Boston, 5 cents from Chicago to Boston, and 2 cents from Washington to Boston.

In 1864 the Western Union Telegraph Company had approved a plan to construct a telegraph line from the United States overland to Europe, by way of Bering Strait and Asiatic Russia, but the plan for a direct cable beneath the Atlantic, as opened in 1866, brought the work to a stop, at a great financial loss, because it had been well under way.

* * *

The first Atlantic cable was completed on August 6, 1858. Queen Victoria sent a message of congratulation and good will to President Buchanan in the United States, and the message was

[3] C. A. Cooper, *An Editor's Retrospect of Fifty Years of Newspaper Work*, pp. 66-70, 166, 176-90. A brief account of how the telegraph was extended in Great Britain itself, and how it was put to good use by the press.

printed by the New York *Sun*. President Buchanan had been suspicious that the message might be a hoax, so improbable did it seem that words could be sent beneath the sea, and he hesitated for some time before replying, lest he be made to seem ridiculous.[4]

From August 10th until September 1st this cable was in operation. The first piece of news sent was printed in English papers of August 18, 1858, and reported a collision in American waters between the Cunard steamers *Arabia* and *Europa*.[5] The New York *Sun* of August 17, 1858, contained the first foreign news to be cabled to the United States, a report of the conclusion of a treaty of peace with China by England and France.[6] But the parting of the cable put an end to that form of news communication for eight years.

When the second Atlantic cable was successfully completed on July 28, 1866, both the New York *Herald* and the New York *Tribune* used it almost at once, prior to its use by any British or European newspaper. Representatives of both the *Herald* and the *Tribune* have claimed priority in the use of the cable, but the honors appear to belong to the *Herald*.

Mr. George V. Smalley went to Europe for the *Tribune* in the summer of 1866. From Berlin he sent a dispatch to his paper via London, announcing a sudden break in peace negotiations between Austria and Prussia, then at war, and a halt in the march of the Prussian troops, which had started homewards. The dispatch was of about 100 words and cost $500 to send at the current London-New York rate of £1 a word. This message, so Mr. Smalley believed, was "the first news dispatch which went by cable." [7]

[4] L. A. Gobright, *Recollection of Men and Things at Washington,* pp. 190-91.

[5] Cyrus W. Field, *Cyrus W. Field, His Life and Work* (edited by Isabella Field Judson), p. 113; A. F. Harlow, *Old Wires and New Waves.*

[6] F. M. O'Brien, *The Story of the Sun,* pp. 197-98.

[7] G. W. Smalley, *Anglo-American Memories,* pp. 144-49; James Grant, *The Newspaper Press,* V. 2, 341-49. References to the early use of the Atlantic telegraph. Harry Baehr, Jr., *The New York Tribune Since the Civil War.*

For the *Herald* James Gordon Bennett, Jr., had ordered cabled, even at a cost totaling $7000, the entire speech of King William of Prussia, as made following the Battle of Sadowa. Sadowa occurred on July 3, 1866, and on July 24th the Austrians were finally crushed at Custozza. The cable was opened for business after July 28th. At a dinner in London on March 10, 1868, to mark the successful laying of the third Atlantic cable, Colonel Anderson of the New York *Herald* said, "I believe I had the honor of sending the first message for the press through the Atlantic cable after it was opened for business. That was a message of peace announcing the end of war in Germany." Mr. Smalley of the *Tribune*, who was the next speaker, did not contradict or correct this statement, which either demonstrates Mr. Smalley's courtesy or justifies the belief that the *Herald* indeed deserves to be credited with the first use of the cable.[8]

In 1870 a cable and land line between England and India was laid by way of the Mediterranean. Land lines multiplied in all parts of the world, sometimes in combination with cables. Two of the longest were, first, the Great Northern Telegraph Company line, a Danish-owned route which connected Great Britain, Denmark and Scandinavia, and then ran across Russia and Siberia to Shanghai, there joining a cable to Japan; and, second, the Indo-European Telegraph Company line, a British-owned company, starting in London and running, by way of the Channel cable, over Germany, through Poland and Russia and Northern Persia to join the Indian government line at the frontier.

In 1870, also, a cable was laid between North America and the West Indies. About five years later a cable was put down in the Pacific ocean, linking North and South America. In 1879 the first French Atlantic cable linked Brest to Massachusetts, with spurs to the West Indies and Brazil. In 1902 a British-owned cable brought Vancouver, Canada, and Australia into direct communication. Germany had five trans-Atlantic cables in 1914, and now has one, since the others were taken over by the Allies as part of the terms of peace. Italy also put down a cable

[8] The speeches are reported in *Cyrus W. Field, His Life and Work* (edited by Isabella Field Judson), p. 241.

to New York and another to the Argentine. British interests put down cables to Africa and to South America, via the West Indies.

*   *   *

The next advance in news-communications methods, comparable in importance to the telegraph and the ocean cable, was the wireless, from which radio was to develop. A beginning in the permanently successful use of the wireless for trans-Atlantic news transmission was made October 17, 1907, by Signor Marconi, who had been experimenting under the direction of the New York *Times*. On that night messages were exchanged direct between the New York *Times* and its London office.[9]

This, however, was not the first use of the wireless for news reporting. The wireless was first used successfully for that purpose by the *Daily Express* of Dublin, Ireland, to report the Kingstown Regatta in July, 1898.[10] It was used again, with equal success, in October, 1899, upon the suggestion of James Gordon Bennett, Jr., to report the America's Cup Race for the New York *Herald*, a service for which young Signor Marconi was paid $5000.[11] The Associated Press also used the wireless to report the Cup Race, at a cost of $25,000.[12]

The Atlantic was first bridged by wireless in December, 1902, with messages between Poldhu, Cornwall, and Cape Breton at Glace Bay, Nova Scotia. The first trans-Atlantic messages went at night, with formal exchanges between the Sovereigns of Great Britain and Italy, both of whom had aided Signor Marconi, and the government of Canada. Representatives of *The Times* of London were present at this ceremony. Later, from Cape Cod, Massachusetts, a message from President Theodore Roosevelt was sent direct to King Edward VII.

In the spring of 1903 the wireless transmission of news from

---

[9] Elmer Davis, *The History of the New York Times, 1851-1921*, pp. 276-86; A. F. Harlow, *Old Wires and New Waves;* O. E. Dunlap, Jr., *Marconi: the Man and His Wireless.*

[10] J. S. Mills, *The Press and Communications of Empire*, pp. 142-43. Other press uses of the wireless, pp. 148-51.

[11] D. C. Seitz, *The James Gordon Bennetts, Father and Son*, pp. 371-72.

[12] M. E. Stone, *Fifty Years a Journalist*, pp. 239-40.

the United States to *The Times* of London was attempted and, for a brief period, the messages continued to be sent successfully and published in *The Times*. Trouble with apparatus soon interfered, however, and continued accidents prevented anything except occasional experiments until the New York *Times* in 1907 began to file a limited schedule of press messages to be transmitted between Glace Bay and Clifden, Galway.[13]

Other isolated use was made of the wireless for news purposes, however, during the intervening years. The method was used by Lionel James, correspondent for *The Times* of London, to report the Russo-Japanese War in 1904.[14] Although Mr. James does not acknowledge it in his autobiography, and may not have known it, the considerable expense of this new departure in war correspondence was shared by the New York *Times*.[15] Wireless was further used in 1905 by a correspondent for the *Daily Telegraph* of London, who was aboard a ship on the Atlantic bound for the peace conference to take place between Russia and Japan at Portsmouth, New Hampshire. He obtained an exclusive shipboard interview with Count Witte, Russian prime minister, and sent it back to London, relaying it by way of four steamers already wireless-equipped.[16]

Wireless service across the Atlantic was not dependable or speedy from 1907 to 1912, but it continued to be used to some extent for news. It was only half as expensive as cable transmission. On February 3, 1908, the service was extended to include regular messages between London and Montreal.[17] In 1912 improvements were made which resulted in satisfactory wireless service and until 1917 American correspondents in Germany, especially, used the wireless regularly.[18] The entrance of the United States into the War, naturally, halted that.

The Marconi wireless system was being constantly improved.

[13] J. S. Mills, *The Press and Communications of Empire*, pp. 151-66.
[14] Lionel James, *High Pressure*, Chs. 17-21.
[15] Elmer Davis, *History of the New York Times, 1851-1921*, pp. 283-84.
[16] J. C. Francis, *Notes By the Way*. With memoir of Joseph Knight, F.S.A., p. 199.
[17] See n. 13.
[18] See n. 9.

Ships were equipped and stations were erected all over the world. By 1904 ships at sea never were out of communication with a land station on one side of the Atlantic or the other. This led to the establishment in June, 1904, of a regular news service on board liners. The *Campania* of the Cunard Line was the first so equipped, although Signor Marconi had experimented aboard the *St. Paul,* returning to England in 1899, and had received the latest news of the South African War while still 66 nautical miles (nearly 76 land miles) from Southampton. In 1900 some ocean liners undertook to install Marconi apparatus, beginning with the Norddeutscher Lloyd Steamship Co. vessels. But the *Campania* set new standards, because it was able to receive messages 1000 miles from a land station.

Wireless telephony was demonstrated in 1919, radio broadcasting of music and speech began in 1920, and in 1923 Signor Marconi developed the so-called "beam" system of directional transmission. Instead of messages spreading out in great concentric circles from the originating station, like rings around a stone dropped into a still pond, the "beam" wireless permitted a message to be projected in a wedge-shaped segment directed at a selected objective. The system greatly reduced the strength of the signals as they were heard elsewhere, outside the "beam" area. It also reduced the amount of power required, resulting in a saving. It increased the privacy of communications, it reduced "interference" and "static," and it increased speed. From this developed "short wave" transmission for spark, voice, and sound, and this form permitted still greater distances to be bridged.

Radio telephony was started in 1927 and, as with wireless telegraphy, it was used by the press at first as a novelty, later as a real aid. The press of all nations uses the long-distance telephone to a great extent, both to gather news and to put it into the offices of publication or into bureaus for relay to those offices.

* * *

The press has had, and probably always will have, a vital interest in every new means of communication, because of the aid it provides in handling the news.

FIG. 13. HOW THE MESSAGE SPANS THE ATLANTIC
For description see List of Illustrations

Mechanical inventions have helped to transform the methods of dispatching press messages. Transmission by automatically operated machines, either over cable lines or radio circuits, has been virtually perfected. By this method, an operator at a Creed keyboard, for example, a keyboard much like that of a typewriter, copies an ordinary written message. But instead of the keys writing letters when struck, they punch holes in a paper tape. The perforated paper tape then is fed into a Wheatstone transmitter machine at the rate of 20 to 400 words a minute. The machine may operate a main transmitter and send out messages on a directional wireless beam, or it may operate printer-telegraph machines in newspaper offices over a wide area, causing them to reproduce the original message.

Assuming that the machine sends the message over the air, in Morse or Continental code, the signals are picked up automatically at the receiving stations, wherever they may be, usually by means of a high-speed operating instrument known as an "undulator." This translates the dots and dashes into a line moving over the tape like a miniature chart. This tape, at a slower rate of speed, passes before an operator at a typewriter, and he is able to transcribe the message into words once more, reading the tape as rapidly as 70 words a minute. Or, the tape, if it is perforated, may be run through an automatic printer-machine that reproduces the message in the form of ordinary written characters, either on another tape, which then must be cut into short lengths and pasted on full sheets, or directly on full sheets, in the manner of a regular printer-telegraph machine.

The same principle has been adapted to the printer-telegraph machine operated over land lines. The operator types the message on the automatic keyboard, which either punches a tape to be run through a high-speed transmitter or operates another automatic typewriter to reproduce the message at the receiving end.

The teletype, operating over wires; the teletypesetter, and other electrically operated devices, telegraphic and wireless both, are being brought into practical use. It is predicted that the time will come when news will be collected by wireless telephone, with reporters carrying miniature portable two-way radio sets by which to maintain communication with the office at all times, even as do police in cruising cars and aviators in flight.

Reuters and Havas have established powerful radio stations from which they broadcast market reports and news to the ends of the earth. The Italian, German and Russian governments also sponsor radio broadcasts of news to Latin America and other parts of the world, while the Japanese government-controlled news agency broadcasts news in the Pacific area.

Almost every known method of news transmission is used somewhere in the world to-day. The dispatch runner, the pony express rider, the carrier pigeon, the news boat, the beacon, the semaphore and signal flags—all among the earliest means—now have gone out of date, but even they are called upon to serve at times.[19]

§ 2. THE CONTROL OF WORLD TRANSMISSION FACILITIES

THERE ARE in the world approximately 3500 cables, extending some 300,000 miles, and chiefly under the management of 24 companies, with 10 companies controlling all except about 50,000 miles of the total.[20]

Crossing the North Atlantic there are 21 cables, of which 16 are American-owned, two are British-owned, and three are French. There are only two cables across the Pacific, one American-owned and stretching from San Francisco to Shanghai, by way of Honolulu, the Midway Islands, Guam and Yap; the other British-owned and reaching from Vancouver, or Victoria, British Columbia, in a straight line to Norfolk Island, where it splits, one branch to New Zealand and the other to Australia.

Far-Eastern communications are facilitated by eight British-owned cables under the Indian ocean. The United States is linked

---

[19] Carrier pigeons still are used in Japan to transmit news from ships to shore quickly, after reporters have boarded arriving liners. Newspapers in the United States and elsewhere use pigeons to convey exposed photographic films from ships to shore, so saving considerable time.

[20] G. A. Schreiner, *Cables and Wireless and their Rôle in the Foreign Relations of the United States*, p. 239; Charles Hodges, *The Background of International Relations*, pp. 467-85; James M. Herring and Gerald C. Gross, *Telecommunications: Economics and Regulation*.

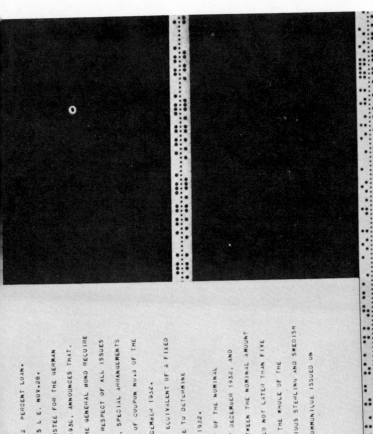

REUTERS

GERMAN GOVERNMENT INTERNATIONAL 5 1/2 PERCENT LOAN.

B A S L E, NOV.28.

THE BANK FOR INTERNATIONAL SETTLEMENTS, TRUSTEE FOR THE GERMAN

GOVERNMENT INTERNATIONAL 5 1/2 PER CENT LOAN 1930, ANNOUNCES THAT,

INASMUCH AS THE PROVISIONS OF ARTICLE VI OF THE GENERAL BOND REQUIRE

THAT THE PAYMENT OF PRINCIPAL AND INTEREST IN RESPECT OF ALL ISSUES

OF THE LOAN SHALL BE EFFECTED ON A GOLD BASIS, SPECIAL ARRANGEMENTS

HAVE BEEN MADE IN CONNECTION WITH THE PAYMENT OF COUPON NO.3 OF THE

STERLING AND SWEDISH CROWN ISSUES, DUE 1ST DECEMBER 1932.

AS THE ACTUAL AMOUNT PAYABLE HAS TO BE THE EQUIVALENT OF A FIXED

GOLD VALUE, AS OF THE DATE, IT IS NOT POSSIBLE TO DETERMINE

THAT AMOUNT UNTIL THE DUE DATE, 1ST DECEMBER 1932.

IN THE CASE OF THE STERLING ISSUE, PAYMENT OF THE NOMINAL

AMOUNT OF COUPON NO.3 WILL BE EFFECTED ON 1ST DECEMBER 1932, AND

A SUPPLEMENTARY PAYMENT OF THE DIFFERENCE BETWEEN THE NOMINAL AMOUNT

AND THE ACTUAL AMOUNT PAYABLE WILL BE EFFECTED NOT LATER THAN FIVE

DAYS THEREAFTER. FOR THE SWEDISH CROWN ISSUE THE WHOLE OF THE

ACTUAL AMOUNTS PAYABLE IN RESPECT OF THE VARIOUS STERLING AND SWEDISH

CROWN COUPONS WILL BE ANNOUNCED IN A PRESS COMMUNIQUE ISSUED ON

1ST DECEMBER 1932. REUTER.

FIG. 14. HOW A MESSAGE IS TRANSMITTED

to Latin America and South America by 10 American-owned cables. Six of them go to the West Indies, three go down the west coast of South America, and one goes down the east coast. South America is linked to Europe by three British cables, one Italian cable, and four other British cables reaching between South America and the West Indies, where other cables provide connections with Europe or the United States.

In total mileage, British companies in 1930 controlled approximately 144,000 nautical miles of cable, American companies, 85,000 miles; French companies, 20,000 miles; and other countries were represented by ownerships totaling 16,000 miles. Private companies operate more than two-thirds of all cables in the world; the rest are government-owned.

The Eastern Telegraph Co., a British concern, owns more than 50,000 miles of cables, representing the largest single unit of operating control in the cable field. Of the American companies, the Western Union owns somewhat more than 20,000 miles of cables and is the largest American owner. The All-America Cables, Inc., and the Commercial Cables Co., the latter controlled by Postal Telegraph, are the other two important United States companies.

*   *   *

The control of world communications facilities proved to be an early advantage to Great Britain. Not only did the country own and control most of the cables, but the supply of gutta percha, essential for the insulation of the submarine lines, was largely in British control. Until after the Great War the control of the principal lines of communication between Europe and North America, South America, Asia, Africa, and Australia was almost entirely British. The ownership of islands and territories all over the world gave Great Britain stepping-stones for the location of cable stations, and permitted full national supervision of the lines.

It was this situation which had an important part in making London the heart, not alone of the British Empire, but of the financial and commercial world. At the center of a network of cables, it was natural and convenient for all concerned to look to London for prices of commodities and stocks. London, as the clearing-house of information on these matters, came to exercise a control. The pound sterling became the standard for world currencies, trading with British houses became easy and convenient for colonies and dominions and non-British countries as well. Liverpool wheat prices, Manchester cotton prices, and London silver prices were among those that became world standards. Reuters, using these cable facilities, became the first world news agency, and London became the world news center. And through it all, the British Government had priority in the dispatch of its messages to and from almost every part of the globe.

When the Great War began this British cable supremacy was one of the chief strategic advantages to the Allies. It enabled Britain to censor and regulate the world flow of news and intelligence. In four hours after Great Britain declared war, Germany's world cable contacts had been cut and the lines subsequently were diverted to Allied purposes. The most important were those reaching North and South America. Only through the Nauen wireless station did Germany subsequently have any direct contact with Allied or overseas countries.

The other nations of the world eventually had come to realize that British control of cable communications gave to that country a great advantage. Although very late in taking action, several of them laid cables of their own, among them France and Germany, both of which acted toward the end of the nineteenth century.

Groups in the United States had had a part in putting down the earliest Atlantic cables, and the United States always has been prominent in the North Atlantic field, but it was not until after 1898 that North American interests began to extend lines to the West Indies, South America, and across the Pacific. Until then the British cables carried messages between the United States and South America, relayed by way of London, at extra cost in time and money, with adverse press conditions and potential political control over all exchanges of messages.

After the Spanish-American War, the so-called All-America cables were laid along the east coast of North America, through the Caribbean to Central America, carried across the Isthmus of Panama, and down the west coast of South America. Known as a "back-door cable," this resulted in more favorable relations between the Americas, and was followed by better business conditions, closer news contacts, and an offset to European cultural expansion in Brazil, Argentine and Chile, particularly. At about the same time, the cable was completed from San Francisco across the Pacific.

Italy put down cables in the Mediterranean; the Netherlands extended cables to its East Indian colonies; and Japan laid cables connecting points in the Far East. Denmark did not take part in the competition for cable advantages but, as already noted, it did build a telegraph line from Copenhagen, across Russia and Siberia, to Shanghai, the line known as the Great Northern route.

* * *

In 1920, as a post-war move, there was held at Washington an International Conference on Communications. It resulted in some changes, particularly in the ownership of more than 15,000 miles of German cables. The two German Atlantic cables, running from Emden via the Azores to Buenos Aires, and from Emden via the Azores to New York, were assigned to the care of the five principal subscribers to the League of Nations, to whom the revenue from their operation was to accrue.

The chief controversy was over control of three cables centering on the former German island of Yap, called the "cable crossroads of the Pacific." President Wilson wanted the island to be neutralized, but Japan ultimately won a mandate over it, while recognizing the United States' claim to equal cable and radio rights there. Control of the three cables centering there was divided. Japan got the Yap-Shanghai line; the United States obtained control of the Guam end of the Yap-Guam cable; the Netherlands got control of the Netherlands Indies end of the Yap-Menado (Celebes) cable. This meant that, for the time, cable communication between Shanghai and San Francisco passed through a Japanese control point, which strengthened the Japanese position, and weakened the position of the United States in China.

Great Britain, which was opposed to the expansion of the United
States interests in the Far East, supported the Japanese in this
dispute, which had been carried over from the so-called Peace
Conference at Versailles to the Washington Conference on Communications in 1920, to the Washington Naval Conference in
1921-1922, and ultimately to another conference in 1922.

In 1919, prior to the later conferences which resulted in only
minor adjustments, chiefly in the German holdings, the ownership of the world's submarine cables was vested in interests of the
following nationalities:

GREAT BRITAIN	51	per cent of the total
UNITED STATES	26.5	
FRANCE	9	
GERMANY	7.5	
DENMARK	3	
SPAIN	1	
ITALY	1	
JAPAN	1	
	100	

Thus it is apparent that three states control more than 86 per
cent of the cables serving the 65 or so countries comprising the
world family.[21] This concentration of control would permit those
national authorities to exert a great influence on international
communications.

To be sure, national governments always hold actual or potential control of the land lines operating within their frontiers. If
not already owned, these lines are at the disposal of military and
other officials. Local governments also control the rights of foreign
companies or governments to land cables on their shores, and
may grant, withhold, renew, or revoke the licenses of foreign
companies doing a local communications business. This right to
revoke licenses has been used on occasions as a club to force
foreign cable companies to exercise an unofficial censorship on
outgoing messages, lest by failing to do so they permit unfriendly

[21] G. A. Schreiner, *Cables and Wireless;* J. Saxon Mills, *The Press and
Communications of Empire;* Charles Hodges, *Background of International
Relations,* Ch. 22.

messages to go, and suffer the penalty of losing their franchises, so sacrificing their investments in equipment as well as the company's good will.

* * *

Apart from submarine cables, there are nearly 7,000,000 miles of land lines in the world. They are divided by continents as follows:[22]

NORTH AMERICA	40	per cent	(Those in Canada and the United States are privately owned.)
EUROPE	36	per cent	(Many of the European lines are government-owned.)
ASIA	12	per cent	(These are all government-owned and operated.)
SOUTH AMERICA	6	per cent	(Some of these lines are financed and owned by foreign interests.)
AFRICA	3	per cent	(Same as above.)
OCEANIA	2.53	per cent	(Same as above.)

99.53 per cent

Telephones, which have long been of use in news gathering, and which, since 1927, have come to be used increasingly for long-distance communications to and from all parts of the world, require more than 115,000,000 miles of wire to service the 35,-000,000, more or less, instruments in the world. These telephones, two-thirds of which are privately owned and operated, are distributed as follows, again by continents:[22]

NORTH AMERICA	66	per cent (59 per cent in the United States)
EUROPE	29	per cent
ASIA	3	per cent
OCEANIA (Including Australia and New Zealand)	2.5	per cent
SOUTH AMERICA	1	per cent
AFRICA	.5	per cent

100 per cent

[22] These figures all are extracted from G. A. Schreiner, *Cables and Wireless;* J. Saxon Mills, *The Press and Communications of Empire;* Charles Hodges, *Background of International Relations*, Ch. 22.

Long-distance circuits, growing more common, linking the most distant places, often in the form of radio telephone, began with a Berlin-Amsterdam circuit in 1896, and continued as follows: Berlin-Paris, 1900; Berlin-Copenhagen, 1903; Paris-London, 1910; Paris-Madrid, 1912; Paris-Amsterdam, 1913; Berlin-Milan, 1914; Berlin-Sofia, 1915, and Berlin-London, 1926. After the Great War the use of the long-distance telephone increased as technical improvements were made in its operation. Trans-ocean communication by radio-telephone began in 1927, when the London-New York circuit was opened. Following that, New York, London, Paris, Buenos Aires, Tokyo and other places were linked by telephone.

In the field of wireless telephony, the United States was able by 1930 to reach 86 per cent of all the telephones in the world, and the same was true of Great Britain. Since then, the percentage has increased.

*   *   *

The new forms of communication employing radio principles, as developed since 1920, have made political control of the cables somewhat less important and have made Great Britain's near-monopoly of the cables correspondingly less important, strategically. Radio communication is cheaper than cables so far as concerns equipment. The servicing is easier and cheaper. It can be used more freely. It reduces costs of transmission. It prevents a nation being bottled up when cables, telephones, and telegraph lines are cut, apart from the development of devices to garble or break up radio waves deliberately. It permits direct communication between sender and receiver.

The United States held the key to the successful operation of radio communication in its control of the so-called Alexanderson high-frequency alternator, a wartime invention. Although the Marconi system was successful, it was not then reliable in all weather conditions. Neither was the system using the Alexanderson alternator, in the beginning, but that device did make it possible for messages to bridge much greater distances with more certainty and increased strength of signals.

British interests tried to buy the alternator at the end of the War, but the United States Government interfered to prevent the sale abroad. Granted to the Radio Corporation of America, for use in transmission, it was so powerful a trump card as to force the Marconi Company, long supreme, to sell its interests in the United States. Then the Radio Corporation of America, controlling the former Marconi contracts in the United States, was able to conclude its own traffic arrangements with Great Britain, France and Germany. In this way, the Radio Corporation of America came to represent a power in world communications comparable to British cable preëminence.

The Radio Corporation offered service across the Atlantic at lower-than-cable rates, the first reduction in the trans-Atlantic rates for twenty years. It also revised the Pacific rates downward. It extended service to 49 countries and reduced the time for transmission very greatly in certain instances.

There was a general improvement in trans-Atlantic communications, beginning in about 1923. Better cables were laid by the long-established Commercial Cable Co., and also by the Western Union Telegraph Co. The International Telephone and Telegraph Corporation, an organization financed by J. P. Morgan & Co., built up telephone systems in Latin America and in Spain, and then invaded North America to form a powerful communications group, embracing the Postal Telegraph-Commercial Cable System and All-America Cables. The Western Union Telegraph Co. remained as an independent and very strong organization. The same was true of the Radio Corporation of America. But there was talk of a merger of all three groups.

The result of this threat in Great Britain, was a merger of cable and wireless interests to present a solid front. To help in this move, there came the "beam" or directional wireless, developed by the British Marconi Wireless Telegraph Co. and put into use in 1924. It had the effect of a reflector behind the transmitting apparatus, permitting wireless broadcasts to concentrate most strength over a rather narrow segment, roughly, a "beam." It gave far stronger signals from the same power, and was preferable in some respects to the cable, especially over distances exceeding 2000 miles. Using the "beam" wireless, the British Government sponsored an Empire communications system linking London with Canada, Australia, South Africa and India. As it developed, the beam system was to be adapted for wireless telephony and rapid facsimile transmission. In 1927 it had reached a point where 200 words a minute could be transmitted from London to Australia.

The new beam system could handle an increased traffic at rates lower than the cables.[23] Used experimentally in 1926-1927, it cut into the cable business and caused friction between the beam system, which was government-owned, and the British Marconi interests (although they had developed the system) and the British cable companies, privately owned, and even with the government-owned cables in the Atlantic and Pacific.

This situation led to the summoning of the Imperial Wireless and Cable Conference in 1927-1928, at which there was concluded a merger of all British communications companies under the title of Cable and Wireless, Ltd., with an operating subsidiary called Imperial and International Communications, Ltd., the present so-called "Imperial," "Eastern," "Empiradio" and "Marconi." It began operations in 1928 over the so-called "Red Network," a cable and wireless system linking all parts of the Empire without once touching non-British soil. This had been an ideal cherished by the British Government since 1910, but even so, its formation did not entirely allay British alarm at American communications plans and accomplishments.

The British merger had been inspired not only as a means of matching a strong British communications organization against

[23] Press rates, as cited by Sir Basil Blackett, Chairman of Imperial & International Communications, Ltd., at the Fourth Imperial Press Conference, London, June, 1930. See the report of that Conference, and also the Company's reprint of the speech, *Empire Communications and the Empire Press*.

LONDON to:	1913	1930	
	Cable	Cable	Radio
AUSTRALIA	7½d	6d	4d
SOUTH AFRICA	3¾d	2¾d	2½d
INDIA	4d	3d	2½d
CANADA (eastern provinces)	5d	2½d	2½d
WEST INDIES	1½d	7½d	7½d

an American, but as a means of providing and assuring an adequate service to knit the Empire. This was demanded with particular insistence by newspaper editors and publishers at every Empire Press Conference. Lower cable rates also were held to be one of the greatest Empire needs, as a means of encouraging the interchange of news and so building a sense of Empire solidarity, and it was urged that a flat rate of one penny a word (2 cents, U.S.) should apply to press messages transmitted between any and all parts of the Empire.[24]

§ 3. GENERAL ROUTING AND RATES FOR PRESS MESSAGES

THE TRANSMISSION of news has become a matter of routine in most world centers. Only extraordinary events, such as wars, adventures of prominent persons, cataclysms of nature, or mishaps involving passenger ships, planes, or trains, send reporters rushing to remote or far places without regard for expense or difficulty. At such times the facts and the pictures become all-important. And it is then that difficulties may arise owing to the disorganization or lack of transportation or transmission facilities.[25]

[24] Robert Donald, ed., *The Imperial Press Conference in Canada, 1920,* pp. 167-68, 173-74. (This is the second Imperial Conference.)

See also: Anon., *A Parliament of the Press: The First Imperial Press Conference, 1909;* H. E. Turner, ed., *The Imperial Press Conference in Australia, 1925.* (This is the Third Conference.) H. E. Turner, ed., *The Fourth Imperial Press Conference, 1930.*

J. Saxon Mills, *The Press and Communications of Empire.* (A Survey based upon reports and addresses at the Imperial Press Conference of 1920.)

The Fifth Imperial Press Conference was held at Capetown in 1935.

[25] Examples include the Riff War in 1926, the Ethiopian campaign in 1935, the Japanese earthquake in 1923, the Russo-Japanese clash along the Chinese Eastern Railway in 1929, the landing of the German transatlantic plane, *Bremen,* at Greenley Island, Labrador, in 1928; the emergency landing of Admiral Byrd's trans-Atlantic plane at Ver-sur-Mer, France, in 1927; the forced descent of the Graf Zeppelin in the south of France in 1929, the Japanese invasion of Manchuria in 1931, and others. At such times enterprising reporters sometimes have used their wits to obtain exclusive control of all transmission facilities, tying them up long enough to insure that their own reports, at least, would be published first. See: Vernon McKenzie, *Behind the Headlines: Journalistic Adventures of Today.*

International conferences, attracting swarms of reporters, per-haps to small towns, sometimes tax the available communications facilities, as well as the housing facilities, but because the needs of the press on such occasions usually have been anticipated, the difficulties are not serious, even if they exist at all.[26]

As technical problems have been solved, an increasing volume of news matter has been transmitted by radio or wireless, terms used synonymously, both by long wave and short wave. Between cities in Europe, and between London and continental cities, the long-distance telephone is used a great deal, sometimes almost to the exclusion of the telegraph, particularly by London news-papers. At prearranged times a correspondent calls his home office, or perhaps a bureau of his paper at a point nearer the home office, which relays the message. Transoceanic telephone calls have become increasingly common in transmitting or gathering news.

There is a growing exchange of news between continents and countries. News entering the United States, as an example, in-creased two and one-half times between 1916 and 1929, while outgoing news quadrupled in that period.[27] The greatest flow of news as between continents is between Europe and North Amer-ica, with the flow westward more than twice the flow toward Europe. Between Asia and North America the cost of transmis-sion over the single existing cable line has been high, which long tended to keep down the volume except at moments of crisis. The development of improved communication by radio and, above

[26] The League of Nations, both at Geneva and in the conferences held under its sponsorship in various parts of Europe, has supervised press fa-cilities so expertly as to make the reporter's work comparatively easy, so far as concerned matters of transmission. The facilities at the London Economic Conference of 1933 represent a case in point. Such conferences have set new records in the number of words dispatched. Political gatherings, sensational court trials, and great sports events also have resulted in heavy files.

[27] M. M. Willey and S. A. Rice, Communication Agencies and Social Life, pp. 171-72. The Willey-Rice study is a part of a more comprehensive study of "Recent Social Trends in the United States" made under the direction of a Committee appointed by President Hoover. See Part II, "The Agencies of Point to Point Communication," Chs. 10-13, pp. 104-54. Also Ch. 14, pp. 156-77.

all, the reduction of press rates, relieved the situation considerably and has increased the flow of news across the Pacific.

The relations between Asia and Europe have been closer, because they are linked by two land lines, as well as by coastwise cables passing through the Indian Ocean, the Red Sea and the Mediterranean. In fact, much of the news of Asia that reaches North America has gone by way of Europe, since that route sometimes is both quicker and more economical.

South America, once linked closely to Europe in a news way, in the years since the beginning of the Great War has established more intimate news relations with North America. Latin America now receives more world news by way of the United States than by way of Europe, although the French Agence Havas is attempting to recapture its former preëminence in that field.[28]

Both Africa and the Antipodes are, as yet, minor factors in the exchange of news, although Australia is in regular news communication with Great Britain.[29]

* * *

A considerable volume of news and editorial matter continues to go by mail. It is called "mail copy." Matter that is not urgent or extremely timely may go that way as a measure of economy. Perhaps, if statistics were available, it would be found that the mails continue to carry most of the news volume.

Much depends upon what one considers to be news. If news ceases to be news 12 hours or 24 hours after it occurs, the implication is that only *events* can be so considered. But that is not true. In the first place, anything is news until it becomes known, and if the mail brings the first information on some subject to a whole population or even a portion of the population one year

[28] It was estimated in 1931 that Latin America received from North American press associations about 30,000,000 words annually, of which 10,-000,000 consisted of news of the United States. C. S. Smith, "News Makes the Americas Better Neighbors," *Quill* (Oct., 1931), pp. 6-7, 15-16.

[29] E. W. Sharp, *International News Communications,* Univ. of Missouri Bulletin (Univ. of Missouri), Vol. 28, No. 3. Vol. No. 45. Journalism Series; Guy Innes, "Cabling the News," *Journalism: By Some Masters of the Craft* (see Anon.), pp. 135-43.

late, or five years late, or even more, that information is still news.[30]

But, in addition, news can be considered to reside in trends, interpretations and analyses as well as in events. There is much background matter or advance matter that also can be mailed, in the case of an anticipated event, such as a conference or a royal wedding or a coronation.

A curious sort of pride in presenting only events of the minute-before-last prevents some newspapers from using mail copy. When they do so, sometimes they put a current date on it, even though that is unethical. Or they may omit the date entirely, with results that sometimes are confusing. But some newspapers, emancipated from such false emphasis on timeliness, present mail copy as just what it is, bearing dates anywhere from a few days to a few weeks old, and no one is the worse for it.

The *Christian Science Monitor* probably uses as much mail copy as any newspaper in the world. The New York *Times,* the New York *Herald Tribune,* the New York *Sun,* the Chicago *Daily News, The Times* of London, and other first class newspapers in the United States, Great Britain, and other countries, follow this procedure. Press associations also send out what they call "news letters" or "clip sheets" containing items and articles for publication, and these services provide some of the most interesting and useful matter in the newspapers.

*   *   *

When the telegraph, the cable and the telephone were new, the charges for their use were high. It cost $5 or £1 to cable a single word across the Atlantic. To-day the "press rate" is 5 cents or

---

[30] The excavations of the tomb of Tut-ankh-amen was big news three thousand years after his burial. The discovery of the remains of Andrée, the Arctic explorer, with his records and equipment, in the north of Canada was news 33 years after his disappearance while making an attempt to reach the North Pole by balloon. These stories, and many others, were news even though so many years had elapsed since the events which they represented. The Great War had been in progress for many months before that fact became known to the residents of some islands and isolated parts of the world, and to those persons it was news, even though it had become history in Europe itself.

2 ½ pence. Yet publishers object that even these rates ought to be lower, and particularly that the rates across the Pacific and between Europe and Australia or New Zealand should be reduced.[31]

The transmission facilities of the world are not perfect, but in the areas where most of the news is being exchanged it is rare for any serious mechanical fault to delay news transit.[32] In the years immediately after the Great War a correspondent, when possible, allowed five hours for the transmission of a message from Paris to New York. Radio competition and the improvement of cable communications reduced the transmission time to minutes, rather than hours, and in some cases to seconds. If one company cannot handle a message promptly, another can; if the cables

[31] At every Imperial Press Conference stress has been put upon the need for cheaper cable rates, with an insistent demand for a rate of 1d (2 cents) a word anywhere within the Empire. See reports of the Conferences. See also: Victor Rosewater, *History of Coöperative News-Gathering in the United States.* Chs. 6, 7, 8, 25, deal with the development of the telegraph and cable rates. The World Press Congresses, at Honolulu in 1921, Geneva in 1926, Mexico City in 1931, also have urged the lower press rates. The League of Nations, too, at its Conference on the Press, has given its endorsement to the lower rate. See also: Keith Clark, *International Communications: the American Attitude;* James M. Herring and Gerald C. Gross, *Telecommunications: Economics and Regulations.*

[32] Useful summaries of the world communications systems, usually with special reference to news transmission, include the following: G. A. Schreiner, *Cables and Wireless.* A guide to cable and wireless communications, with special data in Ch. 6, "The Press and International Communication," pp. 158-89. The Appendix lists cables under government administration; the privately operated, government operated, and government subsidized cables; and the book contains a map of world cable communications, all as of 1924; L. B. Tribolet, *The International Aspects of Electrical Communications in the Pacific Area.* A study of cable and wireless communications in the Pacific area, as of 1929. It gives consideration to national ownership of communications lines and the propaganda values inherent in those ownerships; Charles Hodges, *The Background of International Relations,* Ch. 22, "The Nerves of World Politics," pp. 467-85. A description of the world system of communications, as of 1931, with reading references; F. J. Brown, *The Cable and Wireless Communications of the World,* 2nd rev. ed. Includes the history of the press rates up to 1930; J. Saxon Mills, *The Press and Communications of the Empire.* A survey based upon reports and addresses at the Imperial Press Conference of 1920, and published in 1924; Keith Clark, *International Communications: the American Attitude;* O. W. Riegel, *Mobilizing for Chaos,* Chs. 2, 3, 4, pp. 18-107. Some of the problems inherent in control of world communications.

can promise nothing, there is the radio; if the Paris-New York cables are busy, the message may be relayed to London by wire or telephone and sent from there by cable or radio. Or news originating in Shanghai, for example, may reach New York by way of Moscow and Copenhagen, instead of direct to San Francisco, across the Pacific.

Such round-about routes for news transmission may puzzle the layman. But it is *time,* not distance, that governs when deadlines approach. The routes are constantly being tested by press associations, newspapers, and their correspondents to get faster, more efficient, less expensive transmission.

A regular and ever-present obstacle to quick and certain transmission of virgin news is censorship, whether in wartime or in peace. Censorship on outgoing dispatches is possible where governments control transmission facilities, as they do in most countries; or where they are able to exercise an indirect regulation.

Because the press uses the cables so much it receives a special "press rate," lower than other rates. This means a saving on much traffic, but if immediate transmission is required, and at times of crisis, the press pays the regular rate and even the "urgent" rate, which is still higher, to obtain the fastest service.

The press rate between London or Paris and New York in 1936 was 5 cents or 2½ pence a word, as already noted. Between South America and New York the rate was 14 cents a word, but this was cut to 5 cents a word late in the year. From South America to Europe the rate was 20 to 25 cents a word; this also was cut to 8 to 15 cents. Before the Great War all rates were higher. Even in 1936 the Tokyo rate on an "urgent" message was $2.16 a word. The Shanghai-San Francisco regular press rate then was 25 cents a word, San Francisco-Manila, 12 cents with a 6 cents deferred rate; and San Francisco-Honolulu, 6 cents, with a 3 cents deferred rate. The same rates applied to radio dispatches in 1936.

In addition to the San Francisco-Shanghai cable, there was the British-owned cable in the Pacific, reaching from Vancouver, British Columbia, to Australia, New Zealand and, indirectly, to Hong Kong. It offered a 1922 press rate of 5 cents a word from

Canada to Australia, as contrasted to a 27-cent rate then in effect from San Francisco to Shanghai. The British Government encouraged the interchange of news between parts of the Empire and, through its ownership of certain communications facilities, it was able to provide a rate of 7½ pence (about 15 cents) a word between London and Melbourne, which was a low figure, considering the distance.

The rate for communication between London and portions of the Empire so far away as Australia had long remained high, causing concern to editors and others who wished to keep Australia informed concerning affairs at the center of the Empire, with a view to maintaining Empire loyalty and unity unimpaired.

When the Eastern Extension Co. put in a cable to Australia in 1872 the transmission rate over the 15,000 miles was £9.9.0. for twenty words. In 1875 the single word rate was reduced to 10/8d. The first time that the press was considered entitled to a special rate was in 1886, when the word rate for ordinary messages was reduced to 9/4d., and a press rate set at 2/8d a word. In 1891 this was further cut to 4/- a word for ordinary messages and 1/10d a word at press rate. Some years later this was reduced further to 3/6d for regular and a proportionate press reduction. In 1930 the press rate was 6d a word by cable, and 4d a word by radio.[33]

In some instances the British and Dominion Governments have given financial assistance to the press and press associations in meeting expenses for cable news transmission. Although this assistance has been necessary to insure any considerable transmission of news, it has bothered some editors and officials, as implying that the press is thereby placed under a certain obligation to the government which grants it this subsidy, and such aids and guarantees have lately been declined in certain instances.

There do remain portions of the Empire which cannot receive news direct from Great Britain by cable or wire, although the

[33] Robert Donald, ed., *The Imperial Press Conference in Canada*, p. 172; Sir Basil Blackett, *Empire Communications and the Empire Press*. (Reprint by Imperial and International Communications, Ltd., from the report of the Fourth Imperial Press Conference held in London in 1930.)

wireless is reaching most of them now. The desire to serve them gave impetus to the development of Reuters' wireless news service, which began from Leafield in 1923, and now is serving newspapers throughout the world, broadcasting from Leafield and Rugby by a beam system direct to Montreal, Cape Town, Bombay, Cairo, Shanghai, Tokyo, and other foreign and Empire points.

*   *   *

Because the rates are so high between the Far East and the United States, the volume of news exchanged has been somewhat restricted. And one reason those rates are so much higher has been that there is only the one cable across the Pacific between San Francisco and Shanghai, and that an old one. It can carry only about 100 letters a minute, whereas newer cables across the Atlantic can handle 2500 letters a minute. But, as it would cost $10,000,000 to $16,000,000 to lay a new Pacific cable, there has been hesitation about putting it down, especially with the radio threatening to make cable lines obsolete.[34]

The advent of the radio, in fact, had much to do with breaking the rate schedule from its previous high level. It brought a threat to the cable, more especially in the Pacific area. In 1920, also, the New York *Times* set up its own wireless station to receive foreign news, and the Chicago *Tribune* in 1920 and 1921 was receiving news by wireless direct from Bordeaux, France.

Beginning in 1921, dispatches from the United States to newspapers in Honolulu or Manila could be sent by the United States Navy radio. Congress granted special authorization in 1920 to make this possible. The rate was 6 cents a word to newspapers in Manila, 3 cents a word to those in Honolulu. But that did

[34] It took as much as a hundred hours for a cable message to reach Tokyo from Washington during the naval conference in 1921, so Japanese correspondents discovered, whether sent at regular or at press rates. That was too slow, but if a message was to go at the "urgent" rate it then would cost $3.24 a word, which was excessive. From Tokyo to San Francisco, the time and expense were nearly as great.

Walter Sammis, "Phonetics and Easy Communication Japan's Greatest Needs," *Editor and Publisher* (Dec. 24, 1921), pp. 17, 33; L. B. Tribolet, *The International Aspects of Electrical Communications in the Pacific Area.*

not link the United States directly with China or Japan. It was necessary to pay additional cable or wireless tolls between Manila and Shanghai or Tokyo, bringing the cost up to 24 to 27 cents a word between San Francisco and Tokyo or Shanghai. Beginning in 1922, the Navy radio also began to carry eastbound dispatches, linking Manila with San Francisco, and correspondents in China or Japan could radio or cable their messages to Manila for relay.

The traffic across the Pacific was limited, except in times of crisis or on other rare occasions. But the United Press, shortly after the Great War, began to send a general report of world news to Nippon Dempo Tsushin Sha, a Japanese press association with which it had an exchange arrangement until Nippon Dempo was absorbed by Domei in 1936. It sent a fairly complete news report to the *Mainichi* in Osaka and to the *Nichi Nichi* in Tokyo. The Associated Press in 1922 was sending an average of 1000 words a day from San Francisco to Honolulu, and about 800 to Manila by the Navy radio. It also sent a daily report, totaling about 5000 words a month, to Kokusai (later to become known as Rengo, and now as Domei), the Japanese news agency with which it had exchange arrangements. Other press messages by Navy radio in 1922, as sent from San Francisco to Honolulu, totaled about 3000 words daily; and about 2500 words daily between Honolulu and Guam, and between Guam and Manila.

In 1922 Congress granted a renewal of the press privilege of using the Navy radio, that renewal to continue until June, 1925. Only news messages were acceptable, commercial messages being barred. The Navy radio had stations at San Francisco, San Diego, Seattle, Honolulu, Guam, Manila, Peiping and Pribiloff Island. The press authority was renewed again in 1925, and once more in 1927. When the question of further renewal arose in 1929, however, the Radio Corporation of America, which had become strong, entered a petition that the service to the press be discontinued, since the commercial system was offering a service which, while somewhat more expensive than the Navy radio, was purported to be reasonable.

The Radio Corporation had been operating a service in 1922 between San Francisco and Tokyo, by way of Honolulu, but high rates kept the schedule low. It transmitted a daily news report of about 250 words from San Francisco to Tokyo for the Trans-Pacific News Service, a group organized by B. W. Fleisher, American publisher of the *Japan Advertiser* in Tokyo, to provide news to papers in Japan and China, and to offer an interpretation of Far-Eastern affairs to Occidental papers. It also carried some Associated Press and United Press messages. The press business carried by the Radio Corporation was to increase later.

The Radio Corporation of America, in addition to its service from San Francisco to Tokyo, was able to provide radio communication with points in China, Manchuria and Korea through its Japanese connections. Its press rate in 1922 was 27 cents per word, and $2.16 per word for urgent messages which had to go through at once. This was lower, however, than the cable rate, which was then 32 cents a word for press matter, and $2.88 per word at the "urgent" rate, and it was not much higher than the combined rate for Navy radio plus radio from Guam or Manila to Tokyo or Shanghai.[35]

The Federal Wireless Company, an American-owned corporation, in 1922 was planning to erect a radio station in Shanghai for trans-Pacific communication, with smaller stations at Shanghai, Peiping, Canton and Mukden. It required months of negotiations and months to construct the Shanghai station.[36] A resolution at the Washington Naval Conference had prohibited the use of any government radio station in China, Japan or other Far-Eastern country, and this prevented any coöperative agreement to carry the news to or from those countries by existing government radio.[37]

[35] A good summary of trans-Pacific communications facilities, as they were in 1922, is presented by: John R. Morris, "Navy Radio Must be Speeded to Win Far-East Business," *Editor and Publisher* (July 1, 1922), p. 6.

[36] Much of the foregoing data is from a bulletin published by the Pan-Pacific Union, and quoted in *Editor and Publisher*. See: Anon., "Pacific News Volume Is Increasing," *Editor and Publisher* (Oct. 14, 1922), p. 24.

[37] Anon., "Government Radio Barred in China by Arms Parley Agreement," *Editor and Publisher* (Feb. 11, 1922), p. 6.

A trans-Pacific rate of 9 cents a word for the press was advocated by some North American publishers, and the United Press, represented by its then president, Karl A. Bickel, constantly urged a low Pacific rate. In this, support was found in some Japanese and Chinese press circles. Pending the actual reduction in the rates, which was blocked by political and commercial considerations on both sides of the Pacific, the American press was growing to depend more and more on the Navy radio. Permanent right to use the Navy radio was sought as early as 1925, but it met opposition not only from the growing Radio Corporation of America, as already noted, but also from the Commercial Cables Co., operating the single trans-Pacific cable line.

At length, early in 1925, as a result of negotiations between the United Press and General James G. Harbord, president of the Radio Corporation, an agreement was reached by which the press rate between the United States and Japan was to be reduced from 27 cents a word to 10 cents a word, with a proportionate reduction in rates to and from China. But the Japanese Government declined to approve the plan on the ground that the cable and radio facilities of Japan were not yet great enough to handle the increased volume of business that might be expected to follow so drastic a reduction. At length, in the autumn of 1925, a rate of 22 cents a word was set.

As the radio rate was reduced, cable rates also came down. Beginning in the summer of 1926 the Commercial Cable Co. announced a deferred rate on press service between North America and Manila, Shanghai and Hong Kong. The existing rates had been: New York to Manila, 33 cents; New York to China, 35 cents; San Francisco to Manila, 27 cents; San Francisco to China, 29 cents. The new "deferred" rates, however, were set as follows: New York to Manila, 17 cents; New York to China, 20 cents; San Francisco to Manila, 14 cents; San Francisco to China, 17 cents.

After the disappointing attempt to reduce the radio rate in 1925, it was cut to 18 cents in 1927 and in 1929 it was brought down to a rate which permitted a more liberal transmission of news to and from the Far East. This was a new "deferred" radio press rate of 9 cents a word between North America and Japan. But the "urgent" rate from Japan to San Francisco remained at $2.16 a word. Nor was there any change in the rates from Chinese cities—Shanghai, Peiping, Nanking, Hong Kong— or from Singapore. They continued to range from 12 to 25 cents a word. The same rates were applied to the cable transmission westward, between North America and the Far East.[38]

It was in 1929 that the Radio Corporation of America contested further use of the Navy radio by the press. The matter was referred to a hearing of the Federal Radio Commission, and in the end the Radio Corporation was victorious. In the following year that organization set in operation its new commercial radio station at Shanghai, providing direct wireless communication across the Pacific and opening the way for speedy transmission, which was to be much appreciated in 1931 and 1932.

Following the break-down of world currencies in 1929 and 1930, the rates for cable and radio messages across the Pacific, as well as elsewhere, were upset again, due to confusion in monetary exchange. The Madrid radio-telegraph conference of 1933 resulted in a sharp increase in "urgent" rates for cables.[39] This

---

[38] The New York *Times,* with an excellent foreign news service, expended more than $500,000 on cable and radio tolls in twelve months ending in August, 1927. Although the rates were 5 cents a word for news from London and 5½ cents a word from Paris at that time, with slightly higher rates from Berlin and Rome, the press rate from Tokyo was 21 cents, and from Shanghai it was 31 cents then. This made news from London, as published, represent a cost of about $50 a column, while the news from Tokyo would represent a cost of more than $200 a column, and that from China, between $300 and $350 a column. See editorial in New York *Times* of Aug. 26, 1927. Quoted in *Editor and Publisher,* Sept. 3, 1927. By 1932 the New York *Times* was receiving about 4,000 words daily from the Far East, a great increase due to critical events in Manchuria and China, attending the Japanese invasion. The cable costs alone averaged $500 a day for a time. One of the most expensive days was Feb. 3, 1932, when tolls for matter sent from Shanghai, Tokyo and Manila totaled $685.20. Of this total, $532.80 represented news from Shanghai; $131.04, news from Tokyo; and $21.36, news from Manila. *The Little Times,* house organ of the New York *Times* (Feb. 25, 1932), p. 4.

[39] A. G. West, "Increased Cable and Radio Rates to be Resisted in Congress," *Editor and Publisher* (Dec. 30, 1933), p. 24; A. G. West, "Storm of

was most serious in the Pacific because, as it worked out, it meant that rates were raised very high again, which proved especially burdensome to North American press associations and newspapers because they could not take refuge in such government aid as some other press associations enjoy.

* * *

It was in 1920 that the New York *Times* erected a wireless receiving antenna on the roof, with a receiving set in the building. Here it intercepted reports from ships, and occasionally a distress call gave the *Times* an early lead on a potential story of trouble at sea. Somewhat later, the Hearst newspapers constructed a similar receiving station in New York.

The chief American initiative in converting the wireless into an important adjunct of the world press system for news gathering appears to have been that of the Chicago *Tribune*. On Oct. 14, 1920, the *Tribune* radio station, 9ZN, in Chicago, received its first news dispatch direct from Europe, through the Lafayette wireless station at Bordeaux, France, erected there by the United States Government during the War. It was a receiving station only, at the Chicago end. Similar receiving stations were put into operation by three other newspapers, the New York *Times*,

Protest Follows Rise in 'Urgent' Rate on Cables," *Editor and Publisher* (Jan. 13, 1934), p. 38.

In the latter reference, the following rates to and from New York are cited, as of that date:

Press Rates	Cents per word	Urgent Press	Per word
To London	5	To London	23
From London	7.80	From London	34
To Berlin	7	To Berlin	25
From Berlin	11	From Berlin	38
To Tokyo (full)	22	To Tokyo	82
To Tokyo (deferred)	13	From Tokyo	82
From Tokyo	13		
To Shanghai (full)	24		
To Shanghai (deferred) ..	16		

Above rates, all via Commercial Cable. If via Radio Corporation of America (RCA) or Western Union, "urgent" rate was 88 cents to or from Shanghai, while to or from Montevideo it was 13 cents, or if "urgent," 52 cents.

the New York *American* and the Philadelphia *Public Ledger.*
They received news dispatches from great arc sending stations
at Bordeaux and Lyons, France, and at Nauen, Germany.

Because these receiving stations could not reply direct to the
sending stations, it was agreed in advance that the sending station would send out the call, as for 9ZN, at a given time, say
9 P.M. Chicago time. The Chicago *Tribune* operator would be
ready at that hour to receive messages, in Continental code, and
the stories would be on the cable editor's desk half an hour later,
ready to be prepared for publication. If static spoiled reception
at a certain point, however, the operator was able to get a repeat
by wiring a powerful U.S. Navy radio station at Great Lakes Naval
Training Station, a few miles north of Chicago, and that station
would "break" Bordeaux and have the missing portion repeated.

For almost three months the Chicago *Tribune* received all of
its dispatches from continental Europe in that way, weather
permitting. For the *Tribune,* that totaled about 3,000 words daily.
The system saved hours of transmission time, as compared to the
then-existing system of commercial cable and wireless, and cost
about 30 per cent less.

Early in 1921, the Lafayette station passed into the hands of
the French Government, which reached an agreement with the
newly formed Radio Corporation of America by which all dispatches intended for North America must be handled at the
American end by the Radio Corporation and by Western Union,
with which it had arrangements for land transmission. After that,
the *Tribune* messages were so handled, through Radio Corporation and Western Union. This proved to be slower than the
previous arrangement and, lacking a set filing time to send the
press messages, the dispatching took place at periods often unsatisfactory so far as concerned meeting newspaper deadlines.

Although their radio stations were no longer officially recognized, the *Tribune* and the three other papers which had made
the original arrangement in 1920, continued to listen to the transmission of their news dispatches from Bordeaux and to take
them direct and use them as before. The duplicates, as handled
commercially, would come along several hours later, so meeting

the requirements of form, but by that time the intercepted messages often were being read in early editions of the papers.

At length, however, the various restrictions and complexities of this system induced the four newspapers in the original group to set up a coöperative wireless station at Halifax, Nova Scotia. They formed a Canadian Company, the News Traffic Board, Ltd. This station, operating from six to nine hours a day, beginning in February, 1922, received press messages from Great Britain and from continental Europe, sent by the British General Post Office wireless transmitting station at Leafield, near Oxford. This station attained a considerable speed, amounting to twice that of the cable at the time. It was not always free of interference due to weather conditions, however,[40] and messages had to be relayed at all times from Halifax to Chicago by telegraph. As the old-line telegraph companies were not anxious to aid this competitive communications group, there was frequent transmission delay, overland, and an attempt was made late in 1926 to triple the usual press rate for such messages. Competition, however, between the Western Union, which usually carried the traffic out of Halifax, and the Canadian Pacific Telegraph Co., allied with the Postal Telegraph Co., brought down the rates again after three nights.

Commercial radio companies also were attempting to improve their mechanical services in all countries. The Marconi Companies in Great Britain and Canada put into operation the first "beam" wireless system on Oct. 21, 1926, providing direct transmission between London and Montreal, taking only one minute for the message to pass from the Central Telegraph office in London to the office of the Montreal *Star*.

Radio rates generally are slightly lower than cable rates. The Atlantic rate, for example, is about 4½ cents, instead of 5 cents a word, which is the cable charge.[41]

[40] Information from an address by Joseph C. Northrup of the Chicago *Tribune* at the Medill School of Journalism, Northwestern University. Reprinted in *The Trib*, house organ of the Chicago *Tribune* (Feb., 1922), pp. 1, 4-6; also in *The W-G-N* (Anon.), pp. 101-103, 152.

[41] See note 23, page 114, for other examples of relationship between cable and radio rates.

Broadcasts of the news for radio listeners began very early in the nineteen-twenties. There was some experimental handling of the news in that way, as well. During the political conventions of June and July, 1924, in the United States, some newspapers prepared their news reports in part upon the basis of the broadcasts heard from the convention halls.

In November, 1923, the Reuters' organization in Britain began a Reuterian toll service of commercial messages to all parts of Europe by wireless from Leafield. At length the service was operating entirely around the clock, and it was considered essential to use the Rugby broadcasting station, also. At stated times, news would be broadcast, as well as commercial information, and stations all over Europe and in some other parts of the world would listen in.

In Europe there is only two hours difference in the time between London and Constantinople, extreme points. All commercial messages, as so broadcast, were of use in the Bourses and produce exchanges. In some places where it was received in Europe, the service would be re-broadcast for the benefit of other places where the sets would not pick up the original broadcast. Improvements in broadcast methods later enabled the service, by "beam" system and short wave, to reach the far parts of the world with news and commercial information, on a toll basis and otherwise. So the Reuterian service became the largest of its kind, and made a special effort to provide a supply of news to Empire papers in Canada, Australia, New Zealand, and South Africa particularly. In addition, the service was picked up and used in Hong Kong, Shanghai, and other Far-Eastern places, where quotations on silver, rubber, and other products set the standard for local trade.

In Russia a radio transmission of news started before 1926. At that time a graduate of the Moscow School of Dramatic Expression spoke the news, as provided by the Tass agency, into a microphone in Moscow. In 168 Russian newspaper offices, some of them 3000 kilometers away, the news was taken down, word by word, for use. This relatively inexpensive system for news distribution, without telegraph or telephone wires, was one of the things that helped the Russian press develop as rapidly as it did.[42]

The Wolff agency in Germany began a wireless broadcast of news over an internal wireless telephone system, and later this became a world broadcast of news by means of the Trans-ozean-Nachrichten, a service reaching South America, the Far East, and ships at sea through the Nauen wireless station.

A Helvetian wireless news service reached Swiss newspapers. The Havas agency, despite the Reuter beginning in 1923, has been quoted as asserting itself to be the first big news agency to try to develop radio transmission of the news. In 1931 the Havasian service began to broadcast news to Northern Africa, to South America, and to the Orient. This service continued and was extended in the years following, with an effort to increase the number of places reached. The preparation of this news is a matter of interest to the French Foreign Office. By 1933 the service had a powerful station at Pontoise, near Paris, operating 21 hours a day. It was provided to newspapers at a lower rate than that for cable news because, so it was pointed out, there was no expense for the maintenance of cable facilities.[43]

News service also was being sent to South America by Agenzia Stampa, an Italian organization.

The radio telephone, put into operation in 1927, was used in 1930 by the New York *Times*, the Associated Press and International News Service to get first-hand accounts of developments in the revolution that occurred in Argentina.[44] London newspapers used it at times to telephone to the United States; it was less common for American newspapers to telephone Europe. The first news story radio-telephoned from Europe to Japan went over

[42] Reported by H. V. Kaltenborn, in an address at the Press Congress of the World, Geneva, in September, 1926. See: Walter Williams, ed., *Press Congress of the World in Switzerland*, pp. 57-61.

[43] John W. Perry, "France Plans Propaganda Drive in U. S.," *Editor and Publisher* (April 15, 1933), pp. 7, 34; Anon., "Radio News Takes Europe's Rivalries to South America," *Christian Science Monitor* (Aug. 30, 1933), pp. 1, 7.

[44] John F. Roche, "New Radiophone Feats by Newspapers," *Editor and Publisher* (Sept. 20, 1930), pp. 16, 66.

the air on March 12, 1935, when Webb Miller, European news manager of the United Press, read a dispatch in London to a representative of the Nippon Dempo agency in Tokyo, but by 1937 the Pacific was bridged between North America and Japan, not only by radio telephone, but also in the radio transmission of photographs.[45]

The long-distance land-line telephone continues to be widely used by the press in every country, while in European countries, particularly, correspondents serving British newspapers telephone their dispatches to London regularly. In the same way, European correspondents for newspapers in the United States sometimes telephone their dispatches to a control bureau, or relay point, usually London or Paris, to be edited and sent along.[46]

The telephone sometimes is combined with a radio recording device, or a sort of dictaphone, to speed up news handling and reduce expense. In this system, correspondents telephone their dispatches, which, instead of being taken down by stenographers, are recorded on the dictaphone. This permits the correspondent to speak more rapidly into the telephone, and so saves toll charges on time consumed. The record later is played back at a lower speed, enabling the message to be typed out and used by a London paper, or skeletonized, retranscribed and sent on to the United States.[47]

*   *   *

The development of short wave radio brought new progress in transmission methods. Its first important use for news handling began when Admiral Richard E. Byrd made his first expedition to

[45] Anon., "News Story Phoned London to Japan," *Editor and Publisher* (March 16, 1935), p. 29; Anon. "First Radio Picture Across the Pacific," *Editor and Publisher* (April 17, 1937), p. 90.

[46] G. H. Archambault, "Phone Supplants Wire in Europe," *Editor and Publisher* (April 13, 1935), pp. 8, 11; Anon., "(AP)" (Associated Press), *Fortune* (Feb. 1937), pp. 88-93, 148-62.

[47] Described by Frederick T. Birchall of the New York *Times,* in an address at Columbia University, New York; Anon., "Foolish to Fight a Censor—Birchall," *Editor and Publisher* (Nov. 3, 1934), p. 4; Douglas Dies, "Rebel Phone Censors Have a Sense of Humor (Sometimes), Says UP Man," *Editor and Publisher* (Sept. 26, 1936), p. 16.

the South Polar regions, from 1928 to 1930, as already described. Russell Owen, New York *Times* reporter who accompanied the expedition, sent his stories by short wave radio almost nightly over the 10,000 miles from Little America, where the expedition established a base, to the *Times* building in the heart of New York. The short waves carried his reports at 1,200 words an hour. The New York *Times*, through its syndicate arrangements, relayed his stories to 40 American and Canadian newspapers, and to 17 foreign newspapers, published in Sydney, Antwerp, Prague, London, Milan, Osaka, Rotterdam, Mexico City, Oslo, Copenhagen, Stockholm, Helsingfors, Buenos Aires, La Paz and Cartagena. Only occasionally did weather conditions make reception difficult.[48]

The New York *Times* made another mark in the use of short wave radio for news handling when, on Feb. 17, 1933, it intercepted for publication a 15,000-word Manchurian report of the League of Nations' Committee of Nineteen, broadcast to the world from Geneva. The report was the longest in words ever handled by the *Times*, and it took the longest time, keeping two operators simultaneously busy from 9 A.M. until 7.22 P.M. New York time.[49]

The short wave radio brought a new development, also, in the general use of wireless for transmission of news across the Atlantic. Early in 1928 the United States Federal Radio Commission set aside 20 radio wave bands for trans-Atlantic press communication.

The American Publishers' Committee had been erected on the foundation established in 1922 by the News Traffic Board, Ltd. Mr. Joseph B. Pierson, former cable editor of the Chicago *Tribune*, had been active in establishing the original trans-Atlantic

[48] R. L. Duffus, "Covering the News of Frozen Antarctica," New York *Times* (Feb. 10, 1929), Pt. 10, p. 4; Anon., "Owen, From Antarctic, Tells Story as Easily as Nearby District Men," *Editor and Publisher* (Feb. 16, 1929), p. 18; John F. Roche, "News of Byrd's Flight Flashed to New York in Split Second," *Editor and Publisher* (Dec. 7, 1929), p. 8; J. W. Perry, "Byrd Story Made Radio History," *Editor and Publisher* (June 21, 1930), p. 12; F. E. Meinholtz, *"Times* Station Made Radio History in 1930," *The Little Times*, house organ of the New York *Times* (Jan. 22, 1931).

[49] Anon., "N. Y. *Times* Set Radio Record in Getting 15,000-Word Report," *Editor and Publisher* (Feb. 25, 1933), p. 8.

wireless transmission of news dispatches in 1920, and he was
trustee of the American Publishers' Commission on Cable and
Radio Communication. By 1928 there were other newspapers
receiving press dispatches through the News Traffic Board's
Canadian station. When the Federal Radio Commission notified
newspapers that it was going to hold general hearings on the
matter of using short wave radio, and on the specific allocation of
the wave bands, Mr. Pierson brought together nine newspapers,
later joined by the Scripps-Howard newspapers and others, making twelve newspapers and press associations, to form a committee and to represent the interests of the press before the
Commission.

This group was organized as the American News Traffic Corporation. Members were the Chicago *Tribune,* the United Press
Association, the Los Angeles *Times,* the San Francisco *Chronicle,*
the New York *Herald Tribune,* the New York *World,* the *Christian Science Monitor,* the New York *Times,* the Scripps-Howard
newspapers, the Consolidated Press Association, the Philadelphia
Public Ledger, and Universal News Service.

To this group, on Dec. 22, 1928, was granted 40 clear short
wave radio channels, 20 of them for intra-continental use and 20
of them for inter-continental use. It was required by the Federal
Radio Commission that newspapers agree to open their stations
to all newspapers and press associations without restrictions, the
newspapers taking part on the understanding that the American
News Traffic Corporation was to be a public service corporation.[50]

At length, after six months of controversy over the allocation
of the wave lengths, there was organized in July, 1929, a $1,000,-
000 corporation called Press Wireless, Inc., erected on the foundations of the American News Traffic Corporation, with Mr. Pierson
remaining as trustee for the press. To this group, organized as a
public utility corporation, were allotted the 20 transoceanic wave
bands, while the 20 transcontinental wave bands were reserved to

[50] The origins of this plan are told by: George H. Manning, "Publishers
Propose Ten Companies to Control Press Radio Channels," *Editor and Pub-
lisher* (Dec. 1, 1928), p. 26; Anon., "Joe Pierson Wins Short Wave Radio for
U. S. Inter-Press Telegraphy," *The Trib,* house organ of the Chicago *Tribune*
(Feb., 1929), p. 5.

the press for later assignment, probably to Press Wireless, Inc. This newly formed corporation would assign various wave lengths, in requisite numbers, to newspapers and press associations, and generally would act to provide a *bona fide* service to the press of the United States on an equitable basis, permitting any accredited correspondent to file dispatches.

The Hearst newspapers protested this arrangement, as they had the original allocation,[51] and the case was referred to the Court of Appeals of the District of Columbia, with an answer to the Hearst objections filed by the Federal Radio Commission.

In March, 1930, the 20 transcontinental short wave bands, which had been held by the Federal Radio Commission, were at last granted to Press Wireless, Inc. This grant was attacked by the Radio Corporation of America Communications, Inc., a subsidiary of the Radio Corporation of America, which appealed to the District of Columbia Court of Appeals, on the ground that the assignment of all frequencies in the short wave band to Press Wireless, Inc., and commercial organizations, stood in the way of developing a "truly national system of domestic communication" by the Radio Corporation of America, which it was contended would best serve the public interest. It held that the Radio Corporation of America was more fully able to comply with the standards set down by the Federal Radio Commission.[52]

By that time, however, Press Wireless, Inc., had started to operate on the transoceanic bands, beginning Sept. 15, 1929. Its rate was lower than any other communications route and, although transmission was not always reliable at first, it found active interest among publishers in the United States and in some other countries. Five American newspapers made up the original membership. They were the Chicago *Tribune*, the Chicago *Daily News*, the *Christian Science Monitor*, the Los Angeles *Times* and the San Francisco *Chronicle*. Purchase of stock in the corporation

[51] Anon., "W. R. Hearst Files Protest to Proposed Allocation of Radio Wave Bands," *Editor and Publisher* (Feb. 9, 1929), pp. 5-6; G. H. Manning, "Ask Annulment of Radio Allocations," *Editor and Publisher* (Mar. 9, 1929), p. 15.

[52] Anon., "R.C.A. Seeks Press Wave Bands," *Editor and Publisher* (April 5, 1930).

was open to all American newspapers on the same general terms as those given the five newspapers holding shares at the time. It was, and it remains, a public service corporation in a legal sense, obliged to accept for transmission and reception the press dispatches filed by any correspondent or newspaper, provided the subject matter involved is intended for publication in the press, and provided payment is guaranteed.

Radio stations were erected near New York, Chicago, Boston, Los Angeles and San Francisco. These five stations were in operation by April, 1930, handling about 15,000 words a day, which was considered just a beginning.

Independent wave bands, beyond the 40 granted to Press Wireless, Inc., went to Universal Service Wireless, a Hearst organization serving all Hearst newspapers. This grant was made in December, 1929. In 1931 the Hearst newspapers formed the American Radio News Corporation and received permits and licenses, despite the protest of Press Wireless, Inc.[53]

In January, 1931, the Federal Radio Commission granted permission to Press Wireless, Inc., to erect 19 short wave stations for national and international press communications purposes. This marked the conclusion of the litigation in the District of Columbia Court of Appeals over the assignment of the 20 national wave bands and seven of the international wave bands.[54]

By September of 1931 direct wireless transmission of news from Paris to the United States had begun. A powerful transmission station in France was placed at the disposal of American correspondents, as well as a station in England. Most of the dispatches were received in the United States either at Needham, Massachusetts, or Little Neck, Long Island, New York, and distributed from there. Dispatches from the United States and Canada, intended for the French press and other continental

[53] A general history of the formation of Press Wireless, Inc., appears in: Ben Kartman, "Dailies Fighting for Freedom of Air to Improve Exchange of News," *Editor and Publisher* (April 12, 1930), pp. 5, 46. James M. Herring and Gerald C. Gross, *Telecommunications: Economics and Regulation*, pp. 90, 300.

[54] G. H. Manning, "Press Wireless Given Permit for Network," *Editor and Publisher* (Jan. 24, 1931).

destinations, were transmitted from Hicksville, Long Island. By 1932 about 15,000,000 words of press material were being transmitted annually from continental Europe to the United States, and about 3,000,000 words from the United States flowed toward Europe.

In a general way, these figures imply that the American newspaper reader has more information at hand about European affairs than the European reader has about American affairs. This may be taken to indicate a growth in Americans' interest in world affairs. Newspapers do not believe there is any widespread or strong interest in foreign affairs, but they know that there is an *increasing* interest. The average better-type American newspaper to-day prints far more news from Europe, and from other parts of the world, than it did in 1913, and infinitely more than it did in 1900.

What has happened in the United States also has happened in other countries, in greater or less degree, for the entire world is becoming aware of itself as a unit, rather than as an agglomeration of diverse peoples without common interests, evidence of nationalism to the contrary notwithstanding.

In this change from arid provincialism to rich cosmopolitanism the unfolding communications system of the world plays a part so vital that even such statistics as must be used to tell its story cannot quite obscure its vast importance.

CHAPTER IV

OBSTACLES TO THE FLOW OF NEWS

THE Censor was an official of Roman times who imposed taxes and who regulated the manners and morals of a community. The censor in more recent times has been one who examines books, plays, motion pictures and works of art, to determine whether they are fit to be placed before the public, or are likely to exercise an immoral, subversive, or otherwise undesirable influence. During the last two generations, and especially during periods of national crisis, censors have given close attention to the press and to the news or other matter published.

§ 1. CENSORSHIP

THE CENSORS presume to say what is best for the public to see, hear or read on any given subject. Since all thoughts, beliefs and opinions are based entirely upon what information and impressions reach one, it is clear that the acts of the censor in releasing or withholding information tend to determine what the public is to think on the subject involved.[1] In a Democracy, where sound

[1] L. M. Salmon, *The Newspaper and Authority*, Chs. 2-6. This exceedingly able study of censorship, from the beginning of recorded history, considers, in successive chapters, the "Theory of Censorship," "Preventive Censorship," "Punitive Censorship," "Results of Censorship," and "Regulation of the Press," all up to 1923.

O. W. Riegel, *Mobilizing for Chaos*, Ch. 5. Considers "Nationalism and the Corruption of the News" in a most enlightening way, as of 1934; Will Irwin, *Propaganda and the News*, Ch. 18.

W. B. Graves, *Readings in Public Opinion*, Chs. 31, 32. Considers "Censorship and Public Opinion" and "Public Opinion in War Time," and has an excellent bibliography.

Kimball Young and Raymond D. Lawrence, *Bibliography on Censorship and Propaganda*, Univ. of Oregon Publication (March, 1928), Journalism Series, V. 1, No. 1; L. T. Beman, ed., *Selected Articles on Censorship of Speech and the Press*.

public opinion is most essential, freedom from censorship is seen to be an imperative and basic principle of the political theory.

Censorship is imposed by the government of a country, or by local authorities, ostensibly in the interest of "accuracy." Since printing began it has been common for rulers and governments to try to control what their peoples know, or think they know, about affairs at home and abroad.

Some governments have sought, also, to control reports appearing in the presses of other countries.[2] Perhaps never have these practices been more general than at present.[3]

Censorships of the cruder sort, imposed by force and accompanied by heavy-handed penalties, died away in many countries of Europe after Metternich's time, and did not reappear until the Great War. Then more subtle methods were widely used to control the press and to govern what the public should know.

Bismarck, who was a master of propaganda, said that the best way to deceive the public was to tell it the truth, for he knew that journalists generally would attribute secret motives to purposes frankly stated. All who deal in public opinion depend in part upon the short memory of readers. Secret funds also have been used to influence the press in some countries. More recently, flattery and appeals to the honor of the journalist and editor, and to the alleged civic responsibility of controlling heads of newspapers have been means to induce them to keep silence or else to take certain attitudes. These men sometimes are rewarded with titles, decorations, and diplomatic or other appointments.

*   *   *

Following the Great War, one of President Wilson's "fourteen points" most quoted was that calling for "open covenants of

[2] M. E. Stone, *Fifty Years a Journalist*, pp. 243-78; Walter Lippmann, *Liberty and the News*, pp. 44-58.

[3] In about 1770 Benjamin Franklin is said to have tried to get the American colonial viewpoint expressed in the London press, but without success due to the government control of the press in England. The Revolution followed, in part, because British people had insufficient understanding of, or interest in, the colonial situation. It is invariably true that censorship, by bottling up the truth, may postpone but cannot avert conclusions.

peace openly arrived it." This was altered to read, merely, "open covenants openly arrived it," and there was wide agitation for removal of censorships everywhere. It was expected that a very large measure of what Wilson had at another time called "pitiless publicity" would be permitted to bathe the negotiations surrounding the peace settlements at Versailles and elsewhere. Hundreds of correspondents representing the presses of almost every country were in and about Paris and Versailles, but they found, to their chagrin, that official news sources were extremely secretive, and that, while the *word* "censorship" was not used, the *effect* was much the same.[4] They were forced to seek their news from individual and unofficial sources, and this sometimes resulted in what appeared to be premature and unauthorized reports—the anathema of governments.

The Paris peace conference was only the first of numerous international conferences that followed the War. At some of them news was easy to get, at others it was difficult, at all of them there was a great deal going on behind the scenes that might or might not become available to the press, officially or unofficially. There was no formal censorship, only a continuation of the pre-war type of secret diplomacy. This was inevitable, to a great extent, since the transition from older methods could hardly have been made overnight. Such a change, like all far-reaching social changes, could only follow a long period of public education and preparation. In any case, there is indeed something to be said for negotiations carried on quietly, without artificial, press-stimulated

[4] William Allen White, "Tale That Is Told," *Sat. Eve. Post* (Oct. 4, 1919), pp. 19, 158-65; Anon., "Story of the Futile Fight at Paris That Ended in Disaster," *Editor and Publisher* (Oct. 1, 1921); Irving Brant, "Old Sin of U. S. Press Agonizing the World," *Editor and Publisher* (Feb. 3, 1923), pp. 5-6; Harold Nicolson, *Peacemaking, 1919*, pp. 123-24. Mr. Nicolson observes (p. 124) that "there are only two ways of dealing with a democratic Press. The best way is to tell them everything; that bores them stiff. The second best way is to tell them nothing, which at least provides them with the glory of a 'secrecy' stunt, which provides a highly pleasurable form of conciliatory leakages. It was this flabby method which was adopted by the Conference of Paris." He rebukes the officials for poor press organization and relations at the Conference, where the best correspondents ignored such official news sources as existed, and built their own.

emotions, which are certain to follow when every step is conducted in full public view.[5]

With the signing of the peace treaties, wartime censorships were dropped, either promptly or gradually, in Great Britain, France, the United States, Germany, Italy, and various other countries. The neutral Netherlands and Scandinavian countries never had had any restrictions of the sort. Was the free press to become a reality everywhere? Some of the new countries declared for the freedom of the press, notably Czechoslovakia, where a special provision to that effect became part of the Constitution. So did the new China, and so did the new Germany under the Weimar Constitution. But not Russia, by that time under the Soviet Government.

Then came one crisis after another, political and economic, with a train of social results in every case. Crisis is like war in that it may demand a temporary surrender of liberties to save a whole structure from toppling into ruins. The populace of such countries, almost beside themselves at the course of events, are only too willing to give responsibility for righting matters to some man or group promising a solution.

The Balkan lands were seething, and censorships were imposed whenever matters became too disturbed. The Fascisti took over the Italian Government, and imposed a strict censorship. Spain found itself in difficulties, and its papers were censored, as were outgoing dispatches. Japan and China became involved in problems of crisis-proportions, followed by censorships there, also.

[5] Mr. Wilson himself did not mean that there should be no private negotiations. A memorandum approved by the President and used by Colonel House in preliminary discussions at Paris with M. Clemenceau and Mr. Lloyd George referred to the "open covenants openly arrived at" point as follows: "The purpose is clearly to prohibit treaties, sections of treaties or understandings that are secret. The phrase 'openly arrived at' need not cause difficulty. In fact, the President explained to the Senate last winter that his intention was not to exclude confidential diplomatic negotiations involving delicate matters, but to insist that nothing which occurs in the course of such confidential negotiations shall be binding unless it appears in the final covenant made public to the world."

This is quoted, and the entire subject matter discussed by Walter Lippmann in "Today and Tomorrow: When Diplomacy Is Too Open," New York *Herald Tribune* (Jan. 8, 1933).

South American countries careened with revolution, and censor-ships appeared. Germany threw out the Weimar Constitution and, under the Third Reich, established its own severe censorship. Intolerance, nationalism, suspicion all demanded more censorship, plus a campaign of propaganda for consumption at home, and sometimes abroad as well.[6]

By 1930 the world was living under a blanket of censorship, breathing air thoroughly tainted with propaganda. This situation grew even more acute in the years following. The number of countries with free presses were few, and there was doubt about some of those. The whole trend seemed to be toward increased control of all channels of information, and especially toward regu-lation of the press.

In the entire world, the only countries where newspapers were free to speak without government permission, and from which foreign correspondents could send dispatches without official ap-proval, however hidden or indirect, were the United States, Great Britain, France, Switzerland, the Netherlands, Denmark, Nor-way, Sweden, Canada, Australia, New Zealand and South Africa. Here are 12 countries out of all in the world, and only four of these—the United States, Great Britain, France and Switzerland—can be classified as important news sources, and only three of them as "great powers." The rest of the world, some 700,000,000 persons out of a world population of 2,000,000,000—or more than a third—are being fed with information that is biased and dis-torted to serve divers purposes.[7]

[6] Anon., "Your Mirrors of Europe." (By a Foreign Correspondent.), *Sat. Eve. Post,* Dec. 9, 1922, pp. 5, 145-50. Presents some of the correspondents' experiences with censorship.

[7] Albin E. Johnson, "700,000,000 Served by Censored Press," *Editor and Publisher* (Jan. 11, 1930), p. 9; Albin E. Johnson, "300 Million Citizens of Europe Living Under Iron Rule of Censorship," *Editor and Publisher* (June 30, 1934), pp. 34, 38. Mr. Johnson, in this article, includes Czechoslovakia among the countries where no censorship exists, but other correspondents classify Czechoslovakia as a country maintaining a "covert censorship." Belgium, also commonly regarded as a "free press country," is said to have a "covert" censorship. These covert restraints are charged by Walter Duranty, in "Censors in Europe Extend Their Sway," New York *Times Magazine* (June 2, 1935), pp. 8, 20. It is generally agreed that censorships change with the times, with conditions, and with administrations.

FIG. 15. CENSORSHIP MEETS SPANISH DEFIANCE

For description see List of Illustrations

The purpose of censorship, as applied to the domestic press of a nation, commonly is to prevent the dissemination of statements that might disturb the *status quo,* and also to build up a public state of mind favorable to the government's program, whether that be the fighting of a war or the continuance of its own tenure of office, by controlling what the public knows. Statements such as might incite to riot, violence or disorders; others which might shake public confidence in the government, or those tending to undermine the moral or ethical standards of the people all are barred from the press by censorship, where it exists.

In all negotiations, whether national or international in character, a difficulty is instantly created when the press broadcasts to the public the fact that such negotiations are going on. Such publicity may hamper free and amicable discussions between the conferees, and reduce the chances for a favorable outcome, because the relations, once they are in the press, become a matter of trading advantages, and the honor apparently goes to the negotiators who bring back the best bargain. Diplomats, under such circumstances, are virtually forced to make their appeals to the public, with all its prejudices, rather than to the representatives of the other people. The merits of the case cease to have primary importance. For this reason, those who apologize for censorship say

Constantine Brown, "Censors Grip Most of World's Press," *Editor and Publisher* (Apr. 21, 1934), pp. 15, 66; Anon., "Government News Control Widening," *Editor and Publisher* (Apr. 21, 1934), p. 6.

George Seldes, "The Poisoned Springs of World News," *Harper's* (Nov., 1934), pp. 719-31. Also appears in Ch. 14 in Mr. Seldes's book, *Freedom of the Press*. Will Irwin, *Propaganda and the News*, Chs. 17-19.

Albin E. Johnson, "150 Million 'Mental Robots' Are Pawns of Dictators in European War Scare," *Editor and Publisher* (Sept. 7, 1935), pp. 5, 16. Asserts that people of Italy, Germany, Russia are regimented by rigid censorships, receive only "official" news, and are kept uninformed about outside developments. All but three English papers were banned from Italy at one period in 1937, and all Italian correspondents in London were ordered home. Arnaldo Cortesi, "Mussolini Recalls London Reporters," New York *Times* (May 9, 1937), p. 1.

That the difficulties of European editors began shortly after the Great War is indicated by Otis P. Swift, in "Jails, Duels, Bombs, Fate of Europe's Editors," *Editor and Publisher* (July 14, 1923), p. 5; Seymour Berkson, "Facing the Foreign Censor," *Journalism Quarterly* (March, 1936), pp. 7-16.

that open covenants openly arrived at are impractical and that foreign affairs, particularly, should be carried on privately.[8]

It is possible to make a plausible case for censorship, in some instances. The danger arises, however, from the fact that once the bars are down to censorship in one circumstance it becomes difficult to prevent its use in other circumstances. Before long, a constant censorship is likely to exist, and there is no assurance that it will be administered wisely and unselfishly, rather than by persons acting in the interest of privileged groups or individuals and without regard for the public welfare. Censorship makes dictatorship possible, and no dictatorship is possible without a censorship.[9] If a censorship is held to be a need, moreover, it implies that the standard of general intelligence is so low that the public could not act wisely in its own interests.

A censorship upon outgoing news dispatches usually is based on an attempt to persuade the world that all is well in that particular country. Opinion in the great investing countries—the United States, Great Britain, and France—has in past years been most important to other nations where governments and private business have wished to borrow money, and hence have wanted a "good press," e.g. favorable publicity, in those money-lending lands. This desire has provided an economic reason for censorship.

Sometimes there is a political reason, as when a nation feels that its internal situation is too delicate to warrant free discussion either at home or abroad, perhaps because the government fears a possible adverse effect not only upon its currency exchange rate, credit balance, or volume of tourist travel, but also upon actual government policy, tenure of office, personnel, or administrative authority.

[8] D. P. Heatley, *Diplomacy and the Study of International Relations*, pp. 265-68.

[9] Will Irwin, *Propaganda and the News*, Ch. 18. The technique used by what Mr. Irwin calls "the new aristocracy" is to cut off the supply of pure news in the country, and replace it with propaganda, intended to persuade the populace to accept the ideas that the rulers wish to have accepted. "Deprive the populace of real news, and you disarm it," is the axiom governing censorship. "No class can govern without full and accurate information," it is said, and the rulers have that, which is one reason they remain the rulers.

A government's fate may actually seem to rest on the maintenance of a strict censorship, particularly of the domestic press.
This would be true during a period of crisis or internal change,
and, as some countries have been in a state of almost perpetual
crisis for years at a time, censorship has found a seeming justification.

A third occasion when censorship is invoked is in wartime, when
it undoubtedly is necessary. Once in a war, it would be reckless
for a government involved to permit the local press, if so disposed,
to print full details about troop movements or to discuss progress
without some restriction. Editors, even inadvertently, could dis-
rupt the morale of the military or civilian population by printing
discouraging, defeatist, or pessimistic reports and commentaries.
Nor would it be any wiser to permit correspondents for the foreign
press to provide the enemy with aid or comfort through such
reports.[10]

The need for a peacetime censorship is far more dubious, however, particularly on outgoing dispatches. If a government does
maintain a censorship, if it does expel correspondents whose reports do not agree with official ideas of what should be said, if it
suppresses outspoken newspapers within its own borders, then the
world tends to believe that the government must have something
unfavorable to conceal. Censorship, therefore, has taken on a
rather disreputable air. Because of this, governments which place
restrictions either upon domestic journals or upon outgoing reports, sometimes deny that censorship exists, or they may insist

[10] As this book is not primarily a history of journalism, the history of
wartime censorship need not be considered in these pages. Useful references
to the subject, however, include the following: F. L. Bullard, *Famous War
Correspondents;* J. H. Stocqueler, *The Life of Field Marshal the Duke of
Wellington,* 2 vols.; W. F. P. Napier, *History of the War in the Peninsula
and in the South of France, from 1807 to 1814,* new rev. ed., 6 vols.; J. B.
Atkins, *The Life of Sir William Howard Russell,* 2 vols.; Sir Edward T.
Cook, *The Press in War-Time;* Will Irwin, *Propaganda and the News;* Eric
Fisher Wood, "The British Censorship," *Sat. Eve. Post* (Apr. 28, 1917), pp.
5-7, 101-102; (May 5, 1917), pp. 18-19, 105-106; Marcel Berger and Paul
Allard, *Les Secrets de la Censure pendant la Guerre;* Paul Allard, *Les Dessous
de la Guerre;* Maj. D. L. Stone, "Press and Mail Censorship in Wartime,"
Editor and Publisher (Aug. 14, 1926), p. 5; (Aug. 21, 1926), p. 8.

that the press is free, at least "within the social order," as the phrase goes; and declare it is intended simply to insure accuracy.

* * *

There are five outstanding types of formal and semi-formal censorship:

1. *A censorship on matter intended to be printed and circulated in the domestic press.* This exists at present in its clearest form in Russia, Italy and Germany. Sometimes the domestic censorship is officially admitted, as it is in Russia; sometimes it is not admitted, as is the case in Italy; and sometimes it is boldly announced as though it were a virtue, which is the German way.

2. *A direct censorship-in-advance on outgoing matter,* whether dispatched by telegraph, cable, radio, or even by telephone. This exists in Russia, and it is common in wartime or during periods of crisis. It sometimes is evaded by sending dispatches by mail or by telephoning them out of the country. Spain used its control of the telephone during the Civil War of 1936-1937 to oblige correspondents to submit outgoing dispatches to the censors before telephone connections would be permitted them.

3. *An indirect and usually unacknowledged censorship of outgoing messages* of some or all descriptions. This exists, for example, in Italy, and occasionally even in France. It may be an active censorship, it may mean only a delay, or it may be merely supervisory. Perhaps the heads of communications companies are threatened with having their company franchises canceled if they permit unfriendly messages to pass over the facilities they control. This means that they themselves must set up a supervisory censorship to protect their interests, while the country itself is able to deny that it maintains any censorship. This method was originated in Argentina.

4. *A direct or indirect post-publication censorship on domestic newspapers.* Offending words, sentences, or paragraphs may be gouged out of the type after it is set, or the pages may be made up again after the censor has seen page or galley proofs and indicated his objections. An entire edition may be confiscated if it contains objectionable matter. Or the newspaper, as punishment, may be

suppressed for a period of time, or even permanently, if it has offended authority or transgressed the rules. Or the editor may be fined, jailed, exiled or otherwise penalized. This form has been used, with variations, in Italy, in Japan, in Spain and elsewhere.

5. *A direct or indirect censorship affecting foreign correspondents before or after publication of their dispatches.* They may be reprimanded by government officials for "inaccurate" reports, they may be denied further access to news sources or the use of transmission facilities, they may be misled, deliberately, with a view to discrediting them; existence may be made unpleasant or even hazardous for them in various ways, or they may be asked to leave the country. A correspondent may be accompanied on trips into the country by a government official or agent, who tries to direct the correspondent in such a way that he will see or hear nothing displeasing to the authorities. The very presence of this representative may so intimidate natives of the country that they would not dare tell anything unfavorable, even if they wished to, and they may do the opposite, trying to advance their own interests by saying what they know the government would like to have them say. This has occurred, among other places, in Russia and Poland.

Perhaps correspondents will even be offered direct or indirect bribes, they may be given official honors to win their friendship, or they may be given certain social advantages. Apart from those methods, a correspondent's employer at home may be poisoned against him through complaints of inaccuracy coming from official government sources, directly, or from that government's local diplomatic or consular representatives, or through nationals of the "offended" country living in the community where the paper bearing the dispatches is published, and acting at the suggestion or request of the consul.

* * *

One of the subtlest and yet most effective censorships which any government or official can use is that called the "censorship of confidences." That is, the correspondent is taken into the confidence of the official, he is told the government plan, the real "inside story," something that is to occur, what some high official has said—but he is enjoined that the information is given to him "in confidence." It is, he is told, "for your own information," it is "background material," but not to be used, and certainly not ascribed to the true source.

Such are the ethics of journalism, that a correspondent who learns something "in confidence" does not betray that confidence, even if it means that he is "scooped" on the story by a colleague. In a sense, of course, this is enlightened self-interest, because he knows very well that he will not be told anything else if he betrays one confidence. Yet it has not been uncommon, in the United States, for newspaper reporters to go to jail for contempt of court rather than reveal a source of confidential information.

So effective is the censorship of confidence that many statesmen use it deliberately, sometimes with the added flourish of asking the correspondent's opinion, or even advice; perhaps flattering him so that he tends to forget he is a reporter and begins to dream that he is a statesman, with power to shape the destinies of mankind. This type of censorship is used in national capitals and at international conferences. It may reach editors, publishers, and owners, whose reticence is insured or aid enlisted at the price of a dinner or a social evening with President or Premier.

To avoid being so gagged, some correspondents have refused to accept any confidential information. If they know in advance that they are to be told something in confidence, they will decline to hear it because they may be able to get the same information elsewhere, and use it, while if they had accepted it in confidence from this statesman, they would feel bound to keep silence.

President Theodore Roosevelt was much given to using the method, speaking with the greatest frankness to journalists, sometimes telling them things they already knew, but muzzling them by saying that it was to be considered confidential. Mr. Lloyd George did the same thing.

Sometimes a government may believe a censorship is essential to protect its people from over-sensational journalism, or to protect what seem to be perfectly proper activities against too-inquisitive or mischievous reporting by an unscrupulous domestic press or against irresponsible, inaccurate, or viciously unfriendly reports by journalists representing foreign, and perhaps hostile, papers. Nevertheless, any censorship is dangerous because it invites the commission of abuses by a government protected against the judgment of a populace well informed by full press reports. Under a censorship, the press no longer can serve as a "check" on the government, which is one of its useful functions in lands where freedom of expression exists, and one of the reasons for its being guaranteed freedom in those countries.

* * *

Correspondents with a love of facts do not submit meekly to censorships or other restrictions. Information can be mailed out, and, particularly when the envelope is marked for a private address, there seldom is any interference. Press dispatches sometimes are sent out in diplomatic mail pouches, especially from Russia, Italy and Germany. Occasionally the correspondent's copy is carried out of the country by some friend or agent, and mailed in another country, or delivered in person to a newspaper office or control bureau. Codes have been used. Even a telegraph or cable censorship sometimes is evaded by sending the message to a private address, and at full rates, instead of at press rates.[11]

The chief device for eluding the censorship in recent years has been the telephone, supposed to be protected from interference by international convention. This protection does not always hold good, however; it did not in Spain in 1936.

And yet, a vast amount of news leaves every country. In many of them it must pass the censor and, knowing that it must, the correspondent is influenced, perhaps unconsciously, to shade his story here and there in a way that he believes will meet the censor's requirements. Unless the reader has a super-human ability to read between the lines, therefore, he too is going to get a shaded opin-

[11] Otis P. Swift, "Americans Find 439 Ways to Buck Censor," *Editor and Publisher* (June 23, 1923), pp. 5-6.

During the War a defiance of German control of the press in Belgium resulted in the publication and distribution throughout the War of *La Libre Belgique* in the German-occupied portion of the country. The German authorities never could discover where it was being printed. J. Massart, *The Secret Press in Belgium;* Webb Miller, *I Found No Peace,* pp. 39-52, 197-99.

ion, if not from one story then perhaps from a week of stories, or a month of stories, and that may accomplish the very purpose the censorship is intended to produce.

A government seeking to control foreign opinion does not always own itself defeated by mere evasions. It does not like to expel a correspondent outright, because that may be regarded as a tacit admission that he has spoken too truthfully. Yet many a correspondent has been expelled. There also are other means by which he can be forced to leave. He may be made uncomfortable in petty ways, denied access to officials or to officers, information may be unaccountably "lost" or "unavailable" when he appears, his friends and acquaintances may be annoyed or persecuted until they are afraid or unwilling to give him further information, with the ultimate result that he ceases to be of much use to his paper. In Russia the correspondent may leave the country on a visit and then be denied a reëntry visa, which accomplishes the desired end without the necessity of expelling the man.

*   *   *

One weapon most governments have, and some use, is a virtual monopoly of communications. In almost every country of the world except the United States the facilities of communication, and sometimes of transportation as well, are owned by the government.[12]

Just as it was found convenient to form a Postal Union to facilitate the exchange of mail between nations, so there was formed a Telegraph Union, with a membership of 81 states and headquarters at Berne, Switzerland. The Union has, with general consent, extended its authority to other forms of communication, as human ingenuity has devised them, including the telephone in international use, and the wireless. It holds meetings every five years, and sometimes oftener, to consider matters of importance in world communications. Following the 1932 meeting at Madrid its name was changed to "International Telecommunications Union."

---

[12] In the United States, Congress passed legislation in 1935 providing for a Federal Communications Commission and empowering the government to take control of all communications in time of emergency.

Meetings concerned with these matters have been held in past years at Madrid, The Hague, Washington, Lisbon, Berlin, Copenhagen, Cortina, Paris, Brussels and, the first meeting, at St. Petersburg in 1875. Regional conferences also have been held from time to time.

It is obvious that, if a government has control over transmission facilities, it can control what is to enter or leave the country by telegraph, telephone or wireless. The abuses to which such complete control of the communications might be put, however, has induced the nations assembled in meetings of the Telegraph Union to restrict the privilege. Theoretically, no government is entitled to cut telephone communications with another nation, or to cut telegraph or wireless communications.

In practice, of course, such agreements have been and always will be ignored in wartime. And even in peacetime, while lines of communication are not cut, governments do delay messages filed for transmission, and sometimes "kill" them entirely. Messages are garbled with a purpose, or changed. Telephone lines are out of order, connections are granted only on condition that the news message meets official approval, or connections are poor when it pleases the government to have it so, although all bad connections are not, of course, to be attributed to any such cause.

Certain governments would like to have more absolute control over the communications so that it would not be necessary to resort to subterfuges by way of bottling up or censoring the news.

Until the time of the Madrid conference the governing clause on censorship was Section 9 of the agreement adopted at St. Petersburg in 1875. It read: "The high contracting parties reserve to themselves the right to stop the transmission of any private telegram which appears dangerous to the security of the State or which is contrary to the laws of the country, to public order or to decency."

The Madrid conference added to that the following provision: "... provided that they immediately notify the office or station of origin of the stoppage of said communication or any part thereof, except in cases where the issuance of this notice would appear dangerous to the security of the state."

Although this agreement to notify the sender of any censored message was considered a step forward, the real victory at the Madrid conference was in preventing certain governments from placing more rigid restrictions on communications which would have been an invitation to make their censorships tighter. These governments had proposed certain changes in Article 9 of the original agreement. Czechoslovakia would have made it read: "...dangerous to the security *or good reputation* of the State or which is contrary to the laws of the country, to public order, *economic interests* or to decency." This change Czechoslovakia sought to justify on the grounds that (a) Foreign press correspondents often send telegrams of which the text is not dangerous to the security of the State, but which can be damaging to its good reputation, and (b) It is necessary to prohibit telegrams, the contents of which are for the purpose of damaging the economic situation of a country, a city, and so on.[13]

Austria, China and Japan proposed somewhat similar amendments. All of these proposals would "authorize governments to limit, prohibit or withhold telegrams dangerous to the security of the State, contrary to the laws of its public order and morality," on condition that "the station of origin be notified except in those cases where such notification would be contrary to public interest."

Although this authorization "to limit, prohibit or withhold" came under special fire of liberal journalistic elements in the United States, it was in general what came out of the Madrid conference and it was hailed as a "victory" merely because the sender was to be notified that his message had been censored. Nevertheless, if it had not been for opposition provided by delegates from Great Britain, the United States, Canada and Russia, the restric-

[13] This was not altogether unfounded. Some dispatches from Germany, for example, during the inflation period there, were alarming, and at least one publisher ordered his Berlin correspondent to send fewer stories about "the stabilizaton of the currency, the reëstablishment of industry. 'Get away from those highbrow topics,' he said, 'and send us a lot of scandal about high life and the way in which the aristocratic people who have been ruined by the depreciation of the mark are now finding a livelihood through all sorts of disreputable and scandalous methods.' " Willis J. Abbot, Silas Bent and Moses Koenigsberg, *The Press: Its Responsibility in International Relations.*

tions might have been made much more rigid. France, Germany and Italy joined the above group in its protests against anything stricter, and the final decision was taken unanimously.

At an earlier Copenhagen Intergovernmental Press Bureau Conference, the United States representatives opposed every form of censorship, direct or indirect, and demanded that the resolutions drafted by the Press Experts' Conference at Geneva in 1927 should be used as a minimum guarantee. Those resolutions provided:

1. That telegrams submitted to censorship should be examined by specialists and dispatched with the greatest promptitude possible.

2. That journalists should be informed of the instructions given these specialists to enable them to make their own dispositions.

3. That they should be informed of the passages suppressed in their dispatches as well as of exceptional delays in transmission, and that they should be given the option of sending or withholding the telegrams which have been either censored or delayed.

4. That the transmission charges paid in advance for telegrams which have either been censored or delayed should be refunded in proportion to the number of words suppressed.

5. That complete equality of treatment should be granted to all journalists without exception.

It is safe to say that every one of these rules has been entirely disregarded by governments which gave their full or tacit approval both to the original Geneva resolutions and to the Copenhagen agreement.

Because the United States was not a signatory of the St. Petersburg convention of 1875—the last previous important treaty governing communications—correspondents for American newspapers never had been able to get official diplomatic support for violations of that convention in which they had been the victims. But by signing the Madrid convention in December, 1932, the United States made available to its nationals abroad, including correspondents, full diplomatic support in any complaints they had occasion to make about the treatment of their dispatches.[14]

[14] The experiences of one correspondent in trying to enlist diplomatic aid abroad are recounted by George Seldes, *You Can't Print That!*, pp. 317-35,

The requirement regularized by the Madrid conference, that notice was to be sent to correspondents when any of their messages were stopped, had a particular advantage for press associations, because they commonly send messages in short "takes"—that is, a paragraph or two at a time—and sometimes one "take" would be held or killed by the censor. The receiving office would be confused at failing to receive some portion of the message, and expensive cables or telegrams would be required to straighten out the matter. Under the new arrangement, the correspondent himself would know what had been held and could act accordingly.[15]

The provision for notification has been fairly well observed since the conference. During the first hectic days of the National Socialist régime in Germany, when a censorship was put into effect, there was so great a delay in notification as to make difficulties both for the correspondent and his newspaper, but this detail was worked out eventually to a point of reasonable satisfaction.

§ 2. PROPAGANDA

ONE OF the oldest and most persistent manifestations of egoism among men has been the preference almost every individual shows for his own opinions and beliefs about any given subject, as against the opinions and beliefs of his neighbor. Not satisfied with preferring his own opinions and beliefs, he seldom will rest until he has persuaded his neighbor to accept, to share, and to fall in with them.[16]

395-408. Since Mr. Seldes's experiences the 1932 conference has altered matters for the better.

[15] A. G. West, "U. S. Must Fight Censorship at Madrid," *Editor and Publisher* (May 14, 1932), p. 7; J. W. Perry, "U. S. Gains Point at Madrid Conference; Censorship Rule Liberalized," *Editor and Publisher* (Nov. 5, 1932), pp. 3-4; A. G. West, "Press 'Victory' Slight at Madrid Radio-Telegraph Conference," *Editor and Publisher* (Feb. 11, 1933), p. 16; Anon., "U. S. Failed to Win Special Status for Press Matter at Madrid," *Editor and Publisher* (Apr. 29, 1933), p. 34. Including report of American delegation to Madrid.

[16] The intolerance for the ideas of others that frequently is associated with the efforts of the religious or social zealot is generally known. It has led to persecution and martyrdom in all ages. The readiness with which those able to do so use the power of the State to enforce their particular

The Church of Rome, holding certain beliefs about mankind in relation to God, sought to propagate its faith. From this origin derives the word "propaganda."[17] Long in good usage as it referred to religious beliefs, the word has gained currency throughout the world since the Great War of 1914-1918, because it was widely used at that time in another sense.

Since then, the word has been applied to any set of opinions or beliefs advanced, directly or indirectly, for the purpose of persuading others to accept certain views. Those views may concern, not only religion, but also theories of government, economic or business practices, political, racial or social questions; ideas about persons, nations, business groups and other general subjects.

Propaganda as a political power has been put to increased use as public education has tended to emancipate the masses from their earlier acceptance of government by the few for the benefit of the few. Even dictatorial or totalitarian governments nowadays profess to serve the public welfare. Under the earlier authoritarian government, the leaders *commanded*. Now they try to *persuade* instead. Hence, for all its perils, the very fact that the leaders use propaganda in government to the extent they do, indicates a sort of advance along the road of civilization.[18]

Propaganda is information with a bias, or impressions with a bias, while objective fact is unbiased, so far as such a thing is humanly possible. The propagandist, by emphasizing certain ideas and obscuring or suppressing others, shuts out the light of truth.

views also is a matter of history. For a discussion of this peculiarity of mankind and its results, see: Walter Bagehot, "The Metaphysical Basis of Toleration," *Literary Studies*, V. 3, pp. 204-225. See also V. 2, pp. 422-437, for a discussion of the relation between the State and propaganda.

It was because rulers believed that their views and wishes should prevail, and because tradition supported this theory among the people, that they were able to muzzle the early presses by licenses and taxes. So the State controlled one important means by which unsanctioned ideas might otherwise be disseminated.

[17] To instruct missionaries of the Roman Church in means of propagating the faith, there is established in Rome the College of the Propaganda in the Via Propaganda Fide, and in that street, by coincidence, the Agenzia Stefani, official Italian news agency, also has its main office.

[18] José Ortega y Gasset, *The Revolt of the Masses,* translated from the Spanish, *La Rebelion de las Masas.*

His task is simplified by censorships and by the readiness of most persons to believe what they want to believe, or to believe what tradition, convention, custom, sentiment, inhibitions or self-interest say they should believe.[19]

* * *

Before the Great War some shrewd minds understood the power of propaganda, although they may not have called it that.

William Cobbett, about 1800, would use a lesson in grammar as a means of propaganda. Ostensibly illustrating the use of the verb "to be," he would write, "To say that 'all Kings and priests *is* liars and oppressors of the poor' is not correct, but it *is* correct to say that 'all Kings and priests *are* liars and oppressors of the poor.' "[20]

During the War of Independence the American Colonies maintained in Holland a bureau which was chiefly concerned with handling propaganda favorable to the colonial cause, seeking support in Europe.[21]

---

[19] Such factors, of special aid to the propagandist, have been called "stereotypes" by Walter Lippmann. See his *Public Opinion,* Chs. 6-10, pp. 79-156.

[20] Cited by the *New Statesman and Nation* (Oct. 15, 1932), p. 439. This periodical comments:

The game of getting a little propaganda across while ostensibly teaching a science has long been practised by economists and other instructors of the young. . . . The latest recruit to this pleasant little art is Mr. R. H. Naylor, the astrologer, who writes in "What the Stars Foretell" in Beaverbrook's Sunday paper [the London *Sunday Express*]:

"The passage of Mars through Leo during October and November will surely disturb France and the French. . . . The Stars of France are not the Stars of Britain and the sooner this is realized the better for us. The stars now show that Britain is once again in danger of shouldering new burdens engineered by French diplomacy."

Again:

"Well called 'The Awakener,' Uranus will, before it leaves Aries two or three years hence, have literally electrified this little island. In British industry the effect of Uranus will be wonderfully constructive. British supremacy in engineering will reassert itself; the day of foreign importers of household 'gadgets' and industrial machinery is gone."

The significance of the propaganda was that Beaverbrook papers then were advocating that Great Britain keep out of diplomatic engagements with continental countries, including France; and were urging a tariff to keep out non-Empire goods and to encourage Empire Free Trade.

[21] Bernard Fäy, *Notes on the American Press at the End of the Eighteenth Century,* p. 24. He refers to *Writings of Franklin,* edited by A. H. Smyth,

A plan for an organized propaganda bureau in England, to influence opinion both at home and abroad, was proposed at about the end of the eighteenth century, but was rejected by the authorities.[22] Napoleon operated what amounted to a "press bureau," and which was, in fact, engaged in propaganda activities.[23] Prince Bismarck was even more aware of the power of propaganda, and used it extensively.[24] There were others—statesmen, industrialists, journalists—who used such skill as they possessed in shaping public opinion for their own purposes.

Louis XI of France (1461-1483) expressed thus early the guiding principle of propaganda in his formula for diplomatic practice, "If they lie to you, you lie still more to them." This principle discounts the value of official government statements, whether affirmations or denials of purposes and views.

British statesmen long have maintained close relations with the press, usually through friendship or acquaintance with editors, not always because they wished to disseminate propaganda through the newspapers, but sometimes because they were sincerely concerned about having a fair presentation of their own and of the government views and purposes. Edmund Burke was one of the earliest British statesmen to appreciate the press for what it was worth, and it was he who first called it the "fourth

V. 1, pp. 45, 146; V. 7, pp. 35, 82; V. 8, pp. 3, 142, 245. Also see Fäy, p. 27, in which he comments upon the fact that the propaganda carried on in Europe by the American revolutionists between 1775 and 1790 never has been adequately studied. He refers to some further references to it in his own *l'Esprit Revolutionnaire* (*The Revolutionary Spirit in France and America*, trans. by Ramon Guthrie), pp. 97-100. Also see: Fäy, pp. 27-28, for references to French and English propaganda organizations in the United States after the War of Independence. He refers, again, to his own *l'Esprit Revolutionnaire*, pp. 2, 5, 239, 252, 259, 280; and to J. F. Turner, "The West in Diplomacy," *American Historical Review*, V. 3, pp. 570-80.

Samuel Adams did much to organize revolutionary sentiment among the colonists before 1775, and has since been regarded as a successful propagandist. John C. Miller, *Sam Adams: Pioneer In Propaganda*.

[22] C. K. Webster, *The Foreign Policy of Castlereagh, 1812-1815*, note, p. 42.

[23] A. Périvier, *Napoleon Journaliste.*

[24] Moritz Busch, *Bismarck: Some Secret Pages of His History*, 3 vols. This is one of the most important books on the subject of government-sponsored propaganda, and its political effects.

estate" as a tribute to its importance. Others whose relations with the press were close and usually cordial enough have included Canning,[25] Palmerston, Disraeli, Castlereagh, Aberdeen, Gladstone, Salisbury, Lloyd George and any number of others.[26]

Government officials and politicians in the United States also have been on intimate terms with the press, while in France journalism and politics have been so interrelated as to be almost indistinguishable. In Germany alone, among the greater countries of the world, statesmen commonly remained somewhat uncommunicative where the press was concerned. But there were exceptions, even in Germany—notably Bismarck, Hammann, and von Bülow, and farther south, in Austria, there was Metternich.[27]

[25] Canning, for example, would have two speeches ready, on some occasions, one to deliver and the other to be published in the press, because he realized that what sounded all right might not look so well in print, and vice versa.

[26] Harold Temperley, *The Foreign Policy of Canning, 1822-1827;* Kingsley Martin, *The Triumph of Lord Palmerston;* C. K. Webster, *The Foreign Policy of Castlereagh, 1812-1815;* J. A. Spender, *The Public Life,* 2 vols.; A. I. Dasent, *John Thaddeus Delane, Editor of "The Times,"* 2 vols.; Frederic Whyte, *The Life of W. T. Stead,* 2 vols.

[27] Moritz Busch, *Bismarck: Some Secret Pages of His History,* 3 vols.; Prince Metternich, *Memoirs of Prince Metternich,* 5 vols.; Otto Hammann, *The World Policy of Germany, 1890-1912;* Prince von Bülow, *Memoirs, 1903-1909.*

"No one has ever rivaled Bismarck in the use of the press. By day and by night (literally) his underlings have to work for the press, preparing, suggesting, summarizing, contradicting. He shows the utmost mastery in the dosage of his poison; sees to it that the news items he wishes to reach the public shall come to Berlin from out-of-the-way corners in Germany or from one of the foreign capitals, so that the public may be impressed by the utterance of ostensibly unprejudiced words. In his own study he dictates the most amazing discoveries about himself, which are then given to the world as if they had been sent from Stockholm to Potsdam. ..." Emil Ludwig, *Bismarck,* p. 478.

Prince von Bülow sometimes was able to prevent Kaiser Wilhelm II from making indiscreet statements in speeches and letters. He it was who had the Kaiser's interview with William Bayard Hale, American journalist, suppressed after it was in type and ready to be published in the *Century Magazine.* The interview, which occurred in the summer of 1908, was only published in 1934 in the *Atlantic,* and then as a sort of curiosity. William Harlan Hale, "Thus Spoke the Kaiser: Lost Document Which Solves an International Mystery," *Atlantic Monthly* (May, 1934), pp. 513-23; Hale,

For some years prior to the outbreak of the Great War, Russia and other countries were, as governments, spending large sums of money to buy the support of newspapers, particularly in France, to further their national aims. Alexander Isvolsky, the Russian Ambassador to Paris from 1906 to 1910, was charged with the distribution of the funds where they would accomplish the most good, from Russia's point of view, and his pay-roll included the names of some of the most widely known newspapers and most prominent journalists and statesmen of France. The same situation unquestionably obtained in other countries of Europe. Commercial and industrial groups, selling munitions and other products, were similarly engaged in buying support.[28]

* * *

Large-scale use was made of propaganda as a weapon of offense as well as defense by all countries involved in the Great War. The primary object was to persuade and unite the entire populace

"Adventures of a Document: The Strange Sequel to the Kaiser Interview," *Atlantic Monthly* (June, 1934), pp. 696-705.

The so-called *"Daily Telegraph* letter," however, went through the German Foreign Office at about the same time—1908—without being recognized as potential dynamite. When it was published as a letter in the London paper its repercussions shook all Berlin, due to the frank and indiscreet statements it contained about international affairs. Von Bülow understood, later, that Alfred Harmsworth had seen the letter earlier, and had refused to print it in the *Daily Mail*, due to objections from the British Foreign Office. Later, it was mailed to the *Daily Telegraph*, since the German Emperor had made it known to his officials that he wanted it published in an English newspaper. Prince von Bülow, *Memoirs, 1903-1909*, pp. 328-30, 341-50, 363.

[28] Documents proving the Russian bribery of the French press were published in serial form by *l'Humanité*, Paris daily, in January, 1924. The articles were conveniently summarized in *The Nation and Athenæum*, London, Feb. 9, 1924. They included letters from Alexander Isvolsky, Russian Ambassador in Paris, to the Russian Government, telling of his successes. The letters originally were published by the Bolshevik Government in *Un Livre Noir*.

See: Anon., *Un Livre Noir: Diplomatie d'avant-guerre d'après les documents des archives Russes, Novembre 1910-Juilliet 1914;* Alexander Isvolsky, *Der Diplomatische Schriftwechsel Isvolskis 1911-1914, herausgegeben von Friedrich Stieve; Memoirs of Alexander Isvolsky*, ed. and trans. by C. L. Seeger; G. Lowes Dickinson, *The International Anarchy, 1904-1914;* Otto Lehmann-Russbuldt, *War for Profits;* S. B. Fay, *Origins of the War*, 2 vols.

of a country concerning the justice of their own cause, and to inspire the purpose of carrying on the War with a single-minded devotion. A secondary purpose was to combat enemy propaganda and weaken the morale of enemy people. A third purpose was to convince the people of other countries that there was only one right view of the War and, if possible, to persuade neutral countries to join forces with the propagandist country, or to aid it in other ways.

It would be untrue to say that the Great War was the first conflict in which the force of propaganda was used. But it was the first conflict in which the word was used to designate that force, and it was the occasion for the most important and extensive use of propaganda up to that time.[29] Both the Allied propagandists and the Central Powers' propagandists were successful, on the whole, in enlisting the support of their own peoples. This end they accomplished by intense programs of disseminating information with a bias and by excluding, through censorship, information that might hinder or hamper their own efforts.

The campaign directed toward neutral countries was successful in some instances, although naturally both sides could not win in that campaign. The fact that the Allies brought more new adherents to their banners is attributable, as the world has come to realize, very largely to the superiority of their propagandists.[30]

[29] H. D. Lasswell, *Propaganda Technique in the World War*. This excellent study of the subject goes back into history to indicate how propaganda was used in earlier conflicts as well. There is a remarkably fine bibliography; P. T. Moon, "War Propaganda," *Syllabus on International Relations*, p. 121; Will Irwin, *Propaganda and the News*, Chs. 11-17.

[30] The extensive publicity organizations built up by Sir Gilbert Parker and by Lord Northcliffe to win the United States to the Allied cause are understood fairly well to-day. The interest of American financiers in the Allied cause also was a factor in tipping the scales. The counter-propaganda in the German interest was directed by George Sylvester Viereck in the United States.

Walter Millis, *The Road to War;* H. Schuyler Foster, Jr., "How America Became Belligerent: A Quantitative Study of War News, 1914-17," *American Journal of Sociology* (Jan., 1935), V. 40, no. 4; Lord Riddell, *War Diary;* B. E. Schmitt, *The Coming of the War*, 2 vols.; S. B. Fay, *Origins of the War*, 2 vols.; J. F. Scott, *Five Weeks; The Surge of Public Opinion on the Eve of the Great War.*

The effort to maintain a solidarity among allied nations was successful, except for Russia, and the campaign to demoralize the enemy was a success so far as the Allies were concerned, but a failure for the Central Powers.

The "atrocity" stories, which revealed in the greatest detail the alleged cruelties practised by German invaders of Belgium and

Campbell Stuart, *Secrets of Crewe House;* F. A. Mackenzie, *Beaverbrook: An Authentic Biography,* pp. 120-38; Hamilton Fyfe, *Northcliffe: An Intimate Biography,* Ch. 15; Wickham Steed, *Through Thirty Years,* V. 2, Ch. 15.

George Creel, *How We Advertised America;* Will Irwin, *Propaganda and the News.*

Paul Allard, *Les Dessous de la Guerre;* Marcel Berger and Paul Allard, *Les Secrets de la Censure pendant la Guerre;* Georges Demartial, *La Guerre de 1914: Comment on Mobilisa les Consciences.*

Sir William B. Thomas, *A Traveller in News,* pp. 106-7. Some of the falsities appearing in the French press during the War for propaganda purposes have been published by the Paris newspaper, *Bonsoir,* under the title, *Anthologie du Bourrage de Crane.* The publication began in serial form in the newspaper in July, 1919, and later it was published in book form. This is cited by E. J. Dillon, *The Peace Conference,* note p. 100.

A study of the causes leading to the Great War in France, Germany and Great Britain, with appropriate consideration of the part played by the press, appears in C. E. Playne, *The Neuroses of the Nations.* This is a study of the German neuroses and of the French neuroses, including evidences of those neuroses in the press, and showing how the tensions increased and finally burst into war; C. E. Playne, *The Pre-War Mind in Britain: An Historical Review.* A study of the British neuroses, in much the same way.

See also: Ludwig Thoma, "The Poison Mixers," *Frankfurter Zeitung* (Mar. 29, 1913); Martin Hobohm and Paul Rohrbach, *Chauvinismus und Weltkrieg,* 2 vols.; Anon., *J'Accuse;* Otfried Nippold, *Der Deutsche Chauvinismus* —Trans. to French, *Le Chauvinisme Allemand.* New Edition, augmented; Prince von Bülow, *Memoirs, 1903-1909,* pp. 185-86. Prince von Bülow quotes a letter from Wilhelm II, in which the Emperor asserted that wealthy individuals in London, although not the government itself, maintained a "system of deliberate, organized agitation" against Germany, using the press of every country. He asserted that 300,000 francs were spent in a single year in the Paris press for anti-German articles.

See also: J. A. Hobson, *The Psychology of Jingoism;* Anon., "The Harmsworth Brand," *The Nation* (London, July 18-Aug. 29); J. A. Farrer, *England Under Edward VII.* Discusses the part of *The Times,* the *National Review,* the *Fortnightly Review,* and other periodicals in making Anglo-German friendship difficult by publishing provocative articles, etc. In regard to the attitude of the British press toward Germany, see also: Prince von Bülow, *Memoirs, 1903-1909,* pp. 26-35, 74-75; J. A. Spender, *The Public Life,* V. 2, pp. 108-15.

France, especially during the early months of the War, were widely circulated in the United States and made a great impression. After the War it was revealed that many of them were fakes, typical of every war, and designed to arouse hatred of the enemy among the Allied people and to gain the sympathy and coöperation of neutrals. They proved their value.[31]

The campaign, intended to bring Italy into the War on the Allied side, and sponsored in Italy itself by the Mussolini brothers, Benito and Arnaldo, was successful, so that in 1915 the battlefront was extended to the Italo-Austrian front, although not until Italy gained a *quid pro quo* in the form of secret treaties giving her the right to an Adriatic port, Fiume, and other concessions.

*   *   *

Wartime experiences taught most governments that they could control public response to their acts most effectively if they would coöperate with the press, since the press was and is the greatest agency for disseminating current information. They followed the lead, more or less, of the League of Nations, which made the Information Section a most important part of the Secretariat, win-

---

[31] Arthur Ponsonby, *Falsehood in War-Time;* Will Irwin, *Propaganda and the News,* Chs. 11-13; G. S. Viereck, *Spreading Germs of Hate;* Norman Angell, *The Public Mind,* Ch. 5; J. D. Squires, *British Propaganda at Home and in the United States from 1914 to 1917;* Anon., "War Propaganda." By One of the War Propagandists, *Sat. Eve. Post* (June 15, June 22, June 29, July 27, Aug. 3, 1929). Articles by George Sylvester Viereck, later rewritten and incorporated in *Spreading Germs of Hate;* J. M. de Beaufort, *Behind the German Veil,* Ch. 6; Kurt Muhsam, *How We Were Lied to—The Official Deception of the German People,* trans. from German, *Wie Wir Belogen Wurden. Die Amtliche Irrefuhrung des Deutschen Volkes;* Hans Thimme, *Weltkrieg ohne Waffen.*

Some of the Allied counter-propaganda is described, not only in Mr. Irwin's book, but in: Walter Lippmann, *Public Opinion,* Ch. 2.

Similar atrocity stories have been told in various wars as a means of rallying the peoples involved. In the Boer War, General Smuts and Louis Botha, as leaders of the Boers, were alleged to have been poisoning wells, shooting prisoners and indulging in other atrocities later ascribed to Germans by Allied propagandists in 1914-1918. Yet, after the Boer War, those gentlemen became highly respected and honored in Great Britain, even as Germany's Field Marshal von Hindenburg became honored and respected in Allied countries after the Great War.

ning reams of publicity, and nowhere more than in the United States, which was not a member of the League! So they established press bureaus, usually in conjunction with the Foreign Office, especially to deal with foreign press representatives, and very often in other departments, as well, to explain their activities to interested journalists.

Even though a government also maintained a censorship on outgoing dispatches, or on the domestic press, it might aid journalists in gathering information about government affairs. At international gatherings, governments would place press relations in charge of some official.[32] It even proved useful to send press officers to certain embassies and legations abroad.[33]

There are two attitudes assumed by governments in their relations with the press. The first attitude, exemplified by the United States Department of State, is that everything that is not secret *has* to be given out. The second attitude, exemplified by the British Foreign Office, is that everything that does not *have* to be given out should be kept secret. Other governments follow one or the other of these attitudes, with slight variations.

There also are two general types of press bureaus dealing with foreign correspondents. One is the central type, such as is maintained by Italy. There one bureau acts as a clearing-house for all government news, or virtually all. The other is the scattered type, well represented in the United States, where each department and many bureaus, also, maintain their own press relations. There also is the circumstance where a government has so limited a con-

---

[32] At the Genoa Conference of 1922 Lord Riddell and, later, Sir Edward Grigg acted for the British delegation, and not only the British journalists, but Americans and others turned to this source as the most informative.

Thomas Lamont acted as American press relations officer at the Young Reparations Conference in Paris in 1929.

[33] Robert T. Pell, who went to the Paris Embassy in 1927, was able to accomplish a good deal, serving the United States.

A somewhat chauvinistic view of the influence exerted on American opinion by these government press bureaus and other pressure groups appears in "Popgun Opinion and Our Foreign Policy," by Richard Washburn Child, former United States Ambassador to Italy, *Sat. Eve. Post* (Mar. 26, 1927), pp. 35, 165-68. Some other governments also assign press attachés to their embassies.

tact with the press as to defy classification in either of these categories. That would be true of Russia and perhaps of Germany as well, so far as the foreign press is concerned, although the native press is almost uncomfortably close to the government. Yet every government knows how to prepare statements for the press, when circumstances arise in which it wishes to make known its attitude.

When a government wishes to win a favorable response for some one of its undertakings it puts out propaganda for consumption at home or abroad, or both.[34] The United States did it during its Latin-American military adventures in the 'twenties. France did it at the time of its occupation of the Ruhr, issuing reports that were totally false, but which would seem to prove the French contention that there was a great need for its troops in the area because of German military activity there.[35] Great Britain has done so at Naval conferences. Italy sought to influence foreign opinion in favor of its Ethiopian invasion in 1935. Japan did the same thing when it invaded Manchuria in 1931.

The purpose of foreign propaganda efforts is to shape opinion in nations which might be induced to loan money or provide some other form of support. The press bureaus and "press clubs" set up by governments, particularly in European countries, thus seek to control what correspondents learn, and what they send out of the country.

Success for these press departments has depended largely upon the skill of the press officers. They must be personally likable, suave, genial, and apparently very frank. Yet they must not tell too much. So, a press officer of the British Foreign Office might disarm correspondents by introducing a subject with a remark such as, "Now, if you will excuse me, gentlemen, I'll give you a little propaganda."

An able and well-liked official of the United States Department of State was skilled in telling the truth without revealing too much.

[34] Pierre Denoyer, "The Press in Europe," address by New York correspondent of *Le Petit Parisien* at Princeton Conference on the Press, 1930. *Conference on the Press* (Anon.), pp. 126-34.
[35] Anon., "Propaganda Out of the Ruhr," *Editor and Publisher* (Mar. 3, 1923), p. 5.

One of his methods was to accept a badly asked question literally, at its face value, and by answering it literally, also, cover up certain facts. Thus, he might be asked:

"Has there been any diplomatic communication between the United States and Japan over the Manchurian situation within the last week?"

"No," he would say, and it was true, so far as it went, for there had been no "diplomatic communication" as such between the two governments. However, the United States Ambassador in Tokyo *had* been instructed in a private cable to talk informally to the Japanese Foreign Minister on the subject. If the question had been phrased to embrace the other possibilities, the answer given would not have sufficed, although another method of evasion might then have been found.

* * *

The Great War, with its vast emphasis on propaganda, and the subsequent outpouring of literature on the subject, gave not only to governments, but to many individuals a new concept of the power which a clever practitioner of the art could exercise over the public. Industry was quick to adapt the new-found force to its own purposes. Advertising men, publicity men and journalists became "counsels on public relations" or "vice-presidents in charge of public relations." The best of them ignored the older publicity tricks of circus and theatrical press agents. Their methods were more urbane.

Instead of trying to outwit the press, tricking the papers into using a story with publicity value, as the old press agents did, the new generation tried to *help* the press. If they "made news happen," it was still news, and could legitimately be used, and many times could not be ignored. They made information available much more readily, and brought an end to a feud that had been waged between the press and big business, and to a lesser extent between the press and politicians or government officials. In this respect they were of service to both parties.[36]

[36] A large literature which has appeared on the general subject of propaganda since the Great War indicates a growing awareness of its importance.

Discussion and argument are a legitimate and necessary part of the social order. It may be natural for a person holding a decided belief on any subject to try to persuade others to accept his view. He believes he is right, as perhaps he is, and in that event he may be doing the other persons a real service by correcting their mistaken ideas and putting them on the right track. In so far as propaganda is an effort to persuade men to accept a given set of beliefs that will promote the public welfare, it may be defensible and right. Yet perhaps that kind of persuasion is not propaganda at all, but education.

It sometimes is said that there is nothing bad about propaganda *per se;* that it may be good or bad and that each case must be judged on its merits. Perhaps that is not quite exact. Argument or debate in an open discussion, with all factors exposed, is one thing. But propaganda is not always so frank in its purpose or motivation. The public receives information, but cannot judge its value, probably does not even recognize it as propaganda, and so does not defend itself against the warped thinking induced.[37]

This literature includes these books of general application: Kimball Young and R. D. Lawrence, *Bibliography on Censorship and Propaganda;* H. D. Lasswell, R. D. Casey and B. L. Smith, *Propaganda and Promotional Activities: An Annotated Bibliography;* F. E. Lumley, *The Propaganda Menace;* W. B. Graves, ed., *Readings in Public Opinion;* Peter H. Odegard, *Pressure Politics: The Story of the Anti-Saloon League;* H. D. Lasswell, *Propaganda Technique in the World War;* L. M. Salmon, *The Newspaper and Authority,* Chs. 12, 13; E. L. Bernays, *Crystallizing Public Opinion;* O. W. Riegel, *Mobilizing for Chaos: The Story of the New Propaganda;* Will Irwin, *Propaganda and the News;* L. W. Doob, *Propaganda: Its Psychology and Technique.*

"Pressure Groups and Propaganda." *The Annals of the American Academy of Political and Social Science* (May, 1935), V. 179; *Propaganda and Dictatorship.* A collection of papers tracing the history of propaganda in present-day Europe, and discussing the function of propaganda in a democratic country. Both are edited by H. L. Childs.

[37] Wickham Steed defined propaganda as "partial and deliberately misleading statements," and adds that propaganda is likely to cause "emotional explosions," since it is intended to arouse sentiments pro or con on the subject in question. Wickham Steed, "The Political Causes of War," *The Causes of War* (A. Porritt, ed.), p. 172.

Another, and a semi-serious definition is: "Propaganda is the art of deceiving your friends without quite being able to deceive your enemies."

An excellent definition, by Will Irwin, appears in *Propaganda and the News,* p. 222: " 'Propaganda' in the pre-war sense," he writes, "meant simply

Some persons, defending the work of the "counsel on public relations," assume that if the source of a statement or the sponsorship of an address or action is known, every one will understand how to appraise it, and discount it as much as necessary.[38] Admittedly, it is better than no indication of source, but it still is not enough.

First of all, relatively few persons are informed about the special attitudes, views, prejudices and interests of the individuals, associations, societies and pressure groups figuring in the news; they are names and nothing more. Second, even when they believe they know about the organization, they may not know its true sponsorship or purpose.

To illustrate: Although they may expect the Navy League in the United States to agitate for a "big navy," will they understand that the organization is not inspired by purely patriotic motives, as it would have the public believe, but that it was started and is largely supported by steel concerns and other industries which profit greatly through the building of war vessels? [39]

Or, how many of the German people knew that the National Socialist party was supported and financed by great chemical and steel groups in Germany, and even in France, groups that would profit financially by Hitler's rise to power, and the consequent rearming of the Reich? [40]

Again, the Société d'Etudes et d'Informations Économique, of Paris, was founded by the Comité des Forges, French steel and armament manufacturers, to produce studies not at all objective, but intended to appear so, while supporting a nationalist, high tariff viewpoint. Do French people, even if they know that the Société sponsored a study, understand who sponsored the Société,

the means by which one spread his opinions. In the modern sense it means a traffic in half-lies for selfish or dishonest ends." It is the "selfish or dishonest ends" which differentiate propaganda in its modern guise from "education," which is altruistic in purpose, and in the public interest.

[38] Ivy L. Lee, *Publicity: Some of the Things It Is and Is Not,* p. 23.

[39] Charles A. Beard, "Big Navy Boys: Who Is Behind the Navy League?" *New Republic* (Feb. 3, 1932), pp. 314-18.

[40] Anon., *Arms and the Men,* pp. 42-46. [Reprinted from *Fortune,* March, 1934.]

with its high-sounding name, when references to it appear in the press?

For each group formed to make propaganda for one purpose, another is formed to make propaganda for the opposite ideas. The result of such propaganda and counter-propaganda, the world over, iterated and reiterated, is not so much to persuade as to breed confusion among the peoples.[41] Not knowing what to believe, a people will take no positive, intelligent action, even on vital subjects. The result is a policy of "muddling," of apathy based on confusion, which means that nothing is done until a situation becomes so acute that action of some kind must be taken to avoid a disaster. But by that time, it may be too late to do more than devise a patched-up solution of an inferior variety. In this way, propaganda becomes a force for evil, forestalling decisions, perpetuating wrongs, and delaying the realization of what is good.

* * *

Yet the ultimate solution for the multiple problem of tendentious news, of propaganda, of censorship, of narrow-minded editors and readers, cannot come through any technical provisions of law. It must come through educating the public to desire a clear and adequate supply of facts, and to want it sincerely enough to support periodicals which provide it.[42]

[41] "Our civilization has stimulated the creation of agencies which live deliberately on the falsification of news. It would, indeed, not be very wide of the mark to argue that much of what had been achieved by the art of education in the nineteenth century has been frustrated by the art of propaganda in the twentieth." H. J. Laski, *A Grammar of Politics* (2nd edition), p. 147.

Dr. Alfred E. Zimmern, authority on education in international affairs, contends that it is possible for a discriminating newspaper reader to gain from that source an understanding of world affairs. Zimmern, *Learning and Leadership*, p. 47. He need only read newspapers "representing various opinions and countries," Dr. Zimmern says, "correcting one bias by another and remembering that the further an account has to travel before it reaches its destination the more outspoken it can often afford to be."

[42] "The best remedy for false and tendentious news is the fullest and freest supply of news"—Lord Cecil of Chelwood, in announcing an opinion of the Sixth Committee to the League of Nations Assembly. In *Coöperation of the Press in the Organization of Peace: Report by the Sixth Committee to the Assembly* (Anon.). (Official No. A.50. 1932. Oct. 10, 1932.)

Propagandists will continue to operate so long as there are those who have strong prejudices or opinions, or so long as there are greedy men. But correspondents and editors can learn to detect propaganda and, even when it must be printed for news reasons, they can label it as such, so providing readers with a discount. When censors have exercised their talents, readers also may be so informed. And, most important, readers may be taught to want facts, rather than flattering support for their own prejudices, and they may be shown how to make proper discounts as they read the news.[43]

[43] "The newspaper Press is often criticized as an influence for evil in international relations. The criticism is unfair. For the evils complained of are not of the newspapers' own creation. They are a response to a public demand. So long as the mass of the reading public remains as ignorant of foreign countries and peoples as it is at present, international relations will inevitably remain one of the most convenient channels for ministering to the craving for what is abnormal and sensational"—Alfred Zimmern, *Learning and Leadership*, p. 46.

Leland Stowe, "The Press and International Friction," *Journalism Quarterly* (March, 1936), pp. 1-6.

CHAPTER V

NEWS OF THE OLD WORLD

GEOGRAPHIES show more than 60 political divisions distributed over the five continents and the islands of the seas. Except for isolated events, most news of wide significance has its origin in about a score of countries, and comes to a particular focus in one or sometimes two cities in each country. It is in these news centers that journalists congregate in greatest numbers. It is there that the more important newspapers are published.[1]

§ 1. LONDON AND THE BRITISH EMPIRE

LONDON is the most important news center in the world, and has been for a very long time. London originates news, and information also flows into it from all parts of the British Isles, the Empire, and the rest of the world.

---

[1] Thoroughly up-to-date characterizations of the press in every country, with a list of leading press associations, appear in the *Political Handbook of the World*, issued annually since 1927 by the Council on Foreign Relations, New York.

A current list of newspapers published in each country, without comments, is to be found in the French *Annuaire de la Presse*. See also: *Europa*, V. 1. This contains references to European newspapers. The German *Handbuch der Weltpresse* presents fairly complete data on many newspapers in virtually all countries.

Lists of newspapers and of journalists taking part in the writing, editing and distribution of news also appear in *Willing's Press Guide* (British); *Annuario della Stampa Italiana* (Italian); *Ayer's Newspaper Directory* (U. S. A.); *Editor and Publisher International Year Book* (U. S. A.); *Annuaire Orange* (French); and other reference volumes.

Good encyclopædias publish, usually, under a "Press" classification, or "Newspapers," convenient summaries of the history of the press in each country. The *Encyclopædia Britannica*, which is kept reasonably up to date, is especially useful.

It is well to recall that London is a focal point for cables from every part of the globe; Great Britain was quick to form a chain of radio stations throughout the world after the Great War; trans-Atlantic and trans-European telephone lines center in London; and British ships and planes carry mails between London and the most remote places. By reason of its Empire, "on which the sun never sets," and its wealth, moreover, London became the financial capital of the world. As the center for trade, London also sets prices for commodities and products almost everywhere.

In the nineteenth century it became imperative for any journal with a claim to leadership in the United States or a European country to have a representative in the British capital. London and some provincial newspapers also began, about the same time, to send their own staff representatives abroad, both to report wars and to report less spectacular but no less important developments in the realms of politics, economics, and social conditions. Such dispatches as these men sent to their newspapers likewise became grist for the foreign newspaper correspondents in London.

Some of the latter correspondents were, in fact, native Britons, usually journalists themselves. They were engaged on a salary of sorts to write weekly letters or more frequent dispatches for a foreign paper, or perhaps several papers. Others, of course, were sent to London especially to serve their newspapers. Occasionally, a non-British citizen would reside in London and serve as correspondent there for a newspaper published in a third country, which mayhap he never had visited. In general, this situation continues to be true, except that the correspondent is increasingly likely to be a citizen of the country to which his dispatches go.

Four British press associations occupy leading positions. Reuters concerns itself with foreign news and has news-exchange arrangements with foreign associations, as already described. The London representatives of the foreign associations are entitled to receive the Reuters' service and edit it for relay to their own central offices at home, whence it may be distributed in brief or extended form, more or less altered, to newspapers entitled to the service in that country.

Besides Reuters, there are others, including the Press Associa-

A PRINCRES & S SALE .
MUNICH FRIDAY. THE FOUR DAYS SALE O THE CONTENTS O THE LEOPOLD
PALACE IN MUNICH THE PROPERTY O THE LATE PRINCESS GISELA O BAVARIA
DAUGHTER O THE EMPERUR FRANZ JUSEF O AUSTRIA WS CON
CLUDD THIS EVNG.   THE SALE NOT ONLY ATTRACTED DEALERS AND
COLLECTRS FRM NEARLY EVERY EUROPEAN CAPITAL BUT WS A SOCIAL EVENT
O IMPORTANCE.

PRINCESS ' S SALE PAGE 2.
IT MARKED THE BREAKING O A LINK WITH THE EUROPE DAYS GONE BY.
AN ASTOUNDING FEATURE WS THE LOW PRICES FETCHD BY ITALIAN REN
AISSANCE FURNITURE , CARVED CHESTS INCLUDG ONE O
VERY RARE WRK DATED ABT 1550 FETCHG PRICES RANGING FRM £10
TO £27.
END PAGE 2.

PRINCESS'S SALE PAGE 3.
TODAYS INTEREST WS CENTRD ON THE SALE O ABT 20 PIECES O
FURNITURE WH THE PRINCESS HD INHERITED FRM HER MOTHER THE EMPRESS
ELIZABETH O AUSTRIA AND WH HD BN ORIGNLLY HOUSED IN THE ACHILLEION
CASTLE IN CORFU. HERE AGN PRICES WR LOW.
THE BEST PRICE TODAY WS REALISD BY " A FISH AND STILL LIFE FIGURES"
BY JOACHIM BUECKHLAER (B 1553) THE DUTCH PAINTER WH FETCHD
£340.

6.34 P.M
              ENGLISH NAVY HELPS GREECE.
ATHENS FRIDAY.-
     MR V. CAVENDISH-BENTINCK THE BRIT
ISH CHARGE D-AFFAIRES CALLED ON THE
PREMIER M. VENISELOS TODAY TO SAY
THAT H.M. GOVT AUTHORISED HIM TO
STATE THAT IF THE ASSISTANCE OF THE
BRITISH MEDITERRANEAN FLEET WAS RE-
QUIRED TO HELP IN THE WORK OF RESCUE
IN ANY OTHER AREA DEVASTATED BY THE
EARTHQUAKES THE GOVERNOR GENERAL OF
SALONICA COULD ADDRESS HIS REQUEST
DIRECT TO ADMIRAL CHATFIELD IN COMM
AND OF THE FLEET. M. VENISELOS THANK
ED H.M. GOVT FOR THEIR KINDNESS.
     SLIGHT EARTHQUAKE SHOCKS HAVE BEEN
FELT IN THE CHALCIDICE REGION TODAY.
              EX.TEL.CO.

FIG. 16. BRITISH PRESS

For description see

R E U T E R S

GERMAN GOVERNMENT INTERNATIONAL 3 1/2 PERCENT LOAN.

B A S L E, NOV.28.

THE BANK FOR INTERNATIONAL SETTLEMENTS, TRUSTEE FOR THE GERMAN
GOVERNMENT INTERNATIONAL 3 1/2 PER CENT LOAN 1930, ANNOUNCES THAT,
INASMUCH AS THE PROVISIONS OF ARTICLE VI OF THE GENERAL BOND REQUIRE
THAT THE PAYMENT OF PRINCIPAL AND INTEREST IN RESPECT OF ALL ISSUES
OF THE LOAN SHALL BE EFFECTED ON A GOLD BASIS, SPECIAL ARRANGEMENTS
HAVE BEEN MADE IN CONNECTION WITH THE PAYMENT OF COUPON NO.5 OF THE
STERLING AND SWEDISH CROWN ISSUES, DUE 1ST DECEMBER 1932.

AS THE ACTUAL AMOUNT PAYABLE HAS TO BE THE EQUIVALENT OF A FIXED
GOLD VALUE, AS OF THE DATE, IT IS NOT POSSIBLE TO DETERMINE
THAT AMOUNT UNTIL THE DUE DATE, 1ST DECEMBER 1932.

IN THE CASE OF THE STERLING ISSUE, PAYMENT OF THE NOMINAL
AMOUNT OF COUPON NO.5 WILL BE EFFECTED ON 1ST DECEMBER 1932, AND
A SUPPLEMENTARY PAYMENT OF THE DIFFERENCE BETWEEN THE NOMINAL AMOUNT
AND THE ACTUAL AMOUNT PAYABLE WILL BE EFFECTED NOT LATER THAN FIVE
DAYS THEREAFTER. FOR THE SWEDISH CROWN ISSUE THE WHOLE OF THE
ACTUAL AMOUNTS PAYABLE IN RESPECT OF THE VARIOUS STERLING AND SWEDISH
CROWN COUPONS WILL BE ANNOUNCED IN A PRESS COMMUNIQUE ISSUED ON
1ST DECEMBER 1932. REUTER.

!141KLE!9DD

477.

CONTRADICTIONS AT LAUSANNE.

FRANCE AND GERMANY AT LOGGERHEADS.

M HERRIOT-S STATEMENT.

(FROM CENTRAL NEWS SPECIAL CORRESPONDENT).

(LAUSANNE   TUESDAY).

THERE WERE EXTRAORDINARY CONTRADICTIONS IN
LAUSANNE   TONIGHT. THE CAUTIOUS BUT
DEFINITE OPTIMISM ON THE BRITISH SIDE
CONTRASTS IN AMAZING FASHION WITH THE
UNRELIEVED PESSIMISM OF THE FRENCH.
THE SUGGESTION OF THE IMMINENT BREAK-UP
OF THE CONFERENCE DOES NOT APPEAR TO BE
JUSTIFIED AT THE MOMENT ALTHOUGH ITS
CONCLUSION AT A FAIRLY EARLY DATE IS
EXPECTED. EVENTS MAY TAKE A NEW TURN TOMORROW
WHEN IMPORTANT CONVERSATIONS ARE TO BE
CONTINUED BOTH BETWEEN THE FRENCH AND GERMAN
EXPERTS AND BETWEEN THE CHIEF POLITICIANS
THEMSELVES.
END 1.

ASSOCIATION NEWS COPY

List of Illustrations

tion, a branch of Reuters concerning itself with domestic news, the Central News and the Exchange Telegraph Co.

Newspapers possessing unusual services of news from at home or abroad sometimes resell their dispatches, in proof or typescript form, to foreign newspaper or press association representatives in London. For example, all proofs of matter to appear in *The Times* of London, are received by London representatives of the New York *Times*, the *Corriere della Sera* of Milan, the *Petit Parisien* of Paris, *Asahi* of Tokyo, and the Argus newspapers of South Africa, and may be used or quoted by those newspapers. The *Morning Post*, similarly, sells its dispatches to the New York *Herald Tribune*, for one, and the *Daily Telegraph* has an arrangement with the Chicago *Tribune*.

The United Press of the United States receives, in its London office, not only the service of the British United Press, but of the Exchange Telegraph and of the Central News, and it gets proofs from the *Daily Express* and the *Evening Standard*. The International News Service also receives the Exchange Telegraph and Central News services at its London office, providing a European coverage as well as a good news basis on which a correspondent may work in London. The Associated Press has its exchange arrangement with Reuters, maintains its London bureau in the same building with that association and receives its service. It also receives the Press Association and the Exchange Telegraph services.

Afternoon newspaper representatives in London rarely have affiliations with the British newspapers because the London afternoon newspapers are indifferent in quality, and also because the correspondents can buy the morning papers and get their news tips without cost. They sometimes receive press association services, however, especially Central News and Exchange Telegraph.

*   *   *

As an originating point for news, London always has been important. It is the center of the British Empire, and all governmental news becomes significant. The Houses of Parliament, the Government ministries, the Royal Family, the law courts, all are active sources. So are the various embassies, legations and consulates. Downing Street and Whitehall are constantly in the world news. In practice, most governmental news of interest abroad emanates from the Foreign Office, the Prime Minister's office, and the Colonial Office. As a business center, London is second to none, and the news of the "City," London's banking and trade section, always is important, with the Bank of England standing as a financial colossus. As a social, artistic, cultural and educational center, London is outstanding. Sports also are important. All of these aspects of the news are reported by the newspapers and press associations.

News, however, is not *easy* to get! There is no great willingness to coöperate with the press, snubs are common, many officials do not submit to interviews, news sources that would be open in the United States—such as hotel registers and police records—are closed in Great Britain, and it is impossible to lift reports from any newspaper, since a certain property right in news has been established, and most newspapers sell the exclusive rights to their news services.

Although most departments of the British Government, since the Great War, have had spokesmen to meet the press and explain government policies, the cabinet members themselves rarely meet journalists, and then usually only to give background information. Members of the government must not be quoted on state affairs and must remain anonymous, save when they make public addresses. This accords with the doctrine of cabinet responsibility, which means that the entire cabinet is bound by anything one member may say, whether in a speech, interview, or otherwise. This unwritten rule makes members cautious about saying anything of importance to the press.

The news department of the Foreign Office does not, as in some European countries, act as a central press bureau for all ministries, gathering data and arranging interviews. Instead, each ministry in London has its own press staff. But the Foreign Office department is the most active, and it is closely allied to the Prime Minister's office. Once a day the press comes in group fashion to ask questions of the department's spokesmen. Ordinarily, only a few jour-

nalists will attend this conference unless there is a crisis of some
sort, or unless news is scarce in other quarters. There rarely are
any "handouts." Instead of such prepared and mimeographed
statements, direct questions are asked, and there are comments
and explanations.

Although this Foreign Office news conference is informal, there
is a tendency on the part of officials to speak guardedly and carefully because the journalists present represent papers of various
opinions and nationalities, and there might be an inclination on
the part of some to misinterpret or sensationalize certain statements, while other statements might be sincerely but completely
misunderstood.

More important work is done in the afternoon, when individual
correspondents call on members of the news staff, often by
appointment, to discuss specific topics. Then information can and
is given with a degree of frankness dependent upon the proved
trustworthiness and character of the individual and his paper.
Much background information, not for publication, is provided.
The callers will be leader writers for British newspapers, special
correspondents of newspapers in various lands, and other journalists, all interested in what lies behind the bare bones of the news.
Few reputable correspondents have had cause to feel that they
were being handed propaganda at these meetings, for the press
staff has won general respect by its ability as well as by its frankness.

What the correspondents write on the basis of these conversations is likely to be used under formulas such as, "it is said in
Whitehall," "in official British circles," or "high officials believe."
There are six or seven American correspondents calling at the
Foreign Office to one from any other foreign press. Next in number are the French and German representatives, but most other
journalists in London take their news second hand through Reuters or some other agency, or through exchange arrangements with
some one of the London papers. If, by chance, a correspondent
picks up information at one of the embassies or consulates, rather
than at the Foreign Office, he will ascribe it to "diplomatic
circles."

The Foreign Office news department receives and reads all the British newspapers, but few others. Instead, an attaché or secretary of each British embassy is expected to read the newspapers of the country with special attention. Unless a story is objectionable, Whitehall does not hear of it. But if it is, the report is forwarded by mail or cable, and the correspondent responsible is invited to call at the Foreign Office press department, where he will be asked about it. The Foreign Office believes that no correspondent wants to be inaccurate or will mind correction if he has been in error. If he merely has been careless, or has "guessed," he is reminded that the official viewpoint always is available. Even if he has been really "mischievous" in intent and action, he will not be barred from further Foreign Office press conferences, although it is quite true that he probably will receive little information of value.

The Foreign Office does not expect that the correspondents will accept without question all they are given. That office does not insist that its own is the correct view or the only right view, necessarily, but the view it gives out is *official,* and should be so regarded.

Correspondents seldom give offence by what they write. But the Foreign Office has found that such troubles as do arise in the publication of news in the foreign press concerning British affairs, come, as a rule, from three sources. One is the prejudice or bias of the newspaper's owner, leading him to demand that news be distorted or treated in a misleading way. The second is the influence on newspaper policy coming from business interests and pressure groups of various kinds, including readers who have strong prejudices. The third is the type of headline that misleads, and it is one of the commonest and most serious sources of trouble. The headline sometimes reveals the editor's lack of information or comprehension, or it deliberately supports one of his prejudices or the special interests mentioned, or, striving for an effect in order to catch the reader's interest, departs from strict accuracy.

Most foreign journalists in Great Britain agree that no official effort is made to impose a censorship or to foist propaganda upon them. Nothing, that is, beyond an occasional protest to a story that is regarded as exaggerated or untrue.[2]

The British press itself does suppress a considerable amount of news. But, as in the censorship during the War, it is largely a voluntary suppression, in the interests of "good taste," tradition, loyalty, or perhaps it is news suppressed under the formula that it is "not in the public interest." A sincere sense of national loyalty or interest in the public welfare dictates such procedure on the ground that some news might create unnecessary panic or distress.[3]

Because of this attitude it has been said that Britain has a "disciplined press," although not a censored press, and the government is capable of asking, or arranging, to have unwelcome news stories withheld from publication, and has done so.[4]

[2] The Foreign Office in 1920 protested the United Press reports about the starving of Lord Mayor Terrence MacSwiney of Cork as too sympathetic to the Sinn Feiners. The United Press had received a telegram at the same time from the Sinn Feiners, complaining that the United Press was too pro-British in the matter. This latter telegram was shown to the Foreign Office official who had complained. He laughed, and there the matter dropped.

[3] Stories about members of the Royal Family, of a sort that might seem to invade their privacy, or might prove embarrassing, usually are suppressed by the British press. An excellent example was the omission by the press in the summer and autumn of 1936 of stories and pictures recording the friendship between Edward VIII and Mrs. Ernest Simpson, a friendship which resulted in his abdication. It even has extended to the extraction of pages from foreign magazines, such as *Time,* and banning foreign papers from sale. Anon., "Restraint of Press Poses British Issue," New York *Times* (Oct. 18, 1936), Part IV, p. 4, col. 8; Anon., "Innocents Abroad," *Time* (Oct. 26, 1936), pp. 21-23; Anon., "Simpson Case a 'Headache' to Press," *Editor and Publisher* (Nov. 14, 1936), pp. 7, 35; Anon., "British Break Gag on Simpson Story," *Editor and Publisher* (Dec. 5, 1936), p. 36; Anon., "Simpson Story Jams Cables, Wireless," *Editor and Publisher* (Dec. 12, 1936), p. 6; Arthur Robb, "Shop Talk at Thirty." (Discussion of suppression of Simpson case news in Britain), *Editor and Publisher* (Dec. 12, 1936), p. 56; Arthur Robb, "Shop Talk at Thirty," *Editor and Publisher* (Jan. 23, 1937), p. 52.

[4] A classic illustration occurred when the British fleet was concentrated in the Mediterranean in the summer of 1935, at a time when there seemed danger of an Anglo-Italian clash. Even though the details of the fleet movements were known to journalists everywhere and were made the basis for prominent reports in some other lands, the British press published almost nothing about them. John Gunther, *Inside Europe* (9th imp.), pp. 236-37.

In addition to the news that it originates, London also receives news from all parts of the world. The multitude of affairs that center in London bring information, and the regular news correspondents for British newspapers and press associations pour in their dispatches by mail, telephone, wireless and cable. Reuters, particularly, and Central News, to a lesser extent, have correspondents in other cities and countries. The more important newspapers with representatives abroad include *The Times,* the Manchester *Guardian,* the *Morning Post,* the *Daily Telegraph,* the *Daily Express,* the *Daily Mail,* the *News-Chronicle,* the *Daily Herald,* the *Observer,* and the *Sunday Times.* These are all morning newspapers, the last two appearing on Sunday mornings. Evening papers publish very little foreign news.

The correspondents on the continent of Europe have transmitted news to London almost entirely by telephone since about 1930. The telephone messages may be relayed through Paris or Berlin. The lines are engaged for several prearranged periods of approximately 20 minutes each during the evening, beginning at

As another example, Sir Austen Chamberlain, then Foreign Minister, in a conference with British journalists at Geneva in 1931 expressed the view that President Hoover of the United States evidently did not think much of the Kellogg-Briand Pact as an aid to peace, since he had just signed a bill appropriating $600,000,000 for the American Navy, and also implied that probably the United States would not help to put teeth in the pact by joining with European nations in enforcing it.

When Whitehall learned that the Foreign Minister had spoken slightingly of the United States, every one of the 17 journalists who had attended the conference was reached individually and asked to suppress the story, in the interest of amity. They did so.

But some American newspaper men heard of the affair through the "Geneva grapevine" (to be explained in the section following, on Geneva), and had cabled stories to New York, where they were used, gathered up by British correspondents there and cabled back to London, where the story then received wide attention, despite the original effort by the government to hush it up. Albin E. Johnson, "International Affairs Need Publicity," *Editor and Publisher* (Apr. 25, 1931), p. 36.

Winston Churchill described the situation when he said during a speech in the House of Commons Oct. 26, 1936, that the British press "has freedom plus responsibility." It is that "responsibility" which is otherwise described as "disciplined." Mr. Churchill's remark was reported in the New York *Times* (Oct. 28, 1936), p. 3. Its specific reference was to the Simpson affair, which had not yet received publicity in the British press.

about 6 P.M. and continuing until midnight. Matter from the Far East arrives by Great Eastern and Great Northern telegraph, while news from South America arrives by Great Western, and that from North America comes by Imperial, Western Union, Commercial Cable, and sometimes by wireless. Regular mail and air mail bring additional matter.

In the telephone system, the correspondent writes his message in full and reads it over the telephone. It is taken down in shorthand or on a dictaphone. This gives the correspondent a little more chance, as a writing man, than he had when cable and telegraph tolls compelled him to be brief, above all. The telephonists in London type out the messages from their shorthand notes or from the cylinder, making a dozen or more carbon copies for distribution to leader writers and special editors as well as for the sub-editors who prepare the news for publication in the usual way.

The dispatches, as received and published, not only become the food for opinion in the nation, but are read with special interest by foreign journalists in the British capital. And, in evaluating what they read, it is important for the correspondents to understand what each one of the British newspapers stands for in its ownership, policy, conscience, influence and competence.[5]

So *The Times* has long been known as a conservative organ, in its tone if not strictly so in its politics. Although not the official spokesman for the government, its policy is at least tolerant toward any government that is in power. It is generally regarded as the best British newspaper, has the best news service, prints more news, and is one of the finest newspapers in the world. It is well informed, it is accurate, it is well intentioned, it is so situated as to be practically beyond pressure by political or commercial or

[5] An excellent and always up-to-date listing of London and British newspapers, periodicals, press associations, journalistic organizations and current press representation of foreign newspapers and agencies in London appears in the reference book *Europa*, V. 1, under "Great Britain—the Press." See also: *Willing's Press Guide* (annual), and *Who's Who in Press, Publicity, Printing*, for useful listings relative to the British press abroad and of the foreign press in Britain; and the *Political Handbook of the World*, under "Great Britain." Circulations are noted in the *Editor and Publisher International Year Book*. Also, Low Warren, *Journalism from A to Z*.

THE ✣ TIMES

LATE LONDON EDITION · LONDON FRIDAY MARCH 31 1933 · PRICE 2d

The Morning Post.
THE EMPIRE'S SENIOR DAILY

LONDON, FRIDAY, MARCH 31, 1933 · LONDON LATE EDITION · ONE PENNY

DATE OF WORLD CONFERENCE

The Daily Telegraph

LONDON, FRIDAY, MARCH 31, 1933 · LONDON LATE EDITION · ONE PENNY

LONDON EDITION

The Manchester Guardian

FRIDAY, MARCH 31, 1933

Daily ✣ Mail
FOR KING AND EMPIRE · BROADCASTING PAGE 6

BRITISH PROTEST TO FRANCE

FRIDAY, MARCH 31, 1933 · ONE PENNY

Daily Express

FRIDAY, MARCH 31, 1933 · ONE PENNY.

Daily Herald

FRIDAY, MARCH 31, 1933 · ONE PENNY

News ✣ Chronicle

FRIDAY, MARCH 31, 1933

AMBASSADOR'S NIGHT DASH FROM MOSCOW

FIG. 17. MORNING NEWSPAPERS OF GREAT BRITAIN

For description see List of Illustrations

FIG. 18. SOME LONDON SUNDAY AND DAILY NEWSPAPERS
For description see List of Illustrations

social interests. It prefers to be right, rather than first with a story, if, of course, it cannot be both. So it sometimes lets itself be "scooped" in preference to using a story not complete and accurate in detail.

It has prejudices, however, reflected in its columns, such as a marked hauteur in its attentions to the Soviet Government. But, generally speaking, its correspondents in foreign countries are capable, and it insists that they must be free agents, unhampered by censorship. Rather than have them submit to government regulations, it has withdrawn correspondents from Russia, Yugoslavia and Brazil. On its staff have been such men as Sir William Howard Russell, Henri de Blowitz, J. D. Bourchier and H. Wickham Steed. Its editors have included John Walter II, John Delane, Thomas Chenery and others. Its triumphs have been many, and, although it passed through a difficult period, it now is occupying once more a preëminent position in world journalism.

The *Morning Post* has a lineage dating back farther than *The Times,* and it has been extremely energetic in its pursuit of news. It has been well edited, at times, and has had some able correspondents, as it has to-day. It has suffered in the esteem of some, however, because of an excessive conservatism. More than *The Times,* it has stood for tradition, the perpetuation of the class system, and has believed in a God-given British national superiority. That it has pleased a large number of readers goes without saying, but the *Morning Post* has become a symbol of bourgeois smugness.

The *Daily Telegraph* is an excellent newspaper, second only to *The Times* for news, but for some reason more respected editorially on the Continent than in Great Britain. It is a competently made newspaper, with an unspectacular but reasonably able news service. There have been some great men on its staff, including Dr. Émile Dillon, long its Russian correspondent. It was one of the first British newspapers to station a permanent correspondent in the United States. Mr. Percy Bullen set up an office in New York in 1905, as its representative, and A. Maurice Low was its correspondent in Washington for many years.

The Manchester *Guardian* is the greatest of three or four excellent provincial newspapers, and by some it has been regarded as the greatest British newspaper. It rose to special fame under the editorship of the late C. P. Scott, whose policy always was one of intelligent and generous liberalism. It has maintained capable correspondents at important points and has permitted them to write freely of events within their own news spheres. Although its volume of foreign news is smaller than that in *The Times,* some discriminating persons consider its reports the best. The generally high average of writing and the liberality of thought reflected, has made the newspaper respected and widely read.

The *Daily Mail* was started by Lord Northcliffe (then Alfred Harmsworth) and Kennedy Jones in 1896 on an adaptation of the formula by which Joseph Pulitzer built the New York *World* to financial success in the years following 1883. The formula worked as well in London as it had in New York, and the *Daily Mail* became the corner stone of the Northcliffe newspaper empire, already founded upon the snippet-weekly, *Answers.*

The *Daily Express* is Lord Beaverbrook's most important newspaper. It is published not only in London, but editions appear simultaneously in several cities of the British Isles. Enterprising and lively, with some alert correspondents, its large circulation has been built with the aid of prize contests, premiums, entertaining editorial features, and racing odds, rather more than upon the quality of its news service, the wisdom of its leaders, or the altruism of its management.

The *Daily Express* is so much like the *Daily Mail,* which it copied, and the *Sunday Express* is so much like its counterpart, the *Sunday Dispatch,* that there is no important difference. All are commercial journals of great prosperity and with circulations of from one to two millions. They are interested in startling their publics, even if they have to give the news to do it, but news usually is subordinated to other appeals unless it is the sort that lends itself to sensational treatment. After Northcliffe's death in 1922, his brother Harold (Lord Rothermere) took over his interests.

The *News Chronicle* is a lineal descendant of the old *Daily News,* edited briefly by Charles Dickens and distinguished for its war correspondence in 1870 and at other times, and of the West-minster *Gazette* and the *Daily Chronicle*. It supported the Liberal party, when there was one, with Lloyd George as one of the owners in the past. It remains liberal and, in many ways, bright, lively, admirable, and of large circulation. Its service of foreign news is good, if more limited than that offered by some of the other papers mentioned. It also has experts writing on financial and other special subjects.

The *Daily Herald*, official paper of the Labor party, and with the Trades Union Congress General Council represented on its directorate, has grown large in size and circulation during the years since 1930, attaining first place among the mass-circulation papers in 1933, with more than two million readers, a height achieved during a mad scramble for circulation. Correspondents watch it, but regard it as generally lacking in authority or full dependability in its news reports.

The *Financial News* is a useful paper for information about business, commerce and finance. It gives the reaction of the City to events at home and abroad.

The *Observer* is published only on Sundays, edited by J. L. Garvin, and owned by Lord Astor. Its articles on most aspects of public affairs and interests are competent. The paper is independent, with conservative leanings.

The *Sunday Times,* owned by the Camrose interests, who also own the *Daily Telegraph,* is another weekly newspaper of a quality very like the *Observer.* It has no relation to *The Times* of week-day publication.

These newspapers, all of which are morning publications, are much read by foreign journalists stationed in London. In addition, they read the *Evening Standard,* the best of the three week-day evening papers published in London. It is owned by Lord Beaverbrook. Its cartoons by David Low and its columns of comment are its most interesting features. The *Evening News,* a Rothermere paper, and the *Star,* owned by the publishers of the *News Chronicle,* are the other evening papers. The *Star,* especially, puts emphasis on horse-racing news and betting odds.

The *Daily Worker,* a Communist paper, is little read.

Some of the good provincial papers, in addition to the Manchester *Guardian*, are the Yorkshire *Post*, the Leeds *Mercury*, the Edinburgh *Scotsman*, the Glasgow *Herald*, the *Western Morning News*, the Birmingham *Post* and the Belfast *News-Letter*. They are read in some London newspaper offices and sometimes by foreign journalists.

Other periodicals which receive careful attention from correspondents in Great Britain include the *Spectator*, *Time and Tide*, the *New Statesman and Nation*, the *Economist*, the *Statist*, some of the quarterlies, and the weekly and monthly reviews, including *International Affairs* and some other publications of the Royal Institute of International Affairs; the monthly publications of the big London banks, government reports, and current books. The correspondent's reading literally is never done.

* * *

So far as concerns the foreign news published in the British newspapers, it is not great in volume, due partly to space limitations. But such news as does appear is of three or four kinds: that which concerns Great Britain and the Empire; that about important political, economic, and social events, and about striking incidents abroad; and news that is of little or no importance, but that is interesting or amusing. Even matters of importance occurring at home may receive scant treatment, judged by American standards.[6]

In what they do print, even some of the more conservative papers show a preference for news of disasters, crime, and the misadventures, escapades, and personal lives of widely known individuals. This has meant the publication of considerable news, some of it true and much of it shamelessly sensationalized, about gang warfare and violence in the United States, about motion

---

[6] At the time of the London Naval Conference of January, 1930, only four London newspapers gave the negotiations consistently prominent position. They were the *Daily Telegraph*, the *News Chronicle*, the *Daily Express* and the *Daily Herald*. Even those papers averaged less than a column each day. Unless something "official" was given out, little or nothing would be published, for there was no disposition shown by British journals or journalists to "dig" for facts or to indulge in interpretative or speculative stories.

FIG. 19. SOME PROVINCIAL PAPERS AND LONDON SUNDAY PAPERS

For description see List of Illustrations

picture actors and actresses, especially about their marriages, divorces, and peccadillos; about wrecks, earthquakes, floods, murders, and personal tittle-tattle from every part of the world.

This sort of news, often "tendentious" in its effect, is largely misrepresentative of the nations from which it is supposed to have come. It sows seeds of misunderstandings by the false impressions it gives. Sometimes it arouses dislike and hatred by presenting provocative accounts without concern for their accuracy or at least without the necessary discounting qualifications.[7] The British press is not a serious offender in this regard, as compared to some national presses, but the picture of the outside world often is misleading.

*   *   *

The number of foreign correspondents in London has, in general, increased from year to year. The membership of the foreign press is constantly shifting. They form two organizations, which makes it possible to know approximately how many there are at a given time. The Foreign Press Association, established in 1888, is the oldest, the largest, the most all-embracing, the most influential. The American Correspondents' Association is smaller, and is hospitable to English-speaking journalists of all lands, including Great Britain.

Many of the news offices are in or near Fleet Street, the journalistic center of London. The press association bureaus are busy

[7] Albert Bushnell Hart, "America in the British Press," *Current History* (May, 1929), pp. 305-307. A minor illustration occurred in 1928 when Miss Amelia Earhart flew the Atlantic, the first woman to do so, and landed in Wales. She was quoted in one British newspaper as having said, "Wal, I sure am glad to be here, and gosh! I sure do want to meet the Prince of Wales." This was a complete fraud and presented a well-mannered and well-educated girl in a ridiculous light. When picked up and reported in the United States it roused ire because many saw it as evidence that Britons wished to belittle a remarkable girl and make sport of a nation. See: Anon., "Fanning Hate Flames" (editorial), *Editor and Publisher* (Sept. 22, 1928), p. 32. References to the United States as "Uncle Shylock," especially in the French press, were in the same classification. Although generally offering to readers the best and most complete foreign news service of any national press, some newspapers in the United States offend grievously in presenting "tendentious" matter.

at all times. Correspondents serving morning newspapers are busiest in the late afternoon and early evening hours, while those serving afternoon newspapers are busiest in the late morning until shortly after noonday. Actually, however, they are busy at any or all times, because the news is developing constantly. That does not mean they will be in their offices, necessarily, because the pursuit of the news may keep them moving about.

There are more American correspondents in London than there are correspondents for newspapers of any other country. Taking, as an example, the staff of a London bureau for a morning newspaper and its syndicate in the United States, procedure will be somewhat as follows:

The office consists of a suite of two or more rooms. A boy may open the office and make it orderly after 8 o'clock in the morning. A secretary-stenographer-assistant will be the next to arrive, and then the "second" man, if there is one as assistant to the chief of the bureau. He will have his regular tasks to perform, either in or out of the office. Perhaps there will be one or two other junior correspondents, who also will proceed without instructions.

The head of the bureau, who is chief London correspondent, and may be director of the paper's European service as well, arrives at 9 or 10 A.M., depending upon the amount of work to be done, or the way in which he has organized it. He reads his mail, which will include some publicity material and several feature articles or queries from freelance writers, communications from his home office and from other correspondents. He disposes of this business by tossing most of the publicity matter into the wastepaper basket, looking over the freelance material and ordering or buying only occasionally. What he buys will be forwarded to the United States. The other mail will be answered as circumstances require.

The correspondent probably has read one or two of the London morning newspapers at breakfast or on the way to the office. Now he reads any others that are important and possibly sees one or two continental papers as well. He is an expert at this job, and reads very quickly, taking in at a glance the general drift of the stories. He gives the closest attention to the most significant devel-

opments in politics or finance, and to social movements of importance or of spectacular character. He may see an opportunity, in
connection with certain stories, to arrange special handling, or to
get a good interview during the afternoon. He looks for human
interest stories, and notices editorial treatment of American or
other news, because this may be of interest in the United States.

Very often he must consider picture possibilities in connection with special articles or feature stories that he is sending. He
watches for items, large or small, in which Americans are involved.
The press associations also will watch such matters, but if the
American comes from a city represented in the newspaper syndicate, or would be of special interest for some other reason, the
correspondent follows up the incident, whether it occurred in London or elsewhere in the United Kingdom. He may do it himself
or have an assistant do it if the story is in London, or he may do
it through a British press ticker service in his own office, through
the newspapers, through news correspondents with whom he has
arrangements, or possibly he can cover the story by telephone.

Very many of the stories he ignores, even when they seem
fairly important or would seem to have an interest in the United
States, because he knows the press associations will verify, elaborate where necessary, and transmit them.

After his analytical reading of the news, the chief correspondent has decided what story or stories should be worked up during
the day. He makes a sort of schedule, possibly only in his mind.
If he has assistants, he may give them assignments, much as a
city editor would do in the United States. Some stories, or at least
certain angles of them, may be covered by telephone from the
office. News reports from the press association, or newspaper
proofs are read by the chief correspondent or an assistant and
evaluated against a fund of background information. Presently,
the chief correspondent may leave the office to visit persons and
places in search of information.

*   *   *

The assistant, or assistants, if they are plural, have arrived
early, and have read the papers with care. During the day they

will cover certain routine sources, or events, some of which have been foreseen. Or they build up features or special articles. They edit dispatches for transmission, or copy to be mailed. So much special study is required in connection with the news, that they must devote some time to research. The day is not always highly productive for the foreign correspondent any more than for a reporter in the home office. But at home or abroad there are times when he more than makes up for the easier days.

At about 1 P.M. the chief correspondent probably goes to lunch. Very often he will take from one to two hours, and will go to a club or restaurant or hotel frequented by politicians, leading business men, bankers, writers, artists, or others who are doing things and who know what is going on. There, also, he will meet other journalists of various nationalities, and they often have interesting news tips to share or exchange, since most of them work for noncompetitive newspapers, often newspapers published in different countries.

The friendships made over a period of time bear fruit at such meetings. Conversations may suggest stories, new light may be thrown on events, unexpected angles may be turned up. But the correspondent must dig to get his story. Any one can read the newspapers, even follow up obvious tips, and rewrite what appears in other publications, but real talent is shown in initiative, resourcefulness and energy in uncovering exclusive stories.

In the afternoon the correspondent may return to the office. On some days he will call on friends and acquaintances and make new ones. He will see or telephone to press officials in Downing Street, in the Foreign Office, in the various ministries. If he can get into the lobbies or galleries of Parliament, and thinks it worth his while to do so, he may go there. In any case, he knows, from reading and conversation, something of what is brewing, and he is digging constantly for more details—enough details to serve as a basis for a story, probably an interpretative story, and—he hopes—an exclusive story.

Once a week or oftener he will call in and see the American Ambassador at the Embassy. He may visit the Consulate. He talks to the commercial attaché and others. He may call at certain hotels to interview prominent Americans, or others stopping in London. He knows that Americans who are close-mouthed with newspaper men at home sometimes become almost garrulous when abroad. There often are special meetings to be covered, either in the afternoon or the evening. The chief correspondent or an assist-ant attends many of these.

Late in the afternoon, or after dinner, the correspondent returns to his office. If he has time, or if there seems reason to do so, he reads the afternoon papers carefully. At any rate, somebody in the office does so, and anything requiring it, is investigated. Loose ends of some story may have to be caught up by telephone. Between 4 and 6 P.M., depending upon circumstances, and some-times later, the chief correspondent begins to write what presum-ably will be·the leading story from London in his paper the next morning. He will use the information he has gathered himself, matter obtained by assistants, matter taken from the London press, or press associations and rewritten for American consump-tion. The correspondent, because he understands the general situ-ation and usually knows the ownership and bias of the newspapers that he has read, can arrive very often at accurate and interesting conclusions.

* * *

After finishing his file, which may be by 5 P.M. but probably is not later than 8 P.M., the chief correspondent may still have a formal dinner or reception or meeting to attend. His table at home will be piled with reports, books, reviews and other matter to be read.

One of the assistants remains in charge of the office. He sees that the copy written during the day goes off by cable or radio, or by mail, and he stands ready to relay messages received by wire or telephone from other European correspondents. He also watches for late news developments originating in London, or reaching there from other sources. At 8 P.M. in London it is only 3 P.M. in New York, so that there is ample time for transmission across the Atlantic, and time to send a considerable volume of matter forwarded from Continental Europe.

The relay job is this: Bucharest or Rome, for example, may be the scene of some event. The correspondent who has gone there, or who is covering for the paper there, files his message at 2 P.M. in Bucharest. Possibly it is delayed, for some reason, and only reaches London at 7 P.M. Even if such a message is telephoned through, direct, the question is, shall it be forwarded to New York? Perhaps it does not seem so important to the London bureau as it did to the correspondent in Bucharest. Possibly later developments in London or Paris have put an entirely new face on the situation. The money spent for getting the message to London has been wasted because the story must be discarded. But that is part of the business, and some such wastage seems unavoidable.[8] Or, on the other hand, perhaps the story can be edited to make it conform to the later developments, and then it will be sent along. That is for the editorial assistant in London to decide, and it gives him a real responsibility. Perhaps a message must be translated from French or German and then be forwarded. If it is something very important it may be sent by cable and radio, both, to insure its earliest arrival in New York, but that would not be usual.

Or a story may come through to London from Moscow or Berlin or Paris, to be relayed to New York over cables from London because some big news in France or Southern Europe has clogged the French cables to New York. The news ticker in the office keeps the correspondent in touch with all that happens during the evening. Proofs come from the London paper with which this American paper has an arrangement, and may provide added information worth forwarding. When the first editions of the London morning papers are on the street all of them are brought in. The correspondent looks through them to see that he has missed nothing. This is about midnight. He may take the papers out with him while he has a midnight lunch. It still is only 7 P.M. in New York, 6 P.M. in Chicago, 5 P.M. in Denver, and 4 P.M. in San Francisco, so that last-minute additions or corrections may be sent.

[8] One American press association estimates that about 15 per cent of the matter received by its London bureau from European sources is not sent on to New York, for one reason or another.

After midnight there is little to do, but it is considered wise to keep the office open until 1 A.M. or even as late as 4 or 5 A.M. There always is a possibility that something unexpected may develop. At 4 A.M. in London it is only 11 P.M. in New York, so that a message sent from London could make the 1:30 or 2 A.M. edition in New York.

Correspondents for those individual newspapers which do not syndicate their dispatches, usually are entirely alone, without assistants, excepting possibly stenographer-secretaries. Such a correspondent may work during the afternoon and evening. He will seek interviews and will hold conversations with friends and officials. He will read the newspapers with care. In the evening he will produce stories covering the subjects of interest to the readers of his newspaper, and will see that those stories are transmitted.

Correspondents in London for Continental newspapers often use the telephone in sending their dispatches, getting a connection at specified times, direct from London to their home offices in Paris, Berlin, Hamburg, Milan, Rome, or elsewhere.

The special correspondent in London for an afternoon paper in the United States works intensively from about 9 A.M. until 1 or 2 P.M., by which time he must file for the afternoon editions on the other side of the Atlantic. Urgent matter can be filed up to 7 P.M. which is 2 P.M. in New York and earlier in cities farther west, but the afternoon papers wish to have as much copy on hand as early as possible so that they can plan their editions most easily. In the afternoon, the correspondent continues to be busy, working up stories for later use, visiting officials and others in London, and perhaps in the provinces. He follows much the same procedure, and depends upon the same news sources as the morning newspaper correspondent.

The press associations must work 24 hours a day, since they are serving newspapers in all parts of the world, with deadlines arriving somewhere at frequent intervals. Also, they are dealing primarily with *events*, which may occur at any moment, rather than with analyses or interpretations or "situation" stories, which concern the special correspondents more particularly. All of this means that the work is especially intense and fast for the press association correspondent with the only "let-down" occurring in the early hours of the morning.

* * *

In London, as at any post, an understanding of the nation's people and the country as a whole is the most useful and most essential equipment for a correspondent. A thorough knowledge of history and economics is very desirable, as it is everywhere, and the correspondent also should be able to adapt his manners and habits more or less to those of the country, if he wishes his personal life to be pleasant.

§ 2. PARIS AND WESTERN EUROPE

PARIS is a center for all of the news of France and its widespread political, commercial, artistic and colonial interests. Much news of Spain and Portugal, of Belgium and Switzerland, and some news of Italy, the Balkans, and even of South America filters through Paris. It is the capital of the Latin world. It is second only to London as headquarters for foreign press services, and every press association or newspaper which has any European coverage at all maintains an office in Paris. A few newspapers have correspondents in Paris and none in London.

France attained a high news importance during the Napoleonic era. It was at about that time that British papers began to reach abroad for reports of events. Both newspapers and press associations developed from rather rudimentary beginnings during the nineteenth century, particularly in their presentation of foreign news. London newspapers maintained correspondents in Paris beginning in 1815. North American newspapers followed considerably later, and in no important numbers until after 1900.[9]

[9] Sisley Huddleston, "Correspondent in Paris," *Blackwood's* (Sept., 1924), V. 216, pp. 321-31. Mr. Huddleston says "the most important executive newspaper post in the world is that of the Paris correspondent of *The Times.* It has great traditions, and Paris has during the past few years become the ·very center of diplomacy." Mr. Huddleston at that period himself represented *The Times* in Paris. He reports that Lord Northcliffe, speaking from the British point of view, "put the capitals outside of Great Britain in the fol-

The Agence Havas, the largest of the French news agencies, whose history already has been noted,[10] parallels in its growth the history of the modern press in France. Havas also controls another French news agency, the Agence Télégraphique Radio, which specializes in political and financial news. The Agence Radio, as it is called, was set up in 1919 to compete with Havas, but subsequently was taken over by the older agency. Where Havas exchanges news with Reuters, the Associated Press, and other agencies belonging to the world league of news agencies, the Agence Radio exchanges news with the United Press.

Havas also controls Fabra, the Spanish agency, and Fabra has withdrawn its representative from Paris. Havas covers the news of Spain and Portugal through this connection. It also has long been active in gathering news of Latin America and providing news to Latin America, but North American agencies have made great advances in that territory since 1915.

Beginning in 1931 the Havas agency began to extend its operations to the radio, broadcasting news throughout France and, by short wave, to the French colonies in North Africa and to South America and the Orient. In 1933, by a liberalization of its exchange arrangements with the Associated Press and other agencies, it became free to sell its service in the United States, and found its first client in a radio group which wished to have foreign news to add to its own domestic reports.

A third major press association in France is the Agence Fournier, an independent organization distributing financial and political information of a somewhat special nature.

Correspondents in France have learned to discount in one way or another almost every item of information that reaches them through the French press or press associations.[11]

lowing order (of news importance): 1. Paris; 2. Washington; 3. Tokyo; afterward came Berlin and other European capitals."

[10] See pp. 55-59.

[11] An annual summary of the French press and press associations appears in the reference book *Europa* under "France—the Press." See also: *Political Handbook of the World* under "France"; *Annuaire de la Press, Française et Etrangère,* for a complete list of publications in France and in other countries; *Annuaire Orange,* under "Les Journaux et leurs principaux collaborateurs."

AGENCE HAVAS

PARIS, Jeudi 5 Janvier 1933
20 HEURES
PREMIÈRE FEUILLE

[Reproduction, récexpédition, communication à des tiers, ou utilisation quelconque, interdites sauf accord avec l'AGENCE HAVAS.]

DÉPÊCHES TÉLÉGRAPHIQUES

FRANCE

Un vœu de la Chambre de Commerce

Lyon, 5 janvier

Au cours de sa dernière séance, la Chambre de Commerce de Lyon délibérant sur le projet de loi relatif aux transports des marchandises par mer, a adopté un vœu qui conclut à l'adoption de l'article 10 du projet, qui, en ce qui concerne...

BELGIQUE

Anvers

Bruxelles, 5 janvier

Le *Soir* publie la dépêche suivante de Luxembourg :

Un remettant en ordre la cellule de Constantinoff, le gardien de la prison a trouvé sur la planchette de la fenêtre jointe en noir, inscrits à l'aide d'un clou des mots en allemand composant des déclarations incohérentes.

« J'ai fait sauter la cathédrale de Kral Torganis, et financé 80.000 levas, police bulgare n'en sait rien ni compagnons de cabaret. J'ai suborné Matievic parce qu'il était un patriote serbe chauviniste. Vive la révolution, vive l'anarchie ! »

Matievic ou plutôt Matijevik est l'autre assassin du curé Koch et a été condamné par la Cour d'assises aux travaux forcés à perpétuité. Ce dernier a fait l'aveu que Constantinoff lui avait raconté qu'il avait assassiné à Paris un riche Bulgare. Ces faits ont été communiqués par les autorités luxembourgeoises aux autorités bulgares qui ont ouvert...

En ce qui concerne l'opposition, il se confirme qu'elle ne pourra pas constituer un parti unique avant le scrutin. Il importe, cependant, de constater que, si tous les petits groupes qui combattaient dans le dernier parlement la politique de M. de Valera tombent d'accord pour un peu plus d'entente, ne sont tous résolus à combattre nettement le Fianna Fail.

Le parti travailliste, qui a pris la décision de soutenir M. de Valera, ira en fin par 25 candidats, le Fianna Fail 90, et celui de M. Cosgrave — favorable au recensement — comprend 153 députés. (Havas)

ITALIE

La perte de l'Atlantique »

Rome, 5 janvier

... Confédération nationale fasciste des entreprises de transports maritimes et aériens à l'occasion de l'incendie de l'Atlantique a adressé au comité central des armateurs en France le télégramme...

I/20/10   (X47)

Washington, 20 octobre

Questionné aujourd'hui au sujet du manifeste international des industriels suggérant une modification des tarifs douaniers, le président Coolidge a répondu :

Bien que je n'aie pas eu le temps d'étudier le manifeste à fond, il me semble qu'on ne peut pas faire grand chose aux Etats-Unis pour stimuler le commerce européen en révisant le tarif douanier américain sans risquer d'abaisser les conditions de vie aux Etats-Unis. Ceux qui ont consenti des emprunts internationaux sont naturellement en faveur d'un libre échange virtuel et il en est de même pour les importateurs, tandis que les ouvriers et les industriels préfèrent le protectionnisme.

Le président a exprimé l'avis .... e intéresse surtout les nations europé.....

On fait observer à Was........

peut modifier la polit.....

question de tarif........

feste, provoqu.......

de la n.......

URGENT

SERVICE SPÉCIAL de l'AGENCE HAVAS

À REMETTRE DE SUITE AU PORTEUR

du NEW-YORK-HERALD

HEURE DE DÉPÔT

SAINT-SIÈGE

Anniversaire

Cité du Vatican, 5 janvier.

Le onzième anniversaire de la mort du Pape Benoît XV tombant le dimanche 22 janvier, les cérémonies funèbres à la chapelle sixtine seront célébrées le lundi 23 en la présence du Pape.

Le cardinal La Fontaine, en qualité de premier cardinal, créé par le Pape défunt, chantera la messe de Requiem en présence du Pape, qui donnera l'absoute devant le catafalque qui sera très élevé près du trône. (Havas)

FIG. 20. NEWS AS IT IS

For description see

SIÈGE CENTRAL
PARIS
55 et 57, Boul. Haussmann
R. C. Seine N° 128,070
Adresse Télégraphique :
TURADIO-PARIS

AGENCE TÉLÉGRAPHIQUE
"RADIO"
Société Anonyme au Capital de 5.000.000 de fr.
INFORMATIONS DU MONDE ENTIER

TÉLÉPHONE :
ANJOU 65-00
65-01, 65-02
65-05, 65-06
65-07, 65-08
INTER : ANJOU
221 - 222 - 223 - 224 - 228
226 - 227 - 232 - 238

" TÉLÉFILS "   7 DÉCEMBRE 1932 - 19 heures 15   n°36

INFORMATION PARLEMENTAIRE

Le communiqué officiel de la Commission des Affaires Etrangères de la
Chambre

PARIS, 7 décembre -
Voici le communiqué remis à l'issue de la réunion de la
commission des Affaires Etrangères

"La commission des Affaires Etrangères, réunie sous la
présidence de M. François Albert, a procédé à un échange de
vues sur la situation extérieure.
"L'audition du Président du Conseil devant avoir lieu ven-
dredi, la commission a décidé d'ouvrir, à la suite de cette audition, un débat sur les dettes franco-américaines.
"A l'issue de ce débat, la commission désignera le rapporteur des propositions de résolution relatives à l'échéance du
15 décembre. (Agence RADIO)

C'EST BIEN LA JALOUSIE QUI EST CAUSE DU DRAME DE LA RUE
LAFAYETTE

SIÈGE CENTRAL
PARIS
55 et 57, Boul. Haussmann
R. C. Seine N° 128,070
Adresse Télégraphique :
TURADIO-PARIS

AGENCE TÉLÉGRAPHIQUE
"RADIO"
Société Anonyme au Capital de 5.000.000 de fr.
INFORMATIONS DU MONDE ENTIER

TÉLÉPHONE :
ANJOU 65-00
65-01, 65-02
65-05, 65-06
65-07, 65-08
INTER : ANJOU
221 - 222 - 223 - 224 - 228
226 - 227 - 232 - 238

SERVICE DE L'ETRANGER

6 DÉCEMBRE 1932 - 13 HEURES 40   N° 10 SH

ETATS-UNIS

LE PAQUEBOT ITALIEN " COMTE DI SAVOIA " DOIT
STOPPER EN PLEINE MER

New-York, 6 Décembre -
De même que le paquebot " Rex ", le transatlantique
italien " Comte di Savoia " qui effectuait son premier voyage
de retour des Etats-Unis, a dû stopper en pleine mer pendant
9 heures, par suite de la rupture d'une conduite au turbo-
générateur. (Agence RADIO)

U.R.S.S.

LE GENERAL CHINOIS SOU-PUNG-WEI AURAIT CHERCHE
A SE REFUGIER EN TERRITOIRE SOVIETIQUE

Londres, 6 Décembre -
Des télégrammes reçus de Moscou et émanant des autorités soviétiques à la frontière mandchoue, affirment que le général chinois Sou-Pung-Wei aurait abandonné les forces rebelles
en Mandchourie et cherché à se réfugier avec son état-major,
en territoire soviétique. (Agence RADIO)

MANDCHOURIE

L'AVANCE DES TROUPES JAPONAISES CONTINUE

Moukden, 6 Décembre -
Une dépêche de Tsitsikar annonce que les troupes japonaises avancent partout avec rapidité. Les rebelles chinois sont
complètement mis en déroute. (Agence RADIO)

SI M. POINCARE POUVAIT
PARLER.

*Voici le bilan financier qu'il tra-
cerait de trois mois d'ordre, d'efforts et de confiance.*

*Des chiffres officiels et inédits
sur*
Nos impôts : Le Trésor : Nos dettes

Dans le cabinet du Louvre, qui
est celui du grand argentier de
France, et où ont passé tour à tour
l'irrésolution, l'inquiétude, l'agitation, l'angoisse, nous avons enfin
depuis dix semaines, vu s'installer
en maîtres souverains le travail,
l'ordre, la méthode. Et la confiance
les a suivis. Et l'argent a suivi la
confiance...

Il ne nous reste plus que dix
mois à parcourir pour qu'une année, où les hauts et les bas s'alter-
nèrent de façon dramatique, soit
close. Au seuil de ces deux der-
niers mois, j'ai pensé qu'il conve-
nait de tracer le tableau exact de
la situation financière de la France.
Et j'ai été frappé à la porte de
l'homme qui a pris le navire dans
la plus effroyable des tempêtes et
qui, l'ayant d'abord conduit en
mer plus calme, tente aujourd'hui
de l'amener au port.

M. Raymond Poincaré m'a-t-il
ouvert ? M'a-t-il parlé ? A quoi bon
le détail ?... Il est entendu que le
président du conseil a prêté serment de ne pas se laisser inter-
viewer. Le serment présidentiel
doit être et sera tenu. Aussi bien
n'était-ce pas des déclarations que
j'étais allé chercher au palais du
Louvre, mais des chiffres. Et ces
chiffres, le président ne pouvait
me les refuser, parce qu'ils appar-
tiennent au public qui y a droit.
Si, n'ayant pas prêté serment, M.
Raymond Poincaré avait pu parler
au journaliste, voici, en lui don-
nant les chiffres, ce qu'il lui aurait
dit : -

LES IMPOTS RENTRENT

— Dans une lettre du 30 septembre au président de la commission des finances de la Chambre, j'ai été obligé de parler du
retard anormal qu'avait présenté
cette année l'émission des rôles.
L'évaluation budgétaire des impôts à recouvrer en 1926 par l'administration des contributions directes, impôt foncier, impôts sur
le revenu, taxe civique, vieilles
contributions-dont une part doit
revenir à l'Etat) était de 7.429 millions. Or, au 31 juillet, c'est-à-dire
au lendemain du jour où le cabinet actuel est arrivé au pouvoir, le
total des rôles émis ne dépassait
pas 66 %. Mais au 30 septembre,
les rôles émis s'élevaient à 6.289
millions, soit 84,6 %. Au 30 octobre, le pourcentage a atteint 90 %.
Le retard est donc comblé.

« Naturellement, les recouvre-
ments suivent de près la courbe
des émissions de rôles. Les con-
tribuables, bien qu'ils aient répondu avec un empressement patrio-
tique à l'appel du gouvernement, ne
payent guère que lorsqu'ils ont reçu leurs feuilles. Plus nous avan-
çons dans l'année, et plus les paye-
ments s'accélèrent. Les moins-va-
lues disparaissent, les plus-values
s'accroissent. Deux exemples seulement : nos vieilles contributions
directes qui, au 31 août, présen-
taient encore une moins-value de
14 %, offraient au 30 septembre
une plus-value de 40 % ; de même,
le recouvrement de l'impôt sur le
revenu qui, au 31 juillet, n'accu-
sait que 8 % d'augmentation sur
les chiffres de 1925, offrait au 30
septembre une augmentation de
33 % sur ces mêmes chiffres. Au
total, l'ensemble de nos recouvre-
ments budgétaires qui, au 31 juil-

DISTRIBUTED IN FRANCE

List of Illustrations

French newspapers, although some of them are very rich, and although many of them have "foreign editors," maintain only limited foreign news representation. For that reason, the newspaper reader of France learns relatively little of foreign affairs from his paper. The newspapers themselves are physically small, so that they do not have space for much news. This reduces the volume of domestic news, also. Most of the papers prefer to depend upon Havas for news, both foreign and domestic, even when they can afford foreign representation, because it would be economically impractical for them to maintain such a system with so little space available in which to print the reports that would be written. Yet, even Havas has only a small foreign representation, preferring to place chief dependence upon its exchange arrangements with press associations to give it coverage abroad.

There are more French correspondents in London than in any other foreign capital, although the French press also is represented in Geneva, Berlin, Moscow, Rome, Buenos Aires, Shanghai, Tokyo, New York and Washington.

Foreign news in French newspapers usually consists of bare facts only. These are submitted to the reader, who may form his own opinion of their significance, or who may turn to the editorial columns for interpretations, which are frequently far from objective. When the item is of importance to France it often is made the springboard, in some newspapers at least, for a longer article, written by an authority and explaining the entire situation from beginning to end. At times, these articles are "inspired" by governmental or other interests. The French foreign correspondent does not need to interpret the news, even to the extent that an American or British correspondent sometimes does; in fact, he is discouraged from doing so. Mail stories are well liked by Paris newspaper editors, especially such stories as have an historical twist that makes them "stand up" for more than the day.

* * *

The foreign correspondent in Paris is nearly as free of restriction or interference as he is in London or in Washington. He has four chief sources of information, even as in London. He may cover a story himself. He may have an assistant, possibly a French journalist, help him cover such news as develops at the Ministry of Foreign Affairs, at some other government ministry, at the Chamber of Deputies, at police headquarters, et cetera. He may have an arrangement to receive advance proofs or special information from some one of the Paris newspapers. He reads the French press carefully for such ideas and suggestions as it may contain.

News of personalities is important to correspondents stationed in Paris, which is a crossroads of the world. This means obtaining interviews and watching for deaths, marriages and divorces, or has in the past. But, in addition, Paris is a vital center for news of political and economic affairs. The government is almost constantly active, and meetings or conferences of international importance gather often in the French capital.[12]

A Paris correspondent for an American morning newspaper puts in a day much like a London correspondent's day. He reaches the office at 9 or 10 A.M., reads the mail and the morning papers, sees visitors, maps out the day's work for himself and his assistants, if any. He lunches at some news center, which may be the weekly meeting of the Anglo-American Press Association, at which distinguished guests sometimes speak. In the afternoon he visits various news sources. He may not call on officials so much in Paris unless he is fluent in the French language, or unless some of the officials speak English. He covers, or has an assistant cover, routine sources, such as the Foreign Office, the Chamber of Deputies, the United States Embassy and Consulate, the American Chamber of Commerce, the American Club, which has weekly luncheons that sometimes are of news importance; perhaps the American Church, the American Hospital, undertakers who do most of the American "business," the big hotels and bars patronized by prominent visitors, and other sources.

[12] Since the Paris Peace Conference of 1919 to 1920, there have been such gatherings as the Dawes Conference of 1924, the Young Reparations Conference of 1929, meetings of the League of Nations Council, the signing of the Pact of Paris (Kellogg-Briand Pact) in 1928, and others.

Journalists representing British or other national newspapers will have their corresponding sources.

Later in the afternoon the correspondent may meet a "tipster" or two. These are persons of various nationalities, men or women of a type indigenous, particularly, to the continent of Europe. For a price, they divulge information that they consider may be of interest. The correspondent also sees French journalists whom he pays to keep him informed on affairs in certain fields of activity. He reads the afternoon newspapers, and then writes his dispatches.

If the correspondent is acting for a London newspaper, or for some Continental paper, he almost certainly telephones his dispatches; otherwise he will telegraph, cable or radio them. An assistant may remain in the office until sometime between 12 midnight and 2 A.M., reading papers and proofs, relaying messages from Berlin, Rome, Madrid or Vienna, and standing ready in the event of need. Correspondents plan their time in Paris as in London, since the hours are the same.

Although the motivating power of France lies in the provinces, it is a curious fact that foreign correspondents rarely go, themselves, into those provinces, except when some striking event calls them. This is understandable, because it is impossible for a correspondent to be everywhere at once, and he *must* be in Paris most of the time, since it is there that the political and other forces make themselves felt, wherever they may originate. A foreign press association may maintain contact with the provinces through native correspondents in the various cities, and some Paris correspondents read certain provincial papers carefully.[13]

Although many papers and press associations have kept full-time staff correspondents at Geneva, it also has been a common practice to have the Paris correspondent go to Geneva when the news warranted. The same was true of important news breaking in Brussels, Madrid or Barcelona. Some Paris correspondents

[13] Leland Stowe, then Paris correspondent for the New York *Herald Tribune,* did the unusual thing in the spring of 1934, when he actually did tour the provinces. Anon., "France: Beyond Paris," *Time* (May 28, 1934), pp. 19-20.

became almost as familiar with one or two of those cities as with Paris itself.

A press association covering France reports the news in greater detail, and more factually than a special correspondent, who selects only certain affairs for attention. Ideally, a press association handles the news through a system modeled on that of an American newspaper covering a large metropolitan district. The United Press illustrates the method in the organization it maintains in France. All the papers are read, and staff members cover everything that should be covered. There also are available as assistants more than a hundred native correspondents in all parts of France, many of them editors of leading provincial newspapers. When news breaks in any part of France, the United Press receives a telephone call or places its own call to establish quick communication with one of these informed persons nearest the scene, and so gains prompt coverage. The news, once written and edited, is "typed off" on a Creed typewriter keyboard in the office, and is in New York in less than a minute, going via Commercial Cables, passing through the Paris office and on to the cable to Newfoundland and the landwire from there to New York.

* * *

News gathering is something of a task in France. First, there is a language barrier, and then there are different customs and habits of thought. "Journalists" are considered a somewhat lower form of life until they become editors, when very often they are as much feared as respected. French reporters, as a class, are underpaid and sometimes turn to what would be unethical practices in Anglo-Saxon countries to find means to augment their incomes. They act as representatives for individuals, causes, organizations or businesses. They write what amounts to publicity for their "clients," and manage to have it appear as news in one or more newspapers, for which they themselves may work. Or they accept what amount to bribes to get items published, or to suppress them. Occasionally even widely known journalists use extortion to extract money where they believe they can do so.

French persons often assume that foreign correspondents are

of the same breed. They ignore reporters if they wish and dare to do so, and their privacy is guarded more than it would be in the United States, although perhaps very little more than in Great Britain. The telephone service has not been very good in Paris, moreover, which has helped them to avoid reporters who might otherwise have reached them in that way.

The police do not, as a rule, recognize journalists—foreign or otherwise—as entitled to any special courtesies in their pursuit of the news. It is partly for this reason that most Paris police news of interest to foreign readers is gathered by French reporters, who are acquainted with the police through long association, and operate on a basis of personal friendship and *quid pro quo*.

Underlings in government offices, or elsewhere, are rarely more helpful to a foreign journalist. Any person who does not know the correspondent socially probably will not answer his questions, for any one of several reasons: Because he does not know the answers, because he sees no personal advantage to himself in bothering to answer, or because he is too lazy or apathetic to find out. The only solution is personal acquaintance, or acquaintance with some one who can introduce the reporter properly and formally to the one who has the information.

Personal acquaintances are of the greatest value to the reporter anywhere, and not least in Paris. Correspondents representing newspapers and press associations spend a considerable amount of time forming acquaintances, entertaining them, trying to do them favors, bringing them information which will win a regular welcome, and offering them chances to make money by writing articles for foreign publications. Many French politicians are journalists, anyway, and some of them write more or less regularly for publications in the United States and Great Britain. They are asked to do so, very often, to win their regard so that correspondents serving the newspapers or press associations for which they write may approach them for information.

* * *

Although the Foreign Office, or the Quai d'Orsay, as it is commonly called, assigns a secretary to meet the press representatives, the relation between the press and the Foreign Office has not been so frank and helpful in Paris as in London or Washington. It is much more difficult to get at the official views.[14]

In Washington all press representatives, foreign and domestic, attend the same press conferences. At the British Foreign Office no distinction is made. In Paris, however, there are two conferences and, in addition, there is a third conference attended by six or eight correspondents for French newspapers in special sympathy with the government or occupying particularly important positions in the journalistic world, and hence useful to the government. To these few favored men the Premier himself, or the Foreign Minister, speaks with considerable frankness.

This is one reason why some French newspapers are especially helpful to foreign correspondents. By reading between the lines of articles in the papers known to be represented at this special conference, a correspondent may discern what the French Government wants the readers of that paper to believe, and from that he sometimes can make useful deductions.

Even though the foreign press is not permitted to attend these inner sessions, some of the favored journalists turn about and sell information so gained to one of the foreign correspondents, and perhaps to other papers in Paris or France, as well. That is to say, one of the favored ones receives a fee for acting as a "tipster" for that correspondent or that newspaper. Moreover, the French Government knows that these men are acting thus, and itself

[14] The problems confronting correspondents in Paris, as elsewhere, have changed since 1914. For example, the relation of government to the press has been much liberalized. In France a secretary at the Foreign Office long had been assigned to meet journalists and explain government policy. When the Associated Press established its Paris office and told the Foreign Minister about the hundreds of newspapers to which it provided news, other American correspondents in Paris were notified that instead of applying to the secretary at the Foreign Office, they might ask their questions of the Associated Press, which would be kept directly informed by the government of France. A delegation of correspondents from the four most important American newspapers immediately waited upon the Foreign Minister to explain that this method would not satisfy competing papers. It was not until the distribution of war news forced a new policy, however, that the system was instituted by which correspondents were able to meet with a responsible Foreign Office official.

makes use of the circumstance to "plant" certain ideas or information with the foreign press. The tipster will not, of course,
betray secrets intended only for his own information because then
he would be stricken from the favored list.

The Foreign Office holds four press conferences daily. The
first is at 12 noon and another is at 7 P.M., both for the French
press. At 12:30 noon and at 7:30 P.M. the foreign press is met
similarly. Communiqués sometimes are given out, and sometimes
foreign correspondents are referred to Havas or to a certain Paris
newspaper for data. This, however, is not considered a satisfactory system, especially because it may mean subscribing to the
Havas service, at considerable expense, or else waiting until some
Paris paper prints the Havas dispatch, which means loss of time.[15]

A new policy in French governmental press relations, intended
to correct the previous faults, was instituted in 1933 under the
direction of M. Pierre Comert, long the successful French director
of the Information Section in the League of Nations Secretariat.
He improved the situation somewhat.[16]

*   *   *

[15] The French Foreign Office, in the past, has been so slow to speak that
it has resulted in unfavorable publicity for the country. So, in the spring of
1932, when the story was current that France was attacking the dollar in
international exchange, there was no denial from the government, although
the story apparently was untrue and could have been disproved.

It was not until the time of the Great War, in fact, that the French
Government made the slightest effort to modernize its press relations. Franklin D. Roosevelt, then Undersecretary of the United States Navy Department, holding an informal press conference in Paris after the entrance of
the United States into the War, gave French journalists their first taste of
such practices, and told them that it was the usual thing in Washington.
This annoyed M. Clemenceau somewhat, since he did not want to see the
older method changed by setting new precedents.

[16] Anon., "France Establishes Propaganda Bureau," *Editor and Publisher*
(Mar. 25, 1933), p. 16. M. Comert disclaimed the word "propaganda,"
however, in an address before the Anglo-American Press Association in
Paris on Jan. 4, 1933. He said that all he hoped to do was: 1. To provide
easy and rapid access to all the news; 2. To remove discrimination against
the foreign newspaper men, since the foreign journalist at the time was
not permitted to gain direct and intimate knowledge of government affairs.
That knowledge was reserved to a few favored French journalists, who in
turn became "tipsters" for foreign journalists; 3. To encourage the frank

France is considered one of the free press countries of the world, and the French press, in truth, is free to print what it wishes. At the same time, no press is free from certain restraints and obligations. The press of France is at the disposal of the French Foreign Office when a united front seems required on any subject affecting the foreign policy of the country. In matters which do not involve the foreign relations of France, the domestic press frequently attacks the government, and otherwise shows unlimited independence.

Yet, free though the press is, neither discipline of correspondents nor censorship is unknown in France. An example of the former occurred in 1928. In that year there was signed an Anglo-French naval agreement. The news that such an agreement had been signed became known, but the exact nature of the agreement itself remained unknown. The uncertainty stood as a threat to Anglo-American friendship, and to Franco-American friendship. Presently, the Hearst newspapers published the agreement in full in the United States, and it proved to be a fairly harmless document after all. But in Paris, the Hearst Universal Service correspondent who had cabled the dispatch was arrested, and held incommunicado by the police for seven hours, questioned, and given his choice of five years in jail or agreeing to leave France within a day or two. He chose to leave France.[17]

exchange of views between the journalists and the government so that the government may learn in advance what effect a proposed or actual French act may have abroad.

The French Foreign Office also objected to the word "propaganda" being applied to its efforts to improve French press relations. The word implied that France sought to "disseminate information that is not true," whereas "all France asks is that the truth shall be made known."

Lucien Romier, "Tribune Libre: La Réforme de Notre 'Propaganda,'" *Le Temps* (Jan. 2, 1933), p. 1.

[17] Anon., *Not to Be Repeated*, pp. 292-95. This book contains a declaration that France classifies all foreigners either as "friends of France," meaning that they approve of everything French; or as "enemies of France," including even those who criticize only one aspect of French life, while approving everything else. Correspondents feel this distinction, perhaps unpleasantly, if they try to be objective, the more so because their home office may consider them pro-French anyway, for reasons cited on p. 40, note 5, ante.

Anon., "France Orders U. S. Correspondent Expelled," *Editor and Publisher* (Oct. 13, 1928), p. 5.

The expulsion of this correspondent was exceptional, because France rarely takes such action. It came about because the correspondent was supposed to have bribed a government official to get a copy of the treaty, and this was regarded as a serious offense.

At times of crisis, moreover, the French Government has been known to impose a real censorship, even though only a temporary one, by bottling up the news for short periods, refusing to let news messages cross the frontiers until it is deemed expedient. Sometimes pressure is brought to bear upon the domestic press as well. Despite the fact that censorship is forbidden by the French Constitution, the letter of the law is evaded by delaying correspondents' dispatches for an hour or more, until the crisis is past, until the government has had time to take certain actions calculated to discount the effect of the news abroad, or until the news contained in the dispatches is so old that it has lost its first publication value.

This method has been used at times of cabinet crisis and resignations, when President Doumer was assassinated in 1932, upon the death of important men, in periods of violence or riot. Although not advertising such actions, the Quai d'Orsay justifies them in private simply by saying that "a government has to protect itself, and has a right to do so." There can be no denying that. Correspondents have evaded the censorship by using the telephone or prearranged code.[18]

---

[18] The news of the Doumer assassination, for example, was telephoned by one press association from Paris to its Berlin office and thence to London. The French censorship stopped all communication with London direct, including the telephone, but forgot the Berlin wire. The story was bottled up, otherwise, for 1 hour and 15 minutes.

When the Chamber of Deputies voted on payment of war debts on Dec. 13, 1932, correspondents worked as long as 18 hours without ceasing. Then the censors held up their messages for two hours after the vote, an act which was protested by the Anglo-American Press Association. Only one report went out, and that reached London by a prearranged code. Although the censors, acting on orders, stopped all debt stories, they did not question the report of a certain sports event, which conveyed the debt information in other terms.

On another occasion, however, the censors were over-suspicious. Then, the routine Bourse quotations sent daily to South America by the United Press aroused the suspicions of an inexperienced clerk in the Commercial

Actually, however, the Foreign Office does not concern itself directly with the censorship. It is the Ministry of Commerce, Posts, Telegraphs and Telephones (P.T.T.) which places men in the cable offices to inspect messages filed and to send them over to the Ministry for further consideration if there is any doubt about them.[19]

The French newspapers are not censored, but are controlled by their loyalties, by government subsidies, and by advertising placed through the Agence Havas, which is itself close to the government and is the recipient of subsidies. Because of this relationship, also, the foreign news and much of the national news distributed by the Agence Havas, may be controlled by the government, especially since it owns all the communications lines in France.

At the beginning of the so-called Stavisky affair in France, early in 1934, strong pressure was brought upon the press to suppress information about it. A Bill was introduced by the Ministry of Justice to make "libel punishable with from one month to one year in prison." In two years Stavisky had spent 3,000,000 francs for press bribes.[20]

Riots in the Place de la Concorde in March of 1934 also resulted in a censorship on outgoing cable messages, a circumstance countered by some newspaper men by telephoning their dispatches to London for use or transmission.[21]

From April to July, 1935, an unofficial censorship on outgoing cables was in effect. It began after Chancellor Hitler, in Germany, issued conscription orders, and it applied to all French military movements. Later it was extended to all news about the value of the franc. All messages dealing with these matters, if filed at the government telegraph, cable, or radio offices, were ordered sent to Cables office. He sent the message to the proper department, and the French "black chamber" worked on it all night, trying to decipher that which was not coded at all.

[19] Constantine Brown, "Censors Grip Most of World's Press," *Editor and Publisher* (April 21, 1934), p. 15.

[20] Leland Stowe, "Propaganda Over Europe," *Scribner's* (August, 1934), pp. 99-101.

[21] Wilfred Barber, "On the Firing Line in Paris Riots," *Editor and Publisher* (Mar. 17, 1934), p. 22.

a central office of the Ministry of Commerce, Posts, Tele-graphs and Telephones for approval there before being dis-patched, and some of them were held up for a time or not sent at all. Again correspondents telephoned their messages to London. When M. Laval became Premier he had the censorship lifted.[22]

* * *

If France has used censorship very seldom, it has used propa-ganda as a weapon at least as much as any other country. Much of the French press has been at the service of the highest bidder wishing to use it as a means to shape opinion, whether that bidder was an individual, a business house, an industrial group or a gov-ernment. Judged by Anglo-American standards, the press, in gen-eral, has been corrupt and venal in France, and still is. As always, there are exceptions, and that must be fairly recognized.[23]

For years munitions makers paid the press for its support, but more recently they have bought several papers outright. The Comité des Forges, the French steel trust, bought *Le Temps,* which is considered the semi-official organ of the Government. The De Wendel family, which virtually owns the Comité des Forges, also owns the *Journal des Débats* and other papers, in whole or in part.[24]

This situation may be rationalized, since advertising is not de-veloped in France as it is in the United States or Great Britain, or even in Germany. The newspapers find support elsewhere.

[22] Anon., "Paris Writers' Objections Halt Censorship on News of France," *Editor and Publisher* (July 13, 1935), p. 12.

[23] Philip Carr, "French Journalism," *Contemporary Review* (June, 1930), V. 137, pp. 760-64. Robert Dell, "The Corruption of the French Press," *Current History* (Nov., 1931), pp. 193-97.

Premier Léon Blum sought by legislation in 1936 to disclose the influences owning and controlling the French press, as well as to strengthen the libel law to prevent unjust and slanderous reports, such as those said to have driven M. Roger Salengro, Minister of the Interior, to suicide in 1936.

Anon., "Blum Forcing New French Press Law," *Editor and Publisher* (Dec. 5, 1936), p. 11. See also: Anon., "Premier Forces Out Havas Director," *Editor and Publisher* (Nov. 7, 1936), p. 45; Anon., "New French Govern-ment Withdraws £30,000 Press Subsidy," *World's Press News* (July 9, 1936), p. 9.

[24] See n. 20, this chapter.

Political parties frequently subsidize papers, but such papers are so biased politically as to be almost worthless as newspapers, and the public realizes that. There remain the other papers, and they obtain their support from persons, groups, and governments, but usually on a *quid pro quo* basis.

For many years the French national budget has made provision for the expenditure of a considerable sum annually for propaganda purposes, to be spent among the newspapers, and otherwise. Indeed almost every government appropriates money for such use. In 1933, however, it became known that the French appropriations called for 33,000,000 francs ($1,320,000) for publicity at home and, more particularly, abroad. The sum would be spent to insure a favorable press, by direct subsidy and bribery, in France and in other countries where the press was open to such propositions; to give support to the Agence Havas, particularly in its radio news service to the Far East and Latin America, and for miscellaneous things, such as the production of travel motion pictures, expenses of lecturers sent to various parts of the world, maintaining information bureaus, scholarships for foreigners coming to France, providing "documentary material to such journals and organizations as may be interested," et cetera.[25]

[25] John W. Perry, "France Plans Propaganda Drive in U. S.," *Editor and Publisher* (Apr. 15, 1933), pp. 7, 34; Anon., "Propaganda Plans Denied," *Editor and Publisher* (May 20, 1933); Ellery Wood, "How France Uses Press of America," *American Press* (May, 1933), p. 3.

The 1933 budget report of the French Foreign Office to the Chamber of Deputies included an estimate of sums to be spent by European countries on propaganda in 1933. They were:

Country	In French francs	
GERMANY	256,000,000	
ITALY	119,000,000	
FRANCE	71,000,000	(Including all departments. The 33,000,000 francs noted above was entirely for the Ministry of Foreign Affairs.)
GREAT BRITAIN	69,000,000	
POLAND	26,000,000	
HUNGARY	23,000,000	
CZECHOSLOVAKIA	13,000,000	
YUGOSLAVIA	13,000,000	
RUMANIA	7,000,000	
TOTAL	597,000,000	(About $24,000,000, or almost £5,000,000)

Under Premier Blum, in 1936, there also was established by decree an inter-ministerial commission formed to coördinate the efforts of diplomatic, commercial, intellectual and tourist services supported by France in foreign countries. In effect, it was to be a publicity and propaganda bureau serving France's interests.[26]

* * *

Much of the French press takes orders from the Foreign Office, so far as concerns its attitude toward foreign nations, and a portion of the funds allotted to the Ministry for secret service and propaganda purposes goes to the newspapers to assure editorial support of government policies. The Minister of the Interior has a similar fund, which goes primarily to the provincial press. Other Ministries, such as Colonies, Beaux-Arts, and Public Works, place smaller sums at the service of publishers.

It is this general practice that makes it possible for the French

These estimates are in the *Projet de Loi*, V. 1. "Budget Général de l'Exercice 1933. Affaires Etrangères" (1933 budget report). Imprimerie Nationale (Paris, 1932), p. 331, Art. 29. Special secret funds for support of newspapers, p. 331, Art. 33. For work in France and abroad. (Oeuvre française a l'étranger), p. 332, Art. 40. Special funds for French information to foreign countries. See Anon.

Projet de Loi, V. 2, Ch. 39 (formerly Ch. 38 in earlier reports), p. 66, "Depenses d'Expansion et Information Française a l'Etranger." Much of the total requested in these pages is for expenses attendant to international conferences, missions abroad, and expenses for the receptions of foreign visitors; for French works in schools, literature, etc., throughout the world. The sums earmarked particularly for the press are not especially large, and are intended to cover the cost of providing information to the press, printing bulletins, and advertising in newspapers and journals of various kinds.

After the proposed budget requests had been acted upon by the Finance Commission of the Chamber of Deputies, a Report was issued:

Adrien Dariac, *Budget Général de l'Exercice 1933 (Affaires Etrangères)*. 2 vols. (A Report made in the name of the Finance Commission responsible for examining the *Projet de Loi*, or estimates, before fixing the final budget allowance.) No. 1535. Chamber of Deputies. 15th meeting. Session of 1933 (Paris, 1933), V. 1, pp. 147, 149, 150-51, 154, 155-59; V. 2, pp. 263-67. Such similar publications are issued by the French Government whenever the question of appropriations is to be considered.

[26] Anon., "Publicity Bureau Created in France," New York *Times* (Oct. 18, 1936); Anon., "Léon Blum Creates Publicity Bureau," *Editor and Publisher* (Oct. 24, 1936), p. 32.

Government to obtain almost unanimous support for any policy. And it is this very unanimous press support that makes public opinion in France tend to rally behind any proposal that the government wants to have supported.[27]

It need not be assumed that every minor issue becomes the occasion for distributing a subsidy, nor should it be implied that French editors and publishers are lacking in patriotic and loyal devotion to the national interest, which would lead them to support the government on most occasions in any case. But the power of the government propaganda fund, nevertheless, cannot be ignored in considering the French press.

Big private business, however, is even more important to the French press than the government, for, while it does not provide such large subsidies, it does give financial aid in other forms. So the steel trust, or Comité des Forges, under the control of the De Wendel family, owns the majority of stock in a score of Paris and provincial newspapers, including *Le Temps, Le Journal, Le Journal des Débats,* and also controls the *Journée Industrielle* and is a power in the management of *Le Matin, L'Écho de Paris,* and the Agence Havas. Most of that control centers, not in the Comité des Forges itself, but in the individual stock ownership of François de Wendel and other persons.

M. François Coty, the perfume and cosmetic manufacturer, at the time of his death, owned *Figaro* and *L'Ami du Peuple.* The oil trust, or Comité des Houillères, also has been reported to hold a

[27] Robert Dell, "Corruption of the French Press," *Current History* (Nov., 1931), pp. 193-97; Otto Lehmann-Russbuldt, *War for Profits;* Anon., "The Reptile Press," *Not to be Repeated,* Ch. 4, pp. 278-89; Francis Delaisi, *La Patriotisme des Plaques Blindes;* Anon., "War Scares and Armament Contracts," *The Secret International: Armament Firms at Work,* Ch. 5, pp. 36-42.

A defense of the French journals and journalists against such charges is written by: Georges Jubin, "Journalism in France: 1933," *Journalism Quarterly* (Dec., 1933), pp. 273-82. He writes (p. 281): "The French newspaper and newspapermen are generally very honest. The 'black sheep' are scarce; and as they will all have been tracked down soon, they will have to give up the game.... In France, government can, from time to time, and most often in the country's interest, ask the papers the favor of silence on some special propaganda, but they will not become permanently domesticated on general principles...."

large interest in *Le Temps*. The Prouvost trust, a textile group with interests in Roubaix, France, and in Pawtucket, Rhode Island, controls *Paris Midi, Paris Soir,* and *L'Intransigeant.* The Banque de Paris et des Pays-Bas finances *La Liberté* and also is said to have an interest in *Le Journal.* The Galeries Lafayette, great department stores, through their owner, finance *Le Populaire,* Paris Socialist paper, and *Petit Provençal* of Marseilles. Jean Hennessy, cognac maker, finances *Le Quotidien* of Paris.

Le Matin has, at various times, received support from big railroad companies, from the textile trust, the oil trust, the Schneider-Creusot munitions firm, the Standard Oil Company, American steel interests, and from the British Hotchkiss and Royal Dutch Shell companies. The paper, more recently, has been said to be financed by the French steel trust and by motion picture interests.

In the average French newspaper there is very little to mark the line between advertising and editorial matter. Publicity notices appear everywhere in the paper, rarely indicated to be such. In reporting sports events, for example, a French paper usually will mention the name of the automobile, airplane, or bicycle used in a race only if the maker pays for the mention. Even when distinguished men make speeches, sometimes, reports do not appear in certain papers unless payment is made, and even then the paper may demand payment on a per-line basis. This is not true of all newspapers, but it is true of some.[28] Favorable reports may be purchased on the financial pages of some newspapers, and in the columns devoted to music, art and literature.

Some individual journalists and editors in France do a lucrative business on the side. A political or foreign editor, for example, will write articles to appear in some small newspaper in the Balkans or in Japan or in a South American country, and he will receive payment out of all proportion to what he has done or what the paper in question could afford to pay him. But actually it is pay-

---

[28] During the investigation of methods used by New York insurance companies in 1905 it was revealed that some New York newspapers had accepted payment of a dollar a line for running news stories written by publicity men for the insurance companies. The newspapers concerned no longer exist. Will Irwin, *Propaganda and the News,* pp. 104-105.

ment for publicity which he arranges in the Paris paper which he serves regularly, and it comes from the foreign government or foreign banks or other interests which expect to benefit from the publicity.

In France the press is not regarded as owing any special responsibility to the people, nor do journalists appear to feel any such responsibility. Consequently ethics have a different basis and both the papers and their makers must be adjudged from their own standard. Premier Blum, in 1936, nonetheless, took steps intended to reform the situation by laws designed to purify the press, even at the cost of some liberty. At the time, the French press was entirely free, and government interference with the journalism of France has been rare. There has been little or no fear of "special interests," the advertiser has virtually no influence, and libel laws have been lax. All of this makes for a lively press.

* * *

As in every country, the press of France—and especially of Paris—is a most important aid to the foreign correspondent resident there. French newspapers, however, do require a bit of understanding. The unit of journalism in the country is not even the newspaper; it is the journalist himself. An individual journalist can make the fame of a newspaper. Signed articles are common and good photographers gain quick fame.

The French newspaper is not so imposing a thing as a London or New York newspaper. No French newspaper is so large as *The Times* of London or the New York *Times*. There are very few newspaper business successes to compare with those of Great Britain or the United States. The French paper has only a limited advertising revenue, the circulation income is not great; and the news service is inferior. In fact, they are not *news*papers at all, in an Anglo-Saxon sense. The chain newspaper idea is only beginning to penetrate France, although there are several papers of mass-circulation.[29]

[29] For an historical and contemplative view of the French press see: Eugène Hatin, *Histoire Politique et Littéraire de la Presse en France*, 8 vols.;

There are two classes of papers in the country: The *journals of information*, which specialize in news; and the *journals of opinion*, or the political press, which print some news, but usually specialize in articles that interpret and comment upon public affairs and the arts, and deal especially with politics. This latter type of newspaper represents about 75 per cent of the Parisian press, and a considerable portion of the provincial press.

Discerning observers, French and foreign both, agree that the provincial press includes newspapers that are superior to any of the Parisian press. They mention with special favor the *Depêche de Toulouse, Progès de Lyon, L'Echo du Nord* of Lille, *L'Ouest Éclair* of Rennes; *Le Petite Gironde* of Bordeaux; *Les Dernières Nouvelles* of Strasbourg, and *L'Eclaireur* of Nice.

Because the French papers are small, physically, and are not obliged by tradition to provide expensive news service, they may be started at comparatively little cost. They frequently do not own their own plants unless they are very well established, and even then a relatively modest outlay is sufficient for presses and typesetting machines required. The papers are supported, usually, by political parties, by groups which want a voice, or by individuals of wealth who may or may not have altruistic reasons for financing a newspaper.

The journals of information are business propositions, and may be supported by advertising and circulation. In such a paper a

Franz Funck-Brentano, *Les Nouvellistes;* Stéphane Lauzanne, *Sa Majesté La Presse;* André Billy, *La Monde des Journaux: Tableau de la Presse Française Contemporaine.*

The chain newspaper idea was introduced in France by Raymond Patenotre, son of a former French Ambassador to the United States, who had become owner of the Philadelphia *Inquirer.* After his death the paper was sold to American interests. Youthful Raymond Patenotre soon after began to develop a group of newspapers in France, adding to others already in the family. His newspapers in 1936 included the *Petit Journal, La Republique,* the Lyons *Republicain, Le Petit Van, La Sarthe* and *Le Petit Nicois.* He also has an interest in *l'Oeuvre* and *Paris Soir.* He appears to be trying to produce good newspapers, with good foreign news service.

The late M. François Coty (Joseph Spoturno) owned several papers at the time of his death, forming a sort of chain, while steel, chemical, textile and oil interests now own or have interests in several papers in France, as otherwise noted.

FIG. 21. SOME FRENCH PROVINCIAL PAPERS

For description see List of Illustrations

FIG. 22. FIVE BIG MORNING PAPERS IN PARIS

For description see List of Illustrations

political article may lead, sometimes on page one, sometimes on page three. Few such newspapers contain more than eight pages, and some have less. Crime has a prominent place. There is relatively little foreign news, but there are well written feature articles, including reports of expeditions and articles about social and economic subjects, sometimes by authorities.

Papers occasionally buy important, exclusive, copyrighted stories. Occasionally they send staff men on long journeys to write "impressions," and the stories resulting from this so-called *"grand-raportage"* often make interesting reading.[30] Some of them have their own correspondents about France, and even abroad, especially in London and Berlin, to supplement the service provided by the Agence Havas, but most depend upon that and other agencies for news. The news and headlines in the press often are inaccurate in facts and implications, but this seems not to disturb the French journalist, who makes no apology, and at times the light treatment of fact is deliberate and intended to accomplish some purpose.[31]

Most French newspaper circulation is through news-stand sales. Subscriptions are rare. Home deliveries are almost unknown.[32] Instead, the circulation is placed under the control of the Messageries Hachette, an agency which buys the papers in bulk and distributes them in Paris, in France, and abroad. This is the general practice in France, so that Hachette has a virtual monopoly on the distribution of all periodicals, and itself occupies a position of great power and importance, not only in France, but in some other Continental countries, where it sometimes controls the distribution of foreign publications.

Because the papers are distributed throughout the country—a feat that is possible since France is comparatively small and

[30] See, for example, those brought together in book form: Jules Sauerwein, *Que va faire l'Amérique?* M. Sauerwein, one of the best known French journalists of the present generation, is foreign editor of *Paris Soir*.

[31] Beckles Willson, "Paris Press and French Public Opinion," *Contemporary Review* (Nov., 1925), V. 128, 574-83.

[32] Out of 1,700,000 daily circulation, for example, *Le Petit Parisien* had only 65,000 mail subscribers in about 1930, and no encouragement is given to that type of circulation.

has its railways running out like the spokes of a wheel from Paris —the first "national" newspapers appeared in France. Like the London press to-day, the Paris press long has included newspapers of widespread circulation. Some now have more than a million readers, and one or two have close to two million.

It is a French habit to change newspapers frequently, but in spite of that the circulations remain fairly constant. Serialized fiction, usually of a superior kind, is used to hold readers to one paper. But, even so, the Frenchman may buy several newspapers in a day. The price is low, and one paper may deal primarily with politics, another with general news, another with business and finance, another with sports, another with literature, the stage and screen, and the arts. If his range of interests is large, he may pay somewhat more for his day's reading material than he would in New York or London, where he would find all of that combined in one larger newspaper.

* * *

The foreign correspondent in Paris must read the press with care, and needs to understand, so far as possible, what interests and attitudes are represented by the various newspapers. The paper closest to the government in power, for instance, must be read attentively because it is likely to express the official view of things. The leading paper of the opposition, similarly, is important, and so are the expressions of individuals who carry weight in French affairs.

The outstanding political papers or journals of opinion in Paris are:

Le Temps.—An important afternoon paper. Although it is awkward in size, very conservative, dull, and not widely read, it does influence leaders of French thought and reflects their views to some extent. It is moderate in its domestic political expression, but rather violent toward some foreign countries. Its "Bulletin du Jour," or leading editorial of the day, published on page one, often is written by a member of the government, or some one equally well informed about affairs, and for that reason it is read with special attention since it is supposed to express, semi-

FIG. 23. LEADING PARIS AFTERNOON NEWSPAPERS
For description see List of Illustrations

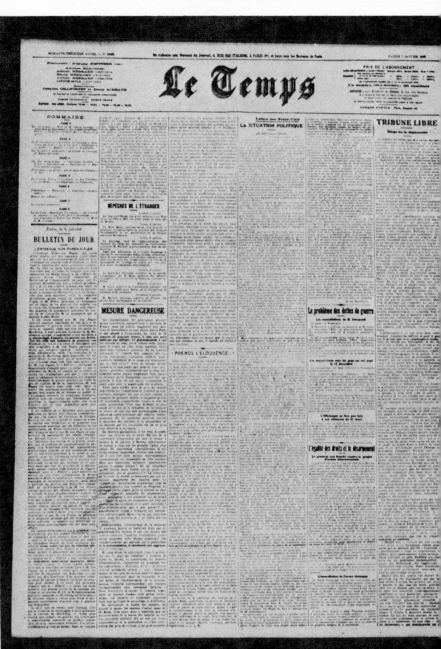

FIG. 24. THE FRONT PAGE OF *LE TEMPS*

For description see List of Illustrations

officially, the views of the Quai d'Orsay or other department of government.[33] The news sometimes is a day or two old when published, although the paper does have some special correspondents in other capitals. It is owned by members of the Comité des Forges and the Comité des Houillères.

Le Journal des Débats.—An extremely conservative and ultra-reactionary, yet semi-official paper. Much like *Le Temps* in some ways, it is more violent. It is the oldest existing paper in Paris, having been started in 1789. It is carefully read by those who wish to follow French affairs, and is widely quoted, particularly for its comment on French foreign policy. It has been very pro-British and anti-American in policy. Independent of the government, it is owned outright by the De Wendels, of the Comité des Forges.

Le Populaire.—Socialist Party organ of which M. Léon Blum has been Director and therefore reflects Popular Front views. Financed by owner of Galeries Lafayette.

La Liberté.—A Catholic nationalist paper, very conservative, nationalist, and anti-American in its views. It is financed by the Banque de Paris des Pays-Bas.

L'Oeuvre.—A paper which formerly supported Left Wing Radicals, and now is controlled by l'Agence Havas, with Raymond Patenotre holding a minority interest. It is a paper well done in a literary way, but without a strong policy at present.

L'Humanité.—Founded in 1904 by Jean Jaures, it now is the French Communist party organ. It is undependable and because it sometimes offends the government, many obstacles have been placed in its way; that is, its telephones do not work at crucial moments, telegrams fail to arrive, et cetera. Henri Barbusse is one of its editors.

L'Ère Nouvelle.—Also a daily of the Left Wing, supported by and supporting the Radical-Socialist party. During the Herriot terms as Premier it served to express government policy, and was closely watched by correspondents for that reason.

---

[33] A former Premier once remarked, humorously, that "to be successful as Premier one must have dexterity in fashioning discreet editorials for *Le Temps.*"

All the papers mentioned are published in the afternoon. Paris is more notable, however, for its morning papers. The journals of the largest circulation are morning papers, because there is time to get them distributed throughout the country during the night and early morning hours, and it happens, also, that most of them are journals of information, rather than journals of opinion.

There are, particularly, the so-called "Big Five," all papers published in the morning, and four of the five placing emphasis on the news. All have circulations of more than a million. They are:

Le Petit Parisien.—This paper has nearly two million circulation, the largest in France and one of the largest in the world. The paper itself is small, as to the size and number of pages. It sometimes is regarded as semi-official. Crime and scandal are prominent in its news columns, but it also has the best foreign news to be found in any French newspaper, with its own correspondents in London, Berlin and Washington. It is owned by Mme. Paul Dupuy, American widow of a French Senator. The paper is directed by M. Pierre Dupuy, brother of the Senator.

Excelsior.—A popular paper devoted to society and class interests, but without political concern, also is owned by· Mme. Dupuy.

Le Matin.—A conservative, nationalist, semi-official, and reasonably accurate paper, founded in 1884 by a group of American newspaper men under French patronage, but which went into other hands a year later. It has a wider news service than any other French newspaper, including a relatively large foreign service. Stéphane Lauzanne, known for his friendship for the United States, is its political editor. Marcel Knecht is prominent in the organization. Maurice Bunau-Varilla is chief owner. The New York *Herald Tribune* receives its proofs. The Comité des Forges is said to have a part interest in it now.

Le Journal.—A rather sensational paper which leads in reportorial initiative. Formerly owned by Henri Letellier, millionaire proprietor of gambling casinos at Deauville and other French resorts, it now is owned by Havas and the De Wendels, of the Comité des Forges. It is one of the few French papers with some

FIG. 25. A GROUP OF PARIS PAPERS
For description see List of Illustrations

FIG. 26. MORE PARIS NEWSPAPERS
For description see List of Illustrations

foreign representation of its own. It has been consistently anti-American.

Le Quotidien.—A Republican paper, but with Socialist leanings. During the nineteen-twenties it was a paper especially well informed, politically, and important to correspondents and others because the Socialist group was then much in power. It is now owned by M. Jean Hennessy, cognac manufacturer.

L'Écho de Paris.—Mouthpiece of aristocratic, bureaucratic, military elements in France. It is nationalistic, conservative, clerical, and appeals to army readers. It is not notably friendly to the United States, among other foreign countries, but it is pro-British. It is more strictly a journal of opinion than the last four papers mentioned. André Geraud ("Pertinax") has won special fame for his foreign and political comment in its columns. The *Daily Telegraph* of London gets its proofs.

Among other morning papers in Paris are:

The New York *Herald Tribune.*—The most important English-language daily in Paris, with European news and a cable service from the United States.

Le Figaro.—A conservative paper of good reputation. It is particularly well written and gives much attention to literary and theatrical affairs.

Petit Journal.—Owned by Raymond Patenotre. Regarded as semi-official, although not strongly political.

L'Action Française.—Organ of the extreme Right, Royalist group. Edited by Léon Daudet. The paper is anti-clerical, and was placed on the Papal Index in 1927 because of its attitude on the relationship of Church and State. It also is anti-parliamentary. Its circulation is small, especially since 1927, but it has an importance because of the faction it represents.

Some of the more important papers in the afternoon field in Paris, not already mentioned, are:

L'Intransigeant.—One of the most widely read of the afternoon papers, running more pages and more advertising than any other French paper, morning or evening. It is conservative and it publishes more news of politics, sports, and more well displayed feature articles than almost any other paper. A thorough journal of information issuing five editions daily. Purchased by Jean Prouvost.

Paris Soir.—Owned jointly by Raymond Patenotre and M. Beguin, sugar and paper magnate. It is an evening journal of information that has won popular favor during recent years, taking the lead in evening circulation in Paris, a position previously occupied by *L'Intransigeant.* Although it does not stress politics, it is Left in its general attitude. The New York *Times* receives its proofs. M. Jules Sauerwein, formerly long associated with *Le Matin,* is foreign editor.

Paris Midi.—Owned by the Prouvost trust, textile manufacturers. It has a special foreign news service, and tries to be impartial and intelligent.

L'Information.—An important and widely read paper devoted chiefly to business and financial news.

Paris probably has more newspapers than any other city in the world, and there are many periodicals, daily, weekly, and monthly, so far unmentioned, but devoted to news and to special interests. Some of them are read with care by foreign correspondents in France. Any list would include, among a great many others, *La République, L'Ami du Peuple, Le Journal Officiel, L'Homme Libre, Le Peuple, Jour, L'Ordre, L'Auto, L'Avenir, La Volonté, Petit Bleu, Journée Industrielle, Victoire, Candide* (weekly), *Gringoire* (weekly), and such others as *l'Illustration, Lu, Notre Temps, Crapouillot, Annales Politiques et Litteraire, Revue des Deux Mondes, Mercure de France,* and *L'Europe Nouvelle.*

§ 3. GENEVA AND THE LEAGUE OF NATIONS

THE LEAGUE OF NATIONS, the International Labor Office, and organizations that have grown up around those two post-war creations have made Geneva a news center of importance to the world. It also has made the attractive Swiss city an active propaganda center. In eclipse during 1936-1937, it may resume its prominence.

The first session of the League Assembly took place in 1920, attracting representatives of 167 newspapers and 20 news agencies.

This number rose as high as 386 correspondents at the Seventh Assembly in 1927, and even higher at other times. At the Disarmament Conference in the winter of 1932 there were 432 journalists accredited. They sent out 420,000 words of copy by telegraph alone, and far more by mail, to say nothing of 618 hours of long-distance telephone time.

Some newspapers and press associations keep representatives permanently in Geneva because so much news develops there, while others have arranged for their Paris correspondents to go to Geneva when events warrant.

The Information Section of the League's Secretariat has made the gathering of news about affairs in which the League is concerned a relatively simple business. The correspondent's task is as convenient as possible. More words have been sent out of Geneva than from any capital of Europe, and they have been published in newspapers of all countries.[34]

The newspaper men in permanent residence at Geneva, and going there frequently for sessions of the League Council or Assembly, or for special gatherings, have formed the International Association of Journalists Accredited to the League of Nations.[35] Through this organization, the journalists arrange with the League's Information Section, so far as necessary, for services of news transmission and for prompt and accurate preparation of documents and other data that they require. Although some of the meetings held in connection with the work of the League are secret, the Information Section usually provides the press with a general account of what transpires therein, while the public meetings are reported in full detail for the press, which also is free to attend or not, as it pleases.

[34] Paul F. Douglass and Karl Bömer, "The Press as a Factor in International Relations." In "National and World Planning," V. 162 of the *Annals of the American Academy of Political and Social Science,* pp. 241-72, especially pp. 245-64. In John Whitaker, *And Fear Came,* a correspondent much at Geneva for the New York *Herald Tribune* describes the situation as it existed there before 1937.

[35] There were 20 correspondents permanently stationed in Geneva in 1936, about 80 others fairly regular in attendance at Geneva, and about 200 bona fide journalist members of the Association.

LEAGUE OF NATIONS.

C/56th Session/Agenda 1.

Geneva, August 29th, 1929.

FIFTY-SIXTH SESSION OF THE COUNCIL.

AGENDA

for the meeting at 11 a.m. on Friday, August 30th, 1929.

———

PRIVATE.

Rapporteur.

1. Adoption of Agenda.

Note. The Secretary-General proposes that items 10,
12 and 14 of the Agenda
should not be taken until after
the opening of the Assembly.

2. Budgetary and Administrative Questions:

Representative
of Persia.

(a)(1) Audit of the Accounts for 1926 of the Grants
of the Rockefeller Foundation towards the Budget
of the Health Organisation.

League of Nations   Information Section

No. 3,878   30th August, 1929.

The first meetings of the 56th session of the Council took
place to-day under the Chairmanship of the Persian representative,
M. Foroughi.

At its private meeting, the Council adopted its agenda and
on the report of the Persian representative, settled several
budget and administrative questions.   It accepted a grant of
723,795 dollars from the International Health Division of the
Rockefeller Foundation for the work of the Health Organisation
from 1930-1934.   It also accepted a sum of 200,000 Swiss francs
from the Rockefeller Foundation for the printing and publication
of currency and banking laws.   It instructed the Secretary-
General to thank the Rockefeller Foundation on its behalf.

Conf. M.E./4.

Londres, 12 juin 1933.

CONFERENCE MONETAIRE ET ECONOMIQUE.

TREVE DOUANIERE.

Table des matières.

I. Résolution adoptée par le Comité du Conseil pour
l'Organisation de la Conférence, le 12 mai 1933.

II. Résolution adoptée par le Conseil de la Société des
Nations, le 24 mai 1933.

III. Adhésions reçues avant l'ouverture de la Conférence.

FIG. 27. THE LEAGUE INFORMATION

For description see

Address of the Honorable Cordell Hull,
Secretary of State and Chairman of the
American Economic Conference, at 3 p.m.
Wednesday, June 14, 1933.

"Mr. President: it is appropriate that the nations
should meet in this great capital to deal with the crisis

C/56th Session/P.V.1(1).

LEAGUE OF NATIONS

FIFTY-SIXTH SESSION OF THE COUNCIL

MINUTES

FIRST MEETING (PRIVATE, THEN PUBLIC).

Held on Friday, August 30th, 1929, at 11 a.m.

President: His Highness Ali Khan Foroughi (Persia.)

Present: All the representatives of the Members of the Council, and the Secretary-General.

**2459. Question of placing on the Council's Agenda of a Petition submitted under Article 304
of the Treaty of Trianon by the Nagykikinda-Aradi-Helyierdekü Local Railway Company:
Communication from the President of the Council.**

The following communication from the President was read: [1]

" Article 304 of the Treaty of Trianon provides that:

" ' With the object of ensu... ...ular utilisation of the railroads of the former Austro-
Hungarian Monarchy owned b... ...mpanies which, as a result of the stipulations of
the present Treaty, will be s... ...itory of several States, the administrative and
technical reorganisation of... ...gulated in each instance by an agreement
between the owning com... ...ally concerned.'

" ' It further states th... ...

" ' Any differenc... ...ding questions relating to
the interpretation of... ...shall be submitted to
arbitrators designe... ...

" In virtue of t... ...any, which
owns standard-gau... ...nes, sent
to the Secretary-G... ...ncil
to designate arb... ...the
Roumanian an... ...any's
petition to th... ...d 22nd,
1929, stating th... ...ts might
desire to make there... ...ecretariat
from the Roumanian C... ...

" ' The Nagykikinda... ...d you, under
Article 304 of the Treaty of... ...n of arbitrators
to settle the outstanding questio... ...operation of the
lines under the sovereignty of the Ki... ...dom of the Serbs,
Croats and Slovenes respectively, and fo... ...hose States, since,
despite repeated efforts, it has been unable t... ...t of these questions.

" ' We beg to point out that we are at pre... ...the Company for the
purchase of its lines.

" ' At the last interview, held a short time ago, a p... ...signed to this end by the
Railway's delegates and our own.

" ' All that remains is to settle a few questions of detail, a matter which will probably
be effected shortly.

[Superimposed card:]

12ᵐᵉ ASSEMBLÉE DE LA SOCIÉTÉ DES NATIONS
Genève, 1931

Carte d'entrée permanente

M ....
Représentant le Journal " ....

Photo

N° ....

Entrée par la porte A

SECTION AIDS THE CORRESPONDENT

List of Illustrations

The Information Section has been called "a publicity bureau par excellence." It is manned by former newspaper men of a score of nationalities. Neither the Northcliffe publicity organization of wartime Britain, nor the Creel bureau in Washington was more successful. The section is similar in some ways to the British Foreign Office press bureau. As the foreign office press bureau attempts to guide the publicity given the departmental activities, particularly in the press, so does the Information Section concern itself with the newspaper attention given to all League meetings and activities.[36]

In addition, however, the Information Section attempts to arouse and maintain the interest of individuals and organizations in the League and what it is doing. Its efforts are aimed, directly and indirectly, at educators, politicians, and writers—those who may do most to spread the gospel.

In its contact with the press, the Information Section releases one or more communiqués almost every day, either at Geneva, or wherever the scene of action may be. Correspondents do not feel they can afford to miss these communiqués, and await them with interest. The Section also keeps in touch with the leading newspapers and press associations of most countries or with their representatives in Geneva, and it stands ready to provide information or assistance of any practicable kind.

*   *   *

Geneva is one of the world's greatest propaganda centers. This is partly because the many international gatherings there attract individuals who represent various national, economic and social groups throughout the world, eager to put their marks upon the activities occurring at Geneva.

These organizations seek to use the League as a sort of sound-

---

[36] Anon., *The League of Nations and the Press* (Information Section, League of Nations, Geneva, 1928); A. E. Johnson, "Publicity in Press Sustains League's Power in International Affairs," *Editor and Publisher* (Aug. 4, 1928), p. 8; Anon., *Present Activities of the Secretariat.* League of Nations Document No. A21, 1932 (Geneva, Sept. 1, 1932). General, 1932, 6; C. Howard-Ellis, *The Origin, Structure and Working of the League of Nations,* pp. 187-88.

ing-board by means of which their ideas, ideals, aims, aspirations and ambitions may receive world-wide attention. Scores of organizations send permanent or temporary representatives to Geneva, especially when the League Assembly is meeting.[37] They bring pressure to bear on League officials, delegates, and especially on newspaper correspondents. The correspondents, however, are far from naïve, and are too busy to go about advancing "causes," so that most attempts to "use" the press fail. The correspondents, for example, are invited to attend numberless meetings sponsored by the propagandist groups, but they rarely go near them.[38]

[37] Anon., *Not to Be Repeated*, pp. 504-11. Here are listed nearly two score organizations with representatives at Geneva, with comments on their activities. The League has nothing to do with them, but cannot bar them from Geneva.

[38] The name of William B. Shearer became known in 1929 because he went to court to sue for money he declared was owed to him for work done in Geneva in 1927, allegedly for the Bethlehem Shipbuilding Corporation, the Newport News Shipbuilding and Dry Dock Company, and the American Brown Boveri Corporation, to protect their interests at the Naval Disarmament Conference. He was able to sow distrust and suspicion behind the scenes. He claimed the doubtful credit for causing the conference to fail, and sought to collect a $250,000 fee, in addition to $50,000 already paid him as recompense by the warship-building firms.

Shearer's influence at Geneva was recorded by Silas Bent in an article, "International Window-Smashing," appearing in *Harper's* for Sept., 1928, about a year before Shearer started his suit to collect fees from his sponsors. In commenting on Mr. Bent's article at the time of its publication, *Editor and Publisher* dismissed the charges in these words: "In discussing newspaper reports of the Geneva Conference, Mr. Bent makes the startling assertion that American reporters listened to representatives of munitions makers and to naval experts. . . . This assertion is simply not borne out by what the more important American newspapers printed." *Editor and Publisher* (Sept. 15, 1928), p. 54. Mr. Bent's article is reprinted in his book, *Strange Bedfellows*, pp. 173-92. See also: Anon., "Journalists and Peace," *New Republic* (Nov. 6, 1929), pp. 311-12; Anon., *Arms and the Men* (by the Editors of *Fortune*).

Other references to the Shearer case follow: Anon., "Source of Attack on U. S. Writers Sought," *Editor and Publisher* (July 23, 1927). Raymond G. Swing, correspondent in London for the New York *Evening Post*, cabled a story on July 19, 1927, quoting the press spokesman at the British Foreign Office as accusing American correspondents at Geneva with "behavior unparalleled in the history of journalism." The story said: "According to the British view, correspondents at Geneva have been dominated by 'men in big Panama hats, with big stomachs, smoking big cigars and spending money

Although the League Information Section exists primarily to assist press representatives in Geneva, and presumably is devoted to the idea of "open covenants openly arrived at," it is perhaps only natural that it bottles up news occasionally, for reasons that seem good enough to League officials. It also is not above flattering, cajoling, and bringing influences to bear on correspondents, where it seems advantageous to do so. An unfailing courtesy is its strongest weapon in putting the journalists in a happy and friendly frame of mind.

The same method is not always effective with every journalist, or even with the same journalist, but the net result seems to establish what is sometimes known as the "Geneva mind" in the correspondent, an attitude favorable to the League and all it stands for.

*   *   *

Journalists in Geneva get their news in various ways. Although League officials, aside from members of the Information Section, are advised not to form friendly associations with correspondents because of the danger of undesirable news "leaks," many high officials and statesmen visiting Geneva do have close friends among the journalists. This gives the latter an "inside" position, and sometimes they actually help to make the news.[39]

freely, who, disguised as journalists, are, in fact, secret agents of the steel trust and other armanent interests.' Instead of trying to get the facts on the British viewpoint first hand from W. G. Bridgeman, head of the British delegation, the American correspondents, the British charge, have taken their information from these secret agents who deliver to them alleged facts supposed to have just come from Mr. Bridgeman and which, upon being published, are proved to be absolutely false."

Without a doubt, this refers to Mr. Shearer. Yet none of the other New York newspapers or press associations appeared willing to follow the lead, although they cabled their London correspondents to check up on the story. The responsible heads of those papers and associations in New York whitewashed the American press.

Raymond G. Swing, "Mr. Swing's Story," *Editor and Publisher* (Aug. 8, 1927). A letter explaining the circumstances in detail, as referred to in *Editor and Publisher* of July 23, 1927, and noted above.

[39] It is said to have been a journalist who brought Maxim Litvinoff and Sir Austen Chamberlain together on an occasion when relations had been broken off between Russia and Britain. An American journalist smoothed

The correspondents attend any of the public meetings that seem promising to them. They get the Information Section's advance agenda for the meetings, communiqués dealing with private and public conferences, special documents of interest and importance. They talk, if they wish, to any of the delegates, and then write their stories, which they may send direct from the League building, where an excellent transmission service is available. The League does not attempt to suppress criticism, nor are correspondents for papers which oppose the League discriminated against in any way.

There have been four distinct types of stories sent from Geneva to the world press:

1. A rather dull, objective story, as for a conservative-type press association.

2. A story a bit more colorful, as for a more lively-type press association.

3. A strongly international story, as for papers friendly to the League idea.[40]

4. A strongly anti-League, isolationist story, as for papers unfriendly to the League.[40]

out a misunderstanding between Mr. Joseph G. Porter, Chairman of the United States House Committee on Foreign Affairs, and Viscount Cecil of Chelwood, when the two were heading their respective delegations to the Opium Conference, held under the League's auspices.

[40] Among pro-League papers have been included the New York *Times,* the New York *World-Telegram, Christian Science Monitor,* Chicago *Daily News,* Boston *Globe,* Springfield *Republican,* Philadelphia *Bulletin,* Baltimore *Sun,* Cleveland *Press,* Cincinnati *Enquirer,* Milwaukee *Journal* (usually), in the United States. In Great Britain: *The Times,* Manchester *Guardian, News-Chronicle, Herald.* In France: *Petit Parisien, Matin, Temps, Oeuvre.*

Among anti-League papers have been included, in the United States: Chicago *Tribune,* New York *Sun,* Boston *Transcript,* the Hearst newspapers. In Great Britain: *Daily Telegraph* (mildly), *Daily Express,* and other Beaverbrook papers; *Daily Mail* and other Rothermere papers. In France: *l'Écho de Paris, Journal des Débats, Intransigeant.*

Among papers classified as neutral and uncertain: In the United States: Kansas City *Star,* St. Louis *Post Dispatch,* the New York *Herald Tribune,* Washington *Post.* In France, actually, all papers are variable in their attitudes and cannot be permanently classified. In Italy, the *Corriere della Sera* was quite consistently friendly before 1935, and so was the *Popolo d'Italia* when Dino Grandi was Foreign Minister. At times such as the Corfu crisis

Because a controversy is popularly regarded as the best page-one story, from Geneva as from anywhere else, there has been a tendency to exaggerate differences at League meetings, and correspondents soon learn what sort of copy their papers want. A correspondent who receives a message reading, "Your 23456 Page One" is vastly cheered. But if he is told, "Your 34567 Page Three Gazette Geneva Page One," he will know something was wrong, from the home office viewpoint, and he will find out what the Gazette correspondent sent and then assume that his own office also wants that sort of copy.

There is a "grapevine" system of news gathering in use in Geneva that has no counterpart in other European news centers. By this method many of the correspondents for papers published in some one country may work on a loosely coöperative basis to get all details of a certain story, in which their own country is expressly concerned. They gather all views and cover all aspects of the story and pool the results. At the same time, correspondents for papers published in other countries contribute to the pool such details as they are best able to obtain.

On very big stories, for example, the general views of persons qualified to speak for the United States, and statements as to the way in which the matter under discussion will affect the United States, will be reported by correspondents for newspapers and press associations of the United States. Correspondents for British newspapers will report their country's spokesmen and interests; French correspondents, their country's, and so on. The total re-

or during the Ethiopian trouble the entire Italian press has turned unfriendly.

In Germany, before Hitler's régime, the Frankfurter *Zeitung*, Berliner *Tageblatt*, Kölnische *Zeitung*, and the Ullstein papers, usually, were friendly to the League, while the Hitler press and the Hugenberg press were unfriendly. Since the Hitler régime began, the German press has been consistently unfriendly to the League. The Russian press seldom was friendly to the League before Russia became a member, but after its admission press cordiality increased. In Japan the press is entirely anti-League and has been since the country began its campaign of expansion.... In China the press is mildly pro-League, although its faith is much shaken by the course of events in which Japan has taken increased sections of China. The South American press is fickle in its attitude toward the League, shifting a good deal, but seldom expressing hostility.

sults will be made known to all groups, so that complete stories may be prepared. Such a thing is only possible in Geneva, for it is the only city where news is so entirely centralized.

Some experienced correspondents consider that Geneva is the most interesting news center in the world. In the various capitals, they point out, much of the news is purely local politics. But in Geneva, the business of the League, the many conferences held there, the presence of world figures, all of whom seem to arrive sooner or later, make the news of wider interest and so more stimulating to cover. Or so it was from 1921 to 1936.

The new League building offers the correspondents three "press rooms" in which to work. They are adjacent to telephone booths from which all the world may be reached, and near telegraph and radio offices. Correspondents are admitted to the same lobbies and refreshment rooms with the delegates, as in the original League building, so that they have opportunity to watch and to talk to the international figures attending the meetings.

Some League meetings are secret, yet it is a rare one whose proceedings and conversations do not become known to the press, at least in essence, through indirect channels. In every meeting there are three attitudes among the participants themselves which makes this inevitable:

1. There are those present who want the news of what happened to become known, whether for altruistic or selfish reasons.

2. There are those who do not want the news to become known, whether for altruistic or selfish reasons.

3. There are those who do not care whether the news becomes known or not.

The third group is the largest, numerically, and it is from its members that correspondents usually get most of their useful private information, probably on the understanding that the source will remain confidential. They may return the favor by getting other information for their informants, as only journalists can do at times.

The busiest periods of the day for the Geneva correspondents are from 11 to 1 and from 5 to 7, that is, after morning and afternoon meetings, when they see delegates and others, and put their ideas together. Then they write their copy, and send it by telephone, telegraph or radio.

A direct radio service was opened for the benefit of correspondents at Geneva on Feb. 2, 1932, through the Société Radio-Suisse. It provides communication between Geneva and New York, Shanghai, Nagoya (near Tokyo), Buenos Aires and Rio de Janeiro. If the correspondent marks his dispatch "Via Radio-Nations" it goes that way. Most dispatches for the Far East began to go by radio almost as soon as the service was made available, although the Great Northern Telegraph continued to be much used, and sometimes was faster than the radio. Dispatches sent by telegraph or cable reach London in four minutes, Paris in less, and New York in eight or ten minutes. Most dispatches for European newspapers go by telephone.

Apart from the Secretariat and the International Labor Office, the great news centers of Geneva are the hotels and the cafés, where journalists and delegates meet and talk, and where correspondents drop in during the evening. There are also the luncheon meetings of the Anglo-American Press Association, a branch of the Paris organization, often addressed informally by leading statesmen. The Association of Journalists Accredited to the League of Nations rarely, if ever, holds social meetings, but it does conduct business sessions.

In practice, correspondents from China and Japan have had more trouble covering Geneva news than any other press representatives. This probably is because they are dealing with a generally unfamiliar civilization. The situation has resulted in the Far-Eastern newspapers depending upon Occidental news services, very largely, with Reuters and the United Press sending almost equal amounts of copy to the Orient. This was particularly true in 1932-1933, during the Sino-Japanese trouble, when a great deal of Geneva news was being used in the Far East.

*   *   *

Foreign correspondents in Switzerland do not read the Swiss newspapers to any extent, with the exception of one or two published in Geneva, where they themselves are congregated. Instead, they read London and Paris papers, which reach Geneva quickly. But there are several good papers published in Switzerland. Among the best, so far as concerns general news presentation, including foreign news, are:

Journal de Genève.—Widely known because published in Geneva, the center of international life visited by people from all over the world, and because printed in French, a language more widely known than German or Italian, the other two languages of Switzerland. One read by correspondents.

Gazette de Lausanne.—The second most important French-Swiss paper.

Journal des Nations.—Geneva. Read by correspondents.

Neue Zürcher Zeitung.—Zurich. The best Swiss paper, in any language, the best informed, the richest. Published in the German part of Switzerland.

Basler Nachrichten.—Basle.

Bund.—Berne. This is the third of the three outstanding papers in German-Switzerland.

In Italian-Switzerland there are no papers of note, only small ones serving an agricultural section of 200,000 persons. The *Corriere della Sera* of Milan has the largest circulation of any newspaper in that section.

The three best papers in Switzerland, in the order of their excellence, are considered to be the *Neue Zürcher Zeitung, Journal de Genève,* and *Basler Nachrichten.* These papers have correspondents, although not always staff men, in Berlin, Rome, Washington, and in Spain, Belgium, Hungary, Poland, and Greece. They have special staff correspondents in Paris and London.

The Agence Télégraphique Suisse is the Swiss press association, an independent agency affiliated with the Associated Press, Reuters, Havas, and other members of the world league of press associations. Its central office is in Berne.

§ 4. BERLIN AND CENTRAL EUROPE

THERE were a half dozen fairly good papers in the present area of Germany earlier than 1790, but that date marks the time when the German press attained a status of some importance. French journalistic influence then was strong in Germany, and the papers were modeled after the Paris press. During the "war of liberation" a crop of new and more Germanic papers sprang up, and the same thing happened again after the upheavals of 1830 and 1848. Most of the new papers did not survive very long, but they did bring to German journalism a new energy.[41]

The German people had preferred books and pamphlets and magazines for their information prior to 1870. After that date, however, the popularity of the newspapers increased rapidly until by the early part of the nineteenth century the daily press in Germany was large and prosperous, and continued so. Certain of the newspapers won world reputations.[42]

The German press was free of censorship virtually from the time the Empire was formed in 1870, with a press law passed in 1874 guaranteeing it, until the beginning of the Great War, although it was not a press free from intimidation through frequent suits for *lèse majesté*. After the Armistice, the revolution in Germany brought the formation of the Weimar Republic, and Article 118 of the Republic's Constitution guaranteed the freedom of the press, which felt no government interference for some years thereafter.

This period of the Second Reich was a happy one for the press in Germany, for it was utterly free. The journalist, whether foreign or native, enjoyed working conditions that were made pleas-

[41] Ludwig Salomon, *Geschichte des deutschen Zeitungswesens,* 3 vols.; Otto Groth, *Die Zeitung, ein System der Zeitungskunde.*

[42] Georg Bernhard, "Die Deutsche Presse," in *Der Verlag Ullstein zum Welt Reklame Kongress Berlin 1929* (see Anon.), pp. 57-79. In this essay Professor Bernhard describes the attitude of German readers toward their newspapers. He points out that the German reader is less critical than readers of other nationalities, that he selects a paper whose opinions correspond most nearly to his own, usually reads only the one paper—or did until the time of the War—and regards it as his own newspaper; he expects it to show an interest in his serious interests, or in his hobbies, such as sports, stamp collecting, or music; he looks to it for instruction, believes what his paper tells him, and accepts the paper's estimates, as stated, or even as implied by the amount of space given, as respects men or affairs. See also: Anon., *Handbuch der Weltpresse.* Offering a brief history of every German newspaper (see "Deutschland") and also of newspapers of other lands.

FIG. 28. A GROUP OF SWISS NEWSPAPERS
For description see List of Illustrations

ant and convenient.[43] Wilhelmstrasse talked more readily and more quickly than any other foreign office, which resulted in the German view on almost every question receiving special prominence, while the French view, by contrast, was obscured and often misunderstood because the Quai d'Orsay wanted to "think it over," and usually spoke last.[44]

When the National Socialist party, under Herr Hitler, took control of the German Government in February, 1933, those circumstances began to change very rapidly. The Hindenburg decree of Feb. 28, 1933, "for the protection of the State and the people" rescinded the Weimar constitutional guarantee of press freedom.

Herr Hitler had declared that "The press is an instrument for the education of the people, which the state has to secure for itself with reckless energy, in order to place the same at the service of the state and nation." The National Socialist party program said: "Since the press is one of the most influential powers in the state, all newspapers infringing upon the public interests shall be prohibited."

"This Government believes that the press must help the Government," said Dr. Joseph Goebbels, in speaking to representatives of the newspapers in March, 1933, soon after his ministry was formed. "To that end criticism may sometimes be necessary, but the criticism must never be of a kind which can be used in other nations to discredit the Reich Government. The Government now foresees the time when the press, through the activity of the new Ministry for Public Enlightenment and Propaganda, will develop into a piano on which it can play." [45]

---

[43] Anon., *Conditions of Work and Life of Journalists;* Anon., "News Men Well Treated in Germany, Returning Correspondents Say," *Editor and Publisher* (May 23, 1925), p. 10.

[44] The earlier state of the German foreign office press relations are indicated by Prince von Bülow, *Memoirs, 1903-1909;* G. V. Williams, "The German Press Bureau," *Contemporary Review* (March, 1910), V. 97, pp. 315-25; Charles Lowe, "German Newspaper Press," *Nineteenth Century Review* (Dec., 1891), V. 30, pp. 853-71.

[45] Robert W. Desmond, "200 Dailies Are Suppressed by Hitler," *Editor and Publisher* (Apr. 1, 1933), quotation, p. 38. This number of suppressed newspapers increased to nearly two thousand in two years. Circulations of some remaining papers fell 30 per cent. Later Dr. Goebbels amended his

Foreign correspondents in Germany found that they were expected to conform to the new government conception of the press. The administration examined copy leaving the country by telegraph or radio, and sometimes delayed it long enough to spoil its value as news. Sometimes a message would not be sent at all, and in that case it might or might not be returned to the correspondent. Mails were opened, telephone conversations were overheard by government agents. Those correspondents who did not bow to government propaganda were reprimanded by the government, and a few were expelled or warned to leave.[46]

The National Socialist régime, soon after it took control, protested to foreign correspondents against sending what was called "unsubstantiated rumor," and made that a basis for holding messages instead of telegraphing them. The censorship on foreign dispatches operated at the Central Telegraph Office. Although it was quite generally considered safe for a correspondent to quote anything that had appeared in German newspapers, sometimes combi-

---

"piano" simile so that the press was to become "a highly sensitive and far-sounding instrument or orchestra on which and with which only those shall play who know how, and in whose hands the Führer himself has placed the conductor's baton." The effect of unanimity and harmony in the press is accomplished by the issuance of instructions as in Italy. Otto D. Tolischus, "A Muzzled Press Serves the Nazi State," New York *Times Magazine* (July 14, 1935), pp. 8-9; Albion Ross, "Goebbels Edits the Popular Mind In Germany," New York *Times Magazine* (Feb. 14, 1937), pp. 3, 27; Otto D. Tolischus, "Step by Step Germany Has Regimented Her Press," New York *Times Magazine* (May 2, 1937), pp. 4-5, 20.

[46] Edgar Ansel Mowrer, correspondent in Berlin for nine years for the Chicago *Daily News,* and president of the Foreign Press Association in Berlin, the organization of correspondents, was so warned, and left. He was one of about 30 correspondents who left Germany before 1935, voluntarily or otherwise. Dorothy Thompson, also an American journalist, was expelled, while a correspondent for *The Times* of London was expelled late in 1935. In periods of crisis the censorship became an even greater problem, as it did at the time of the so-called "purge" on June 30, 1934.

Anon., "Nazi Purging Story Blurred by Censors; Officials Admit Misstatements," *Editor and Publisher* (July 7, 1934), pp. 3-4.

Anon., "Nazis Force Mowrer to Resign," *Editor and Publisher* (Aug. 12, 1933); Anon., "Mowrer Quits Germany; Says Nazis Wouldn't Guarantee His Safety," *Editor and Publisher* (Sept. 9, 1933); G. A. Brandenburg, "Mowrer Denies 'False Reporting' Caused Departure from Berlin," *Editor and Publisher* (Sept. 23, 1933), p. 16.

nations of such items brought objections from German authorities as having been deliberately combined to convey an unwarranted impression.

Foreign newspapers carrying reports unwelcome, or officially disapproved by the administration, are banned from the country, either entirely or for the issues in question.

* * *

Berlin is the news center of Germany, for several reasons. It is the capital, it is a railroad center not only for Germany, but for countries surrounding it as well; it is a hub of Continental diplomacy and politics; it is the greatest aviation center in Europe; it is a communications crossroads, with telegraph, telephone and radio circuits to all of Europe, and especially linking Central Europe and Southern Europe. It is a center for German news, of course, and also for news from Austria, Czechoslovakia, the Balkan areas (Rumania, Bulgaria and Yugoslavia, especially), Russia, the Scandinavian countries (Norway, Sweden, Denmark and Finland), the Baltic countries (Latvia, Estonia and Lithuania), Poland, the Low Countries (Netherlands and Belgium), and parts of Switzerland.

There have been, since the Great War, as many as 200 correspondents from 25 nations or more stationed in Berlin at one time, with even more during important conferences or crises. All important agencies and individual newspapers have representatives in the middle European capital. As in London, those agencies and papers have exchange arrangements locally. So, the Associated Press, Reuters, Havas and others for many years had contracts with the Wolff'sche Telegraphen Büro (full name: Continental-Telegraphen-Compagnie, Wolff's Telegraphisches Büro) which had been established on January 11, 1849, by Dr. Bernard Wolff.

The Wolff agency (WTB) was the official German Government agency, and it distributed news to its own large district offices in Cologne, Frankfurt, Hamburg and other cities, by telescript, or printer telegraph, using the Siemens printer machine. From these points, the news was further distributed to newspapers by wire, telephone or messenger. Beginning in about 1923 or 1924, also,

Deutſche diplomatiſch-politiſche Korreſpondenz

| Charlottenstraße 15B Fernspr.: Dönhoff 3855-70 | Verantwortlich für die Redaktion: Dr. Edgar Stern-Rubarth, Berlin-Schlachted | Berlin SW 68, 10. März 1933 |

8. Jahrgang
Nr. 60

Der Kampf um das Kriegsmaterial.

Wenn überhaupt irgendeins der Themen, die in Genf
zur Erörterung stehen, geeignet ist, der breiten Öffentlich-

BERLINER LOKAL-NACHRICHTEN

WTB Herausgeber: Continental-Telegraphen-Compagnie
Wolff's Telegraphisches Büro Aktiengesellschaft, Berlin SW 68
Fernsprecher: Dönhoff 3856—69 / Charlottenstraße 15 B

Als Manuskript vervielfältigt. Nachdruck und jede Art Verbreitung nur nach besonderer Vereinbarung gestattet
Ohne alle Gewähr

Berlin, den 9. März 1933   Blatt 1

Die S-Bahn im Jahre 1932
================================
Technische Verbesserungen - Ausbau bestehender und
Anlage neuer Bahnhöfe

BLN   Die S-Bahn konnte, obwohl mit der Konjunktur auch
ihre Einnahmen sanken, im vergangenen Jahre im allge-

W. T. B. - Sportdienst

Berlin, 7. März 1933   Blatt: 4

Berufsboxen in Berlin.
Der Berliner "Neue Welt"-Boxring hat in Programm seine
bevorstehenden Kampfabends am Freitag, 10. März einige Um-
stellungen vorgenommen. Der junge Kölner Werner Selle hat

78 * Vortrag des Reichsarbeitsministers beim Reichspräsidenten
     B e r l i n , 11. März. Der Herr Reichspräsident
empfing heute vormittag Reichsarbeitsminister Seldte
zum Vortrag

         Verhaftungen in Gotha
         - - - - - - - - - - -
79 G o t h a , 11. März. Der Arbeitsamtsdirektor und
zwei Direktoren der Ortskrankenkasse wurden
in Schutzhaft genommen.

80 Kein Einmarsch der Japaner in Nordchina?
    -
    T o k i o , 11. März. (Reuter) Wie verlautet, hat der brit-
ische Botschafter die Zusicherung erhalten, dass die Japaner nicht in Nordchina einrücken werden, ausser wenn
sie von den Chinesen dazu gezwungen würden.

83 Der Oberbürgermeister und der Bürgermeister von Magde-
    burg in Schutzhaft genommen
    * M a g d e b u r g , 11. März. Oberbürgermeister
Beuter wurde heute früh von SA-Leuten in seinem Amts-

FIG. 29. NEWS AS IT IS

For description see

Nr. 260. Seite 1.　　　Telegraphen-Union　　　Berlin, 9.März 1933.
　　　　　　　　　　　Vorm.-Dienst　　　　　　(Th.1/1518)

(1 V) Schiffsuntergang bei Hongkong. - 50 Tote.

TU. Hongkong, 9.März. Der chinesische Dampfer "Antung" ist
auf der Höhe der Mofu-Spitze bei Hongkong gescheitert. 50 Menschen
sind ertrunken. Die übrigen 460 konnten gerettet werden. (8101/8716/Q)
　　　Q.

(2 V) Vor der Reise MacDonalds und Simons nach Genf. - Englische Hoffnungen
　　　　　　　　　　　　　　und Besorgnisse.

TU, London, 9.März. MacDonald und Sir John Simon waren, wie die
"Times" meldet, am Mittwoch nicht in der Lage, im Kabinett mitteilen zu

---

DIE KURZFASSUNG

Eigentum der Continental-Telegraphen-Compagnie, Berlin SW 68. Als Manuskript gedruckt. Nachdruck und jede Art Verbreitung
nur nach besonderer Vereinbarung gestattet. Ohne alle Gewähr.

Ausgabe A.　　　Berlin, 10. März 1933.

Weitere Personen in Köln in Schutzhaft genommen.
WTB. Köln, 10.3.　　Bürgermeister Fresdorf, Beigeordne-
ter Meerfeld und der frühere Polizeipräsident von Köln,

Politische Informationen und Notizen

Demokratischer Zeitungsdienst: Berlin SW 11, Bernburger Straße 18　-:-　Fernruf Kurfürst 8163

Berlin, den 8.März 1933. K.

Hitler fährt nicht nach Genf.
═══════════════════════════════
Kabinett und Abrüstungsfrage.
- - - - - - - - - - - -

　　Soweit bisher verlautet, wird Reichskanzler Hitler nicht
nach Genf fahren, da, wie mitgeteilt wird, die innerpolitische
Lage seine Anwesenheit in Berlin erforderlich macht. Von englischer

---

CONTINENTAL-TELEGRAPHEN-COMPAGNIE

CONTI-　NACHRICHTEN-　BÜRO

UNABHÄNGIGER　　(CNB)　　NACHRICHTENDIENST

Eigentum der Continental-Telegraphen-Compagnie, Berlin SW 68. Als Manuskript gedruckt. Nachdruck und jede Art Verbreitung
nur nach besonderer Vereinbarung gestattet. Ohne alle Gewähr. Verantwortlich für Redaktion: Dr. Hermann Diez, Berlin SW 68.

Tagesausgabe.
═-═-═-═-═-═-═-═-═-═
Blatt 1

Berlin, den 8. März 1933.

Dr. v. Winterfeld zu den preussischen Kommunalwahlen.
══

CNB Berlin, 8. März 1933
(Eigene Meldung).

Der stellvertretende Vorsitzende der Deutsch-
nationalen Volkspartei Dr. von Winterfeld erlässt zu
den preussischen Kommunalwahlen folgenden Aufruf:

 # DIE FRÜH-INFORMATION

Korrespondenz zur persönlichen Unterrichtung; nicht zur Veröffentlichung bestimmt
Herausgeber: Conti-Nachrichten-Büro, Berlin SW 68, Charlottenstrasse 15b

Jahrgang 3　　　　　Berlin, den 10. März 1933, morgens.
Nr. 59

Aus München liegt heute früh nur eine kurze Mit-
teilung der Polizei vor, dass die Nacht vollkommen ruhig
verlaufen sei. Irgendwelche Ausschreitungen haben sich also

DISTRIBUTED IN GERMANY

List of Illustrations

the Wolff bureau began a distribution of news in Germany by wireless, some papers receiving it direct from Berlin, and more papers getting it indirectly from regional offices, but still by wireless. They paid for the service. The official news, as distributed more conventionally by Wolff's, was typed on white sheets; the unofficial service was on green sheets, and the sports service was on pink sheets.[47]

The name of the Wolff agency was changed, under the National Socialist Government, to the Deutsches Nachrichten Büro (DNB), representing a merger of Wolff's and the Telegraphen Union, the two German news agencies, the latter owned by Dr. Alfred Hugenberg, industrialist. The Associated Press and other foreign agencies continued with the new agency the arrangement they had had with Wolff's. The Deutsche Diplomatische-Politische Korrespondenz, an agency presenting interpretative articles about foreign and domestic politics and affairs, continued as before 1933, but strictly under official supervision, and as the semi-official voice of the Foreign Office. Arrangements between other foreign press associations and newspapers and Berlin papers were completely disrupted by the formation of the National Socialist Government because the German papers and agencies then began to deal very largely in inspired news.[48]

*   *   *

Foreign correspondents in Berlin operate much as they would in London or Paris, but news is harder to get. Journalists never

[47] See also: Paul F. Douglass and Karl Bömer, "The International Combination of News Agencies," *Annals of the American Academy of Political and Social Science* (July, 1932), pp. 265-68.

[48] Even before the Hitler régime, there was some reason to complain that news emanating from Germany was less than the whole truth. This was not entirely the fault of the correspondents, but was to be traced to an unwillingness on the part of readers at home to accept facts which sometimes conflicted with preconceived opinion. S. Miles Bouton, "False News from Germany," *American Mercury* (Sept., 1932), pp. 30-37.

After the Hitler régime began, the prejudice of readers, strongly unfavorable to methods of terrorism used, also operated to prevent newspapers in the United States, for one place, reporting constructive accomplishments of Hitlerism.

had an easy time in Germany. Search for objective truth now is looked upon with impatience, and when such reports have been published abroad they have been officially damned in Germany, sometimes, as "malicious lies." [49] Many of the correspondent's informants ceased to speak freely or even to recognize him in public, fearing official retribution if the correspondent ever were to write anything that might be interpreted by the government as unfriendly. Ultimately it was made "high treason" for any German to communicate to a foreigner—journalist or not—any information that had been withheld by the authorities from the German press. The penalty for doing so was to be decapitation or banishment to a concentration camp.

Despite difficulties strewn in his path since 1933, the American correspondent has found much in the attitude of mind and national customs in Germany that parallels, in certain ways, what he is accustomed to in the United States. The German does not close his shop or office for two hours at noon, as does the Frenchman. He does not take long weekends, as does the Briton. He does not sleep late in the mornings and talk late into the nights, as does the Spaniard. He does not insist upon advance appointments and formal introductions, as the Briton and the Frenchman often do. He does not so frequently try to sell his opinions as do persons of some other nationalities. And, until 1933, he was somewhat interested in objective truth.

The correspondent has his news sources, of course. News tickers

[49] Karl H. von Weigand, "Gathering News in Gathering Gloom," *Circulation*, publication of King Features (March, 1923), p. 28; Louis P. Lochner, "Berlin as a News Center," *Wisconsin Alumni Magazine* (March, 1927), p. 164; Anon., "Fog of Propaganda Covers Germany," *Editor and Publisher* (July 21, 1934), p. 10; Paul F. Douglass and Karl Bömer, "The Press as a Factor in International Relations," *Annals of the American Academy of Political and Social Science* (July, 1932), Ch. 3. "The Organization of the Foreign Press in a Capital European City," pp. 269-72. A description of the Berlin situation in pre-Hitler days. See also: Karl Bömer, "German Journalism in 1931," *Journalism Quarterly* (Dec., 1931), pp. 435-45; Walter Williams, *Some Observations on the German Press*. Univ. of Missouri Bulletin. V. 33, No. 32 Journalism Series No. 67 (Nov. 10, 1932); Anon., "Sulzberger Gives Modern 'Case History' of Many Pressures on Newspapers." Report of address by A. H. Sulzberger, publisher of the New York *Times*. *Editor and Publisher* (Jan. 9, 1937), pp. 3-4.

are less common, and certainly less valuable, than in London. A variety of press opinion is not available, as in Paris or London. Government offices and officials yield little that is useful in these times, although they once were helpful. But some foreign embassies, legations and consulates are good sources; private persons in positions to know what is happening, both natives and foreigners, are helpful, provided they will tell what they know; hotels, clubs and cafés are, as ever, news exchanges, although not so good as they once were.

The telephone and the airplane have been aids to news gathering and also to news dispatch, for much of the news sent from Berlin goes by telephone to London or Paris, to be used there or relayed. This is especially true since the National Socialist Government began to hold back, censor, or change telegraph dispatches.

Berlin is filled with propaganda. Government offices give out propaganda; the Minister of Public Enlightenment and Propaganda is a member of the council which governs the nation; the newspapers print reams of propaganda; foreign diplomats in Berlin dispense propaganda liberally; and the German capital always has been a gathering place for persons dealing in forged and counterfeited documents.

*   *   *

The German press itself, useful to correspondents in the past, now is much less helpful. For the period of the Second Reich, and even prior to the War, certain of the newspapers were trustworthy and enlightened. For a time during the Second Reich it was even possible to say that the German press was one of the best on the continent of Europe. It was a serious press, although not without its gutter fringe. The papers printed a fair budget of news, in which domestic political affairs outweighed everything else, and some of them maintained correspondents in foreign lands.[50]

[50] In about 1930 there were 13 correspondents for German papers and press associations in the United States alone, because the news from America had more interest for Germans than news from most other countries, to judge by its volume in the German press. The Ullstein house, largest

The press did not publish popular amusement features, such as cartoons, nor did it pander to mass circulation with exaggerated emphasis on crime, sports, or racing odds and returns. Instead, the emphasis, perhaps inspired by the difficult times, was upon economic and industrial problems, literature and the arts.[51]

All of this is changed, however. The National Socialist Government made the press an agency of the State. Newspapers receive daily instructions from the Ministry of Public Enlightenment and Propaganda as to what they may and may not report, and how, including even such details as size of headline and position to be assigned stories in the paper. The number of German correspondents abroad dwindled and most German papers receive their foreign news through the official (or semi-official) Deutsches Nachrichten Büro, Deutsche Diplomatish-Politische Korrespondenz, or, at times, through the German Foreign Office. The daily papers fell off in numbers, news became stereotyped, comment was limited to officially approved expressions, and the press ceased to be much more than a propaganda agency. Even reviews of theaters and music were brought under official control.[52]

publishing unit in Germany, in 1929 maintained 42 chief correspondents at home and abroad, 144 assistant correspondents in the German Reich, and 35 in other countries. In 1936 there were 10 German correspondents in the United States.

[51] A summary of the German press just before the National Socialist Government began: Walter Williams, *Some Observations on the German Press.* A study made under a Carl Schurz Foundation grant. Univ. of Missouri Bulletin, V. 33, No. 32. Journalism Series, No. 67 (Nov. 10, 1932).

[52] The history of the change affecting press and correspondents in Germany is reflected in the following contemporary reports:

Anon., "Gag Decree Stifles German Press," *Editor and Publisher* (Feb. 11, 1933); Robert W. Desmond, "200 Dailies Are Suppressed by Hitler," *Editor and Publisher* (Apr. 1, 1933), pp. 8, 38; Anon., "Editors Differ on Censorship," *Editor and Publisher* (Apr. 1, 1933), p. 8; Anon., "Berlin Writers Resist Pressure; Repression Policies Continue," *Editor and Publisher* (Apr. 8, 1933), p. 8; Mark F. Ethridge, "Reich Press Defeat Held 'Degrading,' " *Editor and Publisher* (Apr. 22, 1933), pp. 13, 78; Anon., "Press Control in Germany," Manchester *Guardian Weekly* (May 26, 1933), p. 411. This reproduces instructions to the German press from the Ministry of Propaganda. The instructions were reprinted in the *New Republic* for June 19, 1935, pp. 152-53; Anon., "Nazi Instructions to Press Cited," *Editor and Publisher* (Sept. 27, 1933); Anon., "German Press to Serve State in Propaganda," *Christian Science Monitor* (Oct. 7, 1935), p. 1; J. E. Williams,

Newspapers published in Germany are, of course, helpful to foreign correspondents, as to intelligent natives, but almost more for what they *do not* report than for what they *do* report. The *Frankfurter Zeitung,* among the better papers of pre-Hitler times, maintained some semblance of independence until the end of 1936, yet even that was negative in that it permitted the paper merely to refrain from joining the chorus of approval for every item of the government program. But it allowed no criticism. Somewhat the same was true of the *Berliner Tageblatt,* which also capitulated completely about Jan. 1, 1937.

The very appearance of the German papers has differed from that of most other national presses. They are small in size—only slightly bigger than the "tabloid" or picture paper—and are often in two sections, neither one very large. The first outside sheet contains news, special articles and editorials. The middle of the paper is occupied by supplementary pages, increased in number as required. Part of these inside pages, and most of the second section, frequently contain a quantity of non-news articles, perhaps written by qualified authorities, dealing with literary, artistic, social or technical subjects. Even a serious journal probably publishes a novel in serial form, as well as numerous novelettes and sketches—this for circulation reasons, as in Paris, to keep readers coming back daily.

The local news in papers published in Berlin and other large German cities is written in a rather naïve manner, with emphasis on personalities and on details, giving the impression to the casual reader that there is much concern with the neighbors' affairs. The

"Journalism in Germany, 1933," *Journalism Quarterly* (Dec., 1933), pp. 283-88. This summarizes the important year of change in Germany; Otto D. Tolischus, "A Muzzled Press Serves the Nazi State," New York *Times Magazine* (July 14, 1935), pp. 8, 9; Reuel R. Barlow, "Nazi Control Is Complete," *Editor and Publisher* (Dec. 7, 1935), p. 9; Franz Hollering, " 'I was an Editor in Germany,' " *Editor and Publisher* (Apr. 25, 1936), pp. 22, 115. (Address before the American Society of Newspaper Editors.) Fritz Morstein Marx, "State Propaganda in Germany," *Propaganda and Dictatorship* (H. L. Childs), pp. 11-31; Anon., "Two German Editors Ousted by Goebbels," New York *Times* (Dec. 24, 1936); F. T. Birchall, "Paul Scheffer Out as Editor in Reich," New York *Times* (Jan. 3, 1937); also n. 46, p. 232 above.

signed article is much in vogue in Germany, as it is in France. Writers and salaried correspondents use pen-names or initials by which they may be identified.

Some of the more prominent German newspapers are published in the mornings. There are not so many afternoon newspapers, and the regular morning newspapers ordinarily do not appear on Monday mornings, because their staff members have Sunday as a free day. There are other weekly papers, however, that appear only on Monday mornings to fill the void.

Whatever was true of individual German newspapers prior to 1933 has ceased to be true since then. The Hugenberg press empire,[53] built up on the foundation laid by Hugo Stinnes, the industrialist, during the inflation period following the War, now is diluted and changed. The great house of Ullstein has been placed under indirect government control.[54] So has the Mosse publishing

[53] It included the *Lokal-Anzeiger*, of Berlin, the *Hamburger Nachrichten*, three other Berlin papers, a chain of provincial papers, nine weeklies and monthlies, six trade journals, many important directories and journals, a book publishing organization, the Telegraphen-Union (TU) press association, second only in importance to the Wolff agency; Wirtschaftsberatung der Provinzpresse (WIRPO), a syndicate providing editorial matter to provincial papers and trade papers; Ala-Haasenstein and Vogler-Daube, two great advertising concerns of dominant influence, the Universum Film Aktiengesellschaft (UFA), producing 75 per cent of all German films and owning more than 150 theaters.

Hugenberg had been president of the Krupp directorate from 1909 to 1918, in the government during the War, a member of the Reichstag after 1920, and a publisher after 1916, but in a particularly important way after 1923 and 1924. He was a supporter of Hitler, and close to him until the London Economic Conference, when a tactless radio address started him toward obscurity. O. G. Villard, "The Press Today: Hugenberg and the German Dailies," *The Nation* (N. Y., Aug. 20, 1930), V. 131, pp. 197-98; Dr. Joachim Schanz, *Die Entstehung eines Deutschen Presse-Gross Verlages*. A privately printed doctoral dissertation in which the Hugenberg press is described. It was published by the Scherl Verlag, the Hugenberg publishing house, Berlin, 1933. Ludwig Bernhardt, *Der Hugenberg-Konzern.*

[54] This great publishing firm, controlled by five brothers, was liberal and progressive. It published four dailies, four weeklies, four class papers, four trade papers, three almanacs or directories, and books. The papers included the *Berliner Allgemeine Zeitung, Vossische Zeitung, Morgenpost,* and *Berliner Zeitung am Mittag.*

Two elaborate souvenir books published by the house of Ullstein describe its history and products, in words and pictures, as shortly before the Hitler

organization.[55] Hundreds of newspapers have been suppressed, all Socialist and Communist papers nearly at once; others have been put under a new direction, or have voluntarily chosen to support the Nazi Government to the smallest detail.

Some newspapers have been started by leaders of the government, and while they are considered highly official in what they publish, they also are the chief propaganda organs. Outstanding among these is the *Völkischer Beobachter* of Berlin and Munich, the Hitler-Goebbels paper and chief press spokesman of the National Socialist Party. Some honored German papers, such as the *Frankfurter Zeitung,* already mentioned, the *Kölnische Zeitung, Hamburger Fremdenblatt* and the *Berliner Tageblatt,* have lost most or all of their old authority, although they may have much the same appearance.[56]

*   *   *

Those Berlin papers read with special care by correspondents include:

Der Angriff.—An official organ of the the National Socialist Party, founded in 1927, and elevated with the party to a position of importance. It was for some time the special mouthpiece of Dr. Goebbels, Minister for Public Enlightenment and Propaganda.

Völkischer Beobachter.—Chief organ of the National Socialist Party. Edited by Alfred Rosenberg. Also published in Munich.

régime. Anon., *Der Verlag Ullstein zum Welt Reklame Kongress. Berlin. 1929.* Published at the time of the International Advertising Association, Berlin Congress, 1929. In English, French and German; Anon., *50 Jahre Ullstein, 1877-1927.* A full history with many illustrations.

[55] The Mosse house published several newspapers, including the *Berliner Tageblatt,* several other important periodicals, had a news agency and an advertising agency of its own, and issued world-known code books, as well as almanacs and other reference books. See also: Anon., "Nazis Take Over Tageblatt; Liberal Policy is at an End," New York *Times* (Apr. 23, 1933), Edit. Sec., pp. 1, 3; F. T. Birchall, "Paul Scheffer Out as Editor in Reich," New York *Times* (Jan. 3, 1937).

[56] Otto D. Tolischus, "A Muzzled Press Serves the Nazi State," New York *Times Magazine* (July 14, 1935), pp. 8-9; O. W. Riegel, *Mobilizing for Chaos* (see "Germany" in Index); Reuel R. Barlow, "Berlin Circulations Are Mounting Despite Nazi Domination," *Editor and Publisher* (Nov. 9, 1935), p. 14.

FIG. 30. SOME IMPORTANT GERMAN NEWSPAPERS

For description see List of Illustrations

Berliner Tageblatt.—An important paper during the First and Second Reichs. Taken over by the National Socialists in April, 1933, and edited until 1937 by Paul Scheffer. Prior to 1933 the editor was Theodor Wolff, one of the most brilliant German journalists.

Deutsche Allgemeine Zeitung.—Reflects interests and views of business elements in Germany.

Deutscher Reichsanzeiger und Preussischer Staatsanzeiger.— Texts of laws, official announcements, and articles.

Germania.—The leading Catholic paper in Germany.

The more important papers published outside of Berlin include:

Frankfurter Zeitung.—For years one of the two or three best papers in Germany, and still somewhat useful.

Hamburger Fremdenblatt.—Long an important paper, and still of some value.

Hamburger Tageblatt.—An organ of the National Socialist Party.

Kölnische Zeitung.—For years one of the two or three best papers in Germany. Still useful.

Münchner Neuste Nachrichten.—Munich.

Leipsiger Neuste Nachrichten.—Leipzig.

Völkischer Beobachter.—Munich edition. Virtually the same as the Berlin edition, and an organ of the National Socialist Party.

In addition, there are newspapers serving as organs of the National Socialist Party published at Essen, Cologne, Hanover, Stuttgart, Breslau, Königsberg, Darmstadt, Dresden, Frankfurt, Bremen, and in other smaller places.

Certain other periodicals in Germany are watched with special care by foreign correspondents. These include the *Europäische Revue, Öst-Europa, Der Stürmer,* anti-Semitic weekly, financial papers and others.

§ 5. ROME AND ITALY

SINCE 1922 Italy has been remade under the administration of Signor Benito Mussolini and the Fascist party. The press has been altered, along with other aspects of Italian life, and the task of the journalist, whether engaged in work on an Italian publication or acting as a correspondent in the country, has been altered accordingly.

Prior to that date, the Italian press laws were based on a royal decree of 1848, and the press had its freedom, although there was some unofficial censorship practised, and the press itself sometimes interpreted freedom to mean license. Earlier than 1848 Italy's papers had been subject to a strict censorship, and were small and unimportant.

Before the Great War Italy was not a center for world news, although some more prosperous foreign newspapers, such as *The Times* of London, maintained correspondents there.[57] Even so, correspondents in Rome usually served several papers in various countries. But the War put Italy on the news map, and since the March on Rome, Italy has been almost constantly in the news.[58]

Using various pretexts, the entire native press of Italy was brought to the support of the Fascist viewpoint between 1922 and 1926. Where peaceful persuasion failed, the recalcitrant papers were suppressed or taken over by those favorable to Fascism, while their publishers and editors, if they did not change their opinions or flee from the country, probably were sent to "the islands." Not only was the domestic press placed under a censorship, but efforts were made to govern what foreign correspondents wrote and sent concerning affairs in Italy, although the correspondent himself usually was shown every courtesy.[59]

[57] W. J. Stillman, *The Autobiography of a Journalist*, 2 vols.; H. Wickham Steed, *Through Thirty Years*, 2 vols.

[58] The number of foreign correspondents in Italy increased from 40 in 1922 to more than 100 in 1932. German correspondents were most numerous in the latter year, French correspondents second in number. The best news reports of Italian affairs published abroad in 1932 were in the German newspapers, in the opinion of the Italian Foreign Office, with papers in the United States and Great Britain following closely. There were 98 foreign correspondents in Rome and 16 in Milan that year, according to the membership list of the Associazione della Stampa Estera in Italia.

[59] Himself a journalist of sorts, Mussolini was ignored and rebuffed by correspondents at Locarno when he went there for the international conference in 1925, while Briand, Stresemann and Chamberlain were guests of the journalists. Albin E. Johnson, "Fascist Dictator Is Snubbed by Press," *Editor and Publisher* (Nov. 7, 1925), p. 11. He also was refused honorary

The censorship in Italy may be said to have grown out of the slaying of Mateotti, a Socialist member of the Chamber of Deputies, in 1924. The youthful Fascist movement was so severely criticized as a result of this act, which was attributed to official instigation, that the Fascist Grand Council put through a decree previously approved but never until then enforced, which provided for two warnings and then a possible suspension of any paper which was displeasing in its contents to a local advisory council. From that time, the press and foreign correspondents in Italy have been subject to supervision or restriction varying somewhat in rigidity and character, with a censorship occasionally admitted to exist, but usually officially denied.

In January, 1925, a second decree increased the powers of provincial prefects to censor the press locally. In June, 1925, the Penal Code was amended to authorize "the necessary measures for preventing and repressing the abuses and crimes committed by means of the press." By 1926, in accordance with decrees of 1925, the newspapers of Italy were unanimously in support of the Fascist Government, and were taking their orders and their cues from official sources.[60] So far as foreign correspondents were concerned, nothing except news favoring, or at least uncritical of Mussolini and the régime, was permitted to leave the country by telegraph, cable, or wireless, while some efforts were made to control the matter leaving the country in other ways.

When correspondents persisted in sending abroad reports of opposition to Mussolini's régime, and unfavorable to it, the government threatened to penalize them. They were to receive sentences of imprisonment for from five to fifteen years for the "publication or dissemination abroad in any form of false, exaggerated or prejudiced reports or rumors about the internal affairs

membership in the National Press Club of Washington in 1928 because he was regarded as "the arch enemy of a free press in our time, and perhaps in all time." G. H. Manning, "Mussolini Is Barred from National Press Club as Enemy of Free Press," *Editor and Publisher* (June 6, 1928), p. 16. See also: George Slocombe, *The Tumult and the Shouting,* Chs. 12, 19.

[60] Mussolini early declared, "I consider Italian Fascist journalism like an orchestra." This was a remark that Dr. Goebbels later paraphrased in application to the German press. Anon., *Not to Be Repeated,* pp. 335-39.

of the state in such a fashion as to hurt the credit or the prestige
of the State abroad; and the performance of any activity which
may hurt national interests." [61]

Although there was early opposition to the Fascist censorship,
the situation ultimately came to be accepted more complacently,
so that by 1930 many correspondents and editors were excusing
its existence, denying that it was a serious handicap, and making
the best of it. Of those who chose to combat the censorship or the
official wishes, a number were expelled.[62]

The next major expression by Rome, after 1930, concerning
restrictions on foreign journalists in Italy came late in 1934, when
Italy had the forthcoming Ethiopian campaign in preparation.
Correspondents then were forbidden to send any news of Italian
military matters, aside from that emanating from official sources,
under pain of being charged with espionage. The list of subjects
forbidden to correspondents was long.[63]

Correspondents willing to praise the régime have been given
special favors, and their work made easier, while their colleagues,
if unwilling to confine their reports to favorable aspects of the
news, have had a lean time.[64]

In Italy the correspondent has no chance to discuss objections
raised to his message. This is partly because the government does
not admit the existence of a censorship.[65] But when messages are

[61] Peter Brooklyn, "Prison Faces Correspondents Who Violate Mussolini's
Latest Decrees," *Editor and Publisher* (Dec. 4, 1926), p. 12.

[62] See George Seldes, *You Can't Print That!*, pp. 69-152. Seldes, corre-
spondent for the Chicago *Tribune*, was expelled from Italy. David Darrah,
also a *Tribune* correspondent, was expelled in 1935. See also: Seldes, "The
Truth About Fascist Censorship," *Harper's* (Nov., 1927), pp. 732-43. See:
David Darrah, *Hail Caesar;* George Seldes, *Sawdust Caesar;* George Steer,
Caesar in Abyssinia.

[63] Anon., "Italy Bans All Military News, Warning Correspondents Not to
Write on Wide List of Subjects," *Christian Science Monitor* (Dec. 18, 1934),
p. 4.

[64] *Ibid.;* see also: George Seldes, "The Truth About Fascist Censorship,"
Harper's (Nov., 1927), pp. 732-43.

[65] Herbert L. Matthews, "Fascists Efficient in Handling News," New
York *Times* (Jan. 31, 1933), Sec. IV, p. 2; A. E. Johnson, " 'Wisecracks'
About Fascism Barred by Newest Italian Censorship," *Editor and Pub-
lisher* (Apr. 4, 1930), p. 24.

filed for transmission over the government-owned telegraph, cable or radio facilities they are whisked by pneumatic tube to the desks of functionaries in the General Post Office, across the street from the main communications office. Officials there read them and either approve them for transmission or delay them for further consideration, perhaps holding them until their news value is lost or reduced. In extreme cases they eliminate or change words, or even put the message aside and do not send it at all. But the correspondent pays for its full transmission in any case. Officials at the General Post Office also read some mail addressed to foreign correspondents and withhold what they do not wish to go through. The envelopes are neatly opened and then resealed with a particular kind of glue which reveals to those who know its nature that they have been inspected.

Although it is true that the telephone has not been interfered with by the censorship in Italy, in the sense that the wires have been blocked, telephone conversations are systematically overheard by officials, with occasional results.[66]

[66] At times the connection has been tampered with in such a way that it has proved impossible to use the telephone. On one occasion a correspondent thought to surprise the government agent whom he suspected of listening to his conversation, so he said suddenly, "You, on the wire, who are not speaking—are you listening?" And a voice answered "Yes." Another correspondent was taken to police headquarters and obliged to listen to a record of a telephone conversation he had had. Such records, automatically made on tapes, are of conversations over telephones known to be used by journalists, diplomats, and even prominent members of the Fascist party. It includes home telephones, as well as office telephones.

The Rome correspondent for a Berlin paper had heard rumors at one time of bread riots in the poorer districts of Rome. In telephoning his day's grist to Berlin, he mentioned that these rumors were about, but said that he had not been able to verify them as yet. For that reason he denied the accuracy of stories which he was told had appeared in some foreign newspapers. Shortly after this conversation, the police called on him, held him for six hours, during which time they took him on an automobile tour of the poorer districts, where no bread riots were to be seen. In addition, he was pumped full of information. "Now," he was told at the end of the tour and detention, "you can see for yourself that there are no bread riots. Why do you send such stories?" It is clear that unless the government had been listening to his telephone conversation, even though they had misunderstood what he had said, they could not have known so quickly that the matter had even been mentioned.

Some authorities in Italy have denied that the attention given outgoing messages by officials in Rome's telegraph offices or elsewhere constitutes a censorship. They prefer to call it a "Revisione," or an effort to insure accuracy, but evidence shows that it goes beyond that at times.

*   *   *

The Italian press itself receives daily instructions from the Ministry of Interior press office, a bureau regarded as so important that Signor Mussolini himself took personal direction of it for a time, and his son-in-law, Count Galeazzo Ciano, later was at its head as Minister for Press and Propaganda. The representatives of the newspapers receive instructions from that department, in person, orally, face-to-face; by "service notes," or by telephone, as to what they may or may not say, should and should not say, and the general attitude that they are expected to assume on a variety of subjects.

Some instructions are of limited importance, others have a considerable significance. To illustrate, one read:

> We draw the attention of all journals to the necessity of a rigorous application of the instructions given to prevent the publication of photographs of slim women. The phenomenon of slim women signifies nothing more or less than diminution of the birth rate.

On another occasion newspapers were asked "not to speak of the automobile accident to Minister Crollananzo." They were asked "to play up the enormous number of travellers on low-priced excursion trains," and "to exult over the defeat of the Weimar Coalition in Germany and the victory of the Hitlerites."

At the time of the Italian naval maneuvers in 1932, newspaper editors were directed:

> Play up the fact that a hundred naval units and thirty submarines participated in the maneuvers. Emphasize the part in the maneuvers taken by the air forces, but do not forget that the navy's part was the most important. Do not

make the mistakes of a Rome paper which gave aviation the biggest headlines.

The great naval maneuvers should be given large front page publicity. Give full accounts and publish photographs of the ships in each edition. Play up the fact that Italy's war fleet is technically very modern, and that it has been completely renewed by the will of the "Duce" during the ten years of the Fascist régime.

In one day's instructions a newspaper is reprimanded for making fun of an anti-fly campaign; another for questioning the efficacy of "cures" at Italian medicinal springs and bath resorts. To this is added: [67]

The newspapers should abstain from making the slightest favorable reference to foreign watering places.

At the time of the Italo-Ethiopian conflict in 1935, and especially when strained relations existed between Italy and Great Britain, the following instructions are presented as having been given the Italian newspapers: [68]

October 23

Do not comment on Hoare's speech. [Speech delivered by Sir Samuel Hoare, British Foreign Secretary, in the House of Commons on October 22.]

Do not comment on the communication of the Italian plans in Ethiopia.

Give space to article from *La Stefan* on Brazil's attitude toward sanctions.

Reproduce—you must reproduce—news from Agenzia di Roma regarding sanctions and France's position. [This news, gathered in Paris, revealed trends in the French press indicating fear there that business would suffer if sanctions were imposed on Italy.]

[67] Marlen Pew, "Shop Talk at Thirty," *Editor and Publisher* (Sept. 24, 1932). These and other instructions reported by Guy Hickok, then Paris correspondent for the Brooklyn *Daily Eagle;* A. J. Zurcher, "State Propaganda in Italy," *Propaganda and Dictatorship,* pp. 35-57; other instructions are cited by George Seldes in *Sawdust Caesar,* ch. 27.

[68] Anon., "Duce's Orders to Press Revealed by N. Y. Anti-Fascist Editor," *Editor and Publisher* (Nov. 30, 1935).

October 24

The account of the Fascist accomplishments in the year XIII [of the Fascist régime] must appear with emphasis in all newspapers.

Quench the correspondence from Asmara regarding Count Ciano, especially the headlines—cut down emphasis on the air squadron "La Desperata" (an organization to which Mussolini's two sons belong).

In the speech by Mussolini to the press, there must be taken out in the third paragraph the word "profound" which follows the word "justice."

In the message to the Black Shirts, in the sentence which starts with "Legionair della Rivoluzione" the words "you must" must be corrected as follows: "you shall"; and the words "you must" which come next must be corrected as follows: "you can."

October 29

As regards England as well as France and Germany, keep an attitude of reserve. Instead, give much emphasis to our internal activities. Put into relief the inauguration of our public works and especially of our University City.

Give space to the bulletins regarding limitations and economies on the consumers' needs, putting into relief that Fascist Italy answers with self-denial and a spirit of sacrifice to the iniquitous sanctions.

October 31

Comment on the telegram which the rabbit and poultry raisers sent Il Duce.

Devote entire front page to the ceremony at the inauguration of University City. Give it much prominence. Comment on Il Duce's speech.

In reference to the answer of the United States Government to the League of Nations, it is opportune that the comments of the Italian press be generally limited to the noted substantial confirmation of the neutrality stand by the United States. On the other hand, as regards the maintenance of the peace in Europe, put into relief the illusions of indirect encouragement to the action of the League that may be caused by the reading of the note of the American Secretary of State. Comment with the utmost reserve without appreciations that could reveal satisfaction for the American note to Geneva.

*   *   *

The ability of the government to command the support and coöperation of the domestic press and of individual journalists and editors, has made it possible to institute a propaganda within Italy itself that converted the population to a fairly unanimous point of view.

During the Ethiopian difficulty, for example, the Italian people were subjected to a press campaign of hate directed against Great Britain. The leader of this symphony of opinion seemed to be *Il Giornale d'Italia,* with its editor, Dr. Virginio Gayda, wielding the baton.

Before the Ethiopian affair, the hate campaigns were turned against Yugoslavia and France. Headlines would provide the clues to the articles. *Il Resto del Carlino* would head a report of an action in Yugoslavia, "A Ridiculous Yugoslav Manifesto" (Dec. 21, 1932). With it would appear a news story, an editorial, and a second news story, all aimed at Yugoslavia. In the *Gazetta del Popolo* of Turin, at about the same time, was a story about very anti-Italian expressions appearing in *Le Temps* of Paris.[69]

One purpose of such campaigns against another nation—the "enemy at the gates"—always has been to take the minds of the people off troubles within the country itself. This, in the opinion of observers, explains the campaigns in the Italian press, and certainly the method is time-honored. Another purpose, it has been said, is to keep the world reminded that Italian interests must not be ignored.

One observer has expressed the view that the Italian press is given considerable freedom in its handling and comment on foreign affairs in return for its acceptance of a considerable restriction in handling and commenting upon domestic affairs.

Italian embassies, legations and consulates watch the news of Italy appearing in the foreign newspapers. Offensive stories are

[69] The Italian Foreign Office admits the tendentious character of some of the news published. It declares such news is induced by public agitation and feeling, and is not inspired by the government. Asked whether the instructions to the Italian press might not cover such a situation, to produce restraint if desired, the Foreign Office representative shrugs and protests that that is an internal press matter and out of his hands, since the internal press relations are controlled by the Ministry of the Interior.

forwarded to Rome by telegraph or cable, if they warrant that attention, and the correspondent who sent the story may be called in to the Foreign Office press department and informed of the official displeasure. In some instances, the Foreign Office has summoned correspondents new in Italy to see how they would react to criticism. If, as a result, they "toned down" future dispatches, that of course pleased the government very much.[70]

Domestically, the censorship operates voluntarily, to a certain extent. The loyal Fascists now in control of the press know what it is "good form" to say, even as the journalists of Great Britain know what may properly be printed there. Hence, they seldom make mistakes. Agenzia Stefani, the official press association, distributes only what the government wants distributed, and the government press office keeps the newspapers informed and instructed on general policy, as already shown.

The foreign press deals with Foreign Office officials, who answer questions, arrange interviews and maintain general surveillance over what correspondents learn and write. If a correspondent persists in being unfriendly he will find news sources closed to him, and friends, acquaintances and assistants may have life made difficult for them until they realize why, and shun the correspondent.

The government has been known to try to discredit such a correspondent with his newspaper at home, perhaps by misleading him, deliberately, on a piece of information, and then denouncing him as inaccurate and unreliable when he falls into the trap. The Italian consul, or perhaps even the Ambassador, in the correspondent's native country will appeal to the publisher of his newspaper, try to convince that gentleman that the correspondent is unfair, inaccurate, or mischievous, and suggest that he ought to be transferred, if not discharged. Italians who are advertisers in the paper are persuaded to complain, and threaten to cancel advertising unless the paper ceases to print such allegedly inaccurate reports. In such ways, among others, the Italian Government has been known to try to get an unwelcome correspondent out of the

[70] On one occasion, the German Ambassador in Rome officially protested to the Italian Government against an harangue directed at Herr Mueller, then correspondent for Germany's Wolff agency in Rome.

country, preferably without expelling him, an extremity which is not considered to be good publicity. When foreign publications themselves offend, they may be excluded from Italy. All but three British papers were banned for a period in 1937 because of their attitudes toward Italy's part in Spain's civil war.[71]

The Foreign Office issues, each week, a review of the foreign press, *Rassenga Settimanale della Stampa Estera,* reprinting favorable comments upon Italian affairs extracted from newspapers all over the world, some of them extremely obscure, translated into Italian, and distributed for use by Italian papers. They are intended to prove how favorably Italy under the Fascist Government is regarded abroad.

* * *

The lot of the individual journalist in Italy was undeniably improved by the Fascist régime. Bribery, blackmail, and other undesirable practices were rooted out. Wages and employment were bettered. But the Decrees of November, 1925, affecting the press, placed stringent regulations upon the publication of news or opinion in the press of Italy, or its dissemination abroad. They were such as to deprive even the most honorable journalist of his freedom, and operated to standardize the press.[72]

Fascist spokesmen maintain that strict regulation of the Italian press is necessary because of conditions in the country. Prior to the Fascist régime blackmail was a common journalistic practice. Editors and publishers escaped responsibility for what was written or published in their papers. Conditions for newspaper men were

[71] Four correspondents covering the Italo-Ethiopian campaign in Ethiopia were expelled by Italian army officers in May, 1936, after the capture of Addis Ababa. *Editor and Publisher* (May 23, 1936), p. 43. Three American correspondents were expelled from Italy itself between 1922 and 1936. They were George Seldes and David Darrah of the Chicago *Tribune,* and Henry T. Gorrell of the United Press. John Giglio of the London *Daily Herald,* was expelled in 1936. George Steer, correspondent for *The Times* of London, also was expelled from Ethiopia. See note 62, p. 246 ante; note 7, pp. 142-143 ante.

[72] A. E. Johnson, "Italy's Press Helpless in Iron Grip of Dictator Mussolini," *Editor and Publisher* (May 11, 1929), p. 24; H. L. Matthews, "Fascists Efficient in Handling News," New York *Times* (Jan. 21, 1933).

LIRE 3.60

MINISTERO DEGLI AFFARI ESTERI
UFFICIO STAMPA

RASSEGNA SETTIMANALE

DELLA

STAMPA ESTERA

| ANNO 7° | 13 DICEMBRE 1932 (XI) | FASC. 49 |

PER LE CONDIZIONI DI ABBONAMENTO VEDI RETRO

SOMMARIO

GIORNALI

Mod. 110

AGENZIA STEFANI

Fondata nel 1853 - ROMA - Via Propaganda N. 27

L'abbonamento ai servizi dell'Agenzia Stefani è personale. L'Agenzia si riserva ogni diritto contro la comunicazione e la pubblicazione non autorizzata, fatta con qualsiasi mezzo, delle sue notizie ed informazioni.

L'Agenzia non assume alcuna responsabilità per eventuali errori o ritardi che potessero verificarsi nei suoi servizi

GENOVA 24 = In occasione del giugno genovese che, come è noto, si ripeterà anche nel 1933 con un programma vario che è allo studio, S.E. Ciano, Ministro delle Comunicazioni, ha concesso alla Associazione per lo sviluppo del turismo ligure che ne è promotrice, la riduzione ferroviaria del 50 per cento sulle tariffe ordinarie differenziali da tutte le stazioni della rete per Genova nel periodo dal primo giugno al 2 luglio 1933. I detti biglietti avranno la validità di 5 giorni se emessi dalle stazioni della Liguria e di 10 giorni se emessi dalle stazioni delle altre regioni d'Italia.

---

bb.

AGENZIA STEFANI

ANNO LXXX   ROMA 26 DICEMBRE 1932 ANNO XI   N.1

STEFANI RADIO

PARIGI 26 = Torneo Internazionale natalizio di tennis = Singolare uomini. Primo giro : Rado (Italia) batte Leven (Francia) per 6/4,6/2; Brugnon (Francia) batte Marinsi (Italia) per 8/10,6/2,6/1.

Nelle ottave di finale per doppio misto Barbier-Lesneur (Francia) battono Orlandini-Rado per 6/3.(Radio Stefani)

CANNES 26 = Ecco i risultati della riunione pugilistica organizzata dal Casino Municipale di Cannes: Kessler batte Rusticali ai punti;Cavagnoli batte Beghin per abbandono alla quarta ripresa; Thil batte van Haoke per abbandono alla seconda ripresa.(Radio Stefani)

SANTIAGO DEL CILE 26 = Mandano da Lima che il nuovo Governo peruviano sarà presieduto da José Mathias Manzanilla anziché da Pedro Irigoyen, che resterà ambasciatore del Perù al Cile.(Radio Stefani)

FIG. 31. NEWS AS IT IS

For description see

Stamane nella Sala del Trono, alla presenza del Santo Padre, si è tenuta la Con-

gregazione Generale dei Riti. Ad essa hanno preso parte i Cardinali, i Prelati

officiali ed i Consultori di detta Congregazione, i quali hanno discusso e dato

il voto su due miracoli proposti per la Beatificazione della Ven. Maria di Santa

Eufrasia Pelletier, fondatrice delle Suore del Buon Pastore, morta nella diocesi

di Angers, nel 1868.

Se la votazione e la decisione del Papa saranno favorevoli, la procedura per la

Beatificazione della Ven. Pelletier si può considerare esaurita, perchè manche-

ranno soltanto delle formalità quali sono: la Lettura del Decreto alla presenza

del Papa e la Lettura del Decreto del "Tutò", col quale si autorizza a procedere

alla Beatificazione. La Causa della Ven. Pelletier fu introdotta il 7 dicembre

1897. I processi Ordinari (diocesani) si svolsero nella diocesi di Angers. Il 24

febbraio 1924 ebbe luogo, alla presenza del Papa la lettura del Decreto che riche
conosceva/la proposta Beata ha esercitato le virtù in grado eroico. Il 23 febbra

AGENZIA DI ROMA
BOLLETTINO QUOTIDIANO D'INFORMAZIONI

ROMA (20)   Piazza Capranica, 95 p. p.   Telef. 65-878

Indirizzo Telegrafico ADIR - Roma

ANNO IX° N° 291   MARTEDI 13 DICEMBRE 1932-XI   Foglio II

AUMENTO DI FALLIMENTI IN BELGIO
E DIMINUZIONE DELLE ESPORTAZIONI

Roma,13 L'"Agenzia di Roma" riceve da Bruxelles che dal 1° gennaio al 2
dicembre di quest'anno, i fallimenti in Belgio sono stati complessivamente
1.037 contro 742 nel corrispondente periodo dell'anno scorso.

AGENZIA DI ROMA
BOLLETTINO QUOTIDIANO D'INFORMAZIONI

ROMA (20)   Piazza Capranica, 95 p. p.   Telef. 65-878

Indirizzo Telegrafico ADIR - Roma

ANNO IX° N° 296   LUNEDI 19 DICEMBRE 1932-XI   Foglio I

L'INDUSTRIA ELETTRICA IN ITALIA
UN CAPITALE INVESTITO DI 11 MILIARDI E 851 MILIONI

Roma,19 L'"Agenzia di Roma" informa che alla data del 1° dicembre scorso,
le imprese elettriche in Italia risultavano ammontare complessivamente a
1.202 con un capitale di 11.851.785.000 lire. Di esse 503 erano società
anonime con un complesso di capitale azionario di 11.543.252.000 lire;
668 imprese non anonime con 220.783.000 lire di capitale investito; e 31
imprese esercenti anche attività accessorie con un capitale di 87.750.000
lire.

Frattanto l'energia elettrica consumata in Italia segna un si-
gnificativo se pur lieve aumento. Dal 1° gennaio a tutto ottobre, tra energia prodotta e energia importata in Italia si sono consumati 8.396,796.000
kilowatt-ora con un aumento di 7.980.000 Kwh. rispetto al corrispondente
periodo del 1931.

(AGENZIA DI ROMA)

DISTRIBUTED IN ITALY

List of Illustrations

uncertain and their status was low. Matters now are much improved in that way.[73]

The Agenzia Stefani, set up in Turin in 1854 by Guglielmo Stefano, has become the leading news agency of Italy. It is an affiliate of the Reuters-Havas-Associated Press league, was an official government agency in other years, and under Fascism it became one of the more potent devices by which the government was able to distribute controlled news to the press. At present, the Stefani agency distributes most of its news in mimeographed form by bicyclists, who go to the various newspaper offices in Rome, and to the offices there of representatives for provincial newspapers. Most provincial papers in Italy do maintain correspondents in Rome. They select what is wanted from the Stefani service and telephone it to their provincial offices, along with the day's instructions from the government press department, telling what news is to be used, and how.

The Stefani service is of three kinds: (1) The so-called Radio service is a selection of foreign news. Despite the name, it is neither received nor distributed by radio, and is not a very fast service of foreign information. (2) The Regular service consists chiefly of national news. (3) The Financial service is faster, and the news comes chiefly from Milan, by telegraph. The chief stock exchange is in that city, although there are smaller exchanges in Rome, and the northern city also is Italy's chief business and industrial cen-

---

[73] An interview in 1929 with Angelo Guidi of *Il Messaggero,* of Rome, held these to be facts: "Italy needs Mussolini now," he is quoted as having said. "In a few years the country may be granted more freedom. But today that is impossible. The censorship imposed is not so much political as it is a moral question. The censorship is handled by the prefectures. A paper is assembled without any government supervision and the first copies printed are submitted to the prefecture. He cuts out offending material, or sequesters the copy of the paper. There are papers opposing Mussolini in Italy. But it is true they are not allowed to inflame their readers against him. Nor do they care to. Mussolini is a great popular hero. The Italian press hesitates to say anything against him. He might not punish. But the fascisti would." Anon., "Mussolini Dignified Journalism in Italy, Rome Newspaper Man Says," *Editor and Publisher* (Feb. 9, 1929), p. 24. See also: Anon., *Conditions of Work and Life of Journalists;* Ermanno Amicucci, *Le Contrat de Travail des Journalistes.* (French translation of a summary of conditions and advantages of work for Italian journalists.)

ter. Stefani is purely official, and it presents both foreign and domestic news.[74]

The Agenzia di Roma is directed especially toward the production and distribution of political and financial news, with interpretation. It is less cut-and-dried than Stefani, and less general, but equally loyal to the régime. Except for Stefani, it is the only Italian agency maintaining representatives outside of the country. It may go so far, in its interpretation, as to discuss and criticize to some extent the actions of the government, but no real opposition is tolerated to any policy that has been definitely decided upon by the central authority.

Thus, the press—newspapers as well as press associations— have a certain liberty, a freedom within the régime, a responsibility to aid the State, and this is the basis for claims, sometimes made, that Italy's press is free. Fascismo demands devotion to a "United Italy," and the press must accept this fundamental concept.

* * *

Rome is not quite a first-water news center, in the same sense as London or Paris, but it is active, nevertheless, and important because of the implications involved in news of Fascism and its undertakings, as well as for the things that actually happen in Italy.

Because of the air of force and oppression that exists, especially in Rome, it has been said that Italy "must be felt—not explained." No opposition is recognized, and only one official opinion is tolerated. For this reason, the press is useless as an index to minority or dissenting views or even impartial views. Everything, at least of a political or economic nature, which reaches publication in the Italian press bears the stamp of official approval, or it does not appear, for the Italian press is an instrument of the State. There have been one or two unsanctioned newspapers, but they have been of no special importance and usually of short life. The Vati-

[74] Manlio Morgagni, "L'Agenzia Stefani," *Annuario della Stampa Italiana* (see Anon.), 1931-1932, pp. 359-66. A description of the history and service of the Italian news agency, written by its President and General Director.

can newspaper, the *Osservatore Romano,* published in Vatican City and so beyond Fascist censorship or control, is one which, at times, has displayed some reportorial and editorial independence.

The news of the Vatican is of interest to the correspondent in Italy. In years past, the office of the Papal Secretary of State was the chief news source there, but neither the correspondents nor the Vatican were satisfied with the results. Although there is now a regular Vatican press representative, he is strictly unofficial, so far as the Vatican is concerned. He visits the Vatican, knows what is going on there, and produces a mimeographed sheet every day, which he distributes to his clients on a paid, syndicate basis.[75]

For general news of Italian affairs, apart from official statements and viewpoints emanating from the government offices, correspondents find that much background material, especially of an opposition character, is to be had at foreign embassies and legations. Even though these are unofficial sources, and usually cannot be quoted, they are extremely helpful.

As in France, and apart from the conditions of Fascism, there is unwillingness among Italians, including many government officials, to express definite views on some subjects, particularly political topics, and sometimes on matters of no apparent moment. This has made difficulty for the correspondent. His questions too often draw a shrug and the reply, *"Non risulta,"* an untranslatable phrase meaning, roughly, "there is nothing new along that line."

Yet, some Italian journalists and editors will tell a foreign correspondent, if they trust him, about news known in Italian newspaper offices, but which will not appear in the Italian press—not promptly or frankly, at any rate. But some such news may go abroad without objection.[76] Or, it may be something definitely political. There are correspondents, too, who are more favored than others in that they are permitted a rather surprising degree of frankness in their dispatches.

[75] Relations between press and Vatican in other years are described by H. Wickham Steed in *Through Thirty Years,* V. 1, Chs. 4-5.

[76] This may be an account of an explosion, which could be regarded as reflecting upon Italian industrial efficiency, or which may imply political unrest, but which for its own reasons the government does not wish to become generally known and commented upon in Italy.

The Italian Government gives a somewhat greater amount of coöperation to the foreign press than many European nations, although the information provided is more one-sided than that provided by some others. The Foreign Office in Rome talks with the correspondents through its press officers; correspondents are permitted, occasionally, to talk to Mussolini; interviews are arranged quite readily with lesser officials of the government, and sometimes with other persons of importance; statistics are brought together from various departments of government; books are obtained for correspondents, to help them; trips are arranged, lower rail fares are provided. While all of this is convenient for correspondents, it permits the government to keep a certain supervision over what appears in the foreign press. The government also maintains an attractive press club for correspondents in good standing, meaning those not unfriendly.

* * *

Despite this government coöperation, however, the other circumstances make facts the hardest and most elusive things to find in Italy. Getting the news is the chief problem for the correspondent.[77] Facts are not in the press, and those who know what is going on seldom will speak frankly or impartially. The result is that the conscientious correspondent must read and study constantly, everything relevant to Italian affairs, and he must talk with and question those persons able to clarify the situation for him, whenever he has the opportunity to meet them. Some correspondents believe that about two years of study is necessary to understand the Fascist viewpoint and to learn how to estimate and comprehend a non-vocal opposition view. In the next breath, they add that three or four years is all that most correspondents can endure in Italy, under present circumstances, partly because the constant repression does tend to "get on the nerves," and partly because there is only a limited amount of work to do in the actual business of covering the news.

A special correspondent for a foreign newspaper may not send

[77] For that matter, facts always were difficult to dig out in Italy, according to the testimony of correspondents there in pre-Fascist days.

a so-called spot news story more than once in three days during some periods, apart from routine reports of financial markets and mail copy of a semi-feature variety. The real job is study.

The press association correspondents have a harder task than the "specials" because they must keep sending the news, and more details, constantly, and they have a harder time satisfying local authorities.

One special correspondent may say that he has had little trouble with censorship of his copy, and that "only a nitwit would have" because it is possible to express things in a way that will not give offense. On the other hand, a press association bureau chief reports having had his messages delayed on occasion, and even edited by the censor with words, phrases and sentences deleted and changed.

Having obtained the news, and prepared his dispatch, the correspondent may file it for dispatch by telegraph, cable, or wireless. But there is an increasing use of the telephone. The Rome correspondent for an American afternoon paper may call Paris or London, and does so usually about noon. Later news may be filed up to about 5:45 P.M. in Rome, which is 4:45 P.M. in London and Paris, and 11.45 A.M. in New York, time enough to make the afternoon editions with important news. The morning papers file between 8 and 9 P.M. in Rome, and rarely later except when the Grand Council holds a session, or some other extremely important event occurs. The Grand Council sessions start at 10 P.M. and may go on until 5 A.M. or longer. After such a meeting a communiqué is issued to the press.

*   *   *

The Italian press, like the German—and before the German— is revealing for what it does not print as well as for what it does print. Certain newspapers are watched with special care by discerning journalists, and excerpts from those papers may be sent abroad when they are believed to represent the official view of the government, or some other attitude.[78]

---

[78] *Il Popolo d'Italia,* of Milan, for example, is Mussolini's own paper, which he edited until 1922, and which was edited by his brother, Arnaldo, until he died, and now is edited by a nephew. It is considered to reflect the

FIG. 32. ITALY'S "NATIONAL" NEWSPAPERS
For description see List of Illustrations

Since the press never is entirely devoted to controversial matters or politics and economics, however, it is fair to say that articles about the drama, the arts, literature, and some other topics are well done in Italian newspapers. Crime and scandal, although never so prominent in the press of Italy as in the press of certain other countries, has been reduced to the minimum and is kept off page one, by government order. It was overemphasis on such news by a few papers, and a tendency in some quarters to use the press as an instrument for blackmail, that gave the Fascist Government a plausible excuse for muzzling the entire press.

Italian interest in politics always has been strong enough to warrant the publication *in extenso* of political speeches and serious matter that would have received short shrift in most newspaper offices of the United States or Great Britain. It was Mussolini's wish that the Italian press should be conservative and that it should educate and enlighten readers. Since the Fascist Government took office the press in Italy accordingly has become more serious in tone and the volume of foreign news has increased.

There are in Italy two classes of papers. What may be called "national papers" go all over Italy and have considerable influence and importance. The "localized press," on the other hand, does not reach readers much beyond the immediate place of publication, yet it may be important as representing special points of view, particularly on internal political attitudes.

The "national papers" include the *Corriere della Sera*, of Milan; *La Stampa*, of Turin; the *Gazzetta del Popolo*, of Turin; *Il Giornale d'Italia*, of Rome; *Messaggero*, of Rome; *Tribuna*, of Rome; and *Il Popolo d'Italia*, of Milan.

Lavoro, of Genoa, is a "localized paper" which has something of a national importance because it is permitted to be more critical and outspoken than others.

government opinion. *Il Giornale d'Italia*, of Rome, edited by Dr. Virginio Gayda, also is considered to be close to the government. Dr. Gayda's editorials were quoted throughout the world during the Italian invasion of Ethiopia in 1935 and 1936, because he was considered to be saying in blunt and realistic terms what the Italian Government itself could not say officially. Papers owned by Italo Balbo and other prominent Fascist party members also are carefully read.

The *Corriere Padano,* of Ferrara, is a "localized paper" that is important because it expresses General Italo Balbo's ideas. Similarly, *Regima Fascista,* of Cremona, is important because it is edited by Roberto Farinacci, former Secretary of the Fascist party, and a Life Member of the Grand Council.

La Stampa, of Turin, has a double importance because it is not only a national newspaper of merit, but is edited by Augusto Turati, another former Secretary of the Fascist party.

The *Corriere della Sera,* of Milan, was considered the greatest newspaper in Italy before the Great War, and during the War it was considered by some to be the greatest newspaper in Europe, if not in the world, because it tried to report events without prejudice and to penetrate the propaganda fog. It remains an important newspaper, but it went under a new management late in 1925, a management friendly to Mussolini.[79] Although called the "Courier of the Evening," the paper actually appears in the morning, except on Mondays, when the first edition reaches the streets and starts into the country at 12 noon and is eagerly bought by the people, who have seen no newspaper since Sunday morning. The circulation is 600,000 to 700,000 daily. It has special correspondents in Paris, London, Vienna, Berlin and New York, and it maintains a considerable staff in Rome to cover it on the news there, to get the government news and instructions, to select and edit the Stefani file, and to forward it all to Milan. It has exchange arrangements with *The Times* in London and *Le Matin* in Paris.

Only one cable reaches this paper daily, and that is from New York. Most of its news from the United States is gleaned from that which *The Times* of London provides. A considerable amount of material also arrives by mail and by telephone. The paper, which had a foreign correspondent in Paris in 1876,[80] its first year

[79] Anon., "Albertini Gave Italy First Modern Daily," *Editor and Publisher* (Dec. 26, 1925), p. 11. Senator Luigi Albertini, Managing Director of the *Corriere della Sera,* is referred to. The paper had been founded in 1876. He came to it in 1898 and made a great paper of it. He and it had a great and good influence on all Italian journalism. He was forced out under the Fascist régime.

[80] The old *Seccolo,* of Milan, already had a correspondent in Paris at that time, and the *Tribuna,* of Rome, later sent a man to Paris. The *Corriere della*

FIG. 33. LEADING "LOCALIZED" NEWSPAPERS OF ITALY

For description see List of Illustrations

of existence, is in telephone connection nightly, for several periods of a number of minutes each, with Paris (93 minutes), London (42 minutes), Berlin (21 minutes), Vienna (21 minutes). The Russian news comes through the London and Paris exchange arrangements.

Italy is an important center for Balkan news, and the *Corriere della Sera* provides a fair budget of that information, coming to it through Vienna, for the most part. It also is the leading paper of Italian Switzerland, which is largely agricultural and has no strong press of its own. The paper depends upon the Agenzia Stefani only for official news and announcements, looking to its own news organization for the rest.

La Stampa, of Turin, which was anti-Fascist at one time, became pro-Fascist in 1925. *Il Mattino* of Naples, formerly anti-Fascist, changed ownership and became pro-Fascist. And so it went. *Il Messaggero*, of Rome, was one of the original pro-Fascist papers. Some Fascist papers were established to replace the anti-Fascist papers that had been suppressed.[81] Smaller newspapers in Italy commonly fill out their news columns by rewriting the foreign news, and other dispatches, from the *Corriere della Sera* and *La Stampa*, the two papers with the best news service. This they have been able to do because of the lax laws in Italy affecting copyright and property right in the news.

One or two other moderately important papers in Italy include *Il Resto del Carlino*, of Bologna, *Il Secolo-Sera*, of Milan, and *Il Lavoro Fascista* and *Il Tevere*, both of Rome. There are also the *Osservatore Romano*, published in Vatican City, and some reviews and quarterlies which receive the attention of correspondents.[82]

Sera sent a man to London soon after 1876, but Paris always has been the most important foreign capital for Italy. The beginning of actual foreign representation for the Italian press is hazy. All the papers to-day do the best they can, considering their limited means.

[81] Philip Schuyler, "Only Two Anti-Fascist Dailies Survive Premier Mussolini's Press Gag," *Editor and Publisher* (Feb. 6, 1926), p. 3. They did not survive for long.

[82] *Annuario della Stampa Italiana.* An annual listing all newspapers and Fascist journalists, with a vast amount of information concerning the press and news gathering in Italy during the year indicated. For other lists of newspapers in Italy, see *Europa*, under "Italy"; *Political Handbook of the*

§ 6. MOSCOW AND THE U.S.S.R.

IT HAS been difficult for the world to consider the news from or about Russia, uncolored by prejudices. Regardless of prejudices, however, the Soviet remains big with news importance, partly because so many millions of persons are affected in Russia itself, a country reaching halfway around the globe, and partly because the ideas being tried there are causing profound changes in thought everywhere.

Journalistically, Russia's earliest newspapers were established by direction of Peter the Great, first at Moscow and then at St. Petersburg, to report the progress of the war with Sweden. The first gazette, the *Viedomosti,* appeared in Moscow in 1702. Periods of crisis, such as the time of the French invasion in 1812, the Polish insurrection of 1830, the Crimean War of 1854, and the war with Japan in 1904 all brought more lively journalistic times, but the limited literacy in the country kept papers few and circulations relatively small, and no political journalism existed at all until after 1905, and then under marked restrictions.

Before the Great War, Russia was not an active source of news, although the Associated Press-Reuters-Havas group had its exchange arrangement with the Petrograd News Agency,[83] of Tsarist Russia. A foreign journalist went to Russia occasionally, but there was no thorough coverage of news originating there.[84] The press was heavily censored and the outgoing news also was colored to suit official wishes. Even Russia's participation in the Great War did not induce the dispatch of war correspondents to the Eastern front. A few went there, but not in the numbers that had covered the Russo-Japanese War in the Far East in 1904.

World, under "Italy"; and other reference sources as noted in n. 1, this chapter; Adolph Dresler, *Geschichte der Italienischen Presse,* 2 vols. Includes a history of the Italian press to 1933-1934. A German study.

[83] Russia was opened to the world in a news way through the efforts of Melville E. Stone, general manager of the Associated Press, who had interviews with the Tsar and his officials in 1904, and gained a relaxation of the news censorship. Melville E. Stone, *Fifty Years a Journalist,* pp. 263-78.

[84] As correspondent in Russia for the London *Daily Telegraph* from 1886-1914, Dr. Émile J. Dillon was an exception, since he remained there permanently, and was the greatest journalist authority on pre-war Russia.

When the Tsarist Government was overthrown in March, 1917, the Kerensky Government was set up. That government itself was replaced in November, 1917 (October, according to the Julian calendar used in Russia), by the Bolsheviks under Lenin and Trotsky. The apparent desertion of the Allied cause in the War angered many in Allied countries, and frightened many more with the Communist threat to established institutions. With the lack of proper news coverage in Russia, those fears were reflected in many ill-informed and exaggerated news reports, some of them possibly manufactured out of whole cloth for their propaganda value, others doubtless resulting from poor news organization in Russia and prejudice at home.[85]

Virtually the only satisfactory foreign correspondence from Soviet Russia before 1920 was that appearing in the Manchester *Guardian* and written by Mr. Arthur Ransome. He was in Russia, he investigated with great care before he wrote, and he wrote about significant subjects. It was not always "spot news," but it was accurate, objective, valuable.[86]

[85] See Walter Lippmann and Charles Merz, "A Test of the News," supplement to the *New Republic*, Aug. 4, 1920. This is a study of the news reports about Russia that appeared in the New York *Times* between March, 1917, when the Kerensky Government went into power, and March, 1920. It professed to show that "the news on one matter of transcendent importance to America has been dubious." It showed "how seriously misled was the *Times* by its reliance upon the official purveyors of information." It showed "that certain correspondents are totally untrustworthy because their sympathies are too deeply engaged." It "indicates that even so rich and commanding a newspaper as the *Times* does not take seriously enough the equipment of the correspondent." It "shows further that at critical periods the time-honored tradition of protecting news against editorials breaks down. The Russian policy of the editors of the *Times* profoundly and crassly influenced their news columns. The office handling of the news, both as to emphasis and captions, was unmistakably controlled by other than a professional standard."

This report was instrumental in inducing the New York *Times* to send Walter Duranty as its correspondent to Moscow, which was opened to foreign journalists at about that time. There he remained for years and won praise and confidence, not to mention the Pulitzer Prize of 1932, for his reports of events and trends in Russia.

[86] Much of his correspondence is collected in book form. See: Arthur Ransome, *The Crisis in Russia*. See also: Arno Dosch-Fleurot, *Through War to Revolution*, Chs. 7-14. The experiences of a correspondent in Russia at the time of the Revolution; Negley Farson, *Way of a Transgressor*, Ch. 33.

In 1918 the Petrograd News Agency had been seized by the Bolsheviks, and reorganized as the Rosta agency, which became known as the Tass agency (full name, Telegrafnoje Agentswo Ssojusa) in 1925.

So far as concerned Russian news in the United States, the change for the better began in August, 1921, when Walter Duranty went to Moscow for the New York *Times*. It was further improved in January, 1923, when the United Press began a news exchange with the Rosta agency. Presently the Associated Press followed suit. In its earliest years the Bolshevik Government had not wanted the foreign press represented in Russia.[87] After 1921, however, an increasing number of correspondents went there, and to-day only a few newspapers maintaining extensive services lack correspondents there.[88] The service is as good as possible, considering the existence of a strict censorship, and considering a lingering prejudice against the Soviet Government. Even where a correspondent is able and impartial, therefore, editors at home sometimes are at least capable of damning his best objective efforts by cutting, filling, and rewriting, by the headlines and divisionals they give a story, and by the pictures and picture captions and cutlines that they select or produce for the occasion.[89]

* * *

The work of the correspondent in Russia differs sharply from his work in almost any other capital of the world. There is a different concept of news there. Political campaigns are lacking, there is no parliament, no politics, in fact; no labor troubles worth mentioning, very little news of court cases, and not much in the way of personality stories. In some respects, Italy and Germany have come to resemble Russia in these aspects of news—or the lack of it. On the other hand, there is the news of the economic,

[87] Walter Duranty, *I Write as I Please.*

[88] Those which do not have correspondents in Russia include *The Times* of London and the Chicago *Tribune*.

[89] The Chicago *Tribune* and the Hearst newspapers in the United States conduct an almost unceasing campaign against all things smacking of Communism.

social and political reconstruction of a vast country, and a more tremendous story would be difficult to find.[90]

Although Moscow and Leningrad look like other European cities in most ways, some commentators believe the people are almost as different from Europeans in character as are the Chinese. This makes Russia something of a puzzle to new correspondents, who must learn to regard its people and events, not by any standards with which they were familiar in other lands, but in the light of the fact that the country is different, and so vast that it differs within its own boundaries. Preconceived ideas and prejudices must be cast aside, for only then can correspondents begin to understand what they are trying to report, and only then can they begin to produce stories that reveal Russia somewhat as it is.[91]

The news in Russia has to be dug out, bit by bit. The government is superficially friendly, but the correspondent receives from it very little coöperation in trying to get interviews or information, and the higher officials are almost inaccessible.[92] The gov-

[90] Edwin W. Hullinger, "Battling for News in Bolshevik Russia," *Editor and Publisher* (Jan. 7, 1922), pp. 5, 16. This recounts the experience of the correspondent in Moscow in the early days of the Soviet Government; F. A. Mackenzie, "Getting the News out of Soviet Russia," *Editor and Publisher* (Mar. 7, 1925), pp. 5-6; Mackenzie, "A Foreign Correspondent in Soviet Russia," *Journalism by Some Masters of the Craft* (see Anon.), pp. 145-49.

[91] John F. Roche, "Uninterpreted News of Russia Puzzles Prejudiced World, Says Duranty," *Editor and Publisher* (June 4, 1932), pp. 5-6; Walter Duranty, "Not 'Anti-Bolshevik'" (Letter commenting upon above article), *Editor and Publisher* (June 25, 1932). This reference is a most edifying explanation of the Russian attitude toward the press and of the task confronting the foreign correspondent in Russia. See also: Walter Duranty, "Soviet to Attend World Press Parley," New York *Times* (Jan. 10, 1932); Duranty, *I Write as I Please;* Duranty, *Russia Reported. 1921-1933.*

[92] When American correspondents obtained interviews with Stalin, with his mother, and with his wife in 1930, after long efforts, it was regarded as something most remarkable. Anon., "Stalin Interview Won After Year's Work," by Eugene Lyons, United Press Correspondent, *Editor and Publisher* (Nov. 29, 1930), p. 10. The only previous interview Stalin had granted was with four Japanese newspaper men, representing the Osaka *Mainichi,* in 1926; Anon., "First Red Lady." (Ralph W. Barnes, correspondent for the New York *Herald Tribune*, interviews Mme. Josef Stalin.) *Time* (Dec. 14, 1931); Anon., "Soso was Good!" (H. R. Knickerbocker, then represent-

ernment controls all of the newspapers, so that no opposition or minority view is to be found there. The government also regards the domestic press as an instrument of propaganda that belongs to the State, and while they may not tell lies in their newspapers, neither do they always tell all the truth. The correspondent will read, or have read to him, most of the papers, and from them glean useful material, but not enough to free him from the necessity of looking farther.

Direct personal investigation and observation, such interviews as he can obtain, and occasional visits to institutions maintained by the State will be valuable. Personal relations that he can develop with persons who know what is going on will provide the correspondent with material, if those persons are not afraid to talk. Official statements and acts give him the basis for much else that is newsworthy. Communiqués from the Foreign Office or other departments convey the bare bones of some news. Foreign diplomats, foreign engineers and specialists, visitors, and foreign business representatives are good sources, but all take time to develop. The file of Tass news, when available, may help.

In some instances, the government has restricted the freedom of correspondents, at least to the extent of refusing them permission to visit areas where difficulties—famine or resistance to the authorities—were supposed to exist, and barring them from prison camps, forced labor areas, et cetera. The language, too, has presented difficulties to correspondents, and long residence commonly is necessary to master it. Without that knowledge, traveling is not very profitable, for it prevents the correspondent gaining a proper understanding of the people and the country.

Interviews with officials, even when obtained, are likely to be unsatisfactory. Most of them require that the correspondent send in his questions in written form, to be answered or ignored, as the official chooses, and often without the correspondent and official meeting face to face. Minor officials and private persons are much too afraid that the secret police will take reprisals if they dare

ing the New York *Evening Post* and other Curtis-Martin newspapers, interviews Stalin's mother.) *Time* (Dec. 8, 1930), p. 24; Anon., "High Soviet Officials Hard to Interview," *Editor and Publisher* (Nov. 7, 1931), p. 42.

to speak with any freedom at all. Those persons who are known or believed to have talked to a correspondent may be held responsible if he writes something unwelcome to the government, and retribution may be swift and silent.[93]

The success of a correspondent in Russia depends very greatly upon his ability to read and speak the difficult language of the country, to look between the lines in the newspapers, to piece together scraps of information gleaned here and there, and to see whatever he is permitted to see with more than ordinary eyesight. Even then he is restrained somewhat by the official censorship and by a self-imposed censorship which leads him to temper his language if he wishes to remain at his post. Because of this general situation, there is extensive opportunity for interpretative writing in the Soviet, and a correspondent's chief opportunity to get an exclusive story is based upon intelligent and penetrating judgment.

The mere physical effort required to live in Moscow and to get about to places where the news may or may not be found has, in the past, been intense. Some officials have issued releases in the early morning hours. Improved communication facilities have obliged correspondents to work nearly all night, as well as all day, to protect themselves against missing some important story which should reach the home office promptly. And once the news has been rounded up and written it must be taken or sent to the Soviet Press Bureau in the Commissariat of Foreign Affairs for submission to a censor. The copy must be signed and stamped by one of the censors before it will be accepted for transmission. And after it is stamped, it must be carried to the telegraph office.

For all of these reasons it takes time to get the news in Russia. The correspondent needs patience and he must work hard. It is an enormous country, news facilities are indifferent, and he himself rarely gets away from Moscow. Yet he must keep his home office satisfied, for it is expensive to maintain the correspondent in Russia at all, perhaps with an assistant and a secretary. He must be there long enough to build up news contacts, and that is

[93] So Russian secretaries or assistants to foreign correspondents have been held responsible personally when the correspondents have written objectionable material, and have been punished.

why his value tends to increase in proportion to the time he remains, more than in almost any other post, even though he may leave at intervals to refresh his viewpoint.

* * *

The censorship itself has been less of a problem to correspondents in Russia than in some other countries because it is routine in character, and permits a human, open relationship between journalist and censor. Most copy passes without question and in some doubtful cases the censor is willing to discuss the matter with the correspondent, enabling him to rephrase the story to meet objections. In general, therefore, the Soviet censorship has stood as the frankest and the most satisfactory type—if there must be such a thing as censorship.

Russia had a censorship long before the Soviet Government came into power. In 1904 Melville E. Stone, then general manager of the Associated Press, went to St. Petersburg, interviewed the Tsar and high officials in an effort to gain their coöperation in making the news of Russia more easily available to the rest of the world, and to arrange a relaxation of the censorship.[94] Although his efforts were not without results, much of the good was rather quickly undone by the situation which arose in Russia at the time of the war with Japan in that same year, and by the 1905 revolutionary outbreak.

After the 1917 Revolution the press of Russia was completely subjugated, and foreign correspondents were, at first, unwelcome. When they were admitted, it was only under sharp restraint.

In 1923 a group of correspondents called on Maxim Litvinoff, then Assisant Foreign Commissar, to ask the complete lifting of censorship on foreign dispatches. They contended that the censorship was hurting Russia, that conditions were not nearly so bad as people in other countries were led to believe because, with a censorship known to exist, they supposed matters were worse than reported. To this Litvinoff replied that there was no censorship of fact, or even of opinion, but that the censorship was con-

[94] M. E. Stone, *Fifty Years a Journalist*, pp. 263-78; Anon., *"M.E.S." His Book*, pp. 139-58.

fined solely to eliminating unverified rumors, or the biased or untruthful reporting of alleged facts. He contended that Russia was in a state of semi-war, and surrounded by enemies, so the government could not abandon the censorship entirely.

All newspapers in Russia are government-controlled. The transmission facilities are owned by the government. This permits the government to supervise the contents of the newspapers and to keep an especially careful watch on outgoing news reports. A correspondent is permitted to mail out his copy. Usually the mail is not inspected, but sometimes it is, and because copy occasionally fails to reach its destination a carbon duplicate often is sent just in case one is held by the mail censor. If the correspondent telephones doubtful messages to Berlin or London, he risks having the connection broken should he report certain kinds of news.[95]

In such ways it is possible for a correspondent to evade the censorship, but if he does so, and has sent out statements that are considered untrue, unfriendly, or undesirable by the government he may find that news gathering has become more difficult for him. Or, if he leaves the country for any reason he may be refused a visa to return. Seldom will he be expelled outright.[96]

[95] The correspondent in Moscow for the Associated Press, Mr. Stanley P. Richardson; and the correspondent there for the New York *Herald Tribune,* Mr. Ralph W. Barnes, evaded the censorship on the arrest of the British engineers of Metropolitan Vickers Co. in Moscow in 1933, preliminary to their trial, by telephoning to their Berlin bureaus.

[96] A woman writer for the London *Daily Express* was expelled in November, 1932, however, because she wrote a series on Russian prison camps without having seen such a camp, since they are closed to the public. She did go to the general neighborhood of a camp, but her stories were without much foundation.

Paul Scheffer, Moscow correspondent for the *Berliner Tageblatt* for some years, and then regarded by many persons as perhaps the best correspondent in Russia, left the country for a visit to Germany and was refused a visa to return. Punitive measures also were taken against his secretary.

Georges Lucianni, correspondent in Moscow for Havas and *Le Temps* of Paris, had the same experience, but he appealed to the French Government, which promptly threatened to bar all Russian correspondents from France unless Lucianni was permitted to return to Moscow. The Soviet Government relented and gave him his reëntry visa.

Walter Duranty nearly was refused a reëntry on one occasion, due to a misunderstanding in Moscow concerning the source of his information on a certain story. See: Walter Duranty, *I Write as I Please,* pp. 259-70.

If a message is to go by telegraph or cable, the correspondent must take his completed dispatch to one of the four censors in the Commissariat of Foreign Affairs. They read it and either pass it for transmission, or make changes, which the correspondent is permitted to see. Because of the opportunity this gives him to learn what is and what is not objectionable, and then to fix the copy so that it makes good sense, the Russian style of censorship is preferred by the correspondents themselves. Yet no other country uses that style.[97]

There are no written rules to guide correspondents. Usually they are permitted to cable anything that has appeared in the Soviet press, although exceptions sometimes are taken to interpretation or manner of combining facts gleaned from the press. Phraseology is important, and words are sharply considered.[98]

[97] Anon., "Russian Censorship is Fair Says Bickel," *Editor and Publisher* (Aug. 9, 1930), p. 16; F. P. Stockbridge, and I. D. Levine, "Russian Press Gives False View of U. S.," *American Press* (Aug., 1931), pp. 1, 42-44; Anon., "Russia and Italy Press Censorships Described by United Press Men," *Editor and Publisher* (Mar. 28, 1931), p. 24. George Seldes, *You Can't Print That!*, pp. 153-62.

W. H. Chamberlin, *Russia's Iron Age*, Ch. 7, pp. 129-51, "Government by Propaganda." Mr. Chamberlin, after more than a decade in Russia as correspondent for the *Christian Science Monitor* reports that the censorship had become more severe, rather than less, since he described it in his earlier book, *Soviet Russia* (rev. ed.) where he said (p. 394), "since the later part of 1925 there have been no repressive measures against foreign journalists," and he details the relations between government and correspondents (pp. 394-96). The Soviet censor like any other censor, Mr. Chamberlin described as "interested, not in the factual truth of the message which is submitted to him, but in the effect which its publication will produce in the country to which it is being sent." Russia, he says, had more things to conceal since 1929, and so the censorship had been made tighter and correspondents had been kept under surveillance and refused the right to travel, especially to famine areas. Correspondents whose reports were not "objective," as the authorities called it, were refused renewals of their visas if they left the country, and, so they were kept out without the Soviet Government's having to explain why it "expelled" them.

Soviet officials also attempt to discredit a correspondent, sometimes, if what he writes is objectionable to them, by trying to undermine his position with the home newspaper office.

[98] For example, if the food situation is "acute" it may be called "difficult," while if it is "desperate" it may be called "acute," so says Mr. Chamberlin.

The censors are selected for their loyalty to the régime and for the knowledge of languages. Although occasionally it is possible to write a thing subtly enough to escape the censor, it then may be so subtle that it will escape the reader of the newspaper in which it appears!

At times of special crises in Russia the censorship becomes stricter than at other times. A subject absolutely barred for discussion is the G.P.U., or the secret police, and its methods. Speculative stories are discouraged; it is not considered justifiable for a correspondent to discuss what the government *may* do, or what *may* happen, since he cannot know. Personalities, gossip or fact, about Stalin or others, or anything discreditable about high officials is censored, although there was a tendency to relax the near-ban on such subjects late in 1935.

When famine has gripped the country, correspondents not only have had difficulties with the censorship, but have been forbidden to visit the districts most affected. The reports of Lenin's death,[99] of the expulsion of Trotsky, and even of such events as the crash of the great airplane, *Maxim Gorky,* in 1935, although the latter cast no reflection on the government, were delayed for hours or days.

The censorship and the peculiar situation under which the correspondents work in Moscow make it unusual for any person to get an exclusive spot news story there. Factual stories come from official sources as a rule, and other stories seldom evade the censorship.

Because their correspondents in Russia would not be completely free to go and come, to write without censorship or without being repeatedly expelled (so making it necessary to break in new correspondents), two prominent newspapers, *The Times* of

[99] Isaac Don Levine, a Chicago *Tribune* correspondent then stationed in Moscow, anticipating Lenin's death, had arranged with the London office of his paper to dispatch the message, "send me hundred pounds," as a code to indicate that the Russian leader had died. As an apparently harmless private message, it went through promptly. The correspondent had visions of a great "scoop." The next morning he had a reply from the London office, "Why want hundred pounds. Too much." Because a man in the office had not known about the code and took the message literally, the paper lost a two-day "beat" on the story, for the censorship lasted that time.

London and the Chicago *Tribune,* maintain no correspondents to Moscow, although they have them stationed in most other capitals.[100] Instead they have correspondents in Riga, the capital of Latvia, just over the Russian frontier. From that outpost they attempt to report the news of Russia, and contend that they can do an effective job.[101] Those correspondents have their sources of information, both within and without the country, and they read the newspapers from Russia with special attention.

Readers sometimes tend to believe that the news received from Riga may be more reliable than the news received from Moscow itself, simply because Riga is free from censorship. On the other hand, such places adjacent to Russia are centers of rumor and doubtless of intrigue, and sometimes such news dispatches reflect these uncertain factors. This has annoyed the Soviet Government to an extent where the Latvian Government was asked to expel certain correspondents, but this demand was refused. It is notable, however, that the most important news of Russia has come from Moscow itself.

The Russian censorship never has prevented able correspondents from reporting almost anything that is true and important. Only occasionally has news been bottled up, and then seldom for long.[102]

[100] *The Times* also would maintain no correspondent in Russia late in 1905 after the "Red Sunday" in St. Petersburg. *The Times's* correspondent, Mr. Braham, had been expelled by the Russian Government for supposed revolutionary sympathies. This induced Mr. Walter to refuse to maintain regular representation in the then-capital. Lionel James, *Times of Stress,* p. 68.

Henry Wales, then Paris correspondent for the Chicago *Tribune,* made a trip through Russia in the spring of 1931 and wrote stories. Some of his copy was censored. One dealt with unhappy conditions among the Kulaks in exile camps at Archangel. The censor refused to pass the story on the ground that what might be true of conditions in one place might not necessarily be true in another, yet it would give a general impression that all were alike. Anon., "Wales Stories Censored," *Editor and Publisher* (April 4, 1931).

[101] As to the merits of this contention, critics have suggested that they might as well try to cover the news of the United States from Havana, Cuba; Tiajuana, Mexico; or from Montreal.

[102] Eugene Lyons of the United Press, interviewed in *Editor and Publisher,* Mar. 28, 1931, said that in three years in Moscow, from 1928 to 1931, there had been perhaps a half dozen occasions when stories known to every

Soviet Russia also has become the classic example of a state that is inseparable from propaganda. The State is warmed and sustained by propaganda at home, and through the censorship and the Third International, which officially is no part of the government, it seeks to shape opinion abroad.

Every agency is bent to propaganda purposes in the Soviet. The press, including every form of printing; the radio, the motion pictures, the poster, the theater, the opera, the schools, the lecture platform, tourism—even sports, and work itself—all are devoted to welding every person into the great machine which is Soviet Russia.

By excluding opposing ideas and ideals, by ridicule of that which is unlike Marxism as interpreted in Russia, by presenting foreign events and ideas from an especially manufactured point of view, by rewards for those who prove their unquestioning acceptance of what they are told to believe, by iteration and reiteration of ideas, by uniting all citizens through exaggerated threats of danger from a common foe, by stirring appeals to the idealism that is dormant in everyone—by such means the State is welded. Where it is not effective, force is used to make it so.[103]

one were not permitted to be sent out of the country for a certain period of time. The expulsion of Trotsky was one story so bottled up, the explosion of a bomb in the headquarters of the G.P.U. (Cheka) was another. See also: Lyons, *Moscow Carrousel;* Lyons, *"To Tell or Not to Tell,"* Harper's (June, 1935), pp. 98-112; George Seldes, *You Can't Print That!,* pp. 153-245.

[103] W. H. Chamberlin, *Russia's Iron Age,* Ch. 7. Mr. Chamberlin points out (p. 141) that, powerful as it is, Soviet propaganda is yet not an invincible weapon. "When the economic shoe is pinching too sharply, the official statements lose their effect. A Ukrainian peasant who knows that his brother and some of his friends perished during the famine will not be impressed, except unfavorably, by a newspaper assurance that poverty has ceased to exist in the Soviet Union; and few workers are stupid enough to believe that the annual forced loans are really voluntary."

The trials of Russian engineers, technicians, professors, writers, etc. in Moscow in 1928, 1930 and 1931, and the trial of British engineers there in 1933, and of the Trotskyist faction in 1937, were intended very largely for propaganda purposes, proving to the Russian people the need for solidarity against the sinister attempts to sabotage the great plans. These trials were expertly stage-managed, broadcast by radio to the nation, and so used to best propaganda advantage. Bertram W. Maxwell, "Political Propaganda in Soviet Russia," *Propaganda and Dictatorship* (H. L. Childs), pp. 61-79.

But it must be noted that the government propaganda in Russia is directed less at the foreign correspondents or at foreign opinion, than at the Russian people themselves. The correspondents are not bothered directly, although the controlled press, the censorship, and the restraint on their travel, their movements and their personal contacts—so far as it is operative—acts as indirect propaganda.

*　*　*

The Russian press itself is called a free press by Russian officials. It is free *within the social order*.[104] That is, it is a Soviet press, pledged to the Soviet idea, but not limited in its activity within the party. It may be compared to the Italian or German presses in this way: In Italy or Germany the newspapers are ostensibly under private ownership, but they do not dare to publish anything that could be interpreted as being in opposition to the government, and they do not dare to criticize the dictator. In Russia the press is government-owned, not intended to make money or entertain readers, but to aid the State. It is free to criticize officials of the party and to suggest reforms, although within limits, and in practice it has seemed to make some difference who does the criticizing.

A Communist party censor is a member of every newspaper staff, and it is his function to read proofs of articles before they appear, making changes that seem desirable to him. In many ways, the journalist of Tsarist Russia did not have so good a life as he does to-day in Soviet Russia, where he enjoys certain

[104] John A. Brogan, Jr., "Opinion in Russia Is Subordinated to General Welfare of State," *Editor and Publisher* (Jan. 13, 1934), p. 20; W. H. Chamberlin, *Russia's Iron Age*, Ch. 7, pp. 129-51. Mr. Chamberlin points out that pre-war Russia had 859 papers, circulating 2,700,000 copies daily. When he wrote in 1934, official figures showed 9700 papers in Soviet Russia, circulating 36,000,000 copies. About 3000 of the 9700 were only small propaganda sheets issued by political departments in country districts twice a week, or as factory newspapers, issued at irregular intervals; Chamberlin, *Soviet Russia*, Ch. 18, pp. 387-403; Vladimir Romm, "The Press of the U.S.S.R.," *Journalism Quarterly* (March, 1935), pp. 20-26. Mr. Romm, Tass correspondent in Washington and elsewhere, was one of the defendants in the Trotskyist trial of 1937.

privileges and a wage scale considerably better than that of most workers.[105]

The percentage of literacy in Russia was extremely low before the Revolution, and the Soviet Government is making every effort to teach the population to read and write, with the result, also, that the numbers of newspapers and the newspaper circulations are growing as more persons become literate. The papers are smaller than those published in the United States or Great Britain, due in part to limited paper supplies, and very serious as a rule.

News within Soviet Russia is gathered and distributed by the Tass agency (Telegrafnoje Agentstwo Ssojusa, also translated as meaning the Telegraphic Agency of the Soviet States) which is an affiliate of the Associated Press-Reuters-Havas group. Tass also has an exchange arrangement with the United Press. It is the official Russian news agency, and has representatives in New York, London, Paris, Vienna, Geneva and Shanghai. The foreign bureaus of the agency deliver to Russia all the foreign news that it is to get.[106] It seeks out the news that will tend to prove that the views supported by the Soviet Government are correct, and that seem to show capitalist nations in difficulty, such as labor troubles, financial failures, serious crime, graft, miscarriages of justice, crop failures, drouths, floods, riots, violence and threats of war. All of this is supposed to make the Russian people more satisfied with their own lot.

Local news and domestic news is covered by the Tass agency, also, and the day's news budget is distributed by this government-owned agency to the government-owned press. The radio is used to a great extent in Russia, where telegraph systems are limited. The news is read over the air, and is taken down in two hundred or more newspaper offices in the country.

[105] Albin E. Johnson, "Russian Newspaper Men Privileged Workers Under Soviet Régime," Editor and Publisher (Nov. 23, 1929), p. 32; Anon., "Newspapermen Highly Favored in Russia, Returned Writer Says," Editor and Publisher (Oct. 17, 1931); Anon., Conditions of Work and Life of Journalists.

[106] Tass in 1934 sent about 20,000 words in cablese monthly from the United States alone to Moscow headquarters. Anon., "Tass Director sails for Moscow; Has Exchange Hook-Up with U.P.," Editor and Publisher (Dec. 1, 1934), p. 12; Kenneth Durant, "Soviet News in the American Press," Journalism Quarterly (June, 1936), pp. 148-56.

The news of Russia that is most important domestically concerns industry, education and agriculture. The biggest story, and a never-ending one, is the progress of the Soviet development. The theater is considered educational, and is much in the news. Important speeches are printed in full, and serialized if they are very long. There have been no entertainment features such as appear in newspapers in Great Britain and the United States. Only recently has any attention begun to be given to so-called human interest news of personalities, crimes, scandals, sports, and the use of photos and cartoons.[107]

No opposition political views are mentioned in the press, and all papers are alike so far as concerns expressions of political policy. But the papers vary in that each appeals to a special group of readers, based chiefly upon diverse occupational or educational interests, apart from the obvious geographical differences. Some attain large circulations, and some contain well-written articles on serious subjects. The foreign news used is limited in volume and its selection and presentation has seemed to be determined by its possible political effect. There is no effort to keep readers informed of world affairs merely for the sake of the knowledge itself. Most of what is printed, is printed for a purpose.[108]

The two outstanding papers of Russia to-day are both published in Moscow, and are read with special attention by Russians and foreign correspondents alike. It is from these papers that correspondents most frequently select matter for quotation. The papers are *Izvestia* (meaning "News"), official organ of the Central Executive Committee of the U.S.S.R. and the all-Russian Executive Committee; and *Pravda* (meaning "Truth"), the official organ of the Central Committee and Moscow Committee of the Communist party. *Izvestia* had a 1936 daily circulation of

[107] I. D. W. Talmadge, " 'Human Interest' In Soviet Press; Newspapermen Win Victory," *Editor and Publisher* (May 16, 1936), p. 16; Walter Duranty, "Soviet Brightens Newspaper Pages," New York *Times* (Feb. 5, 1937).

[108] Anon., "Soviet Propaganda fails to 'Click' Says Writer Back from Russia," *Editor and Publisher* (Nov. 26, 1927), p. 20; Vernon McKenzie, "Soviet Soldiers Have Own Newspapers," *Editor and Publisher* (Nov. 16, 1929), p. 13; R. W. Beckman, "Big News—In Russia," *The Quill* (Dec., 1928), pp. 12-13; F. P. Stockbridge and I. D. Levine, "Russian Press Gives False View of U. S.," *American Press* (Aug., 1931), pp. 1, 42-44.

FIG. 34. A GROUP OF RUSSIAN NEWSPAPERS

For description see List of Illustrations

more than two million, a figure which is growing. *Pravda* had a 1936 daily circulation of nearly three million, also growing.

Both the number and the circulations of newspapers in Russia are constantly increasing, and the circulations could rise more rapidly if they were not artificially restricted due to shortage of newsprint paper.[109] Nearly all use the Cyrillic alphabet. Those which are of special importance to the foreign correspondent, in addition to *Izvestia* and *Pravda,* include:[110]

Za Industrializatsiyu ("Industrialization").—Chief organ of the People's Commissariat for Heavy Industry.

Sotsialisticheskoye Zemledelie ("Socialist Agriculture").—Organ of the Union Commissariat for Agriculture.

Ekonomicheskaya Zhizn ("Economic Life").—Organ of People's Commissariat for Finance and Central Committee of the Union of Financial Workers.

Komsomolskaya Pravda.—Organ of the Union of Communist Youth.

Krestyanskaya Gazeta ("The Peasants' Gazette").—A tri-weekly paper printing 15 regional editions and circulating about 3,500,000 copies per issue in 1936, the largest in Russia. Organ of Central Committee of Communist Party.

Trud ("Labor").—Organ of the Central Council of Trade Unions.

Gudok.—Organ of the People's Commissariat for Transportation.

Nasha Gazeta ("Our Gazette").—Popular organ of the Union of Workers in State Institutes.

Za Kommunisticheskoye Prosveshcheniye ("Communist Education").—Organ of the People's Commissariat for Education and the Central Committee of the Union of Educational Workers.

[109] Anon., "Soviet Papers have 40,000,000 Readers," *Editor and Publisher* (Nov. 9, 1935), p. 27. Compares to 2,500,000 circulation of papers in Tsarist Russia, on authority of the *Foreign Press,* bulletin published by Association of Foreign Correspondents in the United States. It also shows a 4,000,000 increase since 1934, as see note 104, page 276, ante.

[110] For up-to-date list of Russian newspapers, see *Political Handbook of the World,* annual, under "Russia"; *Europa,* and other references in note 1, page 170, ante.

Za Pischchevuyu Industryu ("Food Industry").—Organ of the People's Commissariat for Food Industry and the Central Committee of the Union of Food Workers.

Sovkhoznaya Gazeta ("State Farm Gazette").—Organ of the Commissariat for State Farming.

Krasnaya Zvezda.—Organ of the Commissariat of Defence.

Sovietskaya Torgovlya.—Organ of the Commissariat of Internal Trade.

Moscow News.—Published daily and weekly for English-speaking persons in the Soviet Union.

Other periodicals are published at intervals, dealing with various subjects, technical and otherwise, and some of these are useful to the correspondents.

Unless they learn the difficult Russian language themselves, correspondents are obliged to depend upon others to read the periodicals for them, and report what is in them, perhaps preparing digests of the more important matter. Yet, this system places the correspondent at the mercy of translators who may also collect pay from the government, or others who wish the correspondent to know or believe only what they want him to know or believe.

§ 7. VIENNA AND SOUTHERN EUROPE

VIENNA was a capital of great importance during the days of the Austro-Hungarian empire. In those times, however, international news organization was loosely formed, and for several years after the Great War the former empire was too depressed to be a great source of news. Such things as happened were covered from Berlin or Rome, with a special correspondent, a "swing man," sent there if conditions became acute. But because it is the best center of communications for South Central Europe, and because Berlin became difficult as a center from which to watch Balkan affairs, Vienna grew to new journalistic importance.[111]

[111] Before the Great War there had been some correspondents of note in Vienna and other Southern European capitals. A few newspapers, such as *The Times* and the *Morning Post* of London kept representatives in those

After the Great War, with Austria so reduced in size, the press of Vienna had a difficult time. Circulations were restricted, and there was little advertising, since there was no money to spend in the country, and hardly enough money to pay the reduced staffs. There were changes in personnel and in the character of newspapers, but some weathered the storm. The Vienna press always had included a few alert and interesting periodicals, and this continued to be true.

Austria itself was of news-importance because of the peculiarly uncertain allegiance of the government—the head with a body. What were to be its relations with Germany, with Italy, with Hungary and the other succession states? These questions, together with stormy political developments in the little country, and in other countries of Southern Europe, provided news of interest. The minorities problems in the succession states, and the struggle for control in such countries as Greece and Yugoslavia made news, so that the number of correspondents making headquarters in Vienna continued to multiply until in 1930 there were enough to form an Anglo-American Press Association.

Correspondents, working as far east as Turkey, have found that journalism there is not in high repute. The press is effectually censored in some countries by holding a writer responsible for what he produces, and an editor or publisher for what he prints. Bribery, blackmail and duels are no small part of domestic journalism. This situation breeds difficulty for the foreign correspondent, who is assumed to be of the same caliber.

Because the countries are small it is possible for a correspondent to cover a number of them with reasonable satisfaction. The press in these various countries gives him only a limited aid be-

places. See: H. Wickham Steed, *Through Thirty Years*, 2 vols. Mr. Steed represented *The Times* in Vienna for some years before the outbreak of the War, and he is credited with having exerted great influence over British opinion by what he wrote; Lady Grogan, *The Life of J. D. Bourchier*. As *The Times* correspondent in Sofia for years, Bourchier played an important ex-officio part in Balkan affairs, and is the only journalist, so far as known, honored by having stamps issued in his memory, as was done by the Bulgarian Government in 1921. The wars in the Balkans between 1850 and 1914 brought many war correspondents to the section, including Archibald Forbes, H. W. Nevinson and William Howard Russell.

cause it is not especially dependable; yet it has a certain value, and there are a few newspapers of reliability.

* * *

The Vienna correspondent must keep his gaze at once upon Austria, Hungary, Bulgaria, Rumania, Czechoslovakia, Albania, Yugoslavia, Greece and Turkey. They are all countries in which a lively sense of politics exists, with accompanying jealousies and passions, so that reactions are likely to become violent. Government interference, conflicting claims, propaganda, censorship, physical obstacles, and even hazards are among the problems of the conscientious journalist.[112]

Six of the nine Southern European countries mentioned— Austria, Yugoslavia, Hungary, Rumania, Czechoslovakia and Bulgaria—comprise about 50,000,000 persons, but with very diverse cultures and characters as between certain sections. For this reason, one of the greatest weaknesses in press coverage of European news is in matter from this area. It is economically unsound, considering the limited volume of news originating there, for newspapers to maintain a full-time staff correspondent in each of the countries. Yet to cover the entire area properly from Vienna

[112] G. E. R. Gedye, "Newspaper Men Have Difficulty in Balkans," *The Little Times,* house organ of the New York *Times* (Sept. 18, 1930), p. 2. Mr. Gedye, Vienna correspondent for the New York *Times,* reports that the Press Department in Bulgaria's Foreign Office surprised him because, unlike most Balkan press departments, it tried to help him to get at the truth, and did not try to fill him with propaganda. This attitude they explained by saying that they knew if he was worth his salt he would get all sides of the story anyway, and they were willing to save him time. They arranged interviews for him with opposition leaders, as well as providing him with the official government views.

See also Anon., *Not to Be Repeated,* pp. 416-18; John Gunther, "Policy by Murder," *Harper's* (Nov., 1934), pp. 651-52. Recounts the experiences of correspondents reporting the assassination of Chancellor Dollfuss in Vienna in 1934; Gunther, *Inside Europe,* Chap. 22; Oscar Jászi, "The Ideologic Foundations of the Danubian Dictatorships," *Propaganda and Dictatorship* (H. L. Childs), pp. 83-102; Anon., "Greece Censoring News Sent Abroad," New York *Times* (Dec. 19, 1936). This reports all telegrams, messages, and some letters as censored, the letters having been examined, stamped as opened "to control foreign exchange," and sent on. So close a mail censorship is unusual.

is not simple. There must be considerable dependence upon native journalists, who often are prejudiced.

Correspondents in the Balkans, as it happens, are almost obliged to sensationalize their news if they are to compete for space in the papers and make any sort of living for themselves. Other cities are providing news which seems of more immediate interest to readers. The result is that unless the news from the Balkan countries stresses controversy beyond its deserts, or is otherwise made exciting, it probably will be crowded out.

*   *   *

The papers in part of Yugoslavia and in some other portions of the Balkan area are printed in the Cyrillic alphabet, as in Russia. All of the papers in Yugoslavia are censored, but more copy by foreign correspondents is commonly stopped by censors in Bucharest, Rumania's capital, than in Belgrade, Yugoslavia's capital.

The Slovenes, comprising an important portion of the Yugoslavian population, are considered the most cultured people in the Balkans, and this is reflected in some of the papers published in that country, notably *Politika* of Belgrade.

Bulgaria, however, also has a large press, including some good papers. There are 33 political parties in the country, with almost every one looking to some paper to express its views. There are 17 dailies in Sofia, the capital, and 300 newspapers in the country, including 50 dailies. The most important are, rather naturally, in Sofia, with *Zora* and *Ezgrev* and *Mir* outstanding.

In Rumania certain newspapers will sell their support to the highest bidder. They will attack or support as is desired. Although much of the Rumanian press is corrupt, and although a censorship is strongly maintained in the country, particularly on outgoing dispatches and on incoming foreign publications, some of the newspapers are quite informative.[113]

[113] Anon., "Streit of *Times* Exiled from Rumania, Protests Rigid Censorship Rules." *Editor and Publisher* (May 29, 1926); Anon., "Drastic Press Law Planned in Rumania," *Editor and Publisher* (Dec. 25, 1926), p. 13. This law provided for the equivalent of a $100 fine and four years' imprisonment for any person sending out news by any means which is offensive to

The press in Greece, Albania, and Turkey is as much at the mercy of dictatorship and censorship as in most of the other countries in Southern Europe.

The correspondent in Vienna reads not only the Vienna newspapers, and other Austrian periodicals which will help him in his work, but he probably reads some German, Italian, French and British periodicals, and he reads or has read and translated for him newspapers and periodicals published in the Balkan countries which may be useful. There are scores of such papers, but among the more important, by countries, are these: [114]

AUSTRIA:

Neue Freie Presse.—Vienna. Long the best known Austrian paper in other countries. Liberal and international in its views, but less respected than it once was. Much of its circulation is in Yugoslavia. Politically, it takes no stand of importance, but is socially and culturally strong.

Wiener Zeitung.—Vienna. Organ of the Vaterlandische Front.

Arbeiter Zeitung.—Vienna. A leading Socialist paper.

Reichspost.—Vienna. Often quoted because of its generally authoritative information on internal affairs. Organ of the Christian Socialist party, of which Dr. Kurt Schuschnigg, the Chancellor, is a member.

YUGOSLAVIA:

Politika.—Belgrade. An independent paper, and one of the best informed in the Balkans. Like many others in Yugoslavia, it is printed in the Cyrillic alphabet, founded on the Greek and used in Russia, Bulgaria, and among the Slovenes of Yugoslavia. It has more than 100,000 circulation, is bigger than most French newspapers, must submit to the general censorship, but is not

the King, Queen, or Crown Prince, or for attacks upon the Constitutional government or the established order of succession to the throne. Presumably this would affect foreign correspondents as well as Rumanian journalists. George Seldes, *You Can't Print That!*, pp. 395-465.

[114] Up-to-date lists of newspapers in Austria and other countries appear in the *Political Handbook of the World, Europa,* etc. See other references in note 1, page 170, ante.

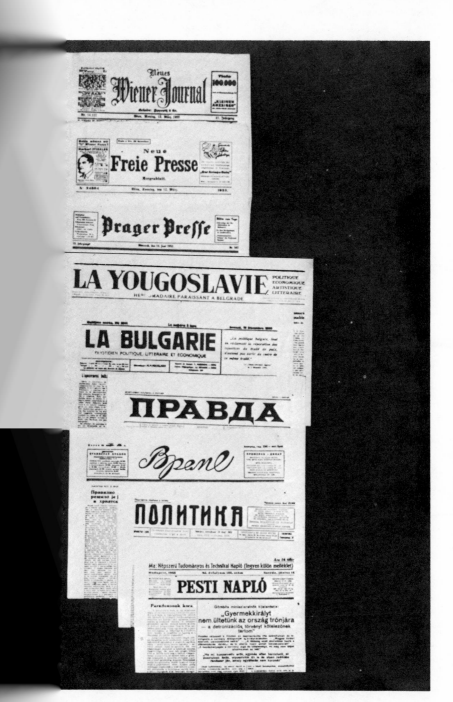

35. A GROUP OF AUSTRIAN AND BALKAN NEWSPAPERS
For description see List of Illustrations

flagrantly nationalistic. On the contrary, it is rather fair in its views and its news affecting relations between the Slavs, Croats and Slovenes. It is somewhat unfriendly toward Bulgaria, however. It carries more foreign news than any other Balkan paper, and has representatives in Berlin, Paris, Geneva, Sofia, and part-time correspondents in London and Vienna. In addition to long and serious articles about political and economic subjects, it runs good articles about the arts.

Vreme ("The Times").—Belgrade. A semi-official paper. Represents the government, and is rather chauvinistic.

Pravda ("Truth").—Belgrade. An important paper, chauvinistic, the only afternoon paper in the capital. Devotes considerable space to general human interest news and news of the arts.

Novosti ("News").—Zagreb. The most important paper in the second most important city, journalistically, in Yugoslavia. This paper is printed in the Latin alphabet, rather ᵗʰan in the Cyrillic, and that is generally true of papers in the Croatian section of the country, centering in Zagreb.

Jutarnji List ("Morning Star").—Zagreb. An independent paper, second in importance in Zagreb.

Obzor ("Outlook").—The oldest Croat paper. Dull. Has correspondents writing to it from all over Europe. Makes a specialty of economic news.

Jugoslavenski Lloyd.—Zagreb. Commercial news.

Yutro ("Morning").—Published in Ljubljana. An independent paper.

BULGARIA:

Zora ("Dawn").—Sofia. The best paper in Bulgaria. Has foreign correspondents in Geneva, Berlin, Bucharest. It minimizes sensation, but it is nationalistic, pro-Macedonian, anti-Serbian, mildly anti-Italian, and generally the best exponent of moderate nationalism in Bulgaria. About 70,000 circulation.

Echo.—Sofia. Communist party paper, of which issues are often confiscated by the government.

Ezgrev ("First Signs of Dawn").—Sofia. A crusading paper, espousing the ideals of truth and right with more vigor than any other paper in the Balkans. It is the most powerful paper in this part of Europe.

Makedonia.—Sofia. A noonday paper, and the organ of the Macedonians in Bulgaria, supported by their organization. It is chauvinistic and aggressive.

Mir ("Peace").—Sofia. An evening paper. Serious and prosperous, printing long and serious articles, but objective in approach. The second best paper in Bulgaria.

RUMANIA:

Universul ("Universal").—Bucharest. A morning paper that is nationalistic, anti-Semitic, widely read and prosperous.

Dimineatsa ("Morning").—Bucharest. A morning paper that is Left Wing, independent, popular, sensational, well informed, and an advocate of government reform. This paper and *Universul* are the two largest in the country.

Adeverul ("Truth").—Bucharest. Evening edition of *Dimineatsa*. Popular and sensational. Supports Peasant party.

Argus.—Bucharest. The best edited and the best written paper in the Balkans. It is semi-official, and devoted primarily to financial and economic subjects.

Dreptatea ("Right").—Bucharest. Organ of the National Peasant party.

Epoca.—Bucharest. A noonday paper. Organ of the Conservative party, and critical of the King.

Neamul Romanesc ("The Rumanian Nation").—Bucharest. Evening paper, representing the National party, and well edited.

Patria.—Published at Cluj. This is a Transylvanian paper of importance, organ of the National Peasant party, and a leading provincial paper.

In Hungary attention goes to the semi-official *Budapesti Hirlap,* the German-language *Pester Lloyd,* the opposition *Népszava,* and the liberal *Pesti Hirlap;* and Czechoslovakia has the official *Prager Presse,* the *Národni Osvobozeni,* which is close to the foreign office, and *Die Zeit,* organ of the Henlein Sudeten German party, and others.

§ 8. MADRID AND OTHER NEWS CENTERS OF EUROPE

BECAUSE they are important cities in their own rights, and because some of them have good newspapers, other European cities occasionally assume special prominence, notably Madrid, Warsaw, Danzig, Prague, Milan, Lisbon, Venice, Hamburg, Leipzig, Cologne, Nuremberg, Bremen, Frankfurt, Munich, Edinburgh, Dublin, Brussels, Rotterdam, Amsterdam, Copenhagen, Stockholm, Zurich, and Basle.

It is through the carefully developed press organization that the news from these and other places is cleared and made available in almost every part of the world, often in great detail. In nearly every country there is at least one press association, and usually an affiliation with the World League of Press Associations.

In every country, also, and probably in every capital, native journalists act as correspondents for foreign newspapers and press associations. A bureau, in Paris, for example, will have made arrangements with individual newspaper men in Lyons, Marseilles, Cherbourg, Havre, Nice, Monte Carlo, Bordeaux, Strasbourg, Biarritz, and elsewhere. Those men will telephone the control bureau in Paris, or telegraph or write, depending upon the urgency of their news, and also depending upon their own ability and news sense. Or the Paris bureau may itself ask them for information. In this way, even a single correspondent or a small bureau in one of the great capitals can, if need be, keep a finger on events all over the country. Each of these regional correspondents will be paid a small retainer fee or space rates or perhaps both for matter he sends that is published.

* * *

The news of Spain filters through Madrid and Barcelona, and both have increased in importance during recent years. The dictatorships of Gen. Primo di Rivera and Gen. Damaso Berenguer, followed by the political revolution in which Alphonso XIII lost his throne, and followed in turn by the social revolution and Civil War, all resulted in censorship locally in Spain, and attracted correspondents to the country in increasing numbers.

The leading news agency, Agencia Fabra, controlled by the French Agence Havas, has offices in Madrid and Barcelona, and covers the Portuguese news, also. It is the official Spanish governmental agency, and is allied with the World League of Press Associations.

Spain has known constant unrest since 1920. The period during which Primo di Rivera acted as "dictator" saw the press placed under certain restrictions, which were made no lighter when General Damaso Berenguer became dictator in his stead. Neither of those Spanish censorships was very strict on outgoing news. The domestic press at that time, however, was obliged to submit page proofs to a government censor, usually stationed in the office. Such material as he designated had to be cut out and the pages remade. Some newspapers, notably *El Sol* of Madrid, objected to the censorship, and, by way of expressing disapproval and disdain for the government, it removed the objectionable sentences and paragraphs, but instead of remaking the pages it left blank holes with inserted blackface notations, "This sentence deleted by the censor," "This article is censored," "This edition has been revised by the Censor," or some similar explanation, intended to rally public opinion against such action. (See Figure 15, p. 142.)

Finally, in February, 1929, the newspapers, by Royal Decree, were commanded to reserve, daily, a definite percentage of space for use by the government to publish what it wished. The things it did wish published were prepared by an administration press bureau and were run. But because the decree failed to consider the possibility, and to forbid their doing it, most papers printed above such stories a notice, *"de incercion obligado"* ("We are forced to print this," or "Forced Publication, by Royal Decree"). This was enough to damn the story so far as concerned its effectiveness as government propaganda.

The domestic censorship under Berenguer was stricter than under Rivera. When it was relaxed there would come such an outburst of anti-monarchial sentiment that it would be clapped back on again. When Rivera resigned, the Madrid editors called upon Berenguer and demanded that the press censorship be removed. They were told that he agreed with them in principle, and that the gag would be removed as soon as practicable, but the editors were warned to be extremely cautious in denouncing the acts of the Rivera régime, and to make no attacks at all on the monarchy.[115]

It was said by Spanish editors, "Under Rivera we knew what we couldn't write; under Berenguer we don't know what we may write." As an illustration, the Law of Public Order, so-called, forbade publication of matter which might be "inciting" or dangerous to the public welfare. Naturally, the interpretation of what might be "inciting" could vary, and could conceivably apply even to a notice of a public meeting or an account of a speech. Previously there had been a censor who examined copy or proof sheets, deleting "adjectives" or inflammatory words. Under Berenguer, however, advance censorship was abolished. Instead, penalties were inflicted after publication for infringements of the royal, the military, or the dictatorial edicts. Rather than risk the penalties, editors took no chances, and that form of censorship became more effective than the censorship-in-advance.

All first editions of papers were carefully examined at the War Ministry. If a warning, telephoned to an editor, was not enough to bring about a change or deletion, then the courts were called upon to prosecute the editor or the publisher. Then the newspapers once more would insert such notices as "This number has been seen by the censor," or "Because of orders from the censors we suspend publication of the History of the Dictatorship," and further indicated that it would appear or continue when circumstances permitted. By such methods the public was kept informed of the censors' work.

And yet, in spite of this elaborate censorship, affecting foreign correspondents as well as local editors, it failed in its purpose of

[115] W. H. Carter, "Dictatorship of Press in Spain," *Forum* (March, 1929), V. 131, 320-29; Albin E. Johnson, "Spain's Press Muzzled But Surly Under De Rivera Dictatorship," *Editor and Publisher* (July 20, 1929), p. 15; Johnson, "New Censorship of Spanish Press Stricter than Primo de Rivera's," *Editor and Publisher* (Mar. 22, 1930), p. 18. Johnson, "Muzzled Press Was Primed to Expose Evils of Dictatorship," *Editor and Publisher* (Dec. 27, 1930); Vincent Sheean, *Personal History,* pp. 62-76, gives his experiences in Spain for the Chicago *Tribune.*

saving the monarchy. Foreign correspondents were arrested, and some were threatened with imprisonment and fines for "exaggeration." [116] It was common for the correspondents to evade the censorship by arranging to have their dispatches carried across the frontier to Hendaye, in France, or to Gibraltar, the British rock, whence they might be telegraphed without interference. These are standard loopholes in the Spanish censorship.

After the abdication of King Alphonso in 1931, the new Constitution of Republican Spain guaranteed the freedom of the press. But newspapers were censored and suppressed much as before, and foreign correspondents continued to be followed and arrested. In fact, scarcely any correspondent who has been any time in the country has escaped spending a few hours or days in Spanish jails, because of some statement he has made in his reports, or because he has attracted suspicion by the persons he has seen in his efforts to get the news. The result was that correspondents, in many cases, went to Spain to gather material, but did not write their dispatches until after leaving the country.[117]

By 1935 the first hopes of the Revolution had been quenched. A strict government press law was approved unanimously by the cabinet, making various provisions, including a censorship on proofs in advance of publication and controlling every means by which information might reach the public. The measure was in force throughout the later months of 1934 and all of 1935. It was lifted early in 1936 to permit what one paper called "liberty with responsibility," but it was not the first time a Spanish censorship had been relaxed, temporarily. The trend of censorship in Spain is indicated by provisions proposed in 1935, but not put into effect then.[118] These restrictions were advocated:

[116] This happened to a correspondent for an important South American newspaper who had pictured a riot scene at Valencia with more vividness than the Spanish authorities considered proper.

[117] Anon., "Says Spanish Routine Balks Reporters" (L. A. Fernsworth, New York *Times* correspondent in Spain, interviewed), *Editor and Publisher* (Oct. 17, 1932), p. 22; Lawrence A. Fernsworth, "Spanish 'Gag' Active Under Republic," *Editor and Publisher* (Apr. 30, 1932), p. 109.

[118] Anon., "Spain Crushes Final Hope of Freedom," *Editor and Publisher* (Feb. 16, 1935), p. 33.

1. In case of war, censorship of troop movements, strategic plans, statistics about military factories, number of dead, wounded, and prisoners, position of troops, operations, riots, supplies or anything which might influence progress of operations, relations with other states, morale of troops or civilian population.

2. In time of epidemic, censorship of statistics about deaths, those affected, movements of travelers, patients or methods of isolation.

3. At times of public calamity or collective movements against principle of authority, censorship of news and comments directed at depressing public spirit or giving heart to disturbing elements.

Other phases of the censorship covered court action, international questions and labor strikes. Papers also were to be forced to publish free of charge and without alteration, government communications and corrections for authorities on matter previously published, with penalties for failure to do so.

The outbreak of civil war in Spain in the summer of 1936 brought difficulties to correspondents trying to gather up the threads of events in a dozen places. Censorship of wartime caliber came into existence in both government and rebel areas, and although correspondents continued to get their messages across the border for transmission, they were far more handicapped than by any previous Spanish censorship. Correspondents in Madrid could telephone their stories from only one place—the telephone building—and censors on duty there would not grant them a connection until they had submitted their copy for inspection, and even then the censor sat beside the correspondent as he read the story into the telephone, listening and checking the copy word for word. Needless to say, the Spanish press itself was closely censored, so that the people did not know what was happening, if they were obliged to depend upon that source of information, as most were.[119]

[119] Anon., "Spain's Revolt Draws Newsmen," *Editor and Publisher* (July 25, 1936), p. 6; Karl H. von Wiegand, "Von Wiegand Tells Difficulties of Covering Spain's Civil War," *Editor and Publisher* (Aug. 15, 1936), p. 6; Robert U. Brown, "Smuggling Undoes Spain's Censors," *Editor and Publisher* (Aug. 29, 1936), p. 11; Anon., "Official Falsehood and Censorship Prevent Clear Picture From Spain," *Editor and Publisher* (Aug. 29, 1936), pp. 11, 42; Douglas Dies, "Rebel Phone Censors Have a Sense of Humor (Sometimes), Says UP Man," *Editor and Publisher* (Sept. 26, 1936), p. 16;

Information tends to center in Madrid during normal times in Spain, and the telephone service between the capital and other places, in and out of Spain, is excellent. But that does not mean that it is simple to get facts. Apart from censorship and a tendency to jail correspondents on various pretexts, the Spanish people are not communicative. They may not talk freely even when they know a correspondent well, and trust him. He must, therefore, engage paid tipsters. Such persons probably are biased, and they may be serving government, or other interests, on the side, but at least they are natives, and know how other natives think and feel, so they do throw light on the real viewpoint, or at least on a viewpoint that they happen to share. To engage several tipsters, representing various shades of opinion, often is the course pursued. Fortunately this has been possible because the fees paid to tipsters in Spain usually are not large. The tipsters and assistants sometimes find themselves in difficulties because of what the foreign journalists write, and those journalists themselves may be followed by spies, who report on their activities.[120]

The Spanish press is neither notable nor especially helpful to the correspondent. The best papers are *ABC, El Sol, Debate, Informaciones, La Voz* and *La Nacion*, all of Madrid; and *La Vanguardia* of Barcelona. Objective news is unknown in the Spanish press, a circumstance that must be considered by foreign correspondents. Readers do not want objective news. In fact, their chief interest is not so much in the events themselves, as in the opinions expressed concerning those events by various writers.[121]

*   *   *

Anon., "Sulzberger Gives Modern 'Case History' of Many Pressures on Newspapers," *Editor and Publisher* (Jan. 9, 1937), pp. 3-4; Anon., "Spanish Coverage Costly Affair," *Editor and Publisher* (Jan. 16, 1937), p. 37.

[120] Vincent Sheean, *Personal History*, pp. 62-76.

[121] Lawrence A. Fernsworth, "Newspapers of Spain Seem Trivial by Our Standards," *American Press* (June, 1932), p. 11; Anon., "Says Spanish Routine Balks Reporters," Interview with L. A. Fernsworth, correspondent for New York *Times, Editor and Publisher* (Oct. 17, 1931), p. 22; Albin E. Johnson, "Spanish Newspapers the Playthings of Political Prejudices," *Editor and Publisher* (June 1, 1929), p. 16.

See note 1, page 170 ante, for references listing Spanish newspapers.

Warsaw, as capital of Poland, serving as a buffer state between Germany and Russia, is a key capital, and while few foreign newspapers or press associations maintain full-time staff correspondents there, all of them keep a careful watch on the city. Its press is entirely controlled by a dictatorial government, and means very little, but there are news sources in the capital to which the journalist may turn.[122]

A censorship on outgoing dispatches also proves inconvenient at times, but less so than in some capitals because the correspondent covering a special event which would receive equally special consideration from the censors, can get out of the country to write his dispatch, or have it taken across the border. Since he probably will not be spending a long time in Warsaw, moreover, he has less reason to fear offending the authorities by flouting their censors.

Like nearby Riga, Warsaw also has been a clearing point for Russian news, brought in by travelers and coming by telephone from Moscow.

* * *

Belgian news commonly filters through Paris. News from Amsterdam, Copenhagen, Stockholm, Oslo and Helsingfors filters through Berlin or London. Much Polish news and news of the Baltic States—Latvia, Lithuania, and Estonia—likewise comes through Berlin or London. Some of the newspapers, especially those of Brussels, Amsterdam, Copenhagen and Stockholm, win special attention from journalists and statesmen of other countries.[123]

Especially important in Brussels are *Indépendance Belge,* with a good presentation of foreign news; *Le Soir,* with the largest circulation of any paper in Belgium.

[122] Anon., "Muzzle is Clamped on Polish Press," *Editor and Publisher* (Nov. 20, 1926). A decree issued by Marshal Pilsudski provided fines and imprisonment as penalties for printing news, *whether true or false,* concerning the State or officials of the State which would cause a public demonstration, or which might be considered derogatory.

[123] Albin E. Johnson, "Happy Medium of Organization Features Swedish Press," *Editor and Publisher* (Aug. 10, 1929), p. 36; Gunnar Bjurman, "The Swedish Press of Yesterday and Today," *Sweden* (see Anon.) (International Press Exhibition Pressa, Cologne, 1928), pp. 9-56.

Relatively little world news comes from Belgium, and that little usually passes through the Agence Havas by its exchange arrangement with the Agence Télégraphique Belge. When something special occurs, a foreign correspondent goes to Belgium, or dependence is placed on coverage by a local journalist with whom an arrangement has been made.

*   *   *

In Amsterdam, a center for journalistic initiative since printing began in Europe, there appears *De Telegraaf,* a leading paper; while in Rotterdam there is published the *Nieuwe Rotterdamsche Courant,* an influential paper that has both morning and evening editions. The *Algemeen Handelsblad,* of Amsterdam, also is above the average. Some of the weekly and monthly periodicals published in the Netherlands and in Denmark are particularly good, and doubtless would have a greater reputation if Dutch and Danish were more generally familiar languages.

The *Berlingske Tidende* ("Berling Gazette") of Copenhagen, is one of the oldest newspapers now published in Europe, having been established in 1749, while the *Dagens Nyheter* of Stockholm, although started in 1864, is one of the most modern newspapers in Europe both in methods and appearance. Nor can *Nya Dagligt Allehanda,* a leading evening paper of Stockholm, be ignored in any such consideration of modernity. Sweden is a progressive country, journalistically, with good newspapers, a free press, and enterprising journalists.

In Oslo, the *Aftenposten,* with morning and evening editions, has a considerable influence and enjoys great prestige. The *Morgenbladet* also is a leading paper. Norway is a stronghold of the free press.

On the whole, the newspapers published in the so-called Low Countries and in the Scandinavian countries are superior to those published in any other continental countries. They are uncensored, impartial and honest.

*   *   *

FIG. 36. SPANISH AND NORTHERN EUROPEAN PAPERS
For description see List of Illustrations

Thanks to the numerous international conferences that have taken place in Europe since the Great War, many other towns and cities that never before enjoyed much news prominence have come into the limelight.

This has been true of Genoa, Locarno, Lausanne, Thoiry, Cannes, Stresa and some others. To these towns have flocked both diplomats and journalists, and from them winged words have flown to the far places.

When the meetings were managed by the League of Nations, as often was the case, the same smooth-working system by which the Information Section simplifies the work of the press at Geneva usually arranged for their housing and feeding, found working places for them, and set up communications facilities by which they might transmit the news.

Even when the meetings were in larger places, such as Paris, London, Berlin or Madrid, with far more adequate facilities, the League's Information Section was in charge of press arrangements, if it was a League meeting at all.

§ 9. THE NEAR EAST, THE MIDDLE EAST AND AFRICA

BOUNDING the Mediterranean Sea and linking Europe with Asia are Syria, Palestine, Arabia, Egypt, Iraq, Morocco, Persia (Iran), Mongolia, Tibet and other political divisions of limited news importance. Some of these countries are under mandate to European powers. British influence is generally predominant in the Mediterranean area, and is based upon the need to protect the Suez Canal and airway routes to India. But France has been in control in Syria, and continues to control part of Morocco, while Italy controls Tunis, Eritrea, Somaliland and Ethiopia. Thus events in the Mediterranean and Near East are likely to have an international flavor.

From the news standpoint, archæological explorations, the politics of oil, resettlement projects, minority problems and native unrest under white domination have been the most important developments in the section during recent years, and hold great potential importance. These have given rise to the Riff War, to

French troubles in Syria, British troubles in Arabia and Egypt, and conflict in Palestine between Arabs and Jews.[124]

Few important newspapers are published in this section of the world. Press correspondents also are few, and they receive little official coöperation from local authorities in an area that is difficult to understand at best, and which is too remote from the newspaper-reading centers to command much interest. Usually the press associations or newspapers of the countries to which the areas are mandated arrange with local residents, sometimes military or professional men, to write, telegraph, or radio any news to London, Paris or Rome, while a crisis brings staff men to the scene. Such news usually reaches the rest of the world through press association affiliations.

In Africa, the British Empire has interests reaching from Egypt, on the Mediterranean shores, to the Union of South Africa, at the extreme southern end. Belgian, Portuguese, French and Italian interests also are represented.

In spite of the relative infrequency with which this continent has come into the headlines, leading press associations, especially Reuters, have arrangements with residents everywhere to cover for them when news breaks.

South Africa is the most important settled area in Africa, with Egypt important in other ways. British in its loyalties, it is connected by cable, telegraph and radio with the mother country. Reuters has a large office in Cape Town, and some other press associations and newspapers have representatives there who keep them informed on matters that may or may not be covered by Reuters.[125]

---

[124] Vincent Sheean, *Personal History*, pp. 333-98; Lothrop Stoddard, *The Rising Tide of Color;* T. E. Lawrence, *Revolt in the Desert;* Lawrence, *The Seven Pillars of Wisdom;* J. A. Spender, *The Changing East;* Upton Close, *The Revolt of Asia.*

[125] Henry M. Collins, *From Pigeon Post to Wireless,* Ch. 11. Tells of organization of Reuters service in South Africa at the time of the Boer War.

CHAPTER VI

NEWS OF THE NEW WORLD

THE FIRST printing press in the western hemisphere was set up in Mexico City in 1535, the second, at Lima, Peru, in 1586, and the third at Cambridge, Massachusetts, in 1639. From these three presses in Central, South, and North America has grown a vast empire of print.

Present-day journalism in this sector of the globe finds its chief centers in New York, Washington, Buenos Aires, Mexico City, Havana and Montreal. In these five centers, above others, most information about Pan-America originates and from them it is injected into the general world stream of news.

§ 1. WASHINGTON AND THE UNITED STATES OF AMERICA

A YOUTHFUL country, the United States of America is yet older than the systematic collection of world news. Since 1800, or thereabouts, the nation has extended its frontiers, and news-gathering methods have more than kept pace.

Almost 2000 daily newspapers, and more than 500 Sunday newspapers, serve a nation of about 125,000,000 persons, circulating more than 35,000,000 daily and more than 24,000,000 on Sundays. Each of these newspapers receives the service of one or more of the regular press associations in the country, while each of the associations has its affiliations with foreign press associations and newspapers, and has its own correspondents in important foreign places. In addition, some individual newspapers maintain foreign staffs.[1]

[1] An up-to-date list of "American News Agencies and Newspaper Representatives" in Europe appears in *Europa*, V. 1, under the heading "Americans in Europe—News Agencies and Newspapers."

It is in New York and Washington that the correspondents for important newspapers and press associations, both foreign and domestic, congregate in the greatest numbers and establish residence. The National Press Club of Washington, with its own building, is one of the most important press organizations in the world. The Association of Foreign Correspondents in the United States has its headquarters in New York. Correspondents move between the two cities, and others, as news requires.

New York City is a center, chiefly, for business and financial news; Washington, for governmental and political news. The headquarters of the press associations are, without exception, in New York. The most important ones are the Associated Press, the United Press, the International News Service and the Universal Service. There are other associations of limited extent and purpose.[2]

The Associated Press, the origins of which have been described,[3] is a coöperative organization of many newspapers in the United States and some elsewhere. It has exchange contracts with important press associations of other countries, and provides an extensive budget of news, foreign and domestic.

The Associated Press, through Melville E. Stone, for many years its general manager, claims to have established the first sustained foreign service in the United States. To-day the Associated Press file may include items during any one day from as many as 200 different places in the world outside of the United States. The agency spent, in 1930, about $12,000,000 to maintain its entire service, including 80,000 correspondents and employees in the United States and elsewhere, with almost 80 bureaus in the United States and almost 20 abroad, and with salaried correspondents in about 190 important foreign cities; and also including the leasing of telegraph wires, cable charges, office rentals and so on.

[2] Victor Rosewater, *History of Coöperative News-Gathering in the United States.* This volume presents an excellent study of the history, organization and practices of the press associations of the country; O. G. Villard, *The Press Today,* Chs. 1, 2, 3, all previously published in the *Nation* (N. Y., Apr. 16, Apr. 23, May 7, 1930).

[3] See pp. 62-65, ante. See also: Anon., *"M.E.S." His Book,* pp. 91-201.

In 1933 it served 1300 papers in the United States and more than one hundred abroad.[4]

The United Press is a younger organization, independent and privately owned. It is just as impartial as the Associated Press, despite the fact that it is a commercial agency instead of a coöperative one, and it serves about as many newspapers of as diverse attitudes. Its history goes back to 1885, but, as known at present, it is the result of the consolidation of three wire associations in 1907.

During the Great War, when the European press associations were busy disseminating propaganda, the exchange of news between the associations in various countries lost much of its value. Neutral countries, especially, found it difficult to obtain impartial news reports. The leading Argentine newspaper, *La Prensa,* of Buenos Aires, seeking an escape from Havas and Reuters, turned to the United Press, which was independent, and did not even have a foreign press association affiliation. *La Prensa* made it financially worth while for the United Press to build up a larger service in Europe during the war years, to make its reports both more factual and more interpretative, so setting a style in news writing that found almost immediate favor in the United States as well as in the Argentine. By the end of the War, the United Press was serving 800 newspapers and had extended its foreign service to all parts of the world.[5]

Continued good work has enabled the United Press to improve its position since the War. Its South American and Far-Eastern news coverage has been especially good, while its European and domestic coverage has shown enterprise and ability. In 1933 it

[4] Kent Cooper, *The Associated Press: An Address* (The Associated Press, N. Y., Oct., 1925); Cooper, *The Associated Press: An Address.* To the American Society of Newspaper Editors (The Associated Press, N. Y., Jan. 16, 1926); Charles Stephenson Smith, "The Associated Press: A Great Adventure in Coöperation," *World's Press News* (Aug. 8, 1929); Dewey M. Owens, "The Associated Press," *American Mercury* (April, 1927), pp. 385-93. Anon., "(AP)," *Fortune* (Feb. 1937), pp. 88-93, 148-62. Bice Clemow, "Where Does the AP Go from Here," *Editor and Publisher* (Jan. 30, 1937), pp. 13, 34.

[5] Stephen Vincent Benét, "The United Press," *Fortune* (May, 1933), V. 7, No. 5, pp. 67-72, 94-104; Webb Miller, *I Found No Peace.* How an

had about thirty bureaus in Europe, South America and the Far East. In that year it served 1,200 papers in the United States and 340 abroad, many of them in South America, and it has the major interest in the British United Press, serving Canadian, British and some Continental papers. It spends about $8,000,000 a year in collecting and distributing the news, and now has exchange arrangements with some foreign newspapers, and a few foreign press associations.

The International News Service is a Hearst-owned service for afternoon papers, founded in 1909. The Universal Service, also Hearst-owned, was started after the War to serve morning papers and especially to provide features and colorful news stories. Both have fairly extensive foreign representation, are for sale to any paper, and have clients overseas and among the general press of the United States, even apart from the Hearst press.[6] Both services were formed to give Hearst newspapers a particular Hearst treatment of news, both foreign and domestic. They are smaller than either of the other two associations mentioned.

All of the North American press associations have extended their coverage to South America since 1916, and have improved their coverage of Far-Eastern news markedly since 1930, due to Japanese activity in that part of the world.

* * *

The services maintained outside of their own communities by individual newspapers of the United States sometimes attain considerable proportions. A good many of them maintain correspondents in New York, where they get advance proofs or copies of stories to appear in such newspapers as the New York *Times*. Even more newspapers maintain Washington correspondents or bureaus. A few have foreign services. Most of the latter services

able United Press man works; Miles Vaughn, *Covering the Far East*. Work for the UP in other parts of the world.

[6] Victor Rosewater, *History of Coöperative News-Gathering in the United States*, Ch. 27.

Anon., "I. N. S. Has Record of Achievement Since Its Organization 25 Years Ago," *Editor and Publisher* (April 21, 1934), pp. 10-11; O. G. Villard, *Some Newspapers and Newspapermen*, pp. 32, 38.

are syndicated to reduce the cost, and some Washington services also are syndicated for use in non-competitive papers in the United States.

It is because of the size of the country, with many non-competing papers and the absence of "national newspapers," in the European sense, that North American papers are able to meet the expenses of maintaining elaborate services, syndicating the news and distributing the costs. The combination makes available to them the best and most complete news service in the world, covering both foreign and domestic affairs.

The American newspapers with extensive foreign representation through staff assignments are the New York *Times,* the New York *Herald Tribune,* the *Christian Science Monitor,* the Chicago *Daily News* and the Chicago *Tribune.* Limited representation has been maintained by the New York *Sun,* the Brooklyn *Eagle,* the Baltimore *Sun* and the Detroit *News.*

The services of the New York *Times,* the New York *Herald Tribune,* the Chicago *Daily News,* and the Chicago *Tribune* are syndicated to other newspapers. The New York *Times* has spent upwards of $500,000 annually on its foreign service for years, and the cost was about a million dollars annually during the war years. The New York *Herald Tribune,* the Chicago *Tribune* and other newspapers spend somewhat less, but it always is expensive to maintain a foreign staff. The Chicago *Daily News,* by another estimate, has spent between $200,000 and $350,000 annually for five columns or more of foreign news a day, which it syndicated.[7]

The New York *Herald Tribune* foreign service is a lineal descendant of the early services maintained by the old New York *Herald* and the old New York *Tribune,* which were merged in 1924, and hence it is the oldest in the United States, dating back to about 1838. It has its own staff correspondents in all primary

[7] The New York *Times* has the most extensive service of any individual newspaper in the United States, or in the world, without doubt. It is a service that is syndicated to other newspapers, in addition to its use in the *Times* itself. Lansing Warren, *"Times* Meets Demands for News From Abroad," *The Little Times,* house organ of the New York *Times* (Sept. 20, 1929), pp. 1-3, 6; Willis C. Bright, *"Times* Growth Extends to Its Foreign Service," *The Little Times* (Dec. 16, 1929), pp. 1-3.

A224
BULLETIN
SAN ANTONIO, TEX., FEB 13-(AP)-FRANK SPENCER MEADOR, YOUNG
INVESTMENT CLERK, WAS GRANTED A DIVORCE HERE TODAY FROM ANNE GOULD
MEADOR, OF NEW YORK, RAILROAD HEIRESS.
HF212PES

A225
LEAD DEFENSE
WASHINGTON, FEB 13-(AP)-TWO UNSUCCESSFUL ATTEMPTS
WERE MADE IN THE HOUSE TODAY TO REDUCE THE $153,474,906 PROVIDED IN
THE WAR DEPARTMENT APPROPRIATION BILL FOR ARMY PAY.

N4

LONDON VIA PRESS WIRELESS 267 24 1112 GMT.

LCPRESS, MONITOR, BOSTON.

LONDON 24110--TALK BETWEEN BRITISH FRENCH MILITARY NAVAL EXPERTS

WHICH BEEN ONGOING PARIS RECENTLY ON SUBJECT COOPERATION IN EVENT

"MAD DOG" ACT IN MEDITERRANEAN ARE UNDERSTOOD TO HAVE NOW BEEN TEMPOR-

ARILY SUSPENDED.

ONE OF CHIEF DIFFICULTIES THAT BEEN ENCOUNTERED ARISES EXFACT THAT

UNDER FRENCH LAW ALL THREE SERVICES ARMY NAVY AIR FORCES TO BE MOB-

ILIZED TOGETHER. LAVAL DECLARES TIS IMPOSSIBLE FOR FRENCH TO MOBILIZE

PART THEIR FLEET TO SEND TO MEDITERRANEAN WITHOUT ALSO CALLING WHOLE

ARMY TO COLORS. THUS IT APPEARS THERE WOULD BE FORTNIGHT'S DELAY

BEFORE FRANCE COULD COME IN FORCE TO BRITAIN'S ASSISTANCE IN EVENT SUDDEN

ONSLAUGHT BY ITALIANS.

ANOTHER PROBLEM HINGES ROUND BRITAIN'S REQUEST BE ALLOWED USE FRENCH

PORTS IN EMERGENCY. FRANCE HAS CONSENTED BUT IT TRANSPIRES MOST POTENT-

IAL FRENCH NAVAL BASES IN MEDITERRANEAN TOO SMALL BE OF MUCH VALUE.

DISCUSSIONS ON THESE AND OTHER TECHNICAL POINTS EXPECTED BE

RENEWED NEW YEAR.

FIG. 38. HOW NEWS
For description see

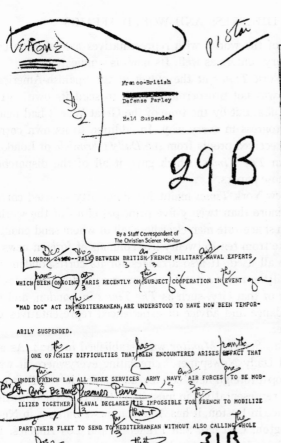

Franco-British
Defense Parley
Held Suspended

29 B

Franco-British

Defense Parley

Held Suspended

Franco-British Defense Parley Held Suspended

By a Staff Correspondent of
The Christian Science Monitor

LONDON, Dec. 24.—The talks between British and French military and naval experts, which have been going on at Paris recently on the subject of co-operation in the event of a "mad dog" act in the Mediterranean, are understood to have now been temporarily suspended.

One of the chief difficulties that has been encountered arises from the fact that under the French law all three services—army, navy and air forces—are to be mobilized together.

"It Can't Be Done"

Premier Pierre Laval declares that it is impossible for the French to mobilize part of their fleet to send to the Mediterranean without also calling the whole army to the colors. Thus it appears that there would be a fortnight's delay before France could come in force to Britain's assistance in the event of a sudden onslaught by the Italians.

Ports Too Small

Another problem hinges round Britain's request to be allowed to use French ports in an emergency. France has consented, but it transpires that the most potential French naval bases in the Mediterranean are too small to be of much value.

Discussions on these and other technical points are expected to be renewed with the new year.

Greece and Turkey Offer Aid

Meanwhile, according to reports from Athens and Istanbul, both Greece and Turkey have offered troops to help defend Egypt in case intensification of sanctions should cause an Italian invasion from Libya. As already reported in the press, a considerable number of British troops and air units have already moved to the neighborhood of Alexandria and a good many more have been brought from India to Aden. But the knowledge that other countries are preparing to co-operate if the need should arise is gratefully noted as indicating a real desire to keep the flag of collective security flying.

More Precautions

It is emphasized that only precautionary measures are being taken. It is also officially declared that complete calm exists on the Egyptian-Libya frontier and it is denied that any clash occurred west of Merus Matruq as reported in some newspapers yesterday.

By a Staff Correspondent of
The Christian Science Monitor

LONDON, 24—TALKS BETWEEN BRITISH FRENCH MILITARY NAVAL EXPERTS,

WHICH BEEN ONGOING PARIS RECENTLY ON SUBJECT COOPERATION IN EVENT OF A

"MAD DOG" ACT IN MEDITERRANEAN, ARE UNDERSTOOD TO HAVE NOW BEEN TEMPOR-

ARILY SUSPENDED.

ONE OF CHIEF DIFFICULTIES THAT BEEN ENCOUNTERED ARISES FACT THAT

UNDER FRENCH LAW ALL THREE SERVICES ARMY, NAVY, AIR FORCES TO BE MOB-

ILIZED TOGETHER. LAVAL DECLARES IS IMPOSSIBLE FOR FRENCH TO MOBILIZE

PART THEIR FLEET TO SEND TO MEDITERRANEAN WITHOUT ALSO CALLING WHOLE

ARMY TO COLORS.   THUS IT APPEARS THERE WOULD BE FORTNIGHT'S DELAY

31 B

BEFORE FRANCE COULD COME IN FORCE TO BRITAIN'S ASSISTANCE IN EVENT SUDDEN

ONSLAUGHT BY ITALIANS.   Ports Too Small

ANOTHER PROBLEM HINGES ROUND BRITAIN'S REQUEST BE ALLOWED USE FRENCH

PORTS IN EMERGENCY.   FRANCE HAS CONSENTED BUT IT TRANSPIRES MOST POTENT-

IAL FRENCH NAVAL BASES IN MEDITERRANEAN TOO SMALL BE OF MUCH VALUE.

DISCUSSIONS ON THESE AND OTHER TECHNICAL POINTS EXPECTED BE

RENEWED. NEW YEAR.

REACHES AMERICA

news centers of the world, with representatives available on call in the secondary centers as well. Its news is syndicated.

The New York *Times* at the outset of the Spanish-American War in 1898 was not prosperous enough to send its own correspondent to Cuba, but by the time of the Great War it had made tremendous progress in every way. In addition to its own correspondence, it received proofs from the *Daily Chronicle* of London, and later from *The Times,* which gave it all of the dispatches received by those papers.

Now the New York *Times* maintains about fifty salaried correspondents in more than twenty-five principal cities of the world, not to mention space-rate men elsewhere, all of whom send enough matter to make from ten to twenty-five columns of foreign news a day if it were all used. It also arranges for its correspondent in each foreign city to receive proofs of news received by some leading newspaper of that city, such as *The Times* in London, and to enjoy the guidance and advice of experienced representatives of that local paper.

The *Christian Science Monitor* was established in 1908. As an "International Daily Newspaper," circulating everywhere, it was quick to develop a foreign news service, and to-day has staff correspondents and representatives in most important centers. With the publication office in Boston, it has American news bureaus in New York, Washington, Chicago, San Francisco and Los Angeles. It does not syndicate its news, but bears the entire cost unassisted. A large volume of mail copy augments its service.

The Chicago *Tribune* service and syndicate grew out of the "query system." Because the *Tribune* had a unique position and considerable prestige in the Mississippi Valley states, editors of other newspapers in that section fell into the habit of writing or wiring the *Tribune* to ask what "inside information" it might have on various subjects. To satisfy this demand, which became especially strong during the Great War, the *Tribune* extended its news service, and sold its stories on a syndicate basis.

The Chicago *Daily News* service, started in 1899, proved to be so good during the early months of the Great War that other newspapers wanted to share it, and so began that newspaper's syndication of its own˙service. It won prestige because of the high quality of its dispatches and its personnel.[8]

* * *

The foreign correspondents in the United States congregate in New York, partly because it is a better cable end than Washington, and partly because it is almost as easy to learn there what is going on in Washington, while at the same time living in the center for financial and commercial news, which usually interests foreign readers at least as much as the nation's political and governmental affairs. The foreign press associations in alliance with the Associated Press have offices in the same building with the Associated Press, while foreign newspaper representatives find it convenient to be in the same buildings with the New York newspapers whose advance proofs they receive.

Although the flow of news out of the United States does not nearly equal the flow of incoming news, the outgoing messages since the War have vastly increased in number, in quality, and in variety.[9]

It is in Washington that the great body of correspondents for national newspapers and press associations gather. Foreign correspondents are tending to go there, also, in increasing numbers.

[8] For a description of how the Chicago *Daily News* foreign service was organized to cover the Great War, see Jason Rogers, *Newspaper Building*, Ch. 18, pp. 145-52. A reprint of an article by Victor F. Lawson, publisher of the paper, which originally appeared in *Editor and Publisher;* Charles H. Dennis, *Victor Lawson: His Time and His Work.*

[9] Warren Bassett, "Why United States is Rapidly Becoming the News Capital of the World," *Editor and Publisher* (Mar. 14, 1925), pp. 3, 27; J. H. Furay, "America—News Gatherer for the World," *The Quill* (June, 1931), pp. 10-11, 15; F. J. J. Merckx, "How a European Correspondent 'Covers' News of This Country," *American Press* (Sept., 1930), p. 34; Harold Butcher, "Foreign Writers Celebrate 21st Year of U. S. 'Coverage' From Abroad," *Editor and Publisher* (Mar. 27, 1926), p. 40; W. W. Davies, "Reporting a Continent," *News, Its Scope and Limitations* (see Anon.) (Univ. of Missouri Bulletin. V. 30, No. 46. Journalism Series No. 37, 1929), pp. 3-9. The work of the correspondent in the United States for *La Nacion* of Buenos Aires; Raymond Clapper, "All Eyes are Turned on Washington," *Editor and Publisher* (Jan. 13, 1934), p. 9; Harold Butcher, "Coverage of New Deal Is Big Job for Foreign Writers in U. S.," by a correspondent for the *News-Chronicle* of London, *Editor and Publisher* (Apr. 7, 1934), p. 16.

The number of out-of-town correspondents in Washington grew, from 65 in 1859, to 183 in 1929, and to 530 in 1933. The membership in the Press Galleries of Congress, which includes many foreign journalists, numbers several hundred. Journalists have been admitted to the galleries of both houses of Congress since the earliest days, and have received an increasing measure of coöperation from officials in their task of reporting the business of government.[10]

While European governments continued to place obstacles in the way of newspaper men before the Great War, the United States Government was pursuing the opposite policy, making it easy and not too unpleasant for journalists seeking facts. Even the President was accessible to certain trusted newspaper men. And, instead of becoming less easy to see, as the years passed, the President became more so.

Some European correspondents, accustomed to being tolerated, at best, in their own countries, and frequently avoided and distrusted, were amazed at the opposite attitude in the United States.[11] They enjoyed equal treatment with the Washington press corps, instead of being received separately by officials—as is often the European way—and there was no restriction upon what they wrote or sent.

* * *

Censorship never has been popular in the United States, even though George Washington himself showed an inclination to clamp an informal muzzle on public discussion of the Jay Treaty in 1794. But despite the definite order from President Washington, the

[10] M. M. Willey and S. A. Rice, *Communications Agencies and Social Life; Editor and Publisher Year Book.* Annual, containing list of correspondents admitted to the Press Galleries. See also: *Congressional Directory.* Issued for each session of Congress; For "First List of Correspondents," reporting House and Senate affairs in 1859, see *Editor and Publisher* (July 21, 1934), p. 118.

[11] H. W. Nevinson, *Last Changes, Last Chances*, p. 231. "In the United States," he wrote of the Washington Naval Conference of 1921-22, "the journalist is held in no contempt, and the highest 'personages' in the country are willing not merely to regard him as an inevitable nuisance, but even to assist his humble endeavors to arrive at the truth."

text of the treaty was sent to the *Aurora,* which published it, following which it was widely reproduced and aroused a storm of public disapproval.[12]

The First Amendment to the Constitution, guaranteeing freedom of speech and of the press, precludes any legal censorship, and so far as such a thing ever has existed in the United States, it has been of private origin, lacking any responsible official support. It has, upon occasions, been attempted locally, despite the constitutional guarantee, and probably more of these occasions have had to do with labor disputes than with anything else. It has taken the form, at times, of threats or actual violence toward newspaper reporters seeking the facts, or of gestures toward the papers themselves. But more often it is made effective through economic power wielded over the press by business men, industrialists and bankers. In such cases, no active enforcement is required because editors and reporters know without being told what they can write and print. It is a "disciplined press," but "disciplined" in the interest of private persons and companies, rather than in the interest of the public.[13]

Another common occasion when a censorship is attempted is when there is an epidemic of a contagious disease, especially in a city which enjoys a large tourist trade that might be curtailed or stopped if general alarm were aroused.[14]

In the years since 1918 a growing belief has developed among correspondents in Washington that they are entitled to know everything that is going on. This has made them increasingly resentful of any official disinclination to speak with the utmost frankness, even if it must be "off the record."

As a defense against the insatiable demands of the press at times when they did not wish to speak, officials have erected a barrier of "contact men," press officials, often former newspaper men, usually able to talk to the journalists in their own language, to explain departmental business intelligently and helpfully, but

[12] Bernard Fäy, *Notes on the American Press at the End of the Eighteenth Century,* p. 17; C. R. Fish, *American Diplomacy,* pp. 119-20.

[13] George Seldes, *Freedom of the Press,* Ch. 2-9.

[14] *Ibid.,* pp. 46-47.

careful never to give out any information that they should not give out.

The Senate has been disturbed at times by publication in the press of actions taken at executive sessions of that body. An effort was made by Senator William Brinton Heyburn, of Idaho, in 1922, to penalize any newspaper printing such news by depriving it of the right to have its representatives in the Senate gallery. Senator David A. Reed of Pennsylvania, in 1925, sought to provide penalties for correspondents or newspapers so transgressing the rules. There have been other suggestions of the same general character, but none ever has received serious consideration.[15]

*   *   *

Most Presidents have had special friends among the press to whom they would speak with extra frankness. Through papers served by these correspondents many stories centering about the White House found first publication. Jefferson, Buchanan, Jackson, Lincoln, Grant, Cleveland, Theodore Roosevelt carried on their relations with the press, usually, through individual newspaper men. Some of the presidents, including Mr. Lincoln, were inclined to be distrustful of the press in general. Much news of the McKinley activities came through his political sponsor, Mark Hanna. Jefferson had had his journalistic spokesman in Samuel Harrison Smith, Buchanan had his L. A. Gobright, Theodore Roosevelt had his O. K. Davis; for Wilson there was David Lawrence, for Hoover, Mark Sullivan.

It had been the custom, prior to Theodore Roosevelt's administration, to cover White House news from the Capitol, a mile away down Pennsylvania Avenue, or through private sources. But Mr. Roosevelt, with a lively sense for personal publicity, began to

---

[15] "It is a matter of fact that Congress as a whole wastes precious little love upon the correspondents as a body. If the gentlemen who do the legislating dared, they undoubtedly would exercise a large measure of control over the news they make. They might not in any event go to the length of enforcing a censorship, but they would like to suppress entirely certain occurrences and to color all the press reports to their advantage." J. F. Essary, *Covering Washington*, pp. 217-18. Arthur Krock, "Press *vs.* Government—a Warning," *Public Opinion Quarterly* (April, 1937), pp. 45-49.

"make" news on Sundays because he knew that interesting page-one stories were less frequent for Monday morning papers than on other mornings. By releasing an announcement or a statement in time for use in the Monday morning papers, he knew that it was more certain to receive a good "play." Also, he summoned press representatives, in a group, to the White House on a few occasions to make special announcements to them.[16]

It remained for William W. Price, then of the *Evening Star* of Washington, to go directly to the White House in the pursuit of news during the latter part of Theodore Roosevelt's administration. He did not himself see the President, nor did he try to enter the White House, but he would speak to Congressmen and others as they left the building, presumably after having seen the President, and try to learn from them the purposes of their interviews with him. Mr. Price got so many exclusive stories in this way that other reporters had to follow suit, and the practice became established. It was then that President Roosevelt ordered that an anteroom in the White House be set aside for the use and convenience of the newspaper men.[17]

[16] Although Theodore Roosevelt, when President, held no general press conferences, he spoke freely to trusted correspondents, telling them much. Sometimes he told them more than they themselves wanted, because much of it was told "in confidence" and so could not be used, whereas they might in some cases have obtained the information elsewhere, and used it, otherwise. Yet he warned them frankly that if he were quoted he would deny the truth of the statement or the accuracy of the quotation. This he sometimes did, and thus was formed the so-called "Ananias Club," composed of men whose veracity was brought into question by Roosevelt's repudiation. In this way, Roosevelt set up his own wall of anonymity, to be used when he found it convenient as a shelter behind which to take refuge. See: Marlen Pew, "Shop Talk at Thirty," *Editor and Publisher* (Feb. 28, 1931), p. 70. This article also sketches the history of presidential press relations to 1931.

[17] Matters have so far advanced that there now exists a White House Correspondents' Association, a formal organization set up to pass upon the credentials of those who would attend presidential press conferences. Its purpose is to keep out propagandists and others with no proper business there, and to facilitate relations between the President and the press in every way possible. From a dozen to 200 correspondents may attend a presidential press conference, depending upon the President and upon the anticipation of newsworthy developments.

A companion organization exists, the State, War and Navy Correspondents' Association, consisting of journalists who cover the affairs of those three

Mr. Taft was the first President to establish formal meetings with the press at group conferences, although they were not held regularly.

President Wilson improved upon the Taft arrangements by holding two press conferences weekly, after Cabinet meetings, on Tuesday noons and Friday afternoons. He was not on particularly cordial terms with the press, however, partly because he was inclined to be impatient under questioning and partly because he resented the curiosity that the press sometimes showed concerning his personal and family affairs.

Beginning in the autumn of 1914, with the Great War in progress, the President received the press less frequently, and he discontinued the meetings entirely after the *Lusitania* was torpedoed in May, 1915. He had found, among other things, that foreign newspaper men at the conferences were promptly relaying all information, including confidential matters, to various embassies and legations. Rather than bar the foreign journalists alone, he took the occasion to end the conferences entirely, although he did see individual journalists, as Theodore Roosevelt had done.

Mr. Wilson was asked to resume regular press conferences, but declined to do so on the ground that they were "a waste of time." "I came to Washington with the idea that close and cordial relations with the press would prove of the greatest aid," he said. "I prepared for the conferences as carefully as for any lecture, and talked freely and fully on all large questions of the moment. Some men of brilliant ability were in the group, but I soon discovered that the interest of the majority was in the personal and trivial

departments of government, all of which happen to be housed in the same building.

The Press Gallery of the Congress of the United States, with both the House Press Gallery and the Senate Press Gallery, each with its Superintendent, considers credentials of journalists who would sit in those galleries. No journalist who is not *bona fide* is acceptable, and if he becomes a publicity representative for any person, group, or organization he must resign, or be expelled.

The aggressive search for spot news in Washington, in contrast to an earlier and more philosophical reporting of affairs in the capital, is noted by Francis E. Leupp in "The Waning Power of the Press," appearing in *The Profession of Journalism* (W. G. Bleyer, ed.), pp. 30-51.

rather than in principles and policies." [18] Although the newspaper men saw him somewhat more often at the Paris Peace Conference, Mr. Wilson never did hold regular press conferences again.

President Harding, a newspaper publisher himself, instituted regular bi-weekly conferences once again, and established extremely friendly relations with the journalists attending. He was genial, frank and easygoing. An incident following one of these conferences, however, resulted in correspondents being required to submit their questions in writing to a presidential secretary not later than fifteen minutes before the conference. Although details differ in accounts of this incident, it appears that the President replied, without sufficient knowledge, to a question involving the foreign policy of the country. His statement, when published, was embarrassing to the State Department, and Secretary Hughes remonstrated with the President. At the next conference Mr. Harding asked the correspondents to put their questions in written form thenceforth, and that practice so became established for ten years, until set aside by President Franklin Roosevelt.

President Coolidge continued the bi-weekly press conferences with almost complete regularity, requiring that questions be submitted in writing. Despite his reputation for taciturnity, he may be said to have enjoyed a "good press." This was partly because he was able to "make" news by talking on subjects not strictly governmental, but very "human," such as his fishing prowess; and partly because, behind the barrier of his conventional anonymity, he was able to say things that would make striking page-one headlines, but which he could deny if the public reaction was unfavorable or if it seemed otherwise expedient to do so.

By the President's "conventional anonymity" is meant the circumstance by which no President is quoted directly unless by specific authorization. President Wilson set this precedent in his second administration, after some earlier unhappy experiences. Seldom has the rule been broken.

Due to this anonymity rule, correspondents who wished to give authenticity to stories built around what the President had said,

[18] George Creel, "Woodrow Wilson, the Man Behind the President," *Sat. Eve. Post* (Mar. 28, 1931), pp. 37-44.

would attribute authority to "the White House Spokesman," "a person close to the President," would refer to "an announcement at the White House," or indulge in comparable circumlocutions. The "White House Spokesman" became a famous individual, and then a subject of jest, until President Coolidge became irritated and asked the correspondents not to use the term any more.[19]

Mr. Coolidge also requested that correspondents refrain from reporting that they had asked questions (in writing, that is) to which he did not choose to reply. Stenographic reports of conferences made by White House secretaries were not available to correspondents, as they had been previously, and a correspondent would be rebuked if he took his own shorthand notes. Some regarded this as a means by which correspondents were being turned into propaganda agents for the president.[20]

Shortly after taking office, President Coolidge had showed a great willingness to please the assembled correspondents. "I notice," he said at the beginning of one conference attended by this

[19] When President Coolidge spent the summer of 1926 at Paul Smith's, New York, a resort, *Le Soir* of Brussels became confused, and decided that "Mr. Paul Smith" was the White House Spokesman himself, and so referred to him in a news report.

[20] The history of presidential press relations up to the Coolidge administration is presented by J. F. Essary, *Covering Washington*, Ch. 5, "Presidents at Home," pp. 83-104.

See also: W. E. Sweet, "Public Opinion and the Chief Executive," *National Conference on Social Work. 1923* (see Anon.), pp. 474-77; J. F. Essary, "President, Congress, and the Press Correspondents," *American Political Science Review* (Nov., 1928), V. 22, 902-9; David Lawrence, "Reporting the Political News at Washington," *American Political Science Review* (Nov., 1928), V. 22, 893-902.

See also: Anon., "White House Corps Urged to 'Strike,'" *Editor and Publisher* (Aug. 18, 1928), p. 22. "The White House Spokesman," however, was a creation of the journalists themselves. The development of this fiction, further details of its operation under Coolidge, and general consideration of the work of the correspondent at the White House appears in an article by David Lawrence, "The President and the Press," *Sat. Eve. Post* (Aug. 27, 1927), pp. 27, 117-18. A statement of the press case against the President, however, is well represented by Willis Sharp, "President and Press," *Atlantic Monthly* (Aug., 1927), pp. 239-45. So far as the "spokesman" system of attribution was concerned, many leading correspondents were ready to defend it. George H. Manning, "Liberalizing of President's Contacts with Press Hoped for from Hoover," *Editor and Publisher* (Jan. 12, 1929), pp. 5-6.

writer, "that the press is becoming less inquisitive. I have fewer questions than usual this morning. I hope that is not an indication that I have failed to answer adequately the questions put to me in the past. I have tried to do so, and I might say that I have always found that you gentlemen quote me accurately and fairly in all your reports. I wish to help you and coöperate with you as far as possible. There are, of course, some questions that for one reason or another I do not feel should be answered at the time they are asked."

Few incidents arose to disturb the relations of President Coolidge with the press. One occurred shortly before Jules Jusserand retired as French Ambassador to the United States, after twenty years. M. Jusserand spoke to an organization of women in Washington, referred to the French war debt owing to the United States, and suggested a moratorium. President Coolidge, asked about this at the next press conference, answered in a way that was interpreted by able correspondents as a rebuke to the French Ambassador. Their stories embarrassed the State Department. The White House, presumably at the request of Secretary Hughes, issued a statement to the effect that any comment by the President had been simply in the nature of a refusal to discuss the Ambassador's address at all.[21]

On four occasions President Coolidge objected to what he considered the failure of the press, either by approval or silence, to support his administration. This was in its handling of the war debts situation, and in its handling of the Mexican-Nicaraguan situation, including the landing of Marines in Nicaragua; and the situation in China at the time. The press was blamed for a presumed misunderstanding of the administration's aims and meth-

[21] This denial provoked Henry Suydam, Washington correspondent for the Brooklyn *Eagle*, to protest the disavowal on behalf of the correspondents, whose accuracy and integrity were brought into question. He challenged the right of the President to refuse to assume the responsibility for what he had said. He departed from the usual journalistic policy, which is to say nothing on such occasions and so permit the public to gain the impression that the newspapers had blundered or lied. Anon., "Brooklyn *Eagle's* Writer Firmly Contests White House Interview Denial," *Editor and Publisher* (Jan. 3, 1925), pp. 3-4.

ods, with a consequent weakening of American foreign policy. These rebukes to the press were interpreted by some as implying that Mr. Coolidge believed the press ought to endorse the administration's foreign policy without question, which was regarded as tantamount to an attempt to gag, muzzle, or censor the press.[22]

Following these and other incidents, the White House Spokesman grew more important.

* * *

When Herbert Hoover was Secretary of Commerce in the Harding and Coolidge cabinets, his relations with the press were exceedingly cordial. When he entered the White House, correspondents expected relations to be even better than they had been under Coolidge.

For about three months after Mr. Hoover became President the White House press conferences were rich and useful. Unlike Mr. Coolidge, however, he was not a President who could "make news," or endure for long the curiosity about his personal life and affairs. Like President Wilson, he found that principles and policies were of small interest to most correspondents, and from that time the Hoover press conferences began to become less useful.

The stock market crash in 1929, with the difficulties following, gave Mr. Hoover endless anxiety and work. The effect and counter-effect of these matters on the press and President resulted in the entire system of press relations going to pieces; questions were ignored and meetings were brief. There were long periods toward the end of the administration when no press conferences would be held, with leading correspondents absenting themselves from such as were held, because no good ever seemed to come from attendance.

The President manifested irritation with the press at times, and especially because of what he considered "news leaks" about both personal and official matters, trivial and otherwise, at the White

[22] Three of these rebukes occurred at press conferences at the White House, on Sept. 18, 1925; Dec. 31, 1926, and early in April of 1927. The fourth was at a public speech, delivered at the twentieth anniversary dinner of the United Press, in New York, on April 25, 1927.

House and at his Rapidan camp in Virginia. There was some justice in his attitude, because, with small things "leaking," important things might "leak," too, unless the source were blocked. Circumstances arising during the depression made the President regard the press as antagonistic. And, for its part, the press sometimes thought it detected a White House disposition to censor or bottle up the news. It may well be true that no President since Lincoln has had to endure so much journalistic abuse as Mr. Hoover, although he had entered upon his administration with every favorable omen.[23]

When Franklin D. Roosevelt became President in 1933 there was a feeling, as when Mr. Hoover took office, that the press was about to enter upon an idyllic relationship with the chief executive. Mr. Roosevelt, as Governor of New York State, had enjoyed excellent press relations. In Washington he resumed regular press conferences, which had almost faded into nothingness under Hoover. He conducted an informal and friendly meeting, gave up requiring that questions be submitted in writing, spoke with the greatest candor, and enjoyed good personal relations with the press, partly because he showed no favors to individuals, as other presidents had done. The conferences proved to be useful to the correspondents as providing "background" material. Mr. Roosevelt himself professed to find them useful because, from the questions, many of which always are asked by correspondents at the

[23] G. H. Manning, "Hoover Liberalizes Press Conferences," *Editor and Publisher* (Mar. 9, 1929), p. 7; Paul Y. Anderson, "Hoover and the Press," *Nation* (N. Y., Oct. 14, 1931), pp. 382-84; Herbert Corey, "The Presidents and the Press," *Sat. Eve. Post* (Jan. 9, 1932), pp. 25, 96-104. Traces the relationship from Taft to Hoover; G. H. Manning, "Strained Air Pervades Press Circle as White House 'Leak' Is Sought," *Editor and Publisher* (July 18, 1931), p. 10; Manning, "President Hoover and White House Corps at Odds over News 'Leaks,'" *Editor and Publisher* (July 11, 1931); Manning, "Joslin Suggests News 'Consultations,'" *Editor and Publisher* (Sept. 19, 1931), p. 7; Manning, "White House Ban on Bank Parley Upset by Correspondents," *Editor and Publisher* (Oct. 10, 1931), pp. 5-6; Paul Y. Anderson, "Is Press Unfair to Officialdom?" *American Press* (Aug., 1932), p. 3; Anon., "An Average American," *Time* (Nov. 18, 1935), pp. 41-46. This is an article about Mark Sullivan, long a correspondent and personal friend of Mr. Hoover, who became his chief apologist; Will Irwin, *Propaganda and the News*, pp. 294-96.

special request of their newspaper editors in various parts of the country, he was able to estimate the drift of public interest and judge the reception of his administration's acts almost at once.

Mr. Roosevelt's conferences remained generally useful. There was no apparent effort on Mr. Roosevelt's part to try to shape the treatment of the news, to bar or eliminate hostile representatives, nor was there more than an occasional disposition to resent personal publicity concerning himself or his family. He professed to realize, when hostile questions were asked, that it was not the correspondent, perhaps, whose attitude was reflected, but an unfriendly publisher hundreds of miles away who was trying to get a statement which would embarrass the President. Such understanding of their own problems pleased the correspondents further, and although most newspapers favored Mr. Landon during the 1936 presidential campaign, the correspondents themselves were almost unanimous in the private preference for Mr. Roosevelt.[24]

* * *

It seems doubtful whether the relations between press and President ever can be entirely harmonious over any extended

[24] Anon., "Correspondents Like Roosevelt," *American Press* (Mar., 1933), p. 3; J. F. Essary, "How Presidents Deal with Press," *American Press* (April, 1933), p. 2; Paul Mallon, "Roosevelt Gets His Story Over," New York *Times Magazine* (Nov. 19, 1933), pp. 1-2, 15; Anon., "Press Conferences: Arthur Krock Explains Why They Are Useful," *American Press* (Dec., 1933), p. 3; George H. Manning, "President Candidly Consults Reporters in Advance of Budget Announcement," *Editor and Publisher* (Jan. 6, 1934), pp. 3-4.

Bice Clemow, "F. D. R. Retains 'Open' Conferences," *Editor and Publisher* (Mar. 2, 1935), p. 9; Samuel G. Blythe, "Ferment," *Sat. Eve. Post* (May 11, 1935), pp. 5-7, 119-21; Frank R. Kent, "Press 'Conferences,'" *American Press* (Feb., 1935), p. 8. Mr. Kent, writing in the Baltimore *Sun*, like Mr. Mark Sullivan, writing in the New York *Herald Tribune*, wrote as an anti-Roosevelt propagandist, rather than as a correspondent concerned with presenting an impartial news picture; Charles W. B. Hurd, "President and Press: A Unique Forum," New York *Times Magazine* (June 9, 1935), pp. 3, 19; Anon., "Roosevelt Press Conferences Make History Book Footnotes," *Christian Science Monitor* (Dec. 30, 1936); Leo C. Rosten, "President Roosevelt and the Washington Correspondents," *Public Opinion Quarterly* (Jan., 1937), pp. 36-52.

period. This is the result of circumstances, and a personal matter, the unfortunate outcome of political influences and differences of opinion concerning official policies.

The tendency of the press usually is to see situations, where possible, in terms of controversy, struggle, and fight, on the theory that conflict makes the most interesting news. Newspaper men also may like a President personally, and bear him no ill will, but some must take orders from publishers at home who are hostile to him and want stories written which present the President and his administration in the worst light. Others are so affected by competition that they will not hesitate to take advantage of something that he has said, even knowing that it will make trouble, and print it as it is, or sensationalize it, "blowing it up" to give it a false importance, simply because of the pseudo-news value this will give it. They want a "good story," at any cost.

Sometimes the correspondents say, with reason, that they are reporters and must *report*. It is for editors, at home, to determine what shall and what shall not appear in print. But editors also are affected by competitive conditions, as well as by various prejudices. Moreover, it is difficult to say, sometimes, when a story should be suppressed and when it should be used, as information to which the public is legitimately entitled. The editor must make the decision. If he is right, he is praised afterward. If he is wrong, he probably realizes it, but then it is too late; critics, who have not had to make the decision, blame him. But for them to attribute all manner of unworthy purposes to him, or to the paper, may be unwarranted.

For instance, President Hoover's proposed moratorium on reparations was discovered by the press through a "leak" in Congressional circles, and it was blazoned before negotiations had been completed, and possibly before the Government of the United States had had time to consult the French Government. Caught unprepared, France considered it and delayed acceptance so long that the value of the plan was virtually lost. Regrettable as this may be, it was not entirely the fault of the press, for even though the White House correspondents might have promised to hold the story a fortnight, until arrangements had been completed, some outside journalist, getting his facts elsewhere, would unquestionably have used the story.[25]

The relation of government and press is important, both in its immediate bearing upon the personal fortunes of officials, politicians, correspondents and newspapers, and also in its effect upon the public interest.[26]

While the correspondents are interested in getting every fact that there is, with everything made available, officials are not always so eager to have this the case. Like the newspaper publication of the steps being taken to capture a criminal, which may help him to escape the law, the newspaper publication of official and diplomatic views, plans and intentions sometimes will spoil all hope of a successful outcome because it crystallizes those views prematurely. It prevents official changes of front for fear of losing prestige, and lets loose passions and prejudices in various quarters, tending to deform further action.

Washington correspondents recognize that the President and Members of the Cabinet, in the public interest, must maintain certain reticences. There is no attempt, therefore, to cross-examine such high officials. They would not be obliged to submit to such questioning, in any event. But Senators, Representatives

[25] This version does not accord with that presented by Drew Pearson and Constantine Brown in *The American Diplomatic Game*, pp. 208-41; Herbert Corey, "The Presidents and the Press," *Sat. Eve. Post* (Jan. 9, 1932), pp. 25, 96-104; J. F. Essary, "The Presidency and the Press," *Scribner's* (May, 1935).

[26] William C. Redfield, "Glimpses of Our Government: Friendly Enemies," *Sat. Eve. Post* (Nov. 15, 1924), pp. 42, 52, 54; Anon., "Politicians and the Press," *Sat. Eve. Post* (Aug. 18, 1923), pp. 25, 72-79; J. F. Essary, "Presidents, Congress, and the Press Correspondents," *American Political Science Review* (Nov., 1928), V. 22, 902-09; David Lawrence, "Reporting the Political News at Washington," *American Political Science Review* (Nov., 1928), V. 22, 893-902; P. W. Wilson, "Reporting Parliament and Congress," *North American Review* (Sept., 1921), V. 214, 326-33; Silas Bent, "Washington Correspondence," *Ballyhoo*, Ch. 3, pp. 79-93; "The Press and the Government." Addresses by David Lawrence, Fred Fuller Shedd, Henry Suydam, Paul Y. Anderson and others at Princeton Conference on the Press, 1930. *Conference on the Press* (see Anon.), pp. 61-93; J. F. Essary, *Covering Washington;* Anon., "The Press," *Washington Merry-Go-Round*, Ch. 15, pp. 321-66; Drew Pearson and Constantine Brown, *The American Diplomatic Game*.

and subordinate officials of government are not always treated with such consideration. The smaller conferences held by the subordinate officials also are a help to most correspondents, who find the size and formality of conferences held by the President and Cabinet members to be obstacles to satisfactory questions.

In the years following the Great War, when governments improved their press relations, some of the wartime lessons have been turned to general use. The propaganda value of a "good press" then came to be recognized, and it was learned that a "good press" usually followed an appearance of frankness. So the United States Government, among others, has made it increasingly easy for a correspondent to cover the affairs of state.

Every department of the government and virtually every division, including the Supreme Court, has its press officer, often a former newspaper man, to gather news from the division, prepare it in proper form, and see that it reaches the press. He also tries to arrange matters so that reports will be as friendly as possible to the department or division itself. Among other things, the impression of worthy activity, conveyed through the news reports over a period of months, may help to obtain an increase in the next year's appropriations, which is a consideration that makes publicity important to government divisions. Department heads have insisted, more and more, however, that all news from their departments must emanate from the accredited press officer, and that no other members or employees are to give out information. It was suggested, late in 1936, that the government might set up a central bureau to maintain contact with the press and the radio, correlating all publicity. General opposition at the time silenced the discussion.

Only when affairs are of the utmost importance, do journalists begin to dig for themselves. It would be impossible, considering the myriad activities of government, for them to give equal attention to every detail. They must concentrate to some extent, and for the rest they are content to depend upon the government press representatives.

In matters that are before Congress it is essential for journalists to watch and listen and study carefully at first hand much

that is going on. Yet, they have considerable help from the Super-
intendents of the Senate Press Gallery and the House Press Gallery, who relieve them of many details, see that the bills under
consideration are available in printed form, and provide other
services. Almost every Congressman and Senator has a Secretary,
and part of the Secretary's duty is to keep his or her employer in
the good graces of the press by providing every possible courtesy
and coöperation.[27]

* * *

The press associations maintain large staffs in Washington,
while leading newspapers are well represented there. Foreign correspondents, who are more concerned with general trends than with
details, depend upon local newspapers to keep them informed on
routine matters. But they must contend with unfavorable time
differences since most of them serve European morning newspapers, and are obliged to file their dispatches when the news-day
is scarcely ended in the United States.

The correspondents in the capital live in reasonable comfort,
but work hard. They must attend conferences, hearings, and meetings; they must see and interview many persons, they must study
many a difficult report, they must be patient seekers after facts
and motives not always easy to discover, despite the system of
"handouts" and publicity; and they must be able to write what
they learn in a way that will capture the attention of readers
usually more interested in events nearer home.

[27] J. F. Essary, *Covering Washington.* Gives an idea of the work corre-
spondents must do in reporting the news of the capital; Robert S. Mann,
"Capital Corps No Propaganda Victims, Writers Tell Journalism Teachers,"
Editor and Publisher (Jan. 4, 1936), pp. 3-4, 12; Turner Catledge, "Federal
Bureau for Press Urged," New York *Times* (Dec. 29, 1936); Anon., "Super
Press Bureau," (Editorial). *Editor and Publisher* (Jan. 2, 1937), p. 28;
Anon., "$1,200,000 for Publicity; That's Uncle Sam's Annual Expenditure,
Says Writer," *Editor and Publisher* (Jan. 23, 1937), p. 40; T. Swann Hard-
ing, "Informational Techniques of the Department of Agriculture," *Public
Opinion Quarterly* (Jan., 1937), pp. 83-96. This department leads all others
in the size of staff and amount of money devoted to information and publicity.
Arthur Krock, "Press *vs.* Government—a Warning," *Public Opinion Quarterly* (April, 1937), pp. 45-49. The argument against a central press
bureau.

The Washington news has become increasingly concerned with economics and social questions, somewhat less with party politics. It has become more concerned with ideas, less with personalities. Its handling requires more learning and less back-slapping.

The correspondent in Washington spends an active day. He must read the New York and Washington papers every morning, and perhaps others as well. He may attend a press conference at the White House twice a week, a daily conference at the State Department or the Treasury Department, or a conference at some other government department. Perhaps he attends a Congressional hearing or investigation; he may listen to a debate in the Senate, or he may have an interview with some legislator, government official, or a visitor in Washington. He may go to a foreign embassy to talk to an official, and he may go to the National Press Club to learn what his colleagues have been doing and thinking. And he must prepare his copy.

In fact, there are so many things for a correspondent to do, so many places that he may go, or must go, in the pursuit of news, that it becomes difficult for one man to do more than a part of it for an American newspaper. For this reason he will specialize on one or two stories, if he is working alone, and follow those wherever they may lead. Or, if he has an informal working arrangement with a colleague for a non-competing paper, if he has an assistant, or if he is only one member of a bureau in the capital, the work will be divided and subdivided. One person covers the White House and all news developing there, another attends to affairs in Congress, one covers the State Department and embassies, another reports affairs at the Treasury Department, or the War Department, or the Navy Department, and so on.[28]

Probably no two newspaper organizations will divide the work in just the same way, but the division of the work does make it

[28] There are many books and articles dealing with the work of the Washington correspondent. Many of them have been cited already. See, especially, note 26, page 318. See also: the *Congressional Directory*. Always contains a list of accredited newspaper correspondents, foreign and native, in Washington; *Editor and Publisher Year Book*. Contains current list of members of the Press Galleries, lists of foreign correspondents in New York and Washington, officers of journalistic clubs and associations, etc.

possible to cover the affairs of government with reasonable efficiency.

The correspondent at Washington usually may depend upon a ticker news service in his office to protect him on the general run of the news, as well as to protect him from being badly "scooped" on the news of Washington itself.

One of his first daily jobs is to go through his mail, which includes scores of mimeographed and printed "handouts" from the numerous government bureaus. Perhaps there will be three or four of value to him. But he does not put such matter directly on the wire to his home office, as some critics have implied. Instead, after throwing most of it away, he sifts what remains, verifies it, gets the other side of the story, rewrites it, and only then does he send the resultant report.

Always, he must consider his deadlines, which may differ in different cities if he is acting as correspondent for more than one paper. He needs to consider any special interests of his readers, such as agriculture, foreign trade, manufacturing, mining, et cetera, and provide coverage on such matters. He selects for attention the news that seems of chief importance or interest in any one day. Then he must manage to cover it thoroughly, if he works for a press association; still more so if he works for a newspaper or syndicate. Rather than wait for lobbyists and propagandists to come to him, or to try to influence him, the canny correspondent goes to them and asks such questions, and obtains such material as he believes will help him in his work.

Correspondents everywhere have found that, space permitting, a complete story is better than a brief one. The emphasis on brevity in recent years has missed the fact that the oversimplification which it requires sometimes tends to distort the truth. The greatest individual journalistic reputations, moreover, and the greatest newspaper reputations, have been based on complete reports.

* * *

Foreign correspondents and all persons who try to keep informed on national and world news find that certain newspapers

FIG. 39. A GROUP OF PAPERS OF THE UNITED STATES

For description see List of Illustrations

and publications in the United States are especially valuable to them.

In matters of foreign news, the newspapers maintaining their own services are particularly worth watching. This means, chiefly, the New York *Times,* the New York *Herald Tribune,* the *Christian Science Monitor,* the Chicago *Daily News* and the Chicago *Tribune.*

These same papers are useful in their reports of domestic affairs, for they all have good news services. In addition, however, such newspapers as the Baltimore *Sun,* the St. Louis *Post-Dispatch,* the New York *World-Telegram,* the New York *American,* the New York *Journal,* the Detroit *News* and a few others also are to be noted. The New York *World-Telegram* represents the Scripps-Howard chain of 24 dailies and 6 Sunday newspapers, and also carries the United Press dispatches. The New York *Journal* and New York *American* represent the Hearst chain of 24 daily and 16 Sunday newspapers, and carry the International News Service and Universal Service dispatches. A number of these newspapers also carry Associated Press dispatches.

The Hearst newspapers and the Chicago *Tribune* are notably provincial and chauvinistic, whereas the New York *Times* and the *Christian Science Monitor* have a broad, world outlook. All have special prejudices in other directions. The Scripps-Howard papers strike something like a happy medium so far as internationalism or nationalism is concerned, but sometimes run heavily to features at the expense of news. The New York *Herald Tribune* is strongly Republican, while the St. Louis *Post-Dispatch* tends to be Democratic, as does the New York *Times.*

Apart from the general newspapers, such specialized papers and periodicals are useful as the *Wall Street Journal,* for business and financial news; the *Nation,* the *New Republic, Fortune, Time, Foreign Affairs, Current History,* the *Forum,* the *Yale Review,* the service of the Foreign Policy Association, the publications of the Council on Foreign Relations, and, of course, reference books, such as the *Congressional Directory,* the *World Almanac,* and others of that type.

THE COUNTRIES of South America were settled by Europeans and, like the United States and its people, have had most of their foreign relations with European nations. It was only when the Great War interrupted trade with Europe that South America began to look to North America and even to the Far East. The business men of North America were ready enough to enter into increased trade relations with South America.

It is an axiom that where one's own interests are concerned, where one's money is invested, where one sells one's goods or obtains raw materials, there one's thoughts turn. So it was that North Americans suddenly wanted more news of South America and South Americans wanted more news of North America.

Prior to 1914, the South American press was fairly well developed in Buenos Aires, Santiago, and Rio de Janeiro, less developed in other places. There was a limited press service of news. The journalistic pattern was European—Spanish, French, German and British. Havas served South America with most of its news about the rest of the world.

The Great War sent transmission rates higher, and propaganda began to be more than generously mixed with the news reaching South America through the usual channels. *La Prensa*, of Buenos Aires, in that circumstance, turned to the United Press, of the United States, for an impartial and enlarged service of world news. The Associated Press and the International News Service, competing agencies, were obliged to follow the United Press both in reporting South American news and in serving news to papers in South American countries, which had no important press associations of their own.

Cable rates were lower from New York than from Europe, which made it more economical for South American papers to subscribe to North American news services than to European services. Soon after the War, the two leading North American press associations, particularly, were serving many Latin American newspapers, and had forced Havas to take a subordinate position. Havas subsequently made strenuous efforts to regain its former lead, and, thanks to a French government subsidy, was able to offer very low rates and to institute a transoceanic wireless news service. But it still did not provide so good an objective schedule of news.

Not only did the news of the world formerly reach South American countries chiefly through Havas, but the news of events in South America reached most of the rest of the world through that French news agency. This circumstance also was changed, and the shift of South American newspapers to patronage of the North American news services resulted, furthermore, in changing the appearance of newspapers below the equator, inducing many of them to pattern themselves more after newspapers published in the United States.[29]

So far, much of the news that South American newspapers have selected to use about other countries, and especially about the United States, has been of a relatively sensational sort. The same has been true of the news of South America in newspapers of the United States.[30] For South American readers, the United States is often pictured through news of crime, governmental and business troubles, marital difficulties of Hollywood stars, and an assortment of miscellany verging on the more fantastic aspects of the news. The same sort of journalistic bill-of-fare has been offered readers of newspapers in Europe. Even the better newspapers of South America, such as La Prensa, have been guilty of this distortion.

[29] C. S. Smith, "News Makes the Americas Better Neighbors," The Quill (Oct., 1931), pp. 6-7, 15-16; Anon., "Reciprocity of Interest Between North and South America," Editor and Publisher (May 8, 1926), p. 18; J. Edward Gerald, "Aspects of Journalism in South America," Journalism Quarterly (June, 1931), pp. 213-23; B. Cohen, "South American Journalism in 1931," Journalism Quarterly (Dec., 1931), pp. 429-34; J. Edward Gerald, "Journalism in South America: 1933," Journalism Quarterly (Dec., 1933), pp. 302-308; C. S. Smith, "News Exchange Brings American Nations Closer Together," Pan.-Amer. Mag. (Nov., 1930), V. 43, 309-15; Joseph L. Jones, "Press Services Tell Americans about Each Other," Pan-Amer. Mag. (Nov., 1930), V. 43, 302-308; A. J. Cruickshank, "International News in the Central and South Americas," Pan-Amer. Mag. (Jan., 1927), V. 39, 217-19; Stephen Vincent Benét, "The United Press," Fortune (May, 1933), V. 7, No. 5, pp. 67-72, 94-104.

[30] Stephen Duggan, Latin America.

The European news that a South American reads is much more likely to concern serious political and economic and social matters. This contrast tends to give readers the impression that Europe is a sane and desirable place, while the United States is a crude, dangerous and insane part of the world. Some motion pictures from the United States have not tended to correct the impression.[31]

* * *

Buenos Aires is the greatest news center in South America, both for incoming and outgoing dispatches. The newspapers published in the Argentine capital are better, on the whole, than those published in any other Latin-American city. There the press associations have their headquarters. There live the representatives of foreign newspapers and syndicates.

Although the press had been free in the Argentine for many years, the political unrest of 1930 brought a censorship, and that was the beginning of other restrictions, some of them indirect but effective. Journalists also have had to face, always, the business of translating dispatches from English into Spanish or Portuguese for the newspapers of various South American countries, or from Portuguese into Spanish or English, or from Spanish into English or Portuguese, Italian, German or French.

A night's work in a press association office, for example, will include the receipt of cables or wireless messages from London,

[31] Will Irwin, "South America Gets Distorted View of U. S." (Syndicated by North American Newspaper Alliance (NANA) to newspapers in the United States. Published on or about Jan. 14, 1929); Jorge A. Mitre, "Untilled International Field for Press." (Address by the Publisher of *La Nacion* of Buenos Aires, before first Pan-American Congress of Journalists, April 8, 1926.) *Editor and Publisher* (April 10, 1926), pp. 27, 64; Anon., "Reciprocity of Interest Between North and South America," *Editor and Publisher* (May 8, 1926), p. 18.

Carlos Davila, who was Chilean Ambassador to the United States during the Hoover administration, earlier had arranged for the press associations to provide South American newspapers with a better balanced diet of North American news. He had been managing editor and publisher of *La Nacion* of Santiago. Anon., *Washington Merry-Go-Round*, p. 296.

See also: W. W. Davies, "Reporting a Continent," *News. Its Scope and Limitations*, pp. 3-9. (Univ. of Missouri Bulletin, V. 30. No. 46. Jour. Series. No. 57. 1929).

Madrid, Gibraltar, Paris and New York. Such messages must be amplified and passed on to an interpreter, who turns them into other languages, as required. The news is sent on to Rio de Janeiro, Brazil, for newspapers in that Portuguese-speaking city and country. Then the spot news from the east coast of South America, which clears through Buenos Aires, is written and sent to New York. A schedule of news, in Spanish, is written and telegraphed to newspapers in Rosario, Mendoza, Cordoba, Montevideo, and other South American cities. During spare moments and in the daytime a certain amount of mail copy is prepared and sent along.

News is not easy to gather in South American countries. Most of the important people have a distaste for personal publicity, except possibly in social matters. Even politicians bow to this convention and, whether sincerely or not, try to escape more than a modicum of publicity.[32] Pictures are difficult to get, and news photographers are few and not very successful. News sometimes develops in the most remote places, virtually impossible to reach. This was true of the Chaco War in 1932-1935, which was scarcely covered at all by the press, foreign or otherwise, and certainly in nothing like the way the Italo-Ethiopian campaign of 1935 or the Japanese campaign in Manchuria in 1931 and 1932 were reported, even though they also were in remote places.

The result of this situation is that South American newspapers have themselves been less concerned with local news, they have developed few press associations, and instead have given major attention to editorial comment, interpretations, discussions of art, literature and the drama, and to foreign news provided by foreign press associations. There is a change promised in South American journalism, however, led by *La Nacion* of Buenos Aires, whose publisher, Jorge A. Mitre, patterning his paper more after the

---

[32] President Irigoyen of the Argentine was especially hostile to the press and smashed several cameras, in addition to rebuffing reporters. Anon., "Nose for News Needed in South America." (Short interview with Carlos Viale, editor of the editorial page of *La Nacion* of Buenos Aires.) *Editor and Publisher* (Nov. 23, 1924); John W. White, "Finds South America Is Everything but Dull," *The Little Times,* house organ of the New York *Times* (Mar. 21, 1932), pp. 1, 2.

North American style, has been rewarded by a show of public interest reflected in circulation increases, and by *La Nacion* of Santiago, when Carlos Davila was its publisher.[33]

* * *

Not the least of the journalist's difficulties in Latin-American countries has been censorship. Most of the countries in that part of the world had nominally free presses between the time they won their independence from Spain in 1820 until about 1930 and years following, when revolutions occurred in several of the countries. Even before that time, however, the presses of some countries were under the control of governments.[34]

One of the more ingenious types of censorship was instituted for the first time, as far as known, in the Argentine. Although no official government censorship of the press was announced or admitted, and the domestic press was, in fact, left free of government restrictions or instructions, the foreign correspondents found themselves somewhat hampered by an indirect censorship. The cable companies are owned by foreign capital, and operate under franchise from the Argentine Government. These companies were informed that if any messages unwelcome or unfriendly to the government were transmitted over the facilities of any one of those companies, the offending company would lose its franchise. That ruling forced the cable companies to set up censorships of their own to protect their investments, while the government was able to say that it never censored the news.[35]

[33] Anon., "Finds U. S. Press Guide for Latin America," *Editor and Publisher* (June 23, 1925).

Carlos Davila, when he was publisher of *La Nacion*, Santiago, changed the complexion of the Chilean press by clearing advertisements from page one, substituting cable news, omitting political essays, adding a drama page, a financial section, and sports pages, and by enlivening the news style. The success that came to his paper as a result induced other papers to follow suit. Anon., *Washington Merry-Go-Round*, pp. 296-97.

[34] Complaints of censorship in Peru and Venezuela were made to the executive committee of the Press Congress of the World in 1922, but those censorships were not abated as a result.

[35] J. W. Perry, "Indirect Intimidation Is New Technique in Foreign News Censorship," *Editor and Publisher* (June 27, 1931), pp. 5-6. The All-America

Much the same method was adopted by Chile and Brazil. The Government of Chile dictated a decree in 1931 forbidding any action tending to introduce "distrust or uncertainty" in national affairs. The penalty for doing so was to be "minor exile in medium to maximum grades." The decree held that those who spread "false or harmful news or information destined to produce or introduce distrust or disturbance in the order, tranquillity and security of the country, in the financial régimes or in the stability of public securities or properties," shall be "guilty of a crime against the interior security of the State," and shall be punished by exile.

Authorities informed foreign writers that the law would be applied to anything appearing in the form of news sent out of Chile which the government deemed "unpleasant" or "injurious," without consideration for the truth of the story. Furthermore, any news bearing a Chilean dateline, appearing in the paper or papers represented by a given correspondent, would be presumed to have been written by that correspondent or, in the case of news distributed by a press association, to have been written by its correspondent in Chile.

In Brazil a somewhat similar indirect censorship was instituted following the revolution of 1931. The provisional government blocked the sending of news from Rio de Janeiro to foreign papers. The result was that much Brazilian news appearing abroad came from the portions of the country controlled by the rebels, to the north and south of Rio de Janeiro. This news was read abroad and taken in good faith, while that which did come from Rio de Janeiro was under suspicion because of the censorship known to

Cables Company in Buenos Aires was informed in June, 1931, that the company would be held responsible for further reports of "bombings" sent over its circuits. Because the Government of the Argentine controls the concessions under which the company operates, officials of the company felt that they should examine copy filed for transmission to prevent any messages imperiling their investments. The New York *Times* was able to evade the censorship on the first day of the revolution when the New York office called Buenos Aires on the radio telephone. The censor had not clamped down on the radio telephone, but he did so the next day. Anon., "The *Times* Overcomes Argentine Censorship," *The Little Times*, house organ of the New York *Times* (Sept. 18, 1930), pp. 1, 4.

exist there. In this way the government censorship became an embarrassment rather than a help to those who instituted it.

Nevertheless, the censorship was continued. The government issued to newspapers and to foreign correspondents a list of instructions which prohibited the following: [36]

BRAZILIAN GOVERNMENT PRESS PROHIBITIONS

1. Spaces in blank in newspapers.
2. References to perturbations or menaces of perturbations of the public order.
3. News on the movement of army, navy, air or police forces; such news will only be allowed to be published when furnished officially by the War, Navy and Justice Ministries.
4. Interviews and declarations of civil and military authorities, political or non-political personalities, which will tend to perturbate the action of the government, the public safety and national economical situation.
5. All references to internal and foreign Communistic activities.
6. News and comments allusive to the financial plan or to the economic situation, or texts that would harm the credit of Brazil.
7. Declarations and comments of foreign political exiles, which in any way would affect the good standing of our international relations or, by contagion, the internal public order.
8. News and comments on the secessional tendency of certain states of the Union.
9. News and comments on the movement of classes (strikes, perturbation of order in factories, etc.)
10. News and comments capable of occasioning unrest among the army and navy ranks, or capable of provoking an unsympathetic feeling between themselves or with the people.
11. News, comments and editorials capable of provoking scandal, public or private, among government employees of immediate confidence of the provisional government.

[36] Reprinted in *Editor and Publisher*, Oct. 26, 1931, in editorial entitled "Brazil's Gag." Further repressive measures, instituted after the November, 1935, rebellion, did away with the last vestiges of constitutional guarantees, all with a view to insuring the "stability of the present régime."

These restrictions left very little for the correspondent to write about without running the risk of immediate arrest and imprisonment for twenty-four hours or more for the first offense, and indefinite imprisonment for a further offense.[37]

The result of the Brazilián censorship was that news of events in that country supplied for foreign use began to come, often inaccurately, from Montevideo in Uruguay; and through amateur radio operators, travelers arriving from Brazil, and by other indirect channels.

But the news from Uruguay itself was censored in 1934 when political unrest worried the authorities: A labor situation was sufficiently serious to result in a strike preventing the publication of any Montevideo newspapers on December 2, 1933, when the Seventh Pan-American Conference was assembling in the capital, with many of the delegates already present. Foreign correspondents on hand to report the Conferences filed cables about the strike, but the messages never were sent. The censorship remained in effect throughout the Pan-American Conference and made difficulties for correspondents.[38]

The Ecuador delegation to that conference, incidentally, pro-

[37] Because he was held to have transmitted to *The Times* of London, certain news dispatches considered prejudicial to Brazil, George H. Corey, the Brazil correspondent for the New York *Times*, was arrested at his home in São Paulo on Dec. 1, 1931. He agreed to leave the country voluntarily, rather than be imprisoned pending a formal trial, the results of which could scarcely be in doubt, considering the attitude of the government.

George H. Corey, "*Times* Man a Victim of Brazil's Censors," New York *Times* (Dec. 27, 1931), Sec. IV, p. 8. Mr. Corey's first conflict with the censorship was over a dispatch telling of a drouth affecting the northeastern states of Brazil. The censor held that this was "injurious to Brazil."

Perhaps the most amazing thing about his departure from the country was that the dispatch for which he was held responsible by the government authorities was written by another correspondent, the correspondent for *The Times* of London, in which paper it appeared. Corey represented the New York *Times*. Yet, Brazilian authorities pointed out that there were Ford companies in the United States, Argentine, Brazil and other countries, and all were affiliated. Hence it was obvious that the New York *Times* and *The Times* of London were the same thing, in effect. Needless to say, this is not true at all. See also: Anon., "Brazil Ousts Writer on False Charge," *Editor and Publisher* (Jan. 2, 1932), p. 7.

[38] Peter F. Kihss, "News Was Censored at Montevideo," *Editor and Publisher* (Jan. 13, 1934), p. 11.

posed a measure which would compel newspapers to publish news favorable to Pan-Americanism, with penalties for failure to do so. This measure was modified, however, until it became a mere invitation to newspapers to do so.

The Argentine Government made an attempt in 1935 to force foreign press associations and newspapers with representation in the Argentine to post a large cash bond for each correspondent. If the correspondent wrote a dispatch that was considered untrue by the government the bond would be forfeited; and the bond was to remain on deposit for three years after the correspondent left the country, still subject to confiscation if anything that he wrote displeased the government. The government itself was to interpret what it regarded as true and untrue in a dispatch. Even the domestic press attacked the wisdom and fairness of this plan, so that it was dropped by the government almost as soon as it was declared effective, and without any bonds having been posted by any one! [39]

Argentina expelled at least one correspondent in 1934 for sending what were described as "exaggerated and untrue" accounts of the Eucharistic Congress at Buenos Aires in the autumn of that year.[40]

Brazil experienced a Communist rebellion in November, 1935, following which the Federal Government imposed new restrictions upon the press to insure the "stability of the present régime," the "maintenance of traditional institutions," and to "forestall the creation of new Communist centers and uprisings." All constitutional guarantees were suspended, and mail, cables, and press were under censorship. Much vital news was omitted from the press, and the public was misled by some things that were published.[41]

Venezuela has long had a strict censorship, while Peru and Mexico have had restrictions in force from time to time. Ecuador,

[39] Anon., "Press Roars Disapproval Over Restrictions Placed on It by Argentina's Edict," *Christian Science Monitor* (Aug. 12, 1925); Anon., "Argentina: Justo, Justice and Joust," *Time* (Aug. 5, 1935), p. 18; Anon., "Argentine Press Gag Is Voided," *Editor and Publisher* (Aug. 24, 1935), p. 8.

[40] Anon., "Press: Argentine Mystery," *Time* (Nov. 19, 1934), p. 34.

[41] Anon., "Communist Moves in Brazil Checked by State Censorship," *Christian Science Monitor* (Oct. 23, 1936), p. 5.

Colombia, Panama and some other countries of Latin America do not have constant censorships, but stand ready to impose them in the event of a political or other crisis.[42] Ecuador was a country with a censored press as early as the nineteen-twenties.

All of these censorships were sharply attacked by speakers at the Pan-American Press Congress, held at Valparaiso, Chile, in January, 1937. At least one correspondent, John W. White, chief South American correspondent of the New York *Times,* also spoke against the censorships at a public dinner in Buenos Aires. He declared they permitted false news to spread, and so hurt the cause of peace.[43]

* * *

Some of South America's newspapers present a good picture of the world, and some are extremely profitable. Political news takes first place in importance. Features are used merely to give variety and a note of a lighter sort to newspapers inclined to be almost too solemn in their subject matter. Spot news treatment in the North American manner, is replaced by analytical and interpretative articles. The stories tend to be both comprehensive and well written, because many journalists have served long apprenticeships in writing politics. Some of them, because of their expert knowledge, are drafted into diplomacy or other government work.

The technical standards of journalism, especially in Argentina, Brazil and Chile, are relatively high, apart from the complication

[42] It was the Chilean delegation to the League of Nations Assembly in 1925, however, which proposed a technical convention of press representatives from all countries, to meet in Geneva, and to determine by what means the press could contribute toward the work of disarmament (a) by ensuring a more rapid and less costly transmission of press news with a view to reducing risks of international misunderstanding, and (b) by discussing all technical problems the settlement of which would in their opinion be conducive to the tranquillization of public opinion in the various countries. Such a conference was held in 1927, with 60 delegates present, representing 36 countries. Anon., *Conference of Press Experts: Final Report,* Conf. E. P. 13, 1927.

[43] Anon., "Censors Accused of Harming Peace," New York *Times* (Dec. 13, 1936), p. 42; Anon., "Conference Blasts S. A. Governments," *Editor and Publisher* (Jan. 16, 1937), p. 41.

due to censorship. In other countries, however, the press is less developed and strict governmental regulations exist, even as they do in the A-B-C countries at times, and papers often are ultra-political in their purposes.[44]

La Prensa and *La Nacion* are the two leading daily newspapers of Argentina, both published in Buenos Aires. Both provide excellent news services, with especially fine foreign reports. *La Prensa* has been estimated to spend the equivalent of $50,000 a month on its foreign news alone. It pays 8 to 15 cents a word on cables from London or Paris or Madrid, and 5 cents a word from New York. Both papers are wealthy, and *La Prensa*, especially, has an ideal of service which induces it to offer to the public free legal, agricultural and health advice, to make its own magnificent library available to all, to provide free musical training to promising persons, and to offer an annual course of lectures by world thinkers.

Both of these papers are carefully read by all foreign correspondents. Although not always entirely impartial in editorial comments, or entirely wise in selection of news, they are as nearly perfect as any newspaper.[45] In fact, *La Prensa* may be regarded as one of the four or five leading newspapers of the world.

*   *   *

In Brazil, the leading newspapers are the *Jornal do Brazil*, the *Jornal do Comercio*, *A Noite*, and the *Correio de Manhã*, all of Rio de Janeiro. In São Paulo, the paper of largest circulation is

[44] Rafael Fusoni, "Chile First Country to Provide Pensions for Newspapermen," *Editor and Publisher* (July 31, 1926), p. 18; Anon., "Editors of Ecuador Suffer Prison and Exile for Press Freedom," *Editor and Publisher* (Mar. 6, 1926), p. 18. Strict restrictions on the press in Chile prevented for years any editorial discussions of public affairs, and censorships have long existed in most other countries of the continent. Yet, it was Chile's representative to the League of Nations Assembly who suggested the Press Conference which met at Geneva in 1927, with group meetings later. See note 42, page 332.

[45] Henry K. Norton, *The Coming of South America*, pp. 238-42; José S. Gollán, *A Modern Argentine Newspaper*. Refers to *La Prensa*. (Literature Series No. 1, Pan-American Union, Washington, D. C., 1930. Reprinted from *Bulletin of the Pan-American Union*, Sept., 1930.) Dr. Maximo Soto Hall, "Extraordinary Services Given Public by Buenos Aires *La Prensa*," *Editor and Publisher* (May 8, 1926), p. 16.

FIG. 40. SOME NEWSPAPERS OF LATIN AMERICA
For description see List of Illustrations

the *O Estado de São Paulo;* it has the largest circulation, in fact, of any paper in the country. With most of Brazil's literate population concentrated in these two cities, which are the political and commercial centers, it is not surprising that they are the journalistic centers as well, although there also are papers in Porto Alegre, Santos, Recife, Bahia, Pernambuco and elsewhere.

The so-called Edwards group of papers in Chile have displayed considerable journalistic initiative, and are the most important in that country. They are the *Mercurio,* of Valparaiso, the chief seaport, and, again, the *Mercurio* of Santiago, the capital. *Ultimas Noticias* is an evening edition at Santiago, and *Estrella* at Valparaiso.

It would not be accurate to say that the other countries of South America are unimportant, whether journalistically or otherwise. But they have not happened to capture wide or regular interest so far, and the world network of news coverage does not deem them of sufficient importance to warrant the placing of permanent correspondent in many of their capitals. The United Press, for example, has bureaus in Lima, Bogota, Caracas, La Paz, and Montevideo. Elsewhere resident journalists are under agreement to serve individual newspapers published abroad, or bureaus of foreign press associations, when the news is of enough interest, but those occasions are rare.

§ 3. HAVANA, MEXICO CITY, AND CENTRAL AMERICA

CUBA, as the key to the Caribbean, has been important in international diplomacy for many years. Havana, as its capital and commercial center, is a local focus of interest. Because of the intimate relations between Cuba and the United States, press associations and some newspapers in the United States have sent staff correspondents there at critical periods, and have depended upon local correspondents at other times.

The leading Havana paper in circulation is *El Pais.* Others of importance are *Diario de la Marina,* representing commercial interests; *El Mundo,* independent and prosperous; *El Crisol,* of large circulation; *El Avance,* and others representing commercial interests, or presenting general news. The older political aspects have been obscured by political events on the island, events which also have placed a censorship on all newspapers.

*   *   *

Mexico, as the most populous neighbor of the United States and as the leading country of Central America, is of considerable news importance. The history of the country has been stormy, except during the administration of General Diaz from 1884 to 1910, until recent years.

The attempts of international capital to develop the resources and potentialities of Mexico, of Cuba, and of Central American and South American countries have been a subject of constant news importance. The construction of the Panama Canal turned attention to things happening in those areas. Oil, fruits, gold, silver, rubber, mineral ores, timber, live stock, coffee, chicle, sugar and other resources have induced capitalists to go into these parts, while archæological and sociological interests have attracted others.

The world receives most of its news about Cuba, Mexico and Central America through the press associations of the United States. The French Agence Havas has some connections there, but is more active in South America. Mexico has a local semi-official news agency called ANTA (Agencia Noticiosa Telegrafica Americana) which is linked with Havas. There is no local press association in Central America except in Honduras.

Correspondents in Mexico keep in touch with Mexican governmental affairs and with the foreign diplomatic and consular officials, with foreign industrial and commercial interests in the country. They must note especially the news of politics, social changes, and the arts. They need to walk a careful line between the objective facts, the Mexican Government official views, the United States Government attitudes, the prejudices which they, their informants, and their colleagues may have; and the policy of the paper or press association they serve. In addition, they must consider the censorship that the government places upon local newspapers, and which it extends to cover outgoing dispatches, especially in times of crisis.[46]

The important local newspapers published in Mexico City are *El Excelsior, El Universal* and *La Prensa.* Considering the large proportion of illiteracy in the country, they have reasonably good circulations.

* * *

The news from the Central-American countries is gathered and written by resident correspondents, who may be native journalists or who may be foreigners engaged in business or professional activities there. Except in times of crisis, the foreign newspapers and press associations do not ordinarily send staff writers to the countries. This situation is somewhat complicated by the fact that in times of crisis, also, a censorship often is placed upon the free transmission of news. This has been true in Nicaragua and elsewhere.[47]

The greatest difficulties in the news relationships of Central America and Mexico with the rest of the world, and particularly with the United States, are two: A tendency on the part of correspondents to sensationalize events and a tendency on the part of some newspaper makers at home to regard that part of the world as slightly comic, or as a field so rich in commercial possibilities as to color the presentation of the news.

[46] George Seldes, *You Can't Print That!,* pp. 315-91; some newspapers in the United States, by maintaining an attitude of hostility and suspicion toward Mexico, have developed anti-Mexican prejudices among their readers. See: O. G. Villard, *Some Newspapers and Newspaper Men,* pp. 27-28, 202-203; Silas Bent, *Strange Bedfellows,* Ch. 14, "Hearst and the Mexican Forgeries," pp. 218-30; Bent, *Ballyhoo,* pp. 81-83; T. G. Turner, *Bullets, Bottles and Gardenias.* Adventures of a reporter for American newspapers and magazines in Mexico; Webb Miller, *I Found No Peace.* Includes references to Mexican experiences.

[47] A. J. Cruickshank, "International News in the Central and South Americas," *Pan-Amer. Mag.* (Jan., 1927), 39, pp. 217-19; Carleton Beals, *Banana Gold;* C. S. Smith, "News Makes the Americas Better Neighbors," *The Quill* (Oct., 1931), pp. 6-7, 15-16.

§ 4. MONTREAL AND THE DOMINION OF CANADA

CANADA, a dominion of the British Empire, although a country of many square miles, at present has a proportionately small population. It is a new country, still being carved out of wilderness in many parts. That being so, it rarely produces what the world press regards as big news.[48]

The native press of Canada is growing, and some of the newspapers are in the first rank. The best known are published in the largest centers, not unnaturally. That means Montreal, Toronto, Ottawa, Winnipeg and Vancouver. Journalists are highly respected and often take leading parts in the government.

Montreal and Toronto are the most important journalistic centers, with several important newspapers published there, and with busy press association bureaus. The Canadian Press is affiliated with the Associated Press and Reuters. The British United Press is affiliated with the United Press in the United States. Some Canadian newspapers, especially those under group ownership, have representatives in London, and Canada always has been a link in Empire communications.

No correspondents have been sent from the United States or from Great Britain to take permanent residence in Canada, but many correspondents have made special trips to Canada, and Canadian journalists act as representatives, sending dispatches to foreign newspapers.

The largest newspapers are the *Star* of Toronto, which, although published in the second city in population, has the biggest circulation; the *Mail and Empire* of Toronto, the *Telegram* of Toronto, the *Star* of Montreal and *La Presse,* a French-language paper published in Montreal. The Winnipeg *Free Press* became an important paper under the direction of J. W. Dafoe. The Southam newspapers, published in Ottawa, Winnipeg, Hamilton, Calgary, Edmonton, and Vancouver, set a high standard of jour-

---

[48] The story of the five little Dionnes, and how they grew, may be said to have kept Canada in the world's press more consistently than any other news from the Dominion.

nalistic excellence. The Canadian press, as a whole, is distinctly high grade.

The press is entirely free in Canada, without governmental restrictions and uncensored. It receives fast news service from London, by beam radio, and from the United States by telegraph. Serving as a link in the "Red Network," much news passes through Canada between London and Australia and New Zealand.

CHAPTER VII

NEWS OF THE FAR EAST

THE POTENTIALITIES of the Orient are incalculable. It has an immediate importance as a field for commercial development, as a battleground for ideas, as the scene of a struggle for local mastery, and as an area in which East and West may some day try their lances.

It is less than a century since the beginning of regular relations between the peoples of the East and those of the West. To-day, it is hardly necessary to say, China and Japan occupy the news leadership of Asia and of the Pacific area.

§ 1. SHANGHAI AND CHINA

CHINA is the largest country of the Far East, both in area and in population. Its culture is oldest and, in certain respects, finest. It was in China that paper and ink first appeared, and there printing began, including printing from movable types. It was in China and in India that the white race began its dealings with the yellow race. Political and commercial interests have prompted the West to turn to the East.

As the British led in the move to develop spheres of interest in the East, it was natural that Reuters should begin to send and receive news there. *The Times* followed later, but that press association and that newspaper were in the journalistic vanguard, and it was through them alone, for many years, that the world learned what was happening in the Far East. At length, American, French and German interests in the East became sufficiently important to warrant their national newspapers and press associations attempting to develop special services.

Lower communication rates encouraged and civil war in China

demanded improved news coverage. The most distinct growth in the representation of papers and press associations of the United States in China dates from the civil unrest there in 1927-1928. American journalistic interest was led by the Associated Press, and was carried on by certain newspapers and by other press associations, with the United Press especially active, until now the North American journalistic position in the Far East is as strong, and perhaps stronger than the British, although the dependence of the East upon Reuters for commercial figures is an important item in any such assessment.

Although Peking remained the capital of China until recent years, Shanghai long has been the commercial center, and, what was more important, the center of communication and transportation. For that reason Shanghai became the journalistic center of China and of the Far East. From there the mail went most speedily across the Pacific, to Europe via the Transiberian Railway, or around through the Suez Canal. Or a message might go by Great Northern Telegraph over Russia to Copenhagen and thence to London and New York, it might go by Commercial Cable across the Pacific to Guam and San Francisco, it might go by wireless to Manila and San Francisco, or it might go by Great Eastern Telegraph to India and thence to London. Messages in the East usually are sent "RTP" (Receiver To Pay), which is supposed to discourage undue delay or suppression. Moreover, from Shanghai's international settlement, foreign correspondents long were able to send their dispatches without censorship or supervision, thanks to the treaties granting foreigners extraterritorial rights. This no longer is true, however.

Peking (Peiping) continues to be an important news center in China, partly because some foreign diplomats remain there even though the Chinese Government has moved its headquarters to Nanking. That city is not so far from Shanghai as to be inconvenient for periodic visits by correspondents. Canton is an important political center in the south of China, and Tientsin is an important center to the north. In addition, Hankow, Mukden, Harbin, and Tsitsihar, the capital of Manchoukuo, are within a Shanghai correspondent's sphere of interest. If he does not go himself to these places occasionally, or perhaps even if he does, he will arrange with some local person—who may or may not be a journalist, or even a person of his own nationality—to keep an eye on events and let him have word if any interesting or important development arises.[1]

* * *

The conditions of work for the journalist in China have become pleasanter in recent years. Even the Chinese journalist, who once had to beg for scraps of news and live on almost nothing, now is able to go nearly everywhere in his search for news, and, although his salary may not be large, when he travels on a story he receives a generous expense account. This change followed the entrance into Chinese journalism of foreign-educated Chinese.

News is not easy to get in China, for all that. China is a very different place in its mental outlook from the United States or Great Britain or France. Distances are great, transportation is slow, and communication is poor. There is no network to forward news of that far interior, stretching back to Mongolia and Tibet.[2]

[1] During the Japanese invasion of Manchuria in 1931 the correspondents faced difficult problems in covering the news, but managed to do it reasonably well under great handicaps and at heavy cost. In fact, the problem began even earlier, during the civil wars in China.

Anon., "Covering China War Stories Against Odds," *Editor and Publisher* (Apr. 2, 1927), p. 7; Charles Dailey, "Getting the News From China," *The Trib*, house organ of the Chicago *Tribune* (April-July, 1928); M. W. Vaughn, "Wild Rumors Hamper China War Coverage," *Editor and Publisher* (Sept. 14, 1929); J. W. Perry, "Manchurian 'War' Costly to Newspapers; Far Flung Area Hard to Cover," *Editor and Publisher* (Nov. 14, 1931), pp. 5-6; Frederick Kuh, "Censorship, Wire Delays, Sub-Zero Weather Vex Manchurian Writers," *Editor and Publisher* (Jan. 9, 1932), p. 20; J. W. Perry, "War-Time Reporting Returns in China," *Editor and Publisher* (Feb. 6, 1932), pp. 9, 45; Miles Vaughn, *Covering the Far East;* La Selle Gilman, *Shanghai Deadline;* Eugene Lyons, ed., *We Cover the World,* Chs. 4, 7, 13.

[2] On Dec. 14, 1932, a violent earthquake was noted by seismological observatories in eight parts of the world. It was calculated as having occurred in the interior of China. Newspapers noted that brief fact. Not until 48 days later did the news came out of China itself, and then it was revealed that 70,000 Chinese in Kansu province had been killed.

Commenting on this great tragedy, Marlen Pew said, "Our news system is geared to essential local interest—we are not bowled over by events in locations far removed. Imagination does not carry to Kansu province. 'Seventy

The correspondent spends a large amount of time simply tracing down rumors, which are prolific, and trying to discover whether there is any truth in them. He must try to foresee news events that are to occur, and try to be on the ground when they do break, even if it means long trips, hardships, patient waiting. The foreign consulates, banking houses, clubs, hotels and business firms are reasonably good sources, especially for news of the foreigners' activities in China. But the news of China itself is a different thing.

Official news comes from the Bureau of Intelligence and Publicity of the Central Government in Nanking, and from Kuo Min, the official governmental news agency. The former is largely a propaganda bureau, favoring the government, with a modicum of real news. The latter is patterned after the better news agencies of the United States and Great Britain, as to its organization, and provides a general coverage of news, both foreign and domestic, but is still too partial to be regarded with much confidence.[3] The Chinese agency, also, is meagerly represented at home and abroad, and its service of domestic news is so unsatisfactory that some of the big foreign agencies keep men in Shanghai, and some have elaborate bureaus and services to provide news to the English- and French-language papers in China.

Courteous as the Chinese may be, they care nothing for publicity, and they are not inclined to talk freely, especially to a stranger. For this reason it is the correspondent who has been in the country for two years or more, long enough to gain some understanding of the history, customs and traditions of the people, and to make friends in various stations and walks of life, who

Thousand Dead in Quake' is worth only a sunk head on page one, assuming indeed that there is no contemporary local news break such as the sudden demise of a prominent citizen or two dead and three hurt in up-town grade crossing accident. In such case the 70,000 dead in China story might run inside, with no harm done. It is our modern concept, also, that Chinese really do not count. We do not think of the race as of other peoples. Stories of large numbers suffering or dying there, in famine, flood, fire or earthquake, no longer shock our senses." Pew, "Shop Talk at Thirty," *Editor and Publisher* (Feb. 18, 1933).

[3] Anon., "Continuous Censorship in China Bars U. S. Grasp of Events," *Editor and Publisher* (Mar. 10, 1934), p. 16.

begins to find that he can write news stories that have depth, and meaning, and substantial interest for readers.

* * *

As in most countries, a wave of nationalism has swept China in recent years. Communism and other forms of unrest also have induced the government to impose a censorship on the local press, and on outgoing dispatches. This gives the correspondent further cause to worry. And, to send a press dispatch at all over the Chinese telegraph or wireless, the correspondent requires a registration certificate from the Chinese Ministry of Foreign Affairs, and a telegraphic card from the Ministry of Communications, entitling him to send messages from five selected cities of China on an RTP basis. Outside of those five cities, his messages will not be accepted at press rates or on an RTP basis. He himself may choose the five cities from which he wishes to be permitted to send messages.

The press in China has been under an increasingly strict censorship since 1928, as one result of the nationalism affecting the country. The Chinese-language press, particularly, is without freedom. Foreign newspapers are not censored, but certain issues may be barred from the mails if something in them displeases the government. Until recent years, foreign correspondents were free to send what they wished, and still are, for the most part, except for news of military matters. But in 1931 the Nanking Government placed censors, appointed by the Ministry of Communications, in the wireless, cable and telegraph offices.

Sometimes, for considerable periods, there was no censorship at all; then an effective censorship suddenly appeared. Nor has China had a censorship in which the correspondent often was permitted to discuss points with the censor, although correspondents ultimately managed to obtain that right. It has been described as "erratic, anonymous and secretive." The effect often was somewhat absurd, as when the words "puppet ruler" were inserted before every reference to the "Emperor Pu-Yi" of Manchoukuo, and in altering "Manchoukuo" to "Manchuria," or referring to it as the dummy state of "Manchoukuo," and then charging the correspondent for these additions. What was cut out, the correspondent might not be informed.

As the native press is subject to government censorship, every paper in the Chinese language must submit matter intended for publication to an official censor. His ruling is arbitrary and there is no appeal from it. The result is that most of the Chinese people, if they are unable to read the foreign-language press, only read what the government wants them to believe. In Peiping and Tientsin, where the Japanese gained control late in 1935, the native press was forced to omit any reference to opposition to the plan for setting up an autonomous state. Efforts appear to have been made (perhaps by way of compensation for lack of objective news), to try to "brighten" some of the Chinese papers— while a very few of them, apparently with official approval, are even permitted a degree of objectivity.

There have been some attempts to force foreign correspondents in China to modify their attitudes, and efforts have been made to expel one or two, but that action never actually has been taken. Because the future of their concessions and investments in China were involved, however, even foreign companies such as the Commercial Pacific Cable Co. and others felt that they must comply with the government wishes and permit the censors to occupy desk-room in their premises.[4]

The censorship in 1935 prohibited the transmission of news pertaining to military or diplomatic affairs, if "disadvantageous to us"; news about agitations, riots, exciting statements endangering the money market, or news pertaining to social welfare or "harmful to good custom."

One way of evading the Chinese censorship in Shanghai was to mail copy to Hong Kong, a British possession, whence it could be transmitted by radio or by telegraph.

[4] Edgar Snow, "The Ways of the Chinese Censor," *Current History* (July, 1935), pp. 381-86; Frederick Kuh, "Censorships, Wire Delays, Sub-Zero Weather Vex Manchurian Writers," *Editor and Publisher* (Jan. 2, 1932), p. 20; L. Z. Yuan, "New Chinese Press Law Prohibits Attacks on Nationalist Party," *Editor and Publisher* (Feb. 21, 1931), p. 44; Hallett Abend, "Free Press Cry in China," New York *Times* (Feb. 9, 1936); Lin Yutang, *History of the Press and Public Opinion in China,* Ch. 13.

This situation, which continued for several years, was somewhat modified early in 1936, so far as it affected correspondents in Shanghai. H. K. Tong, an American-educated Chinese, was placed in charge of the censorship there and altered the system so that correspondents were notified if their messages were to be changed, and could discuss or argue the changes, even as in Russia. Mr. Tong's jurisdiction extended to Peiping and some other places, but there was no certainty that it ever would include more places, or even that it would survive.[5]

* * *

The Chinese language is so difficult that correspondents sometimes live for years in China without mastering it. They work through interpreters. A good many Chinese, especially of the governing and business classes, speak English. Not a few of them have been educated in English or American schools in China or abroad. The correspondent may not attempt to read the Chinese newspapers, although he will have some items translated. As a matter of fact, many of the newspapers and periodicals of China that are important, from the standpoint of news and from the standpoint of the foreign correspondent, are printed in English, with a few in French or German, and most of them appear in Shanghai, Peiping or Tientsin. Nevertheless, the careful correspondent obtains written translations of some articles appearing in certain native papers.

The population of China is about 80 per cent illiterate, which naturally restricts domestic journalism. Nevertheless, the advances in literacy and in the number of newspapers have been considerable, and in view of what has happened in Russia and, to a lesser extent, in Turkey, by way of teaching the population to

[5] Anon., "Continuous Censorship in China Bars U. S. Grasp of Events," *Editor and Publisher* (Mar. 10, 1934), p. 16; Vernon Nash, "Journalism in China: 1933," *Journalism Quarterly* (Dec., 1933), pp. 316-22. Includes discussion of censorship details; Hallett Abend, "Free Press Cry in China," New York *Times* (Feb. 9, 1936); Anon., "New Deal Censor for China Trained in Missouri School," *Christian Science Monitor* (June 17, 1936); Eugene Lyons, ed., *We Cover the World*, Ch. 7, by Hallett Abend, describes the censorship situation up to 1937.

read and write, it is not essential that this condition in China continue indefinitely. As it is, many of those who cannot read, learn by word of mouth what is happening.[6]

The Peiping papers are mostly concerned with political news; those of Shanghai give more attention to economic and commercial news; while those of Tientsin present a reasonable compromise between the two. There are approximately 500 daily newspapers and 2000 weekly and monthly periodicals published in the Chinese language in China, a country with a population of more than 400,000,000. About thirty "foreign newspapers" are owned by American, British, Japanese, German, French and Russian interests. Mukden and Harbin have a few of these. Some of them set a high standard and have considerable prestige.[7]

The one domestic paper that is nearest independent is the *Min Kuo Jih Pao* ("Republican Daily News") of Peiping, and even that is the editorial spokesman of the Nationalist party.

The Shanghai papers that correspondents read most carefully are *Shun Pao, Sin Wan Pao*, the *China Times* and the *Eastern Times*. Both of the latter two are Chinese-owned, despite their names; neither has a strong editorial policy. *Chen Pao,* or the Shanghai *Morning Post,* regarded as the mouthpiece of General Chang Kai-Shek, was suspended in January, 1936, and resumed under the name of *Cheng Pao* ("The Truth.")[8]

The four papers mentioned above "fly the foreign flag," which means that they register at a foreign consulate, at a cost of about $150 a year, paid through a citizen of the country at whose con-

---

[6] N. D. Harris, *International Politics*, V. 2, "Europe and the East," p. 447 n.

[7] Vernon Nash of Yenching University told the American Society of Newspaper Editors in 1928 that Chinese journalism was experiencing a period of renewal. His address was reprinted in *Editor and Publisher,* April 28, 1928, pp. 42, 44. "Most Significant of Chinese Revolts Is Awakening of Journalism"; see also: Roswell S. Britton, *The Chinese Periodical Press 1802-1912;* Vernon Nash, "Chinese Journalism in 1931," *Journalism Quarterly* (Dec., 1931), pp. 446-52; Nash, "Journalism in China: 1933," *Journalism Quarterly* (Dec., 1933), pp. 316-22; Thomas Ming-Heng Chao, *The Foreign Press in China;* H. G. W. Woodhead, *Adventures in Far Eastern Journalism;* Lin Yutang, *History of the Press and Public Opinion in China.*

[8] Anon.. "Chinese Paper Suspends," *Editor and Publisher* (Feb. 29, 1936), p. 24.

sulate the paper is registered. The Chinese owners give the person who is so obliging the position of Director and pay him a salary, but they run the paper. Any official complaint against the paper then has to be taken only with the consent of the consulate at which it is registered. The "consent" is given readily enough when asked, but the "owner" or the "Director" gets sufficient advance notice so that he can forestall the procedure, very often, or at least prepare a defense. This makes the system of registering a sort of insurance for the paper.

Sin Wan Pao, which was established by Americans, now is owned by Chinese, but continues to be registered at the United States Consulate. The other three mentioned are registered at the French consulate. This system has had its roots in the so-called "unequal treaties."

In addition to these Shanghai papers, every correspondent or newspaper or press association bureau in China will receive papers from other cities. Peiping will provide *The Leader,* a Nationalist paper; the *Journal de Peking,* an independent, French-registered paper, or some other. Tientsin provides the *North China Star,* an American-registered paper, or one or two others. Hankow contributes the *Central China Post,* which is British; or the Nationalist Hankow *Herald,* or others. Hong Kong has several to offer, all British or independent, including the *China Mail,* the *Daily Press,* the *South China Morning Post,* the *Telegraph,* or some one or two of the native papers.[9]

[9] For something of the problems of the foreign correspondent's work in China see: Hallett Abend, "Covering News in China Presents Difficulties." *The Little Times,* house organ of the New York *Times* (May 19, 1930), pp. 1, 5; Charles Dailey, "Getting the News From China," *The Trib.,* house organ of the Chicago *Tribune* (April-July, 1928); Miles W. Vaughn, *Covering the Far East;* Eugene Lyons, ed., *We Cover the World,* Chs. 4, 7, 13.

One writer contends that Chinese news does not mean anything reliable unless it is accompanied by sufficient explanation, that is, unless it is interpreted. This raises the question of transmission costs, however, and it also encounters the difficulty that editors in the United States do not always distinguish between editorializing in the news, which is quite properly frowned upon, and interpretation, which is legitimate. Because of their fear of the former, they will not often permit correspondents to interpret the news in the latter sense, with the result that facts are presented without any explanation. So they frequently give an incorrect impression, or else

There also are weekly and monthly reviews that are of importance to the correspondent who is attempting to keep up on the progress of Chinese affairs.

The native papers are published for profit, and hence are careful to avoid printing anything that might result in a libel suit or offend the government. This caution contributes to the colorless character of the press in which the political news is chiefly official propaganda. More attention is given to art, literature, and other "safe" topics, than to domestic or international affairs.

Although paper-making was invented in China, as well as ink-making and the use of movable type, most of the newsprint paper to-day is imported from Sweden, Japan or the United States, and is expensive. For that reason, the publishers refuse to print more copies than is economical, relative to advertising revenue, even though circulations could quite easily be increased.

§ 2. TOKYO AND JAPAN

JAPAN has been a part of the modern world only since 1854, when it was opened to trade through a treaty negotiated by Commodore Matthew C. Perry. The island kingdom developed rapidly from a feudal state into a modern industrial nation.

Although Shanghai has long been the journalistic center of the Far East, there is a trend toward Tokyo that may, in time, transfer the distinction to the Japanese capital. As in China, the Reuters agency provided the world with most of its current information about Japan until about the time of the Great War. Following that period, North American press associations and some newspapers also went into China and Japan, drawn there by news of the Nationalist military campaigns and Communist encroachments in China, and by the earthquake of 1923 and sub-

mean nothing at all to the reader who does not know China. British editors accept interpretation in the news, which makes reports of Chinese affairs in the British newspapers more reliable and intelligible. Since 1921, when he wrote, it must be added that many more American editors have come to recognize the need for legitimate interpretation of the news, not alone from China, but from everywhere. Nathaniel Peffer, "Why News from the Far East Is Often Unreliable and Misleading," *Editor and Publisher* (Nov. 26, 1921), p. 28.

sequent political changes and military adventures in Japan. Some
of them have had their correspondents moving back and forth
between Tokyo and Shanghai, as the news seemed to warrant.[10]

Both Reuters and the Associated Press have contracts with the
leading Japanese news agency, Domei Tsushin Sha (Allied News
Agency), organized in 1935 as a government-controlled agency,
with twenty charter member newspapers, including the leading
Tokyo and Osaka papers and also the Japan Broadcasting Company. Although nominally independent, it was formed with the aid
of the government, which provided funds, and forced its acceptance by the press and by other agencies. It absorbed the Rengo
semi-official agency December 31, 1935, and the Nippon Dempo
Tsushin Sha ("Japanese Telegraph News Agency"), independent,
June 1, 1936.[11] The latter had been allied with the United Press,
of the United States, for the exchange of news, which arrangement was taken over by Domei. There remain smaller agencies

[10] H. E. Wildes, *Social Currents in Japan*. Contains a useful account of
the development of foreign news service in Japan; Kanesada Hanazano,
The Development of Japanese Journalism.

[11] Anon., "National News Body Chartered in Japan," *Editor and Publisher* (Nov. 23, 1925), p. 13; Anon., "Japan's Agency 'Pure,'" *Editor and
Publisher* (Nov. 30, 1935), p. 10. Nippon Shimbun Rengo ("Associated
Press of Japan") had been generally known simply as "Rengo." That association had been formed in 1926 by representatives of 26 Japanese newspapers, as a non-profit-making, mutual news association much like the Associated Press of the United States. Eight newspapers, with 75 per cent of
the total newspaper circulation in Japan, became charter members. They
were the *Asahi* ("Rising Sun"), *Nichi-Nichi* ("Today-Today" or "Day to
Day"), *Hochi* ("News"), *Jiji Shimpo* ("Current Events"), *Kokumin* ("The
Nation") and *Chugai Shogyo* ("Home and Abroad"), all of Tokyo, and the
Asahi and the *Mainichi* ("Every Day") of Osaka. Yukichi Iwanaga, who had
been managing director of the Kokusai Tsushin Sha ("International News
Agency"), the older association, became managing director of Rengo. Kokusai
was disbanded, although previously it had distributed the Reuters and Associated Press services, on an exchange basis, within Japan. Yukichi Iwanaga
also directs Domei.

Anon., "Domei United News Agencies in Japan," *Editor and Publisher*
(June 6, 1936), p. 14; Marlen Pew, "Shop Talk at Thirty," *Editor and
Publisher* (July 18, 1936), p. 48; K. Iwamoto, "Denies Control by 'Domei'"
(letter), *Editor and Publisher* (July 25, 1936), p. 37; Marlen Pew, "Shop
Talk at Thirty," *Editor and Publisher* (Aug. 1, 1936), p. 36; Anon.,
"Japanese News Agency Sets Nationalist Aim," New York *Times* (Nov. 10,
1936).

in Japan itself, covering the news of great cities, such as Tokyo and Osaka.

The Domei agency affirms its purpose as being to serve Japan's interests. It "must not be placed at the service of the press alone," said Yukichi Iwanaga, its president. "It must always function as a public organ, with an eye to the interests of the nation."

Some Japanese newspapers are profitable, print a considerable volume of foreign news, and send correspondents abroad at times on assignments. But they all depend for the most part on Domei and local press associations to provide them with news. Few of them have special correspondents abroad.

* * *

Correspondents for foreign newspapers and press associations stationed in Japan receive much the same sort of treatment that they would in Washington or London. They have their political, diplomatic, social and business news sources. Regular conferences at the Foreign Office ("Gaimusho") several times weekly are helpful, and the discussions incline to frankness. Correspondents are left free to write what they please. Aside from military information and news affecting the Royal Family, there is no censorship on outgoing news dispatches except in times of crisis such as the political assassinations of 1936. As in some other countries, the Foreign Office keeps informed as to what the correspondents are writing about Japan. Anything more serious than an effort to persuade a writer that he is wrong, if he has sent an "unfavorable" dispatch, would ordinarily be rare.

Tokyo, as the capital, is the chief center for the political and diplomatic news of Japan, and the Imperial Hotel is the news headquarters of Tokyo, so far as the foreign press is concerned. The news of Osaka is mainly industrial and financial. Foreign correspondents must keep in close touch, as elsewhere, with governmental, business, diplomatic and personal news. They have their Japanese assistants to help them. Then they try to write their copy to avoid the taboos and sensitivities of the Japanese.

The mail and one trans-Pacific cable line, until after 1920, were the chief means of sending news from Japan to the United States.

Later, there was the United States navy wireless in Manila, useful to North American correspondents, who could cable news from Shanghai or Tokyo to Manila, to be forwarded from there. British and European correspondents could route their dispatches by telegraph across Russia. But regular commercial radio service across the Pacific to North America has relieved the situation since 1930. Rates remain relatively high, however, which is one reason the world has learned no more about Japan and China. The same circumstance has limited the news of the world published in Chinese and Japanese newspapers.[12] A few newspapers have been willing to use some mail copy, which has helped to give them superior services.[13]

Correspondents must deal with the Oriental mind in Japan, even as in China. This means a mind that is cautious, occasionally suspicious, given to indirection, and to saying the expedient thing, the thing that is pleasant at the moment. For this reason, full and correct facts are difficult to get quickly, although the correspondent usually meets with every courtesy in his pursuit of them.

So the correspondent learns to judge trends, and remembers that he is dealing with and writing about a sensitive people, courageous and proud.[14] Frank discussion of Japanese affairs is not, as

[12] M. W. Vaughn, "High Press Rates Chief Bar to Far Eastern Newspapers," *Editor and Publisher* (Nov. 13, 1926), pp. 24, 42.

[13] Anon., "Mail Copy, Not Cable Matter, Tells Real Conditions in Far East," *Editor and Publisher* (Dec. 11, 1926), p. 8.

[14] The Japanese Exclusion Act passed by the United States, and similar legislation in other countries was a blow to the national pride. Casual references to "Japs," mention of the "yellow peril" and slights to the Emperor are almost beyond endurance. A caricature of the Emperor pulling a ricksha, in the magazine *Vanity Fair*, became a diplomatic incident in the summer of 1935, and was taken most seriously both in Tokyo and in Washington, however trifling it seemed to the American public. Some newspapers which are nationalistic to the point of jingoism make the most of such incidents to arouse ill feeling in Japan against the United States.

Anon., "Minor 'Tempest' Rages in Japan over Caricature," *Christian Science Monitor* (Aug. 5, 1935); Anon., "U. S. A. Has Free Press Is Answer to Japan's Protest Over Cartoon," *Editor and Publisher* (Aug. 10, 1935), p. 10; M. W. Vaughn, *Covering the Far East;* Eugene Lyons, *We Cover the World*, Ch. II, Frank H. Hedges on Japan.

Vice-President Fairbanks once said, "One does not have to be afraid of what one's political enemies say; the thing to scare a man to death is what

a rule, resented, but the occasional mistakes do harm to good relations out of proportion to their real importance because they are magnified by jingoes.

*   *   *

Although there was only one newspaper in Japan up to 1862, now there are more than 2000 publications of various kinds. The Japanese people are among the most literate in the world, and they are voracious readers, so that some of the papers have huge circulations. Although, as elsewhere, the sensational press is better read than the conservative press, the Japanese people, even in rural areas, are reasonably well informed about world events and

he may say himself." So an inadvertent remark may be twisted to do harm to the speaker's political or personal prestige, or it may implicate the country in difficulties. This was demonstrated in U. S.-Japanese relations in 1931.

Secretary of State Stimson, in formal press conference in Washington on Nov. 27, 1931, expressed surprise at a report that Japanese troops were advancing on Chinchow, temporary Manchurian capital, in view of assurances Japan had given that no hostilities would develop in that section. In an Associated Press report based upon these remarks, and expressing the United States Government's attitude toward the Japanese aggression, this sentence appeared: "...At first, officials were given the impression that the military party, which is not under complete control of the civil government, simply had run amuck...."

This sentence was included in the cabled report sent to Tokyo for the use of the Rengo agency. There, the dispatch was edited, with quotation marks added, so that Secretary Stimson appeared to have said, in effect, that the Japanese army had "run amuck" in Manchuria.

This created a brief sensation in the Japanese Foreign Office. The Press Spokesman there denounced Mr. Stimson on the strength of the dispatch, and the Foreign Office itself sent a note of protest to the United States. Investigation revealed that the fault had been in the editing of the dispatch, and the Rengo agency took full responsibility for the mistake. So the matter subsided, but the ease with which a serious controversy might arise over a simple remark was illustrated.

"It is easy to create the wrong impression when you join a story of formal statement with an interpretative statement about a given situation," said Jackson Elliott, assistant general manager of the Associated Press, in commenting on the incident, and its journalistic implications. "In my opinion we should always mark the line distinctly between authorized statements of officials and that matter which is our own." J. W. Perry, "Rengo Agency Takes Blame for Dispatch Causing Japan Attack on Stimson," *Editor and Publisher* (Dec. 5, 1931), pp. 5-6.

also about Japanese affairs. Japan's emergence as a world power has aroused the interest of the nation's people.[15]

Most of the newspapers themselves tend to copy the methods of the more sensational papers of the United States, although this has not always been true. The more conservative newspapers copy the British press. They all sell for the equivalent of a cent or less, and appeal to women and children as well as to men in their news and features. They have large reportorial staffs, including many university graduates, covering Tokyo, Osaka, Yokohama, and other parts of Japan as well. Reporters telephone much of their news to their offices, where it is rewritten, often very well, but not always with great accuracy. Carrier pigeons are used to carry notes of interviews aboard liners in Yokohama harbor to the offices. There is less scramble to get exclusive news stories, however, than to publish good editorials, even if they have to be reprinted from some other newspaper.

Until about 1900 the papers were made to appeal to men, but then a change began which resulted in an attempt to interest women as well. Circulations started to climb, as a result. The Russo-Japanese War of 1904 stirred interest among Japanese readers in world affairs. Until about 1909, when there was a move for representative government in Japan, very little political news appeared, but the organization of political parties with definite views brought politics into the press. A great deal of foreign news is published, and prominently displayed. Practically all of it comes from the Domei agency, which gets it through exchange arrangement with the other press associations belonging to the "world league," as well as from some of its own men.

There are many serialized articles, some of them extremely "heavy," and most of them are signed, since anonymity does not please Japanese readers. Sports news and pictures also are popu-

[15] Sojinkwan K. Sugimura, *Random Thoughts on Journalism*. Presents a brief history of the press in Japan, and discusses the journalism of the day; M. Ohta, *Society and the Newspaper*. A discussion of Japanese journalism by the vice-president of the *Hochi Shimbun*, Tokyo; W. Washio, "Black Third Page; Iniquitous Practice in Japanese Journalism," *Trans-Pacific* (Jan. 23, 1926), V. 13, p. 10; Seiji Noma, *Noma of Japan*. Magazine publisher of note in Japan.

lar. The readers themselves contribute one of the most interesting features by writing freely to the papers, and their letters occupy generous space every day. The papers are lively and progressive, on the whole, and creditable products, despite special technical obstacles, and restraints upon them.

Two major problems irk Japanese publishers and editors: *First,* their use, in addition to the 58 characters in the Japanese alphabet, of the Chinese ideograph characters, requiring 3000 to 4500 characters, which is more than even China requires. Because of the nature of these ideographs, no slug-casting machine has been successfully devised to speed production in the country, and composition requires a large staff of hand-compositors. The monotype machine, however, has been adapted to some uses.[16]

Second, a strict government supervision exercised over the domestic press, restricting the opportunity to get or print anything except officially sanctioned information. The government, controlled by a military clique and able to plead the necessity of emergency for the last several years, has ordered the press to print nothing on certain topics, or to limit its account to a specified degree.

* * *

The Japanese Constitution, under the heading, "The Rights and Duties of Subjects," assures to the people the privilege of freedom of discussion. Article 29 states: "A subject of Japan is guaranteed freedom of speech in publication, printing, assemblage and association within the scope of the law." The phrase, "within the scope of the law," is an elastic one, so that although the press is free to a very large extent, the government, dominated by the military group, can and does keep a close watch upon it. Another Article in the same section of the Constitution further qualifies freedom by declaring that the provisions therein are not inviolable in times of emergency. Beyond that, the Peace Preservation Law,

[16] John R. Morris, "Oriental Monotype Speeds Up Work on Japanese Newspapers," *Editor and Publisher* (July 8, 1922); Walter Sammis, "Phonetics and Easy Communication Japan's Greatest Need," *Editor and Publisher* (Dec. 24, 1931), pp. 17, 33.

or the "Dangerous Thought Act," as it is often called, also restricts free expression.[17]

Editors know that if they print news or editorial opinions unwelcome to the government, there may be unpleasant results. For that reason, they are careful, and if in doubt they may ask instructions or explanations at the proper government offices. The government, in fact, sometimes instructs editors as to what they may say, especially in matters of foreign affairs.

The domestic press is restricted much more than representatives of the foreign press in the country. So much so, that as long ago as 1922, Japanese publishers made bold to suggest that the restrictions on the domestic press were inconsistent with its growing size, quality and influence.[18] But the restraint since then on the press has become greater, if anything.

The effect of the restriction has been, in one of its aspects, to place in the hands of the metropolitan police a complete authority over all newspaper contents—news, editorials, pictures and advertising—in what is assumed to be the best interests of the nation. This makes it unwise for any newspaper to print matter which might be regarded as contrary to government wishes, lest the publication offend, and fines or prison sentences be meted out to the editor. In practice, the first copy of a paper off the press goes to the police, who direct changes, or sometimes suppress the issue.[19]

It is not uncommon for a ban to be placed upon the publication

[17] K. Kawabé, *Press and Politics in Japan.*

[18] John R. Morris, "Japanese Publishers and Editors Renew Fight for Liberty of the Press," *Editor and Publisher* (May 20, 1922), p. 18; Anon., " 'Controlling' News," (Editorial), *Editor and Publisher* (Oct. 31, 1936), p. 28.

[19] Both in Japan and China every newspaper has a real editor and a "dummy" editor. The dummy editor is kept on the staff to serve prison sentences or bear responsibility for other unpleasant episodes, official or otherwise, in which the paper becomes involved. See: Anon., "Japanese Suspicious of Correspondents," *Editor and Publisher* (Feb. 2, 1935), p. 29; Hugh Byas, "Japan Has No Official Censor," *World's Press News* (Aug. 1, 1935), p. 11. Reprint from *Contemporary Japan;* A. Morgan Young, "Japanese Press Censorship," *Asia* (Aug., 1935), p. 474-77. Something of the uncertainty and tension that exists in Japanese newspaper offices is indicated by Marlen Pew in "Shop Talk at Thirty," *Editor and Publisher* (Feb. 29, 1936), pp. 44, 48.

of information relating to a particular subject or incident, and the police serve notice to that effect upon the newspapers. This might be to prevent a criminal, for example, being informed of the police efforts to find him. Again, it might bear some relation to political matters. It might be against the publication of certain advertising, as for example of a book disapproved by government officials.[20]

Despite this ban on some stories, Japanese newspapers have a surprising freedom of expression. Editorial comment can be especially fetterless, perhaps more so in provincial papers than in the Tokyo and Osaka papers.

Foreign correspondents do not submit their reports to a censor, as they would in Russia. Nor is their copy likely to be delayed or altered by any censorship such as exists in Germany or Italy. Nevertheless, the foreign correspondent may find that news gathering in Japan is a somewhat difficult task, and if he is under suspicion, or offends in his reports, it will become so difficult as to be almost impossible, and he may even be asked to leave the country.

There was a censorship imposed on military news, either as sent from Tokyo or from the field, during the Manchurian campaign of 1931-1932; also when Japanese forces landed in Shanghai in 1932, during which period radio and other communication met interference; there is restraint upon references to members of the Royal Family, while a definite censorship was maintained for three days in February, 1936, at the time of the army revolt and assassinations of some leading officials.[21] Otherwise, little limitation is placed upon the correspondents unless there seems

[20] The Japanese people have been kept poorly informed of the Japanese army activities in China, due to a censorship on reports from China and Manchoukuo, and also through restrictions on publication in Japan itself. A propaganda organization, somewhat comparable to those in Germany and Italy, has been set up by the government to help guide opinion.

Marlen Pew, "Shop Talk at Thirty," *Editor and Publisher* (Aug. 1, 1936), p. 36; Frank H. Hedges, "Censors in Japan Are Bars to Peace," New York *Times* (Sept. 1, 1936). See also: "Japan number" of *Fortune* (Sept., 1936). Contains references to thought-regimentation in the nation. Hugh Byas, "Japan's Censors Aspire to 'Thought Control,'" New York *Times Magazine* (April 18, 1937), pp. 4, 27.

[21] J. H. Furay, "J. H. Furay Tells of Censorship During 'Incident' in Japan," *Editor and Publisher* (April 18, 1936), p. 34.

reason to believe that they are deliberately mischievous in their intentions.[22]

It is true that the Foreign Office keeps a vigilant watch on what is published in foreign publications about Japan and if there is reason to object, the correspondent assumed to be responsible will be told why the authorities believe his viewpoint incorrect or unjustified. But no intimidation is attempted. The only result, if he does not show a willingness to be fair, as the Japanese interpret the word, is that he probably will find his news sources harder to reach, and then almost entirely barren.

It is not usual for correspondents in Japan to stray far from the regular news sources in Tokyo and Osaka. The government does not encourage them to do so. If they choose to go into the country, however, correspondents may be watched carefully by agents. They sometimes are invited to leave a place, and provincial telegraph offices may refuse to honor their press cards in the sending of dispatches.[23]

* * *

[22] In 1932, John Powell, correspondent for the Chicago *Tribune* in China, was dropped by the Japanese Government from the list of correspondents entitled to receive official communiqués. Later in the year, while covering the Manchurian campaign, he was consistently spied upon. He incurred the displeasure of the Japanese Government, not through his work for the Chicago *Tribune,* but because, as editor of the *China Weekly Review,* published in Shanghai, he had written editorials considered offensive in their references to the Japanese Royal Family, and unfriendly to Japan. Anon., "Japan Drops Powell from Official List," *Editor and Publisher* (Mar. 12, 1932), p. 8; Marlen Pew, "Shop Talk at Thirty," *Editor and Publisher* (Aug. 13, 1932).

In June, 1932, A. T. Steele, New York *Times* correspondent at Mukden, took refuge in the United States consulate in Harbin, because of charges by Japanese officials that he had acted as agent of the League of Nations' Lytton Commission of Inquiry into the Manchurian invasion, and had obtained from General Ma Chen-shan his version of conditions in Manchuria, after the Japanese had prevented the Lytton Commission itself from getting in touch with General Ma. Anon., "U. S. Writer Accused by Japanese," *Editor and Publisher* (June 25, 1932), p. 8.

[23] Anon.,. "Japanese Suspicious of Correspondents," *Editor and Publisher* (Feb. 2, 1935), p. 29; Miles W. Vaughn, *Covering the Far East.* An account of the experiences of an able correspondent for the United Press in Japan and elsewhere.

G. 41. SOME FAR-EASTERN AND PACIFIC PAPERS

For description see List of Illustrations

There are four chief newspapers in Japan, and they are read by, or translated for, foreign correspondents. With morning and evening editions and special supplements to attract readers, they have large staffs to get the news, and large circulations throughout the nation.

The papers are, the Tokyo *Asahi Shimbun* ("Rising Sun Newspaper") and the Osaka *Asahi Shimbun,* both under one management. This two-headed paper is the most influential in Japan. Each one circulates more than a million copies a day so that the combined circulation is about 2,500,000. The Tokyo *Nichi-Nichi* and the Osaka *Mainichi,* also under a single ownership, are independent and popular, circulating nearly as many copies daily as the *Asahi* newspapers. Other important Japanese newspapers are the Tokyo *Miyako Shimbun,* the Tokyo *Hochi Shimbun,* the *Japan Advertiser,* American-owned Tokyo paper in English; the *Japan Chronicle* of Kobe, which is British-owned, and also in English; the *Japan Times* of Tokyo, a government paper in English, and the Japanese-owned and -edited English-language edition of the Osaka *Mainichi.*

There are many smaller papers in Japan, but they are less important, except as they represent special views, and some of them are mere blackmail sheets.

Because of the restraint placed upon the press by the government, the newspapers of Japan are only of limited assistance to foreign correspondents in the country. What they print is far from being the whole story, on many occasions.

§ 3. OTHER NEWS CENTERS IN THE FAR EAST AND THE PACIFIC

THE GREAT sub-continent of India has been a long way from the western world and generally of limited interest to all peoples except the British.

As a part of the British Empire, it is natural that news to and from India should be handled by Reuters, and filtered through that press association to the rest of the world.[24] To-day, not only

[24] The beginning of news communications with India is traced by Henry M. Collins in *From Pigeon Post to Wireless.* This describes the negotiations

Reuters, but *The Times* of London, and one or two other news-papers and press associations maintain direct news contacts with India, although they do not always keep full-time resident cor-respondents there.

At periods of crisis, correspondents representing some North American press associations and newspapers as well as additional British correspondents, and representatives of other national presses, have arrived in India. Calcutta, Bombay, Delhi, Simla, and Lahore are all important centers, commercially or politically, and hence journalistically as well.

Most of the news clears through Bombay, because of communi-cations arrangements, and goes by the Indo-European telegraph line, British-owned, overland to London. In more recent times, the radio has given India a new link with the rest of the world, both for sending and receiving messages, while the airplane has brought it nearer to other lands, in effect.

Although no strict censorship is admitted to exist in India, and some newspaper correspondents going there especially to report unrest among the people have had no difficulty with censorship, others have had the opposite experience.

During the so-called salt riots of 1930 several correspondents went to India from London, Shanghai, and other centers. Some of their dispatches were censored or stopped as being "alarmist" or as too graphic. Other correspondents were extremely frank, but so honestly impartial that their dispatches were not changed or stopped.[25]

Actually, the British Foreign Office in London does not deny that a censorship existed in India at that period, but maintains that it was a very light censorship, intended not to prevent the

leading to the establishment of the Indo-European Telegraph, under Reuters' direction. Chs. 5-8; see also: J. B. Atkins, *The Life of Sir William Howard Russell*. As *Times* correspondent, Russell reported the Indian Mutiny and other events of 1857-1858, V. 1, Chs. 23-28. He returned in 1875 to 1877 for the Prince of Wales' tour, and events following, V. 2, Chs. 20-21.

[25] Anon., "Miller Returns to London After Covering Salt Riots in India," *Editor and Publisher* (July 26, 1930), p. 12 (Webb Miller, European news manager for the United Press); Negley Farson, *The Way of a Transgressor*, Chs. 85-89; Webb Miller, *I Found No Peace*, Chs. 15-21.

truth from going out, but to be certain that the truth *did* go out, rather than mere sensation and falsehood; that it was intended to prevent over-zealous correspondents seizing upon wild rumors, of which there were many, and sending them as fact.

Of course, this justification, however sound, is the same one offered by all nations establishing censorships. Others have defended the British censorship in India as essential because of agitators in the United States, particularly, who were said to be spreading sensationalized reports of conditions in India. A sentimentalist attitude toward foreign affairs held by many persons in the United States has provided fertile ground for propagandists and money-raisers, and the British Government has been frank about its desire to combat their influences.

* * *

Manila and the Philippines have some journalistic importance. The islands provide a stepping stone across the Pacific for communication and transport lines. Also, now that they are no longer dependent upon the United States, their future presents new possibilities.

The larger North American press associations have bureaus in Manila. Others, and a few more enterprising newspapers, are protected on news developing in the islands by newspaper men, chiefly of North American or British training, engaged in regular journalistic work in Manila. Manila has several publications in English, including the *Bulletin* and the *Herald,* and these in turn have their local correspondents throughout the islands, often men in military, educational, or governmental positions.

* * *

Australia and New Zealand, important parts of the British Empire, have their own press relations with Great Britain. Reuters serves the press there with foreign news; some Australian papers have representatives in London, and some of the leading metropolitan dailies own and control the Australian Associated Press, Proprietary, Ltd., with national coverage. There also are regional press associations, but each paper tries to cover its own news over a wide area, with the result that papers, in Sydney and Melbourne particularly, have very large reportorial staffs by contrast with papers in other lands.

The press is patterned upon that of Great Britain. Although entirely free of supervision or censorship, the laws governing it are fairly strict.[26] Journalists themselves have considerable personal prestige, more freedom than they would have in Great Britain in their relations with officials, but less in what they may write than they would have in the United States.[27] The papers have been handicapped by being obliged to import much of their newsprint, and having to obtain the overseas news by cable or radio, at a high cost.

Cable news, in skeletonized form, reaches Melbourne or Sydney from London, New York, Vancouver, San Francisco or Cape Town, as well as from other overseas points. From there it is distributed throughout Australia over the government telegraph system.

*   *   *

Hawaii, one of the outlying territories of the United States, has its governmental, commercial, social and journalistic center in Honolulu. The most important newspapers are published there,

[26] A list of the regional associations in Australia appears on page 69 ante.
Quentin Pope, Chicago *Tribune* correspondent, reported that he was prevented from sending a report from New Zealand about an earthquake in the Gisborne-Wairoa area in 1932. He was told that the quake was not very bad, and that such a message going to the United States would do New Zealand no good. Officials argued that there should be an international agreement to permit stopping transmission of any message detrimental to the country involved. Later, the Mayor of Wairoa expressed concern about the censorship, blaming it for a general apathy to the city's appeal for relief. Anon., "Quake News Censored," *Editor and Publisher* (Nov. 5, 1932).

[27] Guy Innes, "Cabling the News," *Journalism: By Some Masters of the Craft* (see Anon.), pp. 135-43. Speech under auspices of British Institute of Journalists by head in London of the Australian Newspapers Cable Service. Montague Grover, "Finds American Newspapers Most Truthful," *Editor and Publisher* (Aug. 26, 1928), pp. 7, 42; Anon., "Writer Penalized for Protecting Source," *Editor and Publisher* (Aug. 29, 1931), p. 10; Roy L. Curthoys, "Australian Newspaper Men Work Differently Than Here," *Editor and Publisher* (Aug. 5, 1922), p. 8; Anon., "Press of Australia." (Interview with Tom Clarke in *World's Press News*.) Reprinted in *American Press* (Sept., 1934), p. 9.

and there the news is covered and published just as it is on the mainland. The press associations of the United States have bureaus there, as they do in key cities on the mainland. Cable and wireless connect the islands with other parts of the world.

*   *   *

Other islands in the Pacific are not much in the news, but most of them are linked, directly or indirectly, by cable or wireless to other parts, and some local residents, whether professional journalists or engaged in other occupations, act as correspondents for press associations or newspapers, usually for those of the United States or Great Britain, since it is those two countries which have the most far-flung world interests and the most enterprising newspapers. France and Japan also show some journalistic interest in these other parts. The extension of commercial air service across the Pacific promises to give added news importance to the islands and atolls which dot its surface.

CHAPTER VIII

AUTOCRATS OF THE PRESS

NEWSPAPERS are the products of three autocratic groups—the persons who own them, the persons who make them, and the persons who read them. The final pages reflect the virtues and faults, the tastes and interests of all these persons, whose diverse influences form a constant check upon each other.

The owners and editors order, select and prepare all that appears, and they determine how it shall appear. The reader, however, has the last word. He accepts or rejects the final printed product. When the reader-in-the-mass, or the "public," bestows special favor upon any one sheet, other newspaper-makers usually imitate the successful competitor, assuming that the public has indicated its preference by acceptance of a particular style of newspaper.

News, as obtained and written by reporters and correspondents, eventually reaches the desk of an editor. Several editors see each story before it appears in the newspaper. Some of the copy, and all of the proofs reach the managing editor, and perhaps the owner or publisher as well.

In any case, a few men are deciding which of the news reports will be used, in view of the paper's policy; or can be used, in view of the space available. The rest goes into the discard. Some of it may be important, but uninteresting. Some of it may be true, important and interesting, but not in line with the policy of the paper. If not wholly discarded, it may be reduced to small space and used inconspicuously. Or there may not be space in a given edition or day's issue for what would ordinarily be included.

In practice, the news selected for emphasis very often has to do with matters of local interest, even though it may be of no deep importance. To make space, news from farther away may be sacrificed. Foreign news, especially, has been slighted, so that an intelligent understanding or interest in foreign affairs is very limited in most communities.[1]

Throughout these pre-publication processes decisions are being made by editors. They are human, and often they are under pressure of time, so that they may make mistakes. Perhaps they are possessed of certain preconceived ideas or prejudices, or are biased on some subjects, and ignorant on others.

Possibly an editor has had good training in history, or has read widely in that field, but is obliged to make a decision affecting a story about economic matters, with regrettable results. Perhaps he is timid about using some story because he knows that the owner of the paper, or some superior editor, has a prejudice which would be involved. So an editor's fears, stereotypes and mental gaps have an inevitable, even if subconscious, influence upon the writing, selection, editing, and display of news or other material.

To this extent, the reader is not getting straight facts. Somebody, several somebodies, stand in the light, or help him to read the news as they want him to read it.[2]

Good newspaper men do not willingly permit themselves prejudices. Intelligent and conscientious journalists make a special effort to be objective and impartial in handling the news.[3] And,

[1] Julian L. Woodward, *Foreign News in American Morning Newspapers.*
The managing editor of one great newspaper in the United States has said, "Ninety-nine persons out of a hundred are interested in something *other* than foreign news, very much more." He said this although his newspaper has a good foreign service, adding that "a newspaper prints foreign news more from a sense of public responsibility than because it interests many readers."

[2] L. N. Flint, *Conscience of the Newspaper.* Reference to this sort of "color" in the news appears in Ch. 3; F. W. Hirst, *The Six Panics and Other Essays,* pp. 142-64. Mr. Hirst gives considerable attention to the handling of cables by pre-war British newspapers, showing some of the faults and virtues thereof, including something about the injection of propaganda and efforts to make the foreign news look impressive.

[3] Recall Walter Duranty's conscious effort, as noted in *I Write as I Please,* pp. 94-96, 169, 259-66, to rid himself of prejudice in viewing affairs. His effort was patterned upon the expressed method of William Bolitho, of the Manchester *Guardian* and the New York *World.*

on the whole, they succeed very well. They must, because their newspapers are read by all kinds of people, so that a departure from impartiality brings complaints from readers—and enough complaints react upon the editor in charge or upon the writers. Impartiality itself brings complaints from prejudiced readers, who want the newspaper to accept their prejudices as fact. Extremists on both sides regard real impartiality as just cause for complaint. And unfortunately, most editors, or others who have prejudices or "blind spots," rarely recognize them as such.

*   *   *

The policy of a newspaper is dominated by the owner. In practice, he probably takes advice and counsel from trusted editors and assistants, but he also feels the pressure of others less disinterested. If the paper is mortgaged, the bank or other mortgage-holder may bring pressure to influence the newspaper's policy on some subject. If the owner has strong political ambitions, commitments, or partisanship, it may be reflected in his newspaper. It has been common to believe that advertisers—especially large advertisers, such as department stores—have dictated successfully to the owners of newspapers, perhaps through their business offices, and undoubtedly such things have occurred, but less frequently than critics of the press have implied.[4]

[4] Upton Sinclair, *The Brass Check*. In this vitriolic and not entirely accurate study of the press there nevertheless is revealed something of the character of certain newspaper owners; E. A. Ross, "The Suppression of Important News," *The Profession of Journalism* (Bleyer, ed.); pp. 79-96, and bibliography; George Seldes, *Freedom of the Press*, Ch. 2; L. N. Flint, *Conscience of the Newspaper*, Ch. 4; Will Irwin, "The Power of the Press," *Collier's* (Jan. 21, 1911), V. 46, p. 15 et seq.; Will Irwin, "Advertising Influence," *Collier's* (May 27, 1911), V. 47, p. 15 et seq.; Will Irwin, "Our Kind of People," *Collier's* (June 17, 1911), V. 47, p. 17 et seq.; Will Irwin, "The Foe Within," *Collier's* (July 1, 1911), V. 47, p. 17.
Hornell Hart and Susan M. Kingsbury and associates: "The Detection of Journalistic Bias," *New Republic* (Oct. 15, 1930), pp. 230-32. Hart and associates: "Prejudices in Newspaper Headlines," *New Republic* (Oct. 22, 1930), pp. 251-55; Anon., "Counting Room Holds No Menace to Editorial Freedom, Says White." (Press less at mercy of advertisers than of reporters willing to meddle with facts to please proprietors, says Detroit *News* executive.) *Editor and Publisher* (Mar. 10, 1934), p. 18.
John G. McNaughton, "Politics, Not Commerce, Threatens Free Press,

Although it is true that most newspapers try to give to their readers an honest and balanced picture of the world, so far as that is possible, there are newspapers in every country which represent special points of view, politically, economically, socially. The current ideal is one of impartiality and objectivity, so that almost every newspaper tries to give such an impression. In practice, the same newspaper may have a good policy on one subject and a bad policy on another.[5]

It must not be imagined that every story in every issue, even of a prejudiced newspaper, is given special color to underline a special purpose. Most stories are edited merely to make them more concise or to sharpen the point made by the writer. It is only stories related to the newspaper's particular sphere of interest, or stories especially sought, that receive such attention. Stories are selected or rejected as determined by those particular interests, and stories will be edited or headlined with deliberate intent to obtain a desired effect.

Says English Reporter." (Governments are main sources of false and tendentious news, Robert Dell, correspondent of Manchester *Guardian*, says at University of Geneva.) *Editor and Publisher* (July 27, 1935), p. 16.

[5] The Hearst newspapers, the Chicago *Tribune*, and some others indulge in constant agitation concerning the menace of Communism to the world. When the late Cyrus H. K. Curtis owned the New York *Evening Post* and the Philadelphia *Public Ledger*, those papers also engaged in "red-baiting." Although H. R. Knickerbocker, *Ledger-Post* correspondent, was awarded the Pulitzer Prize for "the best foreign correspondence of the year" in 1930, his series of articles from Russia was played under anything but impartial headlines. See: O. G. Villard, "Red Menace and Yellow Journalism," *The Nation* (N. Y., June 3, 1931), pp. 601-603. The Knickerbocker stories were published in book form as *The Red Trade Menace*.

The Hearst newspapers published a series of documents in 1927-1928 purporting to prove a Mexican-sheltered plot against the United States. These later were revealed as forged. Silas Bent, *Strange Bedfellows*, Ch. 14; Ferdinand Lundberg, *Imperial Hearst: A Social Biography*, Chs. 8, 11.

In Great Britain, the Rothermere and Beaverbrook papers present examples of a special bias of a nationalist type, while the *Daily Herald*, Labor paper, presents another form of bias. Every country has its nationalistic press, and many newspapers are biased politically or economically.

As one instance, when Ramsay MacDonald toured Wales in 1924, he was greeted with wild enthusiasm, says one correspondent who accompanied him. Yet the *Daily Mail* reported that his reception had been cold and silent. See: H. W. Nevinson, *Last Changes, Last Chances*, p. 316.

The desire may be to build up a community opinion on any one of many subjects, perhaps with entirely laudable purpose. It may be politics, temperance, economic or governmental theories, financial subjects, national defense, peace sentiment, labor matters, social questions, agricultural policies, et cetera. Perhaps a newspaper will go so far as to conduct a "campaign" on a given subject, as for or against building a new city hall, entering the World Court, raising the tariff rates, obtaining better sanitation, reducing taxes, or something else. Then news stories may be "slanted," that is, written or edited with a nice consideration for the impression they will create. Headlines are written with equal care, and they are supported with pictures, editorials, little "features," and a considerable array of journalistic devices intended to capture attention and bolster sentiment as desired. All of this is propaganda, no matter how laudable its purpose, unless it is preferred to call "laudable propaganda" by the more pleasing name of "education." And, even then, who is to judge what is laudable?

Conspicuous under-attention toward, or disregard of a topic having public interest or importance is quite as likely to have a special effect as a great deal of attention. It has been said that "the power of the press is the suppress." Under-attention can have even more effect than over-attention, since the latter may weary readers without convincing them. Yet, one of the most subtle and effective journalistic devices to sway opinion is *repetition*—a constant hammering, or a gentle but repeated suggestion. The theory is that this will produce its effect just as surely as drop after drop of water can wear away a rock. An idea, if repeated often enough, will implant itself in the mind of the casual reader, or even of the wary one, so that ultimately it will be accepted as a fact; perhaps even embraced by the reader as his own original idea.[6]

[6] Theodor Lessing, M.D., Ph.D., author of a number of philosophical books and volumes of poetry, held himself the victim of persecution by officially reiterated misinformation in Germany. In letters to the Manchester *Guardian* and other newspapers, he reported that the Nazi press, by inspiration of Dr. Goebbels, persecuted him as a Jew, referring to him repeatedly as "the German Lazarus, calling himself Lessing," and putting words into his mouth that he never uttered or wrote. Although he denied that he or any of his

Many a newspaper has had a "black list," too, a private listing of persons whose names never were to be mentioned in its columns or only under certain conditions. Usually this is because the individual has done something or said something personally displeasing to the owner of the paper; occasionally it is a calculated move to blot out a person's reputation in the public memory. By neglecting to report his speeches and refusing to mention his name a press association could go a long way toward sending a politician to oblivion, just as it could lift him from oblivion by the opposite method. Syndicates and individual newspapers possess equal power, upon a smaller scale.

This is the use of *selection* as a device to establish an opinion. So the New York *Times,* prior to 1920, selected news portraying Soviet Russia in an unfavorable light, which helped to establish anti-Communist sentiment in the United States.[7] The British press used similar tactics. In 1919 Prince Peter Kropotkin, reformer, geographer, and avowed anarchist, banished from his native Russia in 1886, and long resident in England, returned to Russia and, later, he reported what he thought of the Revolution and its results. The *Daily Herald,* with Leftist opinions, printed all that he had said favorable to the Revolution; *The Times,* strongly Right in sentiment, printed all that he said unfavorable to the Revolution. And nothing else, in either case. Readers of the *Daily Herald* gained the impression that Kropotkin was favorable to the Revolution; readers of *The Times* were comforted to believe that he felt the Revolution had been a failure in its results. So, while pleasing their readers, the papers misled them.

It is within the power of newspaper owners to print what they wish. What they wish to print is the thing that accords with the sentiments of the moment, their own and their readers'. Thus, when relations were good between Russia and Great Britain, economically speaking, the British newspapers made much of what

ancestors ever had been named Lazarus, "I find myself obliged again and again to refute this statement, but am still referred to in the Nazi press as Lazarus." In spite of himself, Dr. Lessing said, he was becoming known as "Lazarus." See: Lessing (letter), Manchester *Guardian* (May 26, 1933).

[7] Walter Lippmann and Charles Merz, "A Test of the News," *New Republic* (Aug. 4, 1920).

they called the "Russian soul," a beautiful and rather mystic thing compounded of the great art, music, dance, poetry and literature of that country. It had been regretfully admitted, however, that the Russian Government was less admirable, so that when the Kerensky Revolution occurred it was hailed as further evidence of the "Russian soul" acting to improve matters, and it was compared to the French attack on the Bastille. When the Lenin-Trotsky Revolution occurred, however, and the Communist system came to be regarded as holding a threat to the economic system, further reference to the "Russian soul" ceased, and Russia became a place inhabited by bestial, cruel and illiterate persons and their unfortunate victims. Needless to say, neither view was correct, but represented an emotional treatment of the news, entirely unbalanced.

Similarly, at the beginning of 1852, Napoleon III of France was the butt of an attack in the British press, and presently was one of the most hated men among British newspaper readers. Then the German war threatened, the aid of France was desired, and by the end of 1852 Napoleon III had become—in the press— Britain's "gallant ally." The press attack was then diverted to Nicholas of Russia.

In the United States the Hearst newspapers are notorious for their shifts of sentiment, and even adopt attitudes in one city that are opposed to their attitudes in places where it is expedient to take the other view.[8]

On Oct. 7, 1929, the Hearst papers printed an editorial signed by William Randolph Hearst, in which he praised Ramsay MacDonald as a "great Prime Minister, and as a very valuable influence for the whole world." This theme was developed. But, in the Hearst papers of March 29, 1930, Mr. Hearst signed another editorial, or open letter, in which he referred to Mr. MacDonald as "a sly, smooth and tricky diplomat," because, so it was said, he was doing his "utmost to create a pacifist inferior-Navy sentiment in the United States" by "collaborating daily with half-caste American correspondents of international-minded newspapers,

[8] O. G. Villard, *Some Newspapers and Newspapermen*, pp. 14-41, and especially p. 16.

whose publishers wear the decorations of foreign governments for disloyalty to their own."

Although the Hearst papers supported Franklin D. Roosevelt's candidacy in the Presidential campaign and election in 1932, they presently turned against Roosevelt and all his works. Mr. Hearst specifically directed all of his papers, in any references to the "New Deal" to call it the "Raw Deal." Reiteration had helped damn the "World Court," because the Hearst newspapers constantly referred to it as the "League Court," so tying it to the League and all the iniquity Mr. Hearst had for so many years ascribed to that organization.

The *Daily Mail*, which also is opposed to the League of Nations, and to British participation therein, in its issue of October 19, 1935, summarized a Reuters message from Pretoria reporting a speech about the League by General Jan Smuts. The speech was mainly a tribute to the League for its unanimous condemnation of Italy's aggression in Ethiopia, and an expression of gratitude that Britain had given the League its leadership in the matter. The *Daily Mail* account of the address was headed: GEN. SMUTS AND THE LEAGUE, followed by a subhead, in quotation marks, "Scrap it if it menaces peace." Those words were not to be found in the speech itself, as reported in the *Daily Mail* or in *The Times*, and the passages referring to the League in favorable terms were omitted by the *Daily Mail*.[9]

* * *

Propaganda papers always have existed, but deliberate attempts to warp public opinion seldom have been outstandingly successful, and no paper indulging in such an attempt has been regarded as representing great journalism. Newspapers have spoken for political parties, and when the party was popular the newspaper may have enjoyed a large circulation and considerable following among members of the party itself. But, even so, it never could be called a great newspaper because it was more in the nature of a political trade journal. Similarly, there have been newspapers

[9] This treatment was noted by Col. Maurice Spencer in a letter published by the *New Statesman and Nation* (Nov. 2, 1935), p. 633.

whose chief interest was religious news and views, particularly during the nineteenth century, but they, too, have been trade journals, rather than real newspapers.

* * *

But an influence more subtle and more important than direct attempts to make deliberate use of individual newspapers or even of the press as a whole to further special interests, political, financial or otherwise, has been the transformation of the newspaper from a profession to a business.

Once a newspaper was primarily an editorial product, consisting of news and editorial comment, with some miscellaneous features. To-day it is primarily a business product, consisting of advertisements interlarded with news, editorials and features—increased in quantity and quality, but still incidental to the advertising from which the paper derives its chief income. Whereas the newspaper once paid for itself out of circulation revenue, to-day the circulation revenue does not even pay for the white paper on which it is printed.

It would not be accurate to say that the editorial department has necessarily become subservient to the business department. And yet, newspaper-making has become a big business. It is inevitable that it should be so, because the power of a newspaper as an advertising medium has become so clear that merchants and others who stand to benefit by a mass solicitation of trade are ready and willing to use its columns to convey their sales messages to all readers. The growth of newspapers came largely from this advertising patronage, and from the advertising patronage flow not only the costs of operations, but the profits.

Owners of newspapers, and managers and publishers, under these circumstances, began to be business men, rather than editorial men. They regarded publishing a newspaper primarily as a business, to which business rules were to be applied, rather than as a service and a profession. Great sums of money had to be invested to house a newspaper properly, to buy the necessary mechanical equipment, to pay the numerous employees required in the various departments, and to meet fixed charges and general overhead. Large advertising patronage became necessary, and large circulations became prerequisite to large advertising patronage. Mass appeal in the news was required to attract large circulation. Mass appeal meant excitement, struggle, suspense, humor, pathos, horror, thrills—elementary things reaching readers' emotions rather than their minds.

Owners of newspapers, with their managers, publishers and chief editors, concerned with these matters, found themselves associating with other business men, also concerned with similar management problems. In clubs, at play, in trade conferences they met them and came to hold common views. The result was that newspaper-making was transformed into a manufacturing industry, producing newspapers from its factory.[10]

This has been the trend in the United States. It produced Frank Munsey, the Hearst chain of newspapers, and others. It became apparent in Great Britain, producing, among others, Lord Northcliffe, Lord Beaverbrook, Lord Rothermere, Lord Burnham, Lord Camrose, Lord Astor, Lord Kelmsley, Lord Iliffe—the "press lords," as they are called. In Great Britain, these men and their

---

[10] Anon., "Selfish Publishers Block Peace Move," *Editor and Publisher* (Mar. 17, 1934), p. 11. Report of Paul Block Foundation lecture at Yale University, New Haven, on Mar. 11, 1934, by Willis J. Abbot, of the *Christian Science Monitor*.

Anon., "Millionaire Philosophy Is Called Greatest Threat to Free Press," *Editor and Publisher* (Nov. 8, 1934), p. 10. Report of speech by Sir Willmott Lewis, Washington correspondent for *The Times* of London, before the Phi Beta Kappa Association of Philadelphia, Oct. 26, 1934. "When men whose habits are not those of the journalist but those of the money maker obtain control of newspapers," he said, "these men are not thinking in terms of opinion but in terms of the prevailing of their will." He felt this situation was more serious in Great Britain than in the United States, for there, he said, most newspapers have passed into the control of men "who are primarily millionaires and not journalists," and they appear to wish their views to prevail, to enforce their opinions, rather than to make the newspapers that they control each serve as a "clearing house for the opinions of all."

Anon., *Washington Merry-Go-Round*, pp. 321-26, 345-47, 357-58, 365-66. These pages contend that most press correspondents at Washington "are better than the papers they work for," and cite instances in which the prejudice and partisanship of owners have warped the news as written and published.

editors, in most cases, are the products of a rigid class system and an educational routine, which, combined with their social relations, makes them narrow and close-bound in outlook and sympathies.[11] Then the trend was felt in lesser degree in Germany, producing Hugo Stinnes and later Dr. Alfred Hugenberg. It was felt in Japan, and in other countries, although not in all, and in varying degrees.

The business mentality grips and governs most of the press of the United States and of Great Britain. It is a factor of importance in determining what appears in the newspapers and in what way it appears. Because they have great fortunes invested in the publishing properties, owners take every step to protect their investments and, while this is natural, the public often suffers.[12]

Bismarck has been quoted as saying that the peace of Europe could be preserved by hanging a dozen editors. J. A. Spender, himself an editor, has remarked that about six proprietors and a score of writers formulated all important opinions expressed in the London metropolitan press. Napoleon said that he feared four hostile newspapers more than ten thousand armed men. So the power of owners and editors is estimated for good or for bad, and it follows that the public welfare demands that these men should be possessed of honest motives, good intentions, and trained intelligence.

* * *

If newspapers can be no better than the men who make them, it also is true that newspapers can be no better than the persons

[11] Which explains such headline emphasis over this report in the *Daily Express* one day late in 1926:

LADY STANLEY IN A MISHAP
By Daily Express Correspondent

LICHFIELD, Sunday.—John Joseph Jennings, a farm laborer, of Forgelane, Little Aston, was killed yesterday when his motor-cycle came in collision with a motor-car in which Lady [Arthur] Stanley was traveling to Cheshire, near the Shoulder-of-Mutton Inn, Lichfield. The motor-cycle was wrecked.

[12] George Seldes, *Freedom of the Press*, Chs. 2, 3, 6, 17; Stuart Chase and F. J. Schlink, *Your Money's Worth;* Mary C. Phillips, *Skin Deep;* James Rorty, *Our Master's Voice: Advertising;* F. J. Schlink and Arthur Kallet, *100,000,000 Guinea Pigs.*

who read them. Water cannot rise above its source, and newspapers can be no finer than readers are prepared to accept.

Once asked whether he thought the press of the United States ever would be censored, an astute editor replied, "Censorship of newspapers isn't coming—it's here, and always has been here in the form of opinions of subscribers."

When a newspaper tries to present a fair picture of a controversial subject or situation, readers who hold a prejudice accuse it of disseminating propaganda, or at least favoring the opposite view. If a newspaper honestly supports, editorially, either a liberal or a conservative outlook, those holding the contrary view abuse it unmercifully, and rarely even credit it with sincerity. If a newspaper indulges in a bit of quiet humor now and then, in its editorial columns, trying to leaven the lump of public affairs, its efforts almost invariably will be misunderstood by some readers, perhaps not many, but a vocal group, nonetheless.

It is this audience-response, very largely, that makes so many newspapers dull, standardized, heavy-witted and elemental in their handling of everything that matters. With the exception, perhaps, of the arts and sciences, concerning which there is so little general understanding or interest that a few newspapers are able to present intelligent reports without much fear of challenge by readers whose prejudices have been outraged. In the reporting of sports, also, tradition permits considerable latitude.

Beyond that, it is difficult for the press to present a fair picture of any important subject because the facts themselves may be elusive and kaleidoscopic in character. They are difficult to obtain. They are susceptible of varying, and equally logical, interpretations, as to meaning or importance. One fact may be offset by another of apparently equal weight. The whole pattern of facts often must be so simplified and condensed in presentation as to distort the exact truth at times. And, finally, the public acceptance of a fact, or "near-fact," is contingent upon how generally it is made known, regardless of its accuracy. A greater truth may go virtually unaccepted because it has no great circulation to spread it far and quickly.

It has been said that the public always is 25 years behind the

facts in its thinking. So it will accept to-day things that were true
a quarter of a century ago. But other circumstances have changed
in the meantime, which makes what then was wisdom and truth no
longer entirely applicable. The public thought has been unable to
change quickly enough to keep up with changes in actual conditions, and the result is that government practices and commercial
or financial policies are out of joint with the times, bringing on
economic depressions and social unrest. And when affairs change
more rapidly, as in those very periods of crisis, public thought
becomes increasingly confused in its effort to understand what is
happening, and to make its adjustment. It is in such circumstances that dictators sometimes are welcomed.

*   *   *

Business and industry are organized to make their wishes and
opinions felt in government and elsewhere. But because the public
is an amorphous mass it can make its wishes felt only in a crude
sort of way. Even its elected representatives do not wholly represent it. Perhaps, in these circumstances, the press should do so,
striving to protect the public interest wherever it is involved.

The difficulty, however, is that newspaper owners and editors,
acting in all sincerity, but moved by sectional and personal prejudices, might not agree on what constituted the public interest, and
so one newspaper would offset another, as it does to-day. The public, furthermore, is preoccupied with its personal affairs, is inclined
to see very little beyond the end of its own nose, and is only half
educated. The newspaper, fighting strenuously in the public interest, might earn only disapproval for being "radical" or "dull," or
for being "highbrow," "pessimistic," "fault-finding," or even
downright "dishonest."

Editors and publishers have had enough of such disillusioning
experiences to make them doubt the popularity of the truth in
print. It is a mistake, they have found, to be ahead of mass thinking on a subject, for not only does it do little discernible good, but
it makes enemies and bores readers. "We cannot reform the world
single-handed," they say, in effect. "If we tried we would soon go
out of business. Then we could not accomplish even as much as

we are able to do now. So we do the best we can, and hope that the public will be ready for better things in time."

There is much justice in such a view. Until individual taste and understanding have been raised to a certain level by education and by the impact of events, the press will fall short of the ideal.[13]

It is difficult to think of any newspaper in the world that is doing all it might to serve the public welfare. Certain papers have, on occasion, done fine and courageous and praiseworthy things, but there never has been a newspaper which was able, consistently, to represent the public interest, above all others.

A conventional assumption by critics of the press is that all facts may be verified completely, and presented so convincingly and interestingly as to move even the most mentally blind and cloddish readers to act in their own best interests. In this belief, the critics delude themselves. It is a generally accepted belief, too, that communities and nations are alike, which may not be true at all.

But, on the other hand, disillusioned publishers and editors assume that the public never will learn better. This is an opinion that cannot be endorsed, because the battering of realities, combined with more and better educational training and reading, must eventually raise the standards of public thinking, as indeed it has in the past. The press need not stand still, and the more far-seeing editors and publishers are constantly hoping that their public is ready for something better, and they test that hope at intervals.

* * *

It all comes back to the age-old question: "What is truth?" The press at present can answer only in so far as its limitations permit it to do so, and in proportion as the public is ready and willing to receive the answer.

If the press is doing less than it is capable of doing toward the advancement of civilization, the fault is not entirely its own. Its

[13] N. A. Crawford, *The Ethics of the Press*, Ch. 5; H. L. Mencken, "Newspaper Morals," *The Profession of Journalism* (W. G. Bleyer, ed.), pp. 52-67; Ralph Pulitzer, "Newspaper Morals: A Reply," *Ibid.*, pp. 68-78. A discussion of the public reaction to affairs, as reported in the press.

shortcomings are many, but its potentialities are unlimited. It has organized an amazing system for the gathering and redistribution of information. Its shackles, however, will not fall off, and its faults will not disappear, until the almighty reader rises in his majesty and demands an unobstructed news channel and a press made to fit higher ethical as well as technical standards. That demand he can make effective by accepting the better journalism where he finds it, and so encouraging its growth and extension. The press itself can do much more than it has done toward the attainment of the ideal. But public education comes first. More persons must want to be well and truly informed. It is, above all, the Reader's Choice.

BIBLIOGRAPHY

The preparation of this volume has required reference to various sources of information, apart from personal experience, conversation and correspondence. To list each of the periodical references in the bibliography, would inflate it to an inordinate length. For that reason, those references are confined to the page footnotes, and only the periodicals referred to, and the books, are noted here. The references are grouped in two parts: (1) Books and Pamphlets and (2) Newspapers and Periodicals.

I

BOOKS AND PAMPHLETS

ABBOT, WILLIS J., BENT, SILAS, and KOENIGSBERG, MOSES, *The Press: Its Responsibility in International Relations* (Foreign Policy Association, New York, 1928).

ALLARD, PAUL, *Les Dessous de la Guerre* (Paris, 1932). *See also* BERGER, MARCEL.

AMICUCCI, ERMANNO, *Le Contrat de Travail des Journalistes* (Rome, 1929).

ANGELL, NORMAN, *The Public Mind* (New York, 1927).

ANONYMOUS, *Annuaire de la Presse, Française et Étrangère* (Paris, annual).

——, *Annuaire Orange* (Paris, annual).

——, *Annuario della Stampa Italiana* (Rome, annual).

——, *Arms and the Men,* by the Editors of *Fortune* (Garden City, N. Y., 1934).

——, *Associated Press Handbook* (New York, periodically).

——, *Ayer's Newspaper Directory* (Philadelphia, annual).

——, *Conditions of Work and Life of Journalists* (International Labor Office, Geneva, 1928).

——, *Conference of Press Experts, Geneva* (League of Nations, Geneva, 1927).

——, *Conference of Press Experts: Final Report.* Conf. E.P. 13. 1927 (League of Nations, Geneva, 1927).

——, *Conference on the Press* (Princeton University, Princeton, N. J., 1930).

——, *Congressional Directory.* Issued for each Session of Congress (Washington).

———, *Coöperation of the Press in the Organization of Peace.* League Document No. A. 31, 1932. (League of Nations, Geneva, 1932).

———, *Documents Relating to the Preparation of the Press Experts Committee.* League of Nations publication C. 399.M.140. 1926 (Geneva, 1926).

———, *Editor and Publisher International Year Book* (New York, annual).

———, *Encyclopædia Britannica* (London and New York).

———, *Europa.* 2 vols. Encyclopædia (London).

———, *50 Jahre Ullstein. 1877-1927* (Berlin, 1927).

———, *A Guide for Foreign Correspondents: Practices and Principles in the Collection and Dissemination of AP News Dispatches*—pamphlet (New York, 1932, approximately).

———, *Handbuch der Weltpresse* (Berlin).

———, *The History of The Times: "The Thunderer" in the Making, 1785-1841* (London and New York, 1935).

———, *I Accuse (J'Accuse)*, by a German. Trans. by Alexander Grey (New York, 1915).

———, *Journalism: By Some Masters of the Craft* (London, 1932).

———, *The League of Nations and the Press,* pamphlet (Geneva, 1928).

———, *Life and Writings of James Gordon Bennett* (New York, 1844).

———, *Un Livre Noir: Diplomatie d'avant-guerre d'aprés les documents des archives Russes, Novembre 1910-Juillet 1914* (Paris, 1924).

———, *"M. E. S." His Book.* A Tribute and a Souvenir of the twenty-five years, 1893-1918, of the service of Melville E. Stone as General Manager of the Associated Press (New York, 1918).

———, *Modern Journalism, a Guide for Beginners,* by a London Editor (London, 1909).

———, *National Conference on Social Work.* 1923 (Chicago, 1923).

———, *News, Its Scope and Limitations.* University of Missouri Bulletin, V. 30. No. 46. Journalism Series. No. 57. 1929 (Columbia, Mo., 1929).

———, *Not to Be Repeated: Merry-Go-Round of Europe* (New York, 1932).

———, *A Parliament of the Press: The First Imperial Press Conference. 1909* (London, 1909).

———, *Peace Year Book* (London, annual).

———, *Political Handbook of the World.* Council on Foreign Relations. Walter H. Mallory, ed. (New York, annual).

———, *Present Activities of the Secretariat.* League of Nations Document No. A.21. 1932 (Geneva, 1932).

———, *Principles and Instructions of the Foreign Service of the Chicago Daily News,* pamphlet (Chicago, 1930, approximately).

———, *Projet de Loi. Budget Général de L'Exercice 1933, Vol. I, Affaires étrangères* (Paris, 1932).

———, *The Secret International: Armament Firms at Work* (London, 1932).

———, *Swede*n. Published for the International Press Exhibition Pressa. Cologne, 1928 (Stockholm, 1928).

———, *Der Verlag Ullstein zum Welt Reklame Kongress. Berlin, 1929.* Published for World Advertising Convention in Berlin (Berlin, 1929).

———, *The W-G-N* (Chicago, 1922).

———, *Washington Merry-Go-Round* (New York, 1931).

———, *Who's Who in Press, Publicity, Printing* (London, annual).

———, *Willing's Press Guide* (London, annual).

ARNOLD, MATTHEW, *Friendship's Garland* (London, 1871).

ATKINS, J. B., *The Life of Sir William Howard Russell*, 2 vols. (London, 1911).

B., H. A., *About Newspapers: Chiefly English and Scottish* (Edinburgh, 1888).

BAEHR, HARRY, JR., *The New York Tribune Since the Civil War*, Illus. (New York, 1936).

BAGEHOT, WALTER, *Literary Studies*, 3 vols. (London, 1905).

BARRETT, J. W., *The World, The Flesh, and Messrs. Pulitzer* (New York, 1931).

BATES, ERNEST SUTHERLAND (with OLIVER CARLSON), *Hearst, Lord of San Simeon* (New York, 1936).

BEALS, CARLETON, *Banana Gold*, Philadelphia, 1932.

BEAUFORT, J. M. DE, *Behind the German Veil* (London, 1917).

BELL, E. P., *The British Censorship* (London, 1916).

BEMAN, LAMAR T. (editor), *Seected Articles on Censorship of Speech and the Press* (New York, 1930).

BENT, SILAS, *Ballyhoo: The Voice of the Press* (New York, 1927).

———, *Strange Bedfellows* (New York, 1928). See also ABBOT, WILLIS J.. BENT and KOENIGSBERG.

BERGER, MARCEL, and ALLARD, PAUL, *Les Secrets de la Censure pendent la Guerre* (Paris, 1932).

BERNAYS, E. L., *Crystallizing Public Opinion* (New York, 1923).

BERNAYS, ROBERT, *Special Correspondent* (London, 1934).

BERNHARDT, LUDWIG, *Der Hugenberg-Konzern* (Berlin, 1928).

BILLY, ANDRÉ, *Le Monde des Journaux: Tableau de la Presse. Francaise Contemporaine* (Paris, 1924).

BLACKETT, SIR BASIL, *Empire Communications and the Empire Press*, pamphlet (London, 1930).

BLEYER, W. G., *Main Currents in the History of American Journalism* (Boston, 1927).

———, (editor), *The Profession of Journalism* (Boston, 1918).

BLOWITZ, HENRI DE, *Memoirs of M. de Blowitz* (New York, 1903).

BLUMENFELD, R. D., *The Press in My Time* (London, 1933).

———, *R. D. B.'s Procession* (New York, 1935).

BOK, EDWARD W., *The Americanization of Edward Bok* (New York, 1921).

BOURNE, H. R. FOX, *English Newspapers*, 2 vols. (London, 1887).

BOWMAN, W. D., *The Story of "The Times"* (New York, 1931).

BRINCKMEYER, DR. HERMANN, *Hugo Stinnes* (Munich, 1921).

BRITTON, ROSWELL S., *The Chinese Periodical Press, 1802-1912* (Shanghai, 1933).

BROWN, CONSTANTINE. See PEARSON, DREW.

BROWN, F. J., *The Cable and Wireless Communications of the World*, 2nd rev. ed. (London, 1930).

BULLARD, F. L., *Famous War Correspondents* (Boston and London, 1914).

BÜLOW, PRINCE VON, *Memoirs, 1903-1909* (New York and London, 1931).

BURLEIGH, BENNET, *Empire of the East: or Japan and Russia at War, 1904-5* (London, 1905).

————, *The Natal Campaign* (London, 1900).

BURNS, C. DELISLE, *International Politics* (London, 1920).

BUSCH, MORITZ, *Bismarck: Some Secret Pages of His History*, 3 vols. (London, 1898).

BUSSEY, H. F., *Sixty Years of Journalism* (Bristol, 1906).

CARLSON, OLIVER (with ERNEST SUTHERLAND BATES), *Hearst, Lord of San Simeon* (New York, 1936).

CARR, C. F., and STEVENS, F. E., *Modern Journalism* (London, 1931).

CARSON, W. E., *Northcliffe, Britain's Man of Power* (New York, 1918).

CASEY, R. D. See LASSWELL, H. D.

CHAMBERLIN, W. H., *Russia's Iron Age* (Boston, 1934).

————, *Soviet Russia*, rev. ed. (New York, 1931).

CHAMBERS, JULIUS, *News Hunting on Three Continents* (New York, 1921).

CHAO, THOMAS MING-HENG, *The Foreign Press in China*. China Institute of Pacific Relations (Shanghai, 1931).

CHAPLIN, W. W., *Blood and Ink* (Harrisburg, Pa., 1936).

CHASE, STUART, and SCHLINK, F. J., *Your Money's Worth* (New York, 1927).

CHILDS, H. L. (editor), *Propaganda and Dictatorship*. A collection of papers (Princeton, 1936).

CHURCHILL, WINSTON, *My Early Life: A Rowing Commission* (London,, 1930).

CLARK, KEITH, *International Communications: the American Attitude* (New York, 1931).

CLARKE, JOSEPH I. C., *My Life and Memories* (New York, 1925).

CLARKE, TOM, *My Northcliffe Diary* (New York, 1931).

CLOSE, UPTON (JOSEF WASHINGTON HALL), *The Revolt of Asia* (New York and London, 1927).

COCHRANE, N. D., *E. W. Scripps* (New York, 1933).

COLLINS, HENRY M., *From Pigeon Post to Wireless* (London, 1925).

COOK, SIR EDWARD T., *Delane of The Times* (New York, 1916).

————, *The Press in War-Time* (London, 1920).

COOPER, C. A., *An Editor's Retrospect of Fifty Years of Newspaper Work* (London, 1896).

COOPER, KENT, *The Associated Press: An Address*, pamphlet (New York, 1925).

————, *The Associated Press: An Address*, pamphlet (New York, 1926).

CORTISSOZ, ROYAL, *The Life of Whitelaw Reid*, 2 vols. (New York, 1921).

————, *The New York Tribune: Incidents and Personalities in Its History* (New York, 1923).

CRAWFORD, N. A., *The Ethics of the Press* (New York, 1924).

CREEL, GEORGE, *How We Advertised America* (New York, 1920).

CREELMAN, JAMES, *On the Great Highway* (London and New York, 1901).

CROCKETT, A. S., *When James Gordon Bennett was Caliph of Bagdad* (New York, 1926).

CROKER, J. W., *The Croker Papers. The Correspondence and Diaries of the late Right Honorable John Wilson Croker, LL.D., F.R.S., Secretary to the Admiralty, from 1809 to 1830.* Edited by Louis J. Jennings. 3 vols. Second ed. rev. (London, 1885).

DARRAH, DAVID, *Hail Caesar!* (Boston, 1936).

DASENT, A. I., *John Thaddeus Delane: Editor of "The Times,"* 2 vols. (London, 1908).

DAVIES, B. N. L., *Democracy and the Press* (Manchester, 1919).

DAVIS, C. B., *Adventures and Letters of Richard Harding Davis* (New York, 1918).

DAVIS, ELMER, *History of the New York Times, 1851-1921* (New York, 1921).

DAVIS, O. K., *Released for Publication* (Boston and New York, 1925).

DAVIS, R. H., *The Cuban-Porto Rican Campaign* (London, 1899).

———, *A Year From a Correspondent's Note-Book* (New York and London, 1898).

DELAISI, FRANCIS, *La Patriotisme des Plaques Blindes,* pamphlet (Paris, 1913).

DEMARTIAL, GEORGES, *La Guerre de 1914: Comment on Mobilisa les Consciences* (Paris, 1922).

DENNIS, CHARLES H., *Victor Lawson: His Time and His Work* (Chicago, 1935).

DICKINSON, G. LOWES, *The International Anarchy, 1904-1914* (London, 1926).

DILLON, ÉMILE J., *Leaves from Life* (London, 1932).

———, *The Peace Conference* (London, 1919).

DILNOT, FRANK, *The Adventures of a Newspaper Man* (London, 1913).

DONALD, ROBERT (editor), *The Imperial Press Conference in Canada, 1920* (London, 1921).

DOOB, L. W., *Propaganda: Its Psychology and Technique* (New York, 1935).

DOSCH-FLEUROT, ARNO, *Through War to Revolution* (London, 1931).

DOWNEY, FAIRFAX, *Richard Harding Davis: His Day* (New York, 1933).

DRESLER, ADOLPH, *Geschichte der Italienischen Presse,* 2 vols. (Munich and Berlin, 1933 and 1934).

DUGGAN, STEPHEN, *Latin America,* World Peace Foundation Booklet (Boston and New York, 1936).

DUNLAP, ORRIN E., JR., *Marconi: The Man and His Wireless* (New York, 1937).

DURANTY, WALTER, *I Write as I Please* (New York, 1935).

———, *Russia Reported, 1921-1933* (London and New York, 1934).

ESCOTT, T. H. S., *Masters of English Journalism* (London, 1911).

ESSARY, J. F., *Covering Washington* (Boston, 1927).

FARRER, J. A., *England Under Edward VII* (London, 1922).

FARSON, NEGLEY, *The Way of a Transgressor* (London, 1935; New York, 1936).

Fay, Bernard, *Notes on the American Press at the End of the Eighteenth Century* (New York, 1927).

——, *The Revolutionary Spirit in France and America* (L'Esprit Revolutionnaire), Trans. by Ramon Guthrie (London, 1928).

Fay, S. B., *Origins of the War*, 2 vols. (New York, 1929).

Fenn, G. M., *George Alfred Henty* (London, 1907).

Field, Cyrus W., *Cyrus W. Field, His Life and Work*. Edited by Isabella Field Judson (New York, 1896).

Fine, Barnett, *A Giant of the Press* (New York, 1933).

Fish, C. R., *American Diplomacy* (New York, 1923).

Flint, L. N., *Conscience of the Newspaper* (New York, 1925).

Forbes, Archibald, *Memories and Studies of War and Peace* (London, 1895).

——, *My Experiences of the War Between France and Germany*, 2 vols. (London, 1871).

——, *Souvenirs of Some Continents* (London, 1885).

——, *The War Correspondence of the Daily News, 1870* (London, 1871).

——, *The War Correspondence of the Daily News, 1877-1878* (London, 1878).

Forrest, Wilbur, *Behind the Front Page* (New York, 1934).

Fortescue, Granville, *Front Line and Deadline* (New York, 1937).

Francis, J. C., *Notes by the Way*. With Memoirs of Joseph Knight, F.S.A. (London, 1909).

Franklin, Benjamin, *The Autobiography of Benjamin Franklin*. New ed., with introd. and notes and suggestions by William N. Otto (Boston, 1928).

Funck-Brentano, Franz, *Les Nouvellistes* (Paris, 1905).

Fyfe, Hamilton, *Northcliffe: an Intimate Biography* (New York, 1930).

Gardner, Gilson, *Lusty Scripps* (New York, 1932).

Gauvreau, Emile, *Hot News* (New York, 1931).

Gibbs, Philip, *Adventures in Journalism* (New York, 1923).

——, *More That Can Be Told*. Published in London as *Since Then* (New York and London, 1930).

——, *Now It Can Be Told*. Published in London as *Realities of War* (London and New York, 1920).

Gilman, La Selle, *Shanghai Deadline*. A novel (New York, 1936).

Gobright, Lawrence A., *Recollection of Men and Things at Washington* (New York, 1869).

Gollán, José S., *A Modern Argentine Newspaper*. (La Prensa.) Literature Series, No. 1. Pan-American Union, Washington (Washington, 1930).

Grant, James, *The Newspaper Press*, 3 vols. (London, 1871-1872).

Graves, W. B. (editor), *Readings in Public Opinion* (New York, 1928).

Greenwall, Harry J., *Round the World for News* (London, 1936).

——, *Scoops: Being Leaves from the Diary of a Special Correspondent* (London, 1923).

Griffith, Capt. Glyn. See Worsley, Com. Frank.

Grogan, Lady Ellinore, *The Life of J. D. Bourchier* (London, 1926).

Gross, Gerald C. See Herring, James M.

GROTH, OTTO, *Die Zeitung, ein System der Zeitungskunde.* 3 vols. (Mannheim, Berlin and Leipzig, 1928).

GUNTHER, JOHN, *Inside Europe* (London and New York, 1936).

HAMMANN, OTTO, *The World Policy of Germany. 1890-1912.* Trans. by Maude A. Huttmann (London, 1927).

HANAZANO, KANESADA, *The Development of Japanese Journalism,* published by the Osaka *Mainichi* (Osaka, 1924).

HANOTAUX, GABRIEL, *History of the War.* (In Progress.) Paris, 1914 et seq.

HARLOW, ALVIN F., *Old Wires and New Waves* (New York, 1936).

HARRIS, N. D., *International Politics,* 2 vols. (Boston, 1926).

HATIN, EUGÈNE, *Histoire politique et littéraire de la Presse en France,* 8 vols. (Paris, 1859-1861).

HATTON, JOSEPH, *Journalistic London.* Being a series of sketches of the Famous Pens and Papers of the Day. Reprinted with additions from *Harper's Magazine* (London, 1882).

HAYWARD, F. H., and DAVIES, B. N. L., *Democracy and the Press.* (I.L.P. Library, Manchester, 1919).

HEATLEY, D. P., *Diplomacy and the Study of International Relations* (Oxford, 1919).

HEATON, J. L. (editor), *Cobb of "The World"* (London, 1924).

HEDIN, SVEN ANDERS, *With the German Armies in the West.* Authorized trans. from Swedish by H. G. de Walterstorff (London, 1915).

HENNING, A. S., *Government Propaganda,* pamphlet (Chicago, 1927).

HERRING, JAMES M. (with GROSS, GERALD C.) *Telecommunications: Economics and Regulations* (New York and London, 1936).

HIRST, F. W., *The Six Panics, and other essays* (London, 1913).

HOBOHM, MARTIN, and ROHRBACH, PAUL, *Chauvinismus und Weltkrieg,* 2 vols. (Berlin, 1918-1919).

HOBSON, J. A., *Imperialism: A Study* (London, 1902).

——, *The Psychology of Jingoism* (London, 1901).

HODGES, CHARLES, *The Background of International Relations* (New York, 1931).

HOWARD-ELLIS, C., *The Origin, Structure and Working of the League of Nations* (London, 1928).

HUBBARD, H. P., *Hubbard's Newspaper Press Directory of the World.* No longer published (New Haven).

HUBBARD, WYNANT DAVIS, *Fiasco in Ethiopia* (New York, 1936).

HUDSON, FREDERIC, *Journalism in the United States* (New York, 1873).

HUNT, F. K., *The Fourth Estate,* 2 vols. (London, 1850).

HUNT, WILLIAM, *Then and Now: Fifty Years of Newspaper Work* (Hull, 1887).

IRWIN, WILL, *Propaganda and the News* (New York, 1936).

ISVOLSKI, ALEXANDER, *Der Diplomatische Schriftwechsel Isvolsklis 1911-1914, herausgegeben von Frederich Stieve,* 4 vols. (Berlin, 1924).

——, *Memoirs of Alexander Isvolski.* Ed. and trans. by C. L. Seeger (London, 1920).

JAMES, LIONEL, *High Pressure* (London, 1929).

——, *Times of Stress* (London, 1929).

JOHNSON, T. M., *Without Censor* (Indianapolis, 1928).

JONES, KENNEDY, *Fleet Street and Downing Street* (London, 1920).

JONES, SIR RODERICK, *International Conference on the Press*, pamphlet (London, 1927).

——, *Reuters*, pamphlet (Chatham, 1928).

KALLET, ARTHUR and SCHLINK, F. J., *100,000,000 Guinea Pigs: Dangers in Everyday Food, Drugs, and Cosmetics* (New York, 1933).

KAWABÉ, K., *Press and Politics in Japan* (Chicago, 1921).

KINGLAKE, A. W., *Invasion of Crimea*, sixth ed., 9 vols. (London, 1877-1888).

KITCHIN, F. H., *Moberly-Bell and His Times* (London, 1925).

KNICKERBOCKER, H. R., *The Red Trade Menace*. Published in London as *The Soviet Five-Year Plan and Its Effect on World Trade*, and *Soviet Trade and World Depression* (New York and London, 1931).

KOENIGSBERG, MOSES. See ABBOT, WILLIS J., BENT and KOENIGSBERG.

LABOUCHERE, HENRY, *Diary of a Besieged Resident in Paris*, by H. L., 3rd ed. (London, 1872).

LASKI, HAROLD J., *A Grammar of Politics*, 2nd ed. (New Haven, 1931).

LASSWELL, H. D., *Propaganda Technique in the World War* (New York, 1927).

——, CASEY, R. D. and SMITH, B. L., *Propaganda and Promotional Activities: an Annotated Bibliography* (Minneapolis, 1935).

LAUZANNE, STÉPHANE, *Sa Majesté de la Presse* (Paris, 1925).

LAWRENCE, RAYMOND D. See YOUNG, KIMBALL.

LAWRENCE, T. E., *Revolt in the Desert* (London and New York, 1927).

——, *The Seven Pillars of Wisdom* (New York and London, 1935).

LEE, IVY L., *Publicity: Some of the Things It Is and Is Not*. Collection of Addresses (New York, 1935).

LEGIGAN, EUGÈNE, *L'Agence Havas*, pamphlet (Paris, 1929).

LEHMANN-RUSSBULDT, OTTO, *War for Profits* (Hamburg, 1929; New York, 1930).

LIN YUTANG, *History of the Press and Public Opinion in China* (Chicago, 1936).

LIPPMANN, WALTER, *Liberty and the News* (New York, 1920).

——, *Public Opinion* (New York, 1922).

LIVINGSTONE, DAVID, *Life and Finding of Dr. Livingstone* (London, 1897).

LORD, C. S., *The Young Man and Journalism* (New York, 1922).

LOWE, CHARLES, *Prince Bismarck*. New ed. (London, 1898).

——, *The Tale of a "Times" Correspondent* (London, 1927).

LUDWIG, EMIL, *Bismarck* (London and New York, 1927).

LUMLEY, F. E., *The Propaganda Menace* (New York and London, 1933).

LUNDBERG, FERDINAND, *Imperial Hearst, A Social Biography* (New York, 1936).

LYONS, EUGENE, *Moscow Carrousel* (New York, 1935).

——, (editor), *We Cover the World*, by fifteen foreign correspondents (New York, 1937).

MACGAHAN, J. A., *Campaigning on the Oxus, and the Fall of Khiva*, 4th ed. (London, 1876).

————, *The Turkish Atrocities in Bulgaria*. Letters of the Special Commissioner of the *Daily News*, J. A. MacGahan (London, 1876).

————, *Under the Northern Lights* (London, 1876).

————, *The War Correspondence of the "Daily News," 1877-1878*, including the Letters of J. A. MacGahan (London, 1878).

MACKENZIE, F. A., *Beaverbrook: An Authentic Biography* (London, 1931).

————, *The Mystery of the Daily Mail, 1896-1921* (London, 1921).

MAKOWER, S. V., *Notes upon the History of "The Times," 1785-1904* (Edinburgh, 1904).

MALLORY, WALTER H. (editor), *Political Handbook of the World*. Council on Foreign Relations (New York, annual).

MARCOSSON, ISAAC F., *Adventures in Interviewing* (New York, 1919).

MARTIN, KINGSLEY, *The Triumph of Lord Palmerston* (London, 1924).

MASSART, J., *The Secret Press in Belgium* (London, 1918).

MCCARTHY, JUSTIN and ROBINSON, SIR JOHN R., *The "Daily News" Jubilee* (London, 1896).

MCCLURE, S. S., *My Autobiography* (New York, 1914).

MCKENZIE, VERNON (editor), *Behind the Headlines* (New York, 1931).

MCRAE, M. A., *Forty Years of Newspaperdom* (New York, 1924).

METTERNICH, PRINCE, *Memoirs of Prince Metternich*, 3 vols. Edited by Prince Metternich; the Papers classified and arranged by M. A. de Klinkowstrom. Trans. by Mrs. Alexander Napier (London, 1880-82).

MICHAEL, GEORGE, *Handout* (New York, 1935).

MILLER, JOHN C., *Sam Adams: Pioneer In Propaganda* (Boston, 1936).

MILLER, WEBB, *I Found No Peace* (New York, 1936).

MILLIS, WALTER, *The Road to War: America 1914-1917* (Boston and New York, 1935).

MILLS, J. SAXON, *The Press and Communications of Empire*. A Survey based upon the Reports and Addresses at the Imperial Press Conference 1920. The British Empire: A Survey. Vol. 6 (London, 1924).

MOBERLY BELL, E. H. C., *Life and Letters of C. F. Moberly Bell* (London, 1927).

MOON, P. T. (editor), *Syllabus on International Relations* (New York, 1925).

MUHSAM, KURT, *Wie Wir Belogen Wurden. Die Amtliche Irrefuhrung des Deutschen Volkes* (Berlin, 1919).

MURPHY, L. W. (editor), *An Introduction to Journalism* (New York, 1930).

NAPIER, W. F. P., *History of the War in the Peninsula and in the South of France from 1807 to 1814*. New rev. ed., 6 vols. (London, 1851).

NEVINS, ALLAN, *The Evening Post: A Century of Journalism* (New York, 1922).

NEVINSON, H. W., *Changes and Chances* (London, 1923).

————, *Fire of Life* (London, 1936).

————, *Last Changes, Last Chances* (London, 1928).

————, *More Changes, More Chances* (London, 1925).

NICOLSON, HAROLD, *Peacemaking. 1919* (Boston and New York, 1933).

NIPPOLD, OTFRIED, *Der Deutsche Chauvinismus*. Trans. to French, *Le Chauvinisme Allemand* (Berlin, 1913; Paris, 1917). New ed. augmented (Paris, 1921).

NOMA, SEIJI, *Noma of Japan* (New York, 1934).

NORTH, S. N. D., *History of the Periodical Press of the U. S. A.* House of Representatives, 47th Congress, 2nd Session. Miscellaneous Doc. 42, Part 8, Dept. of Interior. Census Office. Census of 1880 (Washington).

NORTON, H. K., *The Coming of South America* (New York, 1932).

O'BRIEN, F. M., *The Story of the Sun* (New York, 1918). Rev. ed. 1928.

ODEGARD, PETER H., *Pressure Politics; The Story of the Anti-Saloon League* (New York, 1928).

O'DONOVAN, EDMOND, *The Merv Oasis. Travels and Adventures East of the Caspian, during the years 1879, 1880-1881,* 2 vols. (London, 1882).

OGDEN, ROLLO, *Life and Letters of Edwin Lawrence Godkin,* 2 vols. (New York, 1907).

OHTA, M., *Society and the Newspaper,* pamphlet (Tokyo, 1923).

O'MALLEY, I. B., *Florence Nightingale, 1820-1856* (London, 1931).

ORTEGA Y GASSET, JOSÉ, *The Revolt of the Masses.* Translated from Spanish, *La Rebelion de las Masas* (New York, 1932).

OWEN, RUSSELL, *South of the Sun* (New York, 1934).

PAINE, R. D., *Roads of Adventure* (Boston, 1922).

PALMER, FREDERICK, *America in France: The Story of the Making of an Army* (London, 1919).

——, *Going to War in Greece* (New York, 1897).

——, *My Year of the War* (London, 1915).

——, *Our Greatest Battle: The Meuse-Argonne* (New York, 1919).

——, *With Kuroki in Manchuria* (New York, 1904).

——, *With My Own Eyes* (Indianapolis, 1933).

——, *With the New Army on the Somme: My Second Year of the War* (London, 1917).

PAYNE, G. H., *History of Journalism in the United States* (New York, 1920).

PEARSON, DREW and BROWN, CONSTANTINE, *The American Diplomatic Game* (New York, 1935).

PEMBERTON, MAX, *Lord Northcliffe: A Memoir* (London, 1922).

PÉRIVIER, A., *Napoleon Journaliste* (Paris, 1918).

PHILLIPS, MARY C., *Skin Deep: The Truth about Beauty Aids* (New York, 1934).

PLAYNE, C. E., *The Neuroses of the Nations* (London, 1925).

——, *The Pre-War Mind in Britain: An Historical Review* (London, 1928).

PONSONBY, ARTHUR, *Falsehood in War-Time* (New York, 1928).

PORRITT, A. (editor), *The Causes of War* (London and New York, 1932).

PRICE, PRISCILLA, *The Life of Sir Henry Morton Stanley* (London, 1930).

PRINGLE, HENRY F., *Big Frogs* (New York, 1928).

RALPH, JULIAN, *The Making of a Journalist* (New York, 1903).

RANSOME, ARTHUR, *The Crisis in Russia* (New York, 1921).

RICHARDSON, J. HALL, *From the City to Fleet Street* (London, 1927).

RIDDELL, LORD, *War Diary,* published in New York as *Lord Riddell's War Diary* (New York, 1934; London, 1935).

RIEGEL, O. W., *Mobilizing for Chaos: The Story of the New Propaganda* (New Haven, 1934).

ROBINSON, HENRY CRABB, *Diary, Reminiscences, and Correspondence of Henry Crabb Robinson, F.S.A., Barrister-at-law.* Selected and edited by Thomas Sadler, Ph.D., 3 vols. (London, 1869), 3rd ed. and corrections and additions, London, 1872.

ROBINSON, SIR JOHN, *Fifty Years of Fleet Street* (London, 1904). See MCCARTHY, JUSTIN.

ROBINSON, SOLON, *Hot Corn: Life Scenes in New York,* illustrated (New York, 1854).

ROGERS, JASON, *Newspaper Building* (New York, 1918).

ROHRBACH, PAUL. See HOBOLM, MARTIN.

RORTY, JAMES, *Our Master's Voice: Advertising* (New York, 1934).

ROSEWATER, VICTOR, *The History of Coöperative News-Gathering in the United States* (New York, 1930).

RUE, LARRY, *I Fly for News* (New York, 1932).

RUSSELL, W. H., *The British Expedition to the Crimea,* rev. ed. (London, 1858).

———, *The War* (London, 1855).

SALMON, L. M., *The Newspaper and Authority* (New York, 1923).

———, *The Newspaper and the Historian* (New York, 1923).

SALOMON, LUDWIG, *Geschichte des deutschen Zeitungswesens,* 3 vols.; V. 1, Oldenburg, 1900; V. 2, Ebenda, 1902; V. 3, Ebenda, 1906.

SAUERWEIN, JULES, *Que va faire l'Amérique?* (Paris, 1932).

SCHANZ, DR. JOACHIM, *Die Entstehung eines Deutschen_Presse-Gros Verlages* (Berlin, 1933).

SCHLINK, F. J. See CHASE, STUART.

———, See KALLET, ARTHUR.

SCHMITT, B. E., *The Coming of the War, 1914,* 2 vols. (New York and London, 1930).

SCHREINER, G. A., *Cables and Wireless, and Their Rôle in the Foreign Relations of the United States* (Boston, 1924).

SCOTT, J. F., *Five Weeks; The Surge of Public Opinion on the Eve of the Great War* (New York, 1927).

SCUDMORE, F. A., *A Sheaf of Memories* (London, 1925).

SEITZ, DON C., *Horace Greeley: Founder of the New York Tribune* (Indianapolis, 1926).

———, *The James Gordon Bennetts, Father and Son* (Indianapolis, 1928).

———, *Joseph Pulitzer: His Life and Letters* (New York, 1924).

SELDES, GEORGE, *Can These Things Be!* (New York, 1931).

———, *Freedom of the Press* (New York, 1935).

———, *Sawdust Caesar* (New York, 1935).

———, *You Can't Print That!* (New York, 1929).

SHAABER, M. A., *Some Forerunners of the Newspaper in England, 1476-1622* (Philadelphia, 1929).

SHARP, E. W., *International News Communications.* Univ. of Missouri Bulletin, V. 28, No. 3. V. No. 45, Journalism Series (Columbia, Missouri, 1927).

SHEEAN, VINCENT, *Personal History,* published in London as *In Search of History* (New York and London, 1935).

SIMONIS, H., *The Street of Ink* (London, 1917).

SIMPSON, J. P., *Pictures from Revolutionary Paris*. Sketched during the first phase of the Revolution of 1848 (Edinburgh and London, 1848).

SINCLAIR, UPTON, *The Brass Check* (Pasadena, Calif., 1920).

SLOCOMBE, GEORGE, *The Tumult and the Shouting* (New York, 1936).

SMALLEY, S. W., *Anglo-American Memories* (London, 1911).

SMITH, B. L. See LASSWELL, H. D.

SMITH, HENRY J., *It's the Way It's Written,* pamphlet (Chicago, 1921).

SMYTH, A. H., *The Writings of Benjamin Franklin* (London and New York, 1907).

SPENDER, J. A., *Life, Journalism and Politics,* 2 vols. (London, 1927).

——, *The Public Life,* 2 vols. (London, 1925).

SQUIRES, J. D., *British Propaganda at Home and in the United States from 1914 to 1917* (Cambridge, Mass., 1935).

STANLEY, DOROTHY (editor), *The Autobiography of Sir Henry Morton Stanley, G.C.B.* (London, 1909).

STANLEY, H. M., *Through the Dark Continent.* New ed., 2 vols. (London, 1899).

STEED, H. WICKHAM, *Through Thirty Years,* 2 vols. (London, 1924).

STEER, GEORGE, *Caesar In Abyssinia* (Boston, 1937).

STILLMAN, W. J., *The Autobiography of a Journalist,* 2 vols. (London, 1901).

STOCQUELER, J. H., *The Life of Field Marshal the Duke of Wellington,* 2 vols. (London, 1852).

STODDARD, LOTHROP, *The Rising Tide of Color Against White World-Supremacy* (London and New York, 1920).

STONE, M. E., *Fifty Years a Journalist* (New York, 1921).

STUART, SIR CAMPBELL, *Secrets of Crewe House* (London, 1920).

SUGIMURA, SOJINKWAN K., *Random Thoughts on Journalism* (Tokyo, 1927).

SYMON, J. D., *The Press and Its Story* (London, 1914).

TARBELL, IDA M., *A Reporter for Lincoln* (New York, 1927).

TEMPERLEY, HAROLD, *The Foreign Policy of Canning. 1822-1827* (London, 1925).

THIMME, HANS, *Weltkrieg ohne Waffen* (Stuttgart, 1932).

THOMAS, W. B., *A Traveller in News* (London, 1925).

THOROLD, ALGAR LABOUCHERE, *The Life of Henry Labouchere* (London, 1913).

TOPLIFF, SAMUEL, *Topliff's Travels,* with a Memoir by Ethel Stanwood Bolton (Boston, 1906).

TRIBOLET, L. B., *The International Aspects of Electrical Communications in the Pacific Area* (New York and London, 1929).

TURNER, H. E. (editor), *The Fourth Imperial Press Conference. 1930* (London, 1930).

——, *The Imperial Press Conference in Australia, 1925* (London, 1927).

TURNER, TIMOTHY G., *Bullets, Bottles and Gardenias* (South-West Press, Dallas, Texas, 1935).

VAUGHN, MILES W., *Covering the Far East* (New York, 1936).

VIERECK, G. S., *Spreading Germs of Hate* (New York, 1930).

VILLARD, HENRY, *Memoirs of Henry Villard,* 2 vols. (London and Cambridge, Mass., 1904).

VILLARD, O. G., *The Press Today* (New York, 1930).

————. *Some Newspapers and Newspapermen* (New York, 1923).

VILLIERS, FREDERIC, *Villiers: His Five Decades of Adventure,* 2 vols. (New York and London, 1920).

WARREN, LOW, *Journalism from A. to Z.* New and rev. ed. (London, 1931).

WASHBURN, STANLEY, *The Cable Game* (Boston, 1912).

WATSON, ELMO SCOTT, *A History of Newspaper Syndicates in the United States—1865-1935* (*Publishers' Auxiliary* publication, Chicago, 1936).

WEBSTER, C. K., *The Foreign Policy of Castlereagh. 1812-1815* (London, 1931).

WHITAKER, JOHN T., *And Fear Came* (New York, 1936).

WHYTE, FREDERIC, *The Life of W. T. Stead,* 2 vols. (Boston and London, 1925).

WIGHT, J., *Mornings at Bow Street* (London, 1875).

WILDES, H. E., *Social Currents in Japan* (Chicago, 1925).

WILLEY, M. M. and RICE, S. A., *Communication Agencies and Social Life.* Part of study of "Recent Social Trends in the United States" (New York and London, 1933).

WILLIAMS, WALTER (editor), *The Press Congress of the World in Switzerland* (Columbia, Missouri, 1928).

————, *Some Observations on the German Press,* University of Missouri Bulletin. V. 33. No. 32. Journalism Series No. 67, Nov. 10, 1932 (Columbia, Missouri, 1932).

WILLIAMS, WYTHE, *Dusk of Empire* (New York, 1937).

WILSON, R. M., *Lord Northcliffe: A Study* (Philadelphia, 1927).

WINKLER, J. K., *W. R. Hearst: An American Phenomenon* (New York, 1928).

WOODHEAD, H. G. W., *Adventures in Far Eastern Journalism* (Hokuseida Press, Tokyo, 1935). Japanese edition of *A Journalist in China* (London, 1934).

WOODWARD, J. L., *Foreign News in American Morning Newspapers* (New York, 1930).

WORSLEY, COM. FRANK and GRIFFITH, CAPT. GLYN, *The Romance of Lloyds: From Coffee House to Palace* (London, 1932).

WYNTER, ANDREW, *Our Social Bees* (London, 1863).

YOUNG, KIMBALL and LAWRENCE, RAYMOND D., *Bibliography on Censorship and Propaganda.* University of Oregon Publication. Journalism Series. V. 1, No. 1, March, 1928 (Eugene, Oregon, 1928).

ZIMMERN, ALFRED, *Learning and Leadership* (London, 1928).

II

NEWSPAPERS AND PERIODICALS

AMERICAN HISTORICAL REVIEW (New York)
AMERICAN JOURNAL OF SOCIOLOGY (Chicago)
AMERICAN MAGAZINE (New York)
AMERICAN MERCURY (New York)
AMERICAN POLITICAL SCIENCE REVIEW (Philadelphia)
AMERICAN PRESS (New York)
ANNALS OF THE AMERICAN ACADEMY OF POLITICAL AND SOCIAL SCIENCE (Philadelphia)
ASIA (New York)
ATLANTIC MONTHLY (Boston)
BLACKWOOD'S MAGAZINE (Edinburgh)
BOOKMAN (New York)
BULLETIN OF THE PAN-AMERICAN UNION (Washington)
CHICAGO DAILY NEWS (Chicago)
CHICAGO TRIBUNE (Chicago)
CHRISTIAN SCIENCE MONITOR (Boston)
CIRCULATION. Publication of King Features (New York)
COLLIER'S WEEKLY (New York)
CONTEMPORARY REVIEW (London)
CURRENT HISTORY (New York)
DAILY EXPRESS (London)
EDINBURGH REVIEW. No longer pubished (Edinburgh)
EDITOR AND PUBLISHER (New York)
FOREIGN AFFAIRS (New York)
FOREIGN PRESS, THE, Bulletin Published by the Association of Foreign Correspondents in the United States (New York)
FORTUNE (Chicago)
FORUM (New York)
FRANKFURTER ZEITUNG (Frankfurt)
GRAPHIC, THE. No longer published (London)
HARPER'S MAGAZINE (New York)
INDEPENDENT. Merged with *Outlook* (New York)
JOURNAL OF THE INSTITUTE OF JOURNALISTS, THE (London)
JOURNALISM QUARTERLY (Iowa City, Iowa, and Minneapolis, Minn.)
LITERARY DIGEST (New York)
LITTLE TIMES, THE, house organ of the New York *Times* (New York)
LIVING AGE (New York)
MANCHESTER GUARDIAN (Manchester)
MANCHESTER GUARDIAN WEEKLY (Manchester)
NATION, THE (New York)
NATION AND ATHENÆUM. Merged with *New Statesman* and *Nation* (London)
NEW REPUBLIC (New York)
NEW STATESMAN AND NATION (London)

NEW YORK HERALD TRIBUNE (New York)
NEW YORK TIMES, THE (New York)
NEW YORK TIMES MAGAZINE, part of Sunday Edition (New York)
NINETEENTH CENTURY REVIEW (London)
NORTH AMERICAN REVIEW (New York)
OHIO NEWSPAPER, THE (Columbus)
OUTLOOK. Now *Outlook and Independent* (New York)
OUTLOOK AND INDEPENDENT (New York)
PUBLIC OPINION QUARTERLY (Princeton, New Jersey)
QUARTERLY REVIEW (London)
QUILL, THE, Organ of Sigma Delta Chi, men's national honorary journalistic
     fraternity (Chicago)
REVUE DES DEUX MONDES (Paris)
SATURDAY EVENING POST (Philadelphia)
SCRIBNER'S MAGAZINE (New York)
TEMPS, LE (Paris)
TIME MAGAZINE (Chicago)
TIMES, THE (London)
TRANS-PACIFIC (Tokyo)
TRIB, THE, house organ of the Chicago *Tribune* (Chicago)
UNITED SERVICE MAGAZINE, THE. No longer published (London)
VIRGINIA QUARTERLY REVIEW (University, Va.)
WISCONSIN ALUMNI MAGAZINE
WORLD'S PRESS NEWS (London)
WORLD'S WORK. Merged with *Review of Reviews* (New York)

INDEX

Great Western Telegraph Company, 180
Greece, 66, 71, 97, 229, 281, 282. *See also* Athens.
Greeley, Horace, 18
Greenley Island, 115 n
Greenwich Mean Time (GMT), Fig. 6
Grigg, Sir Edward, 163
Gringoire, Paris, 218, Fig. 25
Gruneisen, Charles Lewis, 14, 16, 20-21
Guam, 106, 123, 341
Gudok, Moscow, 279
Guidi, Angelo, 256 n
Guizot, Francois P. G., 15
Gustavus Adolphus, King of Sweden, 13

Hachette, 213
Hague, The, 71, 151
Hale, William Bayard, 158 n-159 n
Halifax, N. S., 17, 18, 62, 129
Hamburg, Germany, 13, 191, 233, 287, Fig. 30
Hamburger Fremdenblatt, 242, Fig. 30
Hamburger Nachrichten, 241 n, Fig. 30
Hamburger Tageblatt, 243
Hamilton, Canada, 338
Hammann, Otto, 158
"Handouts" (Communiqués), 164, 176, 222, 260, 320, 322, 358 n
Hands, Mr., 25 n
Hankow, 341
Hankow *Herald,* 348
Hanna, Mark, 308
Hanover, Germany, 247
Harbin, 341, 347, 358 n
Harbord, General James G., 125
Harbor news associations, 54, 62
Harding, Warren G., 311
Harmsworth, Alfred. *See* Northcliffe, Lord.
Harmsworth, Harold. *See* Rothermere, Lord.
Harte, Bret, 75
Havana, 274 n, 297, 335, Fig. 40. *See also* Cuba.
Havas, 57, 65, 73, 106, 117, 131, 193, 202, 207, 209, 213, 215, 216, 229, 233, 256, 264, 271 n, 277, 288, 294, 299, 324, 336. See also *Agence Havas.*
Havas, Auguste, 58
Havas, Charles, 11, 55, 59
Havasian service, 131. *See also* News by radio.

Havre, 287
Hawaii Hochi, Honolulu, Fig. 41
Hawaiian Islands, 106, 362, Fig. 41
Herald, Manila, 361
Hearst newspapers, 127, 135, 203, 225 n 266, 323, 367 n, 370, 373, Fig. 39
Hearst, William Randolph, 4, 65, 71, 300, 370
Hellenic Press Association, 71
Heliograph, 97
Helsingfors, 66, 77, 133, 293. *See also* Finland.
Helvetian wireless news service, 131. *See also* News by radio.
Hendaye, France, 290
Hennessy, Jean, 210, 217
Herriot, Edouard, 215
Heyburn, William Brinton, 308
Hicksville, Long Island, 137
Hindenburg, Paul von, 231
Hitler, Adolf, 167, 205, 226 n, 231, 236 n, 240, 242, 248
Hoare, Sir Samuel, 249
Hoaxes, 61
Hochi Shimbun, Tokyo, 350 n, 359
Holland. *See* Netherlands.
"Holy Alliance," 17
L'Homme Libre, Paris, 218, Fig. 25
Honduras, 71, 336
Hong Kong, 130, 345
Honolulu, 106, 119 n, 122, 123, 362, Fig. 41
Hoover, Herbert, 179 n, 308, 314, 317, 326 n
Horse express (or Pony express), 17. *See also* Communication.
House, Colonel E. M., 141 n
Huddleston, Sisley, 192 n-193 n
Hugenberg, Dr. Alfred, 236, 241, 374, Fig. 29
Hugenberg press, 226 n, 241
Hughes, Charles E., 311, 313
"Human interest" in news, 5, 9, 187, 266, 273, 278, 300, 310, 314, 315, 320, 333, 345
Humanité, L', Paris, 159 n, 215, Fig. 23
Hungary, 66, 207 n, 229, 281, 282, 286, Fig. 35

Iliffe, Lord, 373
Illiteracy, 337, 346
Illustration, L', Paris, 218

INDEX

421

Wilhelm II, Kaiser, 158 n-159 n, 161 n
Wilhelmstrasse (German Foreign office).
See Germany—government relations
with press.
William, King of Prussia, 101
Willington, Aaron Smith, 53, 54
Wilson, Woodrow, 109, 139, 141, 308,
310, 314
Winnipeg, 338
Wireless, 31, 35, 96, 102, 103, 104, 108,
113, 116, 119 n, 122, 123, 126, 127,
128, 132, 133, 179, 236, 245, 260,
325, 327, 341, 344, 352, 363, Figs. 12,
38; wireless telephony, 104, 105, 112,
114. See also Radio.
Wirtschaftsberatung der Provinzpresse
(WIRPO), 241 n
Witte, Count, 103
Wolff, Dr. Bernard, 233
Wolff'sche Telegraphen Buro (WTB),
60, 66, 68, 73, 131, 233, 241 n, 252 n,
Fig. 29
World affairs, 278, 353. See also Public
affairs.
World Almanac, 323
World Court, 371
World League of Press Associations, 38,
60, 65, 67, 68 n, 73, 193, 229, 256,
264, 266, 277, 287, 288, 298, 305, 338,
350, 359
World Press Congresses, 119 n
World trade and relation to cables, 33,
108

World War. See War correspondence—
Great War.
Writing the news, 75, 78, 94, 149, 189,
225, 283, 311-312, 320, 360. See also
News writing, News transmission.

Yale Review, New Haven, 323
Yap ("cable crossroads of the Pacific"),
106
Yenching University, 347 n
Yokohama, 354
Yomiuri Shimbun, Tokyo, Figs. 1, 41
Yorkshire Post, Leeds, 184, Fig. 19
Young Reparations Conference, 163 n,
197 n, Fig. 2
Yugoslavia, 67, 181, 207 n, 233, 251,
281, 282; press, 283, 284, 285, Figs.
1, 35
Yugoslavie, La, Belgrade, Fig. 35
Yutro, Ljubljana, 285

Zagreb, 285
Za Industrializatsiyu, Moscow, 279,
Fig. 34
Za Kommunisticheskoye Prosveshchen-
iye, Moscow, 279
Za Pischchevuyu Industryu, Moscow,
280
Zimmern, Dr. Alfred, 168 n
Zora, Sofia, 283, 285
Zurich, 287

(1)

INTERNATIONAL PROPAGANDA AND COMMUNICATIONS

An Arno Press Collection

Bruntz, George G. **Allied Propaganda and the Collapse of the German Empire in 1918.** 1938

Childs, Harwood Lawrence, editor. **Propaganda and Dictatorship: A Collection of Papers.** 1936

Childs, Harwood L[awrence] and John B[oardman] Whitton, editors. **Propaganda By Short Wave** including C[harles] A. Rigby's **The War on the Short Waves.** 1942/1944

Codding, George Arthur, Jr. **The International Telecommunication Union: An Experiment in International Cooperation.** 1952

Creel, George. **How We Advertised America.** 1920

Desmond, Robert W. **The Press and World Affairs.** 1937

Farago, Ladislas, editor. **German Psychological Warfare.** 1942

Hadamovsky, Eugen. **Propaganda and National Power.** 1954

Huth, Arno. **La Radiodiffusion Puissance Mondiale.** 1937

International Propaganda/Communications: Selections from *The Public Opinion Quarterly*, 1943/1952/1956. 1972

International Press Institute Surveys, Nos. 1-6. 1952-1962

International Press Institute. **The Flow of News.** 1953

Lavine, Harold and James Wechsler. **War Propaganda and the United States.** 1940

Lerner, Daniel, editor. **Propaganda in War and Crisis.** 1951

Linebarger, Paul M. A. **Psychological Warfare.** 1954

Lockhart, Sir R[obert] H. Bruce. **Comes the Reckoning.** 1947

Macmahon, Arthur W. **Memorandum on the Postwar International Information Program of the United States.** 1945

de Mendelssohn, Peter. **Japan's Political Warfare.** 1944

Nafziger, Ralph O., compiler. **International News and the Press: An Annotated Bibliography.** 1940

Read, James Morgan. **Atrocity Propaganda, 1914-1919.** 1941

Riegel, O[scar] W. **Mobilizing for Chaos: The Story of the New Propaganda.** 1934

Rogerson, Sidney. **Propaganda in the Next War.** 1938

Summers, Robert E., editor. **America's Weapons of Psychological Warfare.** 1951

Terrou, Fernand and Lucien Solal. **Legislation for Press, Film and Radio:** Comparative Study of the Main Types of Regulations Governing the Information Media. 1951

Thomson, Charles A. H. **Overseas Information Service of the United States Government.** 1948

Tribolet, Leslie Bennett. **The International Aspects of Electrical Communications in the Pacific Area.** 1929

Unesco. **Press Film Radio,** Volumes I-V *including* Supplements. 1947-1951. 3 volumes.

Unesco. **Television:** A World Survey *including* Supplement. 1953/1955

White, Llewellyn and Robert D. Leigh. **Peoples Speaking to Peoples:** A Report on International Mass Communication from The Commission on Freedom of the Press. 1946

Williams, Francis. **Transmitting World News.** 1953

Wright, Quincy, editor. **Public Opinion and World-Politics.** 1933